C A L I F O R N I A
ARCHITECTURE

CALIFORNIA
ARCHITECTURE

❖

HISTORIC AMERICAN BUILDINGS SURVEY

SALLY B. WOODBRIDGE

FOREWORDS BY JAMES J. RAWLS AND KATHRYN GUALTIERI ◆ INTRODUCTION BY S. ALLEN CHAMBERS, JR.

CHRONICLE BOOKS ◆ SAN FRANCISCO

Printed in the United States of America.

Library of Congress
Cataloging-in-Publication Data

Woodbridge, Sally Burne.
    California architecture: historic American buildings survey
  Sally B. Woodbridge.
        p.   cm.
    Bibliography: p.
    Includes index.
    ISBN 0-87701-553-8. ISBN 0-87701-538-4 (pbk.)
    1. Architecture—California—Catalogs. 2. Historic Buildings.
  —California—Catalogs. I. Title.
  NA730.C2W65 1988
  720′.9794—dc19   88-23688
                                                        CIP

Editing: Judith Dunham
Book and cover design: Seventeenth Street Studios
Composition: Another Point, Inc.

10 9 8 7 6 5 4 3 2 1

Chronicle Books
275 Fifth Street
San Francisco, California
94103

Frontispiece: Golden Gate Park Conservatory, San Francisco

KATHRYN GUALTIERI

This book is a celebration of the distinctive architecture of California. It represents the record of our state's architectural heritage. For those of us who love California, "preservation through documentation," the stated program of the Historic American Buildings Survey, deserves our enthusiastic support and praise.

National Park Service Director William Penn Mott, Jr., became California's first State Historic Preservation Officer in March, 1967. During his tenure as Director of State Parks and Recreation, Mott saw that the Historic American Buildings Survey provided Californians with the best opportunity to survey and record the significant historic buildings in the state. While several of the Department's historic properties had been recorded since the federal program's

inception, Mott suggested that many others should be surveyed through HABS, so that their repair, restoration and maintenance needs could be met.

As a volunteer, I was involved in a summer HABS project on the San Francisco Peninsula in 1974. That experience convinced me of the value of this important program. As California's current State Historic Preservation Officer, I have supported Director Mott's early belief and have coordinated two summer HABS projects in Sacramento, the Leland Stanford house (HABS Stanford Latrop house) and the Governor's mansion, with the directors of the State Parks and Recreation Department.

I look forward to future HABS summer projects in California, and endorse this book which documents all those earlier structures which have been preserved through the Historic American Buildings Survey. May the effort continue!

KATHRYN GUALTIERI *is the State Historic Preservation Officer.*

JAMES J. RAWLS

The architectural heritage of California is rich and varied. Thick-walled adobe missions and presidios survive as remnants of the Spanish frontier. Victorian homes, splendid in their wealth of decorative detail, stand in neighborhoods crowded with craftsmen bungalows. Downtown theaters, embellished with the flowing lines of Art Deco, linger in the shadow of high-rise office buildings, earnestly conforming to the dictums of the International Style.

California's buildings are special "documents" for the study of the state's history. When properly read, they tell us much about the values, life-styles, and institutions of past generations of Californians. They also help us understand the forces which have shaped our own times.

Unlike other documents, such as diaries and collections of letters, historic buildings cannot be filed away in libraries or archives. They are on constant display, available for observation and study by anyone. Unfortunately this accessibility often has been their downfall. Thousands of historic buildings have been destroyed as the land upon which they rested increased in value. In the battle between history and progress, the forces of modernity have usually been triumphant.

When the Historic American Buildings

JAMES J. RAWLS *is Publications Committee Chairman of the California Historical Society.*

Survey (HABS) was created in 1933, its director proposed that "if the great number of our antique buildings must disappear through economic causes, they should not pass into unrecorded oblivion." Thus it was that a systematic program of recording the nation's architectural heritage was begun. Photographs and precise measured drawings were made of nearly 20,000 structures. Of these buildings, about 30 percent have been destroyed since the program began.

In California, the destruction of our architectural heritage has proceeded at an alarming rate. Public outcries have saved many buildings from the wrecker's ball, but others have disappeared without protest. Many buildings have been destroyed simply because people did not know that the structures were historically significant.

The California Historical Society, an organization dedicated to the preservation and promotion of the state's history, became in 1975 the official cosponsor for the publication of *California Architecture,* the HABS California catalogue. The following year, the Society selected the distinguished architectural historian Sally B. Woodbridge to serve as editor of the volume. Now, after more than ten years of dedication and hard work, the book is complete. It is our hope that its publication will lead to a greater appreciation, study, and preservation of California's unique architectural heritage.

ACKNOWLEDGMENTS

Sally B. Woodbridge wishes to acknowledge the help of the many organizations and individuals who contributed information and time to this book. Among them are the many historical societies throughout the state and the other repositories of information about the history of California. Members of the staff of HABS in Washington, D.C., particularly S. Allen Chambers, who chronicled the history of HABS in California in this book, also offered invaluable advice and assistance in the compilation of the catalogue.

Mission San Miguel Arcángel, San Miguel. Among the HABS *records documenting the California missions are copies of earlier illustrations, such as this drawing, showing the mission prior to 1850.*

HABS in California

S. ALLEN CHAMBERS, JR.

HABS—it is among the many acronyms that have been coined to designate various federal agencies. Although most bureaucrats have difficulty recognizing these initials, those involved in the preservation and documentation of historic architecture in the United States have little trouble at all. In fact, over the years HABS has become one of the most familiar terms in the preservation lexicon.

HABS, short for the Historic American Buildings Survey, began in the early 1930s during the height of the Great Depression. Architecture was among the many professions that had been devastated during that period. With the lack of buildings being constructed, it was unnecessary to hire professionals to provide designs. But attempts were being made throughout the country to provide relief.

In Washington, D.C., in November 1933, the Civil Works Administration invited all of the executive departments to suggest ways to alleviate the chronic unemployment. Among those proposed by the Department of the Interior was the brainchild of Charles E. Peterson, then chief of the National Park Service's Eastern Division, Branch of Plans and Designs. The purpose of the program would be "to enlist a qualified group of architects and draftsmen to study, measure and draw up the plans, elevations and details of the important antique buildings of the United States." A project with a dual function, it would hire unemployed professionals and at the same time would inaugu-

rate a permanent, archival record of historic American architecture. Furthermore, it would only take ten weeks! Although the last goal proved unrealistic, the remaining aims were deemed feasible. Now, thanks to the careful planning and organization at the outset, as well as the intrinsic worth of the program, HABS continues its work, and is one of the few federal programs still extant that can trace its lineage directly back to the Civil Works Administration.

By December 1933, Peterson's proposal was approved, $448,000 was allocated, and a headquarters staff was set up. In the field, the country was divided into thirty-nine districts corresponding to the boundaries of the major chapters of the American Institute of Architects. California was divided into two districts: numbers 37 and 38. Along with Arizona, the southern part of the state was District 37. District Officer Henry F. Withey of Los Angeles was authorized to hire a staff of thirty-six. Northern California, that part of the state described as "north of San Luis Obispo and the Tehachapi," was District 38 and, under the leadership of Irving F. Morrow of San Francisco, was authorized a staff of twenty. At the discretion of the district officers, the staffs were to be divided into smaller squads or teams to do the actual field work involved in measuring the buildings.

As plans for the scope and direction of the survey were refined, Washington blanketed the country with a series of circulars and bulletins. *Bulletin 3*, dated December 20, 1933, qualified the rather imprecise term "antique buildings" of the initial proposal as including only those structures dating prior to 1860. Inasmuch as California

S. ALLEN CHAMBERS, JR. *was the Architectural Historian of the Historic American Buildings Survey, 1972–1987.*

had only joined the union ten years earlier, that cut-off date meant that the colonial and pioneer architecture in the state would receive attention, but that anything later than the early statehood period would get short shrift. Fortunately, there was an escape clause: later buildings of exceptional architectural merit or historical interest could be included at the discretion of the district officers and their advisory committees. There was other good news. If the chronological limits were restrictive, the range of building types to be considered was definitely not. In addition to houses, stores, churches, etc., "barns, bridges, mills, toll houses [and] jails" could be surveyed.

Armed with these instructions, the first California HABS teams went into the field. Almost all of the early missions were recorded in the beginning. Because many were then in various stages of repair and had undergone many changes, efforts were made not only to document their current state, but to find and copy visual materials

depicting earlier stages. As an example, HABS documentation on Mission San Antonio de Padua near Jolon in Monterey County consists of seventeen sheets of drawings, nine photographs, and no fewer than forty-seven photocopies of various early drawings, paintings, and photographs.

Missions were the best-represented buildings in this early crop of HABS recording, but attention was also paid to lesser colonial buildings, especially the adobe structures remaining from the first years of European settlement. El Cuartel in Santa Barbara, typical of this genre, reveals how HABS drawings could be (and indeed were) used to foster the revival styles so popular in the 1930s.

Reminders of the early military presence in the state were also recorded by the first HABS teams. In the mountainous central counties, however, the pioneer establishments were neither military nor mission, but were the mining camps of the mid-nineteenth century. Squads from both districts

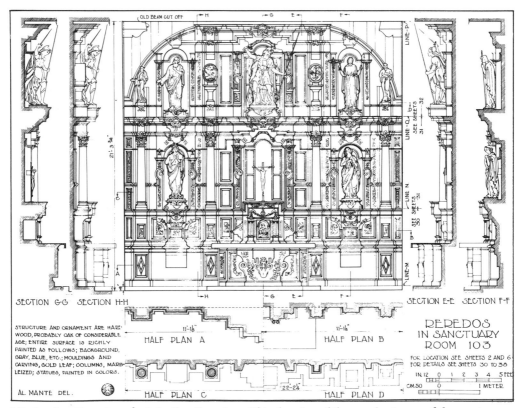

Mission San Francisco de Asís, San Francisco. This drawing of the reredos is one of the most elaborate of the 39 sheets of measured drawings that document San Francisco's famous mission.

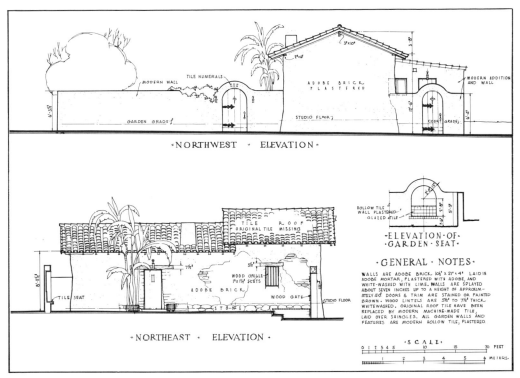

El Cuartel, Santa Barbara. Parts of this remnant of Santa Barbara's Presidio were in some disrepair when the building was recorded in the thirties. Even so, the similarities between it and small houses then being built in the Spanish Revival style seem obvious.

went up into the hills to document these picturesque towns, even to the extent of measuring and drawing such intriguing remnants as tombstones. Roger Sturtevant, later to be best known for his photographs of modern California architecture, documented the Mother Lode towns. The District 38 team assigned to record Knight's Ferry in Stanislaus County took the range of subjects included in the Washington directives seriously. In addition to surveying the normal range of buildings in the town, they also included the covered bridge, the jail, and the firehouse. In some instances it seemed that the teams arrived at a site just in time to record these pioneer structures before they sank into complete oblivion. Yet another "first settler" site—one that fits into neither the mission nor mining category—was recorded in 1934: the Russian compound at Fort Ross.

While the architects in the field were busy measuring and drafting, the Washington staff continued to refine the scope and operation of the survey. Early in 1934 approval was given for an extension beyond the initial ten-week period. Then, in May of that year, final agreements were made among the National Park Service, the Library of Congress, and the American Institute of Architects on a modus operandi for the program. By this Tripartite Agreement, which is still in effect, the NPS administers the program, the AIA provides professional advice, and the Library of Congress maintains the collection and makes the records available to the public. During the same month, the Civil Works Administration program that had initially funded HABS was ended. For the rest of 1934, as well as 1935, operating expenses were provided by Emergency Relief and Public Works funds. By the end of 1934, increased recording activity dictated another division of the country into smaller districts. These new districts, which had been specified in the Tripartite Agreement, were defined to coincide with the territories of the local and regional chapters of the AIA, rather than the major statewide chapters as before.

Fort Winfield Scott, San Francisco. While the 1934 HABS photographer focused his lens on this important nineteenth-century fortification, he also provided a wonderful documentary illustration of the building of the Golden Gate Bridge, already beginning to dwarf the earlier fort.

California was divided into four, rather than two, districts. Recording in the district of northern California, which also included the entire state of Nevada, was still directed by Irving F. Morrow, assisted by William H. Knowles as Deputy District Officer. The Santa Barbara district, which included San Luis Obispo and Ventura counties as well, was directed by Harold E. Burket. Southern California, still including Arizona, but no longer San Diego, continued as a district under the supervision of Henry Withey. The fourth district, which encompassed both the city and county of San Diego, was supervised by William P. Lodge.

The initial HABS program was one planned by architects for architects. Photography and written data, which later became so integral to the survey's documentation, were sorely neglected. *Bulletin 4* instructed recorders simply to jot down the "facts regarding the history of the building within the knowledge of the occupants." No wonder some of the early data cannot be regarded as reliable. In looking at the photographs taken in the 1930s—often the sole record of many a building that has subsequently been demolished—users of the col-

lection shouldn't expect to see great works of art. To photograph the buildings covered in the initial ten-week period, District 37 was allowed the munificent sum of $75 for "film supplies and the developing thereof." District 38 fared even worse, obtaining only $50 for the same purpose.

In 1935 HABS received permanent authorization with the passage of the Historic Sites, Buildings, and Antiquities Act, which is still regarded as one of the landmarks in the legislative history of American preservation. Then, from 1936 until 1941, the Works Progress Administration footed the survey's bills as more buildings were recorded throughout the country. In 1938 and 1941, the documentation that had been produced was published in catalogues. California was represented by almost two hundred structures.

With the beginning of World War II, federally funded employment programs begun during the Depression were terminated. From 1941 to the mid-1950s, however, the HABS collection continued to expand, albeit on a reduced basis. Donations of documentation, primarily from the National Park Service, kept the program going during those lean years.

In 1957, HABS got its second wind, when an announcement was made that the National Park Service would allocate $200,000 from its fiscal-year 1958 appropriations to reactivate the survey. It was all part of the Mission 66 program, by which the park service planned to upgrade its facilities and restore historic properties under its jurisdiction. Thus, in many instances the prime purpose of producing documentation on historic park service properties was to provide actual working drawings for their restoration. By the 1950s, however, what was good for the country was not necessarily good for HABS. The building boom during this time meant that unemployed architects were few and far between. Even though few architects were available to document historic buildings, a plethora of eager young architectural students was willing and able to practice during the summer months the drafting techniques they had been taught during the academic year.

Summer field teams, consisting of four or five architectural draftsmen and an architectural historian, all working under the supervision of a professor of architecture, became, and continue to be, the major source for obtaining new HABS documentation. In addition to providing college credits to the students, this method often affords future architects their first association with architectural history and preservation. At this time, drawings were not the most prominent form of documentation. Photographs and written data began to assume a greater importance. Time constraints, ever-present budgeting problems, and other considerations kept all buildings from being measured and drawn. By contrast, it was comparatively easy, quick, and cheap to prepare photographic and written documentation. Thus began the "photo-data book" concept of documentation, which ideally would complement the drawings, but in many instances had to suffice on its own.

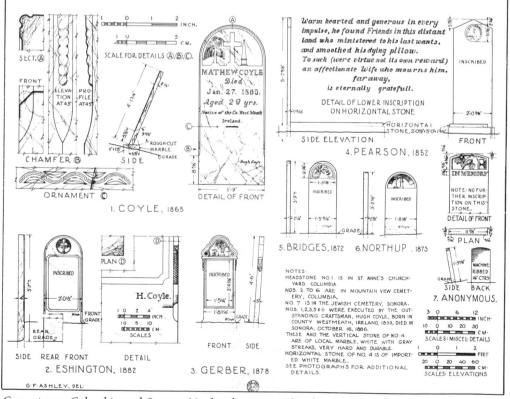

Gravestones, Columbia and Sonora. No detail was considered too insignificant to the early HABS recorders. These stones are among a number of records obtained on early mining towns.

Stone ruins, Mokelumne Hill. Photograph by Roger Sturtevant, 1934. A number of the early HABS *photographs recorded buildings that had long since been abandoned to the elements.*

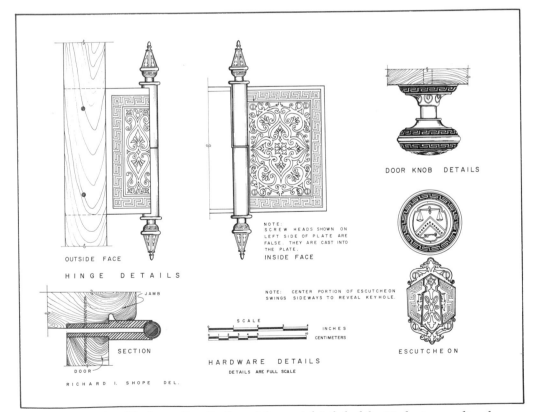

San Francisco Mint, Hardware Details. One of the most detailed of the 22 sheets recording the mint is this—giving full-scale details of the doorknobs and hinges.

During the Mission 66 period, California recordings were handled out of the National Park Service's Western Office, Design and Construction, in San Francisco. Sanford Hill was chief, and Charles Pope, as supervising architect of historic structures, was directly responsible for the HABS program. A number of the historic structures at Yosemite National Park were recorded under Mission 66 auspices. Fortunately, these Mission 66 funds were not restricted to park service buildings, and several of the projects undertaken at the time updated and completed HABS records made in the 1930s. Casa Amesti in Monterey, originally photographed in 1936, was drawn in 1958 by students from the University of California, under the direction of Charles Pope. Other major California landmarks recorded with the assistance of Mission 66 funds were the Sherwood Ranch in Salinas, Fort Yuma in Imperial County, and the imposing Old Mint in San Francisco. In the case of the Mint, which was recorded in 1962, original drawings and other sources were used to document the changes made over the years, and the drawings produced were detailed down to the doorknobs and hinges.

Also documented during this period of resurgence were buildings in the area known as Old Sacramento, that part of the state capital then undergoing radical changes due to highway construction, urban renewal, and—fortunately—preservation interests. Bodie, the Mono County mining town that has been a state park since 1962, was recorded. Among the smaller-scale photo-data projects undertaken in the 1960s were the Governor Pardee house in Oakland, built in 1868, and the elegant Spreckels Mansion across the bay in San Francisco, dating from 1913. As the dates of these buildings indicate, and as had also been the case in the Old Sacramento project, HABS had expanded well beyond its earlier self-imposed restriction of recording only pre–Civil War buildings. Otherwise, the survey might not have had the justification to document what is perhaps the most quintessential Victorian mansion in the nation: the justly famous Carson house in Eureka. Built in 1885-86, the house is now a private club, and the interior is off-bounds to casual visitors. If nothing else, the HABS photographs (of which there are twenty-

eight), certainly prove that the exuberant exterior is matched by the detail and trim inside.

Although a number of individual buildings were documented by HABS in the early and mid-1960s, it was not until 1968 that the first of what would come to be many full-scale summer projects in California was undertaken. This was the *Southern California Project,* which also has the distinction of being among the very first attempts by HABS to document the major landmarks of twentieth-century American architecture. The project was sponsored by the Southern California Coordinating Council for Historic Preservation, a consortium of concerned institutions and organizations. Their "concern" centered around the impressive monuments of modern architecture in Santa Barbara, Los Angeles, and San Diego, many of which were threatened with demolition. Unfortunately, a number of the buildings recorded have since been destroyed. Two of the greatest losses were Irving Gill's Dodge house and the Richfield Oil Building, both formerly in Los Angeles.

This first southern California project was deemed such a success that the coordinating council sponsored a second one in 1969. Then, in 1971, San Diego decided to organize a HABS team on its own. Sponsored by the San Diego Historic Sites Board, the County of San Diego, the San Diego Historical Society, and the local chapter of the American Institute of Architects, the *San Diego Project* was as catholic in its coverage as could be imagined. At one end of the spectrum was the Victorian extravagance known as the Hotel Del Coronado; at the other end was Gill's La Jolla Woman's Club, an austere structure whose simplified forms give only the barest hints of its architectural inheritance from the California missions.

Another method in addition to the summer-team approach of recording was established and used to good effect in California during this period. This was the HABS inventory form, known as HABSI, a one-page sheet on which basic information on a building was recorded and a snapshot attached. A great number of buildings in large areas could be recorded in this manner, utilizing volunteer help, and the most important structures could later be documented in more detail. Many of the buildings on

Oakland's impressive Governor Pardee House was the subject of a HABS *photo-data recording in the 1960s.*

California inventory forms were prepared by students at the University of California at Davis under the direction of Dr. Joseph A. Baird, Jr. With the establishment and growth of the National Register of Historic Places after the passage of the National Historic Preservation Act of 1966 (which depended on similar inventories to be conducted in each state), the HABSI program became redundant and was eventually discarded. Those HABSI forms that were produced, however, have been placed in the Library of Congress and provide an increasingly valuable reference on many structures throughout the country.

Another important innovation of the late 1960s was the establishment of a companion program to HABS. Although canals, mills, and bridges had long been recorded under HABS auspices, a program specifically intended to study such structures was needed. Thus, in 1969, the Historic American Engineering Record (HAER) was

launched. A fully fledged program, HAER has recorded a number of impressive engineering monuments in California.

Although the 1968, 1969, and 1971 HABS summer projects had all been in southern California, northern California soon began to document buildings in the region. Planning for the 1974 *San Mateo Project* had begun as early as 1972 when a Community Heritage project was established by the Junior League of Palo Alto, under the chairmanship of Mrs. Kent Kaiser. In 1973 the committee made a block-by-block survey of historic buildings throughout the county and selected from that list the ones that warranted more detailed HABS documentation. The next year, these were recorded by a six-member HABS team. Among the more unusual buildings documented was the Pigeon Point Lighthouse. The summer project, however, was only the beginning. In December 1974 Kaiser announced to HABS that her group had received permission

Carson House, Eureka. As this detail of the southwest elevation demonstrates, the Carson House is one of the most elaborate architectural confections imaginable.

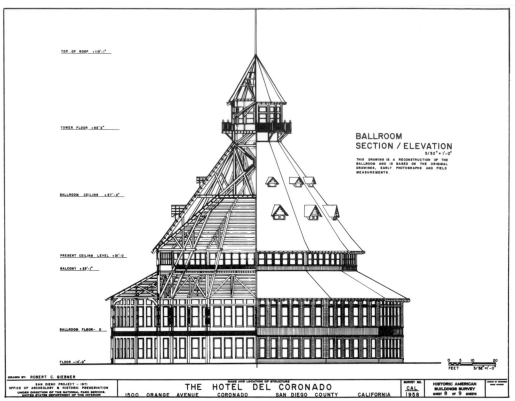

TOP OF ROOF +118'-1"

TOWER FLOOR +88'8"

**BALLROOM
SECTION / ELEVATION**
3/32" = 1'-0"
THIS DRAWING IS A RECONSTRUCTION OF THE
BALLROOM AND IS BASED ON THE ORIGINAL
DRAWINGS, EARLY PHOTOGRAPHS AND FIELD
MEASUREMENTS.

BALLROOM CEILING +57'-0"

PRESENT CEILING LEVEL +31'-0

BALCONY +25'-1"

BALLROOM FLOOR - 0

FLOOR -14'-0"

0   5   10   20
FEET   3/32"=1'-0"

DRAWN BY: ROBERT C. GIEBNER

SAN DIEGO PROJECT - 1971
OFFICE OF ARCHEOLOGY & HISTORIC PRESERVATION
UNDER DIRECTION OF THE NATIONAL PARK SERVICE.
UNITED STATES DEPARTMENT OF THE INTERIOR

NAME AND LOCATION OF STRUCTURE
THE HOTEL DEL CORONADO
1500   ORANGE   AVENUE   CORONADO   SAN DIEGO COUNTY   CALIFORNIA

SURVEY NO.
CAL
1958

HISTORIC AMERICAN
BUILDINGS SURVEY
SHEET 8 OF 9 SHEETS

*Hotel del Coronado, Coronado. This famous resort is one of Southern California's architectural
landmarks. Shown here is the ballroom.*

from Stanford University Press to publish
the results of the survey, along with an expanded text by Dorothy Regnery and photographs by HABS photographer Jack E.
Boucher. Seldom has a HABS project been
presented to the public in such impressive
form as in *An Enduring Heritage* (Stanford
University Press, 1976).

Throughout the 1970s, there was a HABS
team in California practically every summer.
In 1975 the *Second San Diego Project* was
undertaken, and in 1976 Benicia, the early
capital of the state, was the locale. For the
Benicia Project, the Benicia Historical Society provided space and the Exxon Company, U.S.A., which has a huge refinery
there, provided funds. This was the first
HABS recording effort in the United States
funded by a private corporation. In addition
to buildings such as the old state capitol,
the project documented the Benicia Arsenal,

an important military establishment dating
from 1851. As with the San Mateo project,
it was hoped that a publication would result
from the project, and this was realized in
Benicia: Portrait of an Early California Town
(101 Productions, 1980). Project historian
Robert Bruegmann was the author, and
Exxon made another generous grant for the
publication. Once again, the results of a
HABS summer team in California had been
impressively packaged, and as with *An Enduring Heritage,* the Benicia volume went
beyond a strict documentary effort to become an effective preservation tool. Gladys
Wold of the Benicia Historical Society said
it well: "Having capable outsiders come into
town to show such interest in Benicia has
rededicated us to the task of preservation.
. . We've rekindled our grand old dream—
that however Benicia may grow, the aura of
history will remain."

In 1977 the *Santa Clara Project,* or projects, began. This intensive four-year effort, sponsored by the county, resulted in documentation on a number of important structures, among them Welch-Hurst near Saratoga. Both the 1977 and 1978 teams were housed in this fine "rustic revival" log and stone structure. Included in the drawings by the 1978 team were the bungalows of Hanchett Residential Park in San Jose. Although the bungalow as a building type has long been recognized as one of California's contributions to architecture in the United States, this was among the first instances that a group of them was recorded in such detail. The 1979 and 1980 HABS teams included such diverse structures as a 1927 motel, or auto-camp, two gasoline stations, and the unique Yung See San Fong in their work. The latter building, a residence

dating from 1917, can best be described as being in the oriental revival style.

More authentically oriental structures were recorded in another California project in 1979. This was the *Locke Project,* sponsored by the state of California through its Department of Parks and Recreation, the Sacramento Housing and Redevelopment Agency, and the Chinese Historical Society of America. Built between 1912 and 1922 by Chinese farm laborers, this fascinating community consists of four blocks of one- and two-story frame buildings, closely packed together. Something of a "rural Chinatown," Locke is undergoing pressures that it was never built to withstand, and the HABS documentation was undertaken in part to aid in the intelligent planning for the future preservation of this significant and unique community.

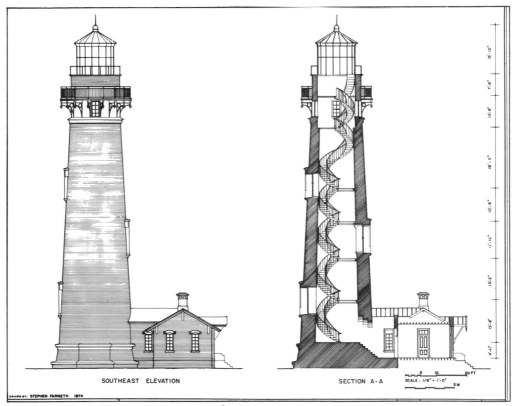

SOUTHEAST ELEVATION   SECTION A-A   SCALE: 1/8" = 1'-0"

DRAWN BY: STEPHEN FARNETH   1974

Pigeon Point Lighthouse, Pescadero vicinity. Although automated in 1974, the original lens and lantern of this 1891 lighthouse remain in place. The structure is the oldest such still functioning in California.

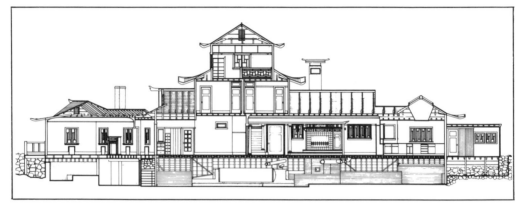

Yung See San Fong, Los Gatos. Santa Clara's individualistic example of what might best be termed "Oriental Revival" was also documented by the Santa Clara team.

For the last several years, the HABS and HAER programs have been regionalized, and California recordings are again being conducted under the direction of reorganized Western Regional Office of the National Park Service, headquartered (as before) in San Francisco. In the summer of 1981, the regional office conducted an inventory of the Presidio of San Francisco as a first step in the development of a program to ensure that the most important structures receive proper preservation or rehabilitation. In the same year, the Western Regional Office and HAER documented the famous San Francisco cable cars, as well as the car barn and tracks. Funded by the city of San Francisco and the Urban Mass Transit Authority, this project was purposely planned to take place prior to a major rehabilitation of this unique transportation system. Then, during the

summer of 1982, another HAER project took place when the U.S. Forest Service sponsored the recording of Hume Lake Dam in Sequoia National Forest.

With the increased recording activity not only in California but in most of the other states, as well as in Puerto Rico and the Virgin Islands, it became apparent that the old 1938 and 1941 HABS catalogues (which had been somewhat updated by the publication of a supplement in 1958) were no longer adequate guides to the collection. Beginning in the 1960s, the first of several state catalogues was published, and others have followed at varying intervals. In publishing catalogues, HABS seeks out interested groups to act as cosponsors, and in California the logical choice was the California Historical Society. When early in the 1970s the first Western Regional Office was closed and operations for

HABS became centered in Washington, D.C., the historical society, which already had so much material on historic architecture in the state was selected to be a logical repository for copies of the HABS records then being sent east. Consequently, in August 1973 the California Historical Society began to maintain an auxiliary HABS collection.

In the beginning, HABS was primarily concerned only with recording and documenting examples of historic American architecture. As the more recent California projects such as San Mateo, Benicia, Locke, and others have demonstrated, the survey is an active proponent of historic preservation as well. This dual purpose—preservation based on proper documentation—is important as part of the nation's effort to ensure

that there will be some evidence of what past generations built and enjoyed. A perusal of the catalogue that follows shows that HABS has recorded far more of California's historic architecture than has been mentioned in this introduction. Conversely, much remains to be done. HABS continues to be a mendicant order, depending on interested cosponsors to fund the projects that enable it to continue to build its collection. The survey welcomes inquiries regarding its program; they should be addressed to the Historic American Buildings Survey, National Park Service, P.O. Box 37127, Washington, D.C. 20013-7127. Only with the assistance of others can we continue the mission to preserve, through proper documentation, our priceless architectural heritage.

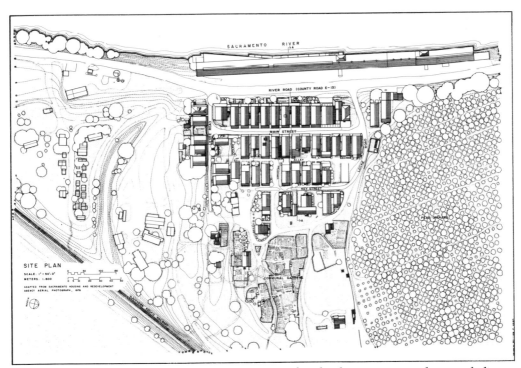

Locke, Sacramento County. This site plan of the town of Locke shows its surroundings, including the pear orchards which furnished income for the residents, and their communal gardens.

Mission San Carlos Borroméo de Carmelo, Carmel, 1839 drawing.

The History of
California Architecture

❖

SALLY B. WOODBRIDGE

Deserved or not, California has enjoyed a long association with Eden. Although the exact origin of this association is obscure, it probably began in 1510 with the publication in Seville, Spain, of a best-selling novel by Garcí Ordoñez de Montalvo, titled *The Adventures of Esplandián.* In it the author describes an island "on the right hand of the Indies . . . very near to The Terrestrial Paradise, which was peopled with black women . . . accustomed to live after the fashion of Amazons. . . . Their arms were full of gold." This island was called California.

Coincidentally, the first Spanish explorers of the Pacific Coast took the peninsula they called Baja, or lower, California for an island. This assumption apparently inspired the connection, perhaps also induced by the long months at sea, between the fictional and the real place. By the time Juan Rodríguez Cabrillo explored the Alta, or upper, California coast in 1542, the name California had taken hold. Father Eusebio Francisco Kino's exploration of the headwaters of the Colorado River at the end of the seventeenth century finally disproved the theory that California was an island.

During voyages of exploration over the next two hundred years, the Spanish began to take seriously England's and Russia's growing interest in the coastal lands that edged the largely unmapped territory north of Mexico. Finally, in 1769, fear of foreign incursions caused Spain to launch a colonial campaign into Alta California. To avoid obligating the viceroyalty's treasury to support military bases, the crown gave the church the dominant role in the campaign. Financial support for the missionary effort came

from the Pious Fund, which was sustained by private donations held in trust by the government. The Laws of the Indies, published in 1681 as the *Recopilación de Leyes de los Reynos de las Indias,* served as the blueprint for settlement through this cooperative effort.

Accordingly, the Franciscan missionaries, escorted by the military, planned a chain of missions along the coast of California. The criteria for siting the mission settlements were clearly stated. Among them were moderate altitude along with a healthful location, proximity to a waterway to ensure both a good supply of drinking water and access to the sea (the communication and supply line to Spain and Mexico), and a native population to receive the gospel.

The missions were established in or near Indian settlements, called *rancherías.* (Since the Spanish believed that they were in the Indies, the inhabitants were called Indians.) The Laws of the Indies emphasized a policy of religious conversion and pacification rather than forceful subjugation of the natives. Although the record of the conquistadores in the New World hardly accords with this policy, the weakness of the empire and the lack of funds for an army to police a hostile population influenced its adoption in California.

According to the plan, the mission lands were to be held in trust by the church for the natives. After a ten-year period of religious conversion and exposure to European civilization, the missions were to become the centers of towns, or pueblos, populated with loyal subjects. The mission churches would become parish churches in a diocese headed by a bishop, and the missionary monks would then move on to new frontiers. But by 1822, when California was transferred to Mexican rule, the acculturation program had barely started. The Indians were neither literate nor prepared for independence from the missions' paternalistic care. Moreover, conflicts between church and state, aggravated by the disintegration of the empire, delayed secularization of the missions until 1834.

The Franciscans' prospects for success had never been promising. Only two monks, or padres, were assigned to administer each mission on a fixed budget. Theoretically, one monk took charge of the spiritual life, and the other, the temporal affairs of the mission. In practice, their roles merged, particularly when the neophytes, as the Indian converts were called, began to number in the hundreds and thousands. While the Indians suffered increasing indignities and abuse, the monks also endured sufficient mental and physical hardships that induced a condition frequently described in official mission correspondence as "pernicious melancholy." Paradise had yet to occur in California.

The settlement campaign began in 1769 when Gaspar de Portolá, the first Spanish governor of Alta and Baja California, led the so-called Sacred Expedition to Alta California to found settlements. Accompanying the expedition was the Franciscan padre, Junípero Serra, who founded the first mission, San Diego de Acalá, on July 16. As *padre-presidente* of the missionary effort, Serra went on to found eight more missions before his death in 1784.

Dependency on ocean supply lines determined the location of the missions in the vicinity of the major harbors of San Diego and San Francisco. Padre Fermín Lasuén succeeded Serra as *padre-presidente* of the missions in 1785 and founded nine more of the twenty-one missions established before Spain lost California to Mexico. Lasuén's first three missions were located near the Santa Barbara channel; the rest of the missions were sited to close gaps in the chain, which reached its northernmost point with the founding of San Francisco Solano in Sonoma in 1823.

The first decades of the nineteenth century were a golden age for the missions.

Through the introduction of a proper plow, extensive irrigation, and foreign plant material, the monks augmented the production of the mission lands. Ultimately, this imported Mediterranean horticulture transformed the state's physical environment.

Horticultural manuals, which included a broad range of plants and trees, were distributed to the missionaries, who acquired seeds from Mexico, South America, and Spain. The abundance of wildflowers, including the royal Rose of Castile, delighted the Spanish, who imported other varieties. Because California enjoyed a Mediterranean climate, pomegranate, fig, banana, olive, citrus, and palm trees grew well in the new land. Thus the Spanish could substitute other crops for the Indians' diet of mice, snakes, insects, acorns, and unpalatable seeds which Lasuén described as "coarse and contemptible."

The Indians' seminomadic way of life also dictated forms of shelter that were as unacceptable to the Spanish as their diet. Typically made of reed frames covered with grass and brush and erected without tools, such structures provided adequate protection in a benign climate. When the insect population became too bothersome, the shelters were burned and replaced. The sophisticated masonry tradition that the conquistadores had found and utilized in Mexico did not exist in California. Thus, among the obstacles to building New Spain in California was the native population's ignorance of tool and building technology. Fate's final trick was to grant the discovery of gold, which had financed Spain's empire in Mexico and Latin America, to her American successors in California.

Although European monastic building traditions determined the mission plan, the Mexican monasteries were the direct prototypes. Buildings were arranged around a quadrangle, with the church generally in the northeast corner. As in Mexico after about 1600, the traditional east-west orientation for the church was not consistently followed. Some churches were oriented north-south; some had sanctuaries in the west ends, and some were detached from the buildings enclosing the court.

The *convento,* or monks' living quarters, where guests also stayed, was perpendicular to the church and sometimes contained a

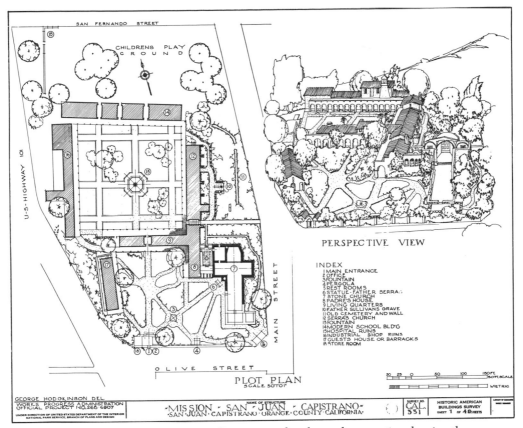

INDEX
1 MAIN ENTRANCE
2 OFFICE
3 FOUNTAIN
4 PERGOLA
5 REST ROOMS
6 STATUE-FATHER SERRA·
7 STONE CHURCH
8 PADRE'S HOUSE
9 LIVING QUARTERS
10 FATHER SULLIVANS GRAVE
11 OLD CEMETERY AND WALL
12 SERRA'S CHURCH
13 FOUNTAIN
14 MODERN SCHOOL BLD'G
15 HOSPITAL RUINS
16 INDUSTRIAL SHOP RUINS
17 GUESTS HOUSE OR BARRACKS
18 STORE ROOM

PERSPECTIVE VIEW

PLOT PLAN
SCALE 50'TO 1'

GEORGE HODGKINSON DEL.
WORKS PROGRESS ADMINISTRATION
OFFICIAL PROJECT NO.265 6907
UNDER DIRECTION OF UNITED STATES DEPARTMENT OF THE INTERIOR
NATIONAL PARK SERVICE, BRANCH OF PLANS AND DESIGN

·MISSION · SAN · JUAN · CAPISTRANO·
·SAN·JUAN·CAPISTRANO·ORANGE·COUNTY·CALIFORNIA·

CAL.
331

HISTORIC AMERICAN
BUILDINGS SURVEY
SHEET 1 OF 4 SHEETS

Mission San Juan Capistrano, San Juan Capistrano, plot plan and perspective showing the arrangement of buildings and also the destruction of the domed nave of the church in the 1812 earthquake.

small chapel. These two buildings, which formed the public side of the mission, were usually preceded by an entrance court called an *atrio.* Since the resident population of monks was very small, the dormitories, refectories, and other buildings typical of large European monasteries were unnecessary. A new building type, the *monjerio,* as the quarters for the unmarried Indian women and young children were called, was usually built into one side of the courtyard along with the infirmary and servants' quarters.

Buildings devoted to the working life of the mission completed the complex. Workshops for weaving, pottery, and other crafts, and storerooms for meat, hides, grain and fruits faced the court. Tanning leather, making soap, and other such activities took place in the courtyard where herbal and flower gardens were also planted. The well or fountain which supplied the compound

with water was an important feature. The guardhouse, manager's quarters, and the Indian villages or *rancherías* were outside the walls. Cemeteries were located just outside the church, typically with a door leading to them from the nave. Stretching beyond the compound were the stables, corrals, irrigation systems, grist mills, pottery and lime kilns, orchards, vineyards, and fields of crops.

◇   ◇   ◇   ◇   ◇

The first mission buildings were stockade structures with walls of poles set close together in the ground, plastered inside and out with mud, and whitewashed with lime. The roofs were made of poles covered with alternate layers of rushes and clay. Structures with walls of adobe (a word derived from the Arabic word for mud, *at-tub*) followed. Strictly speaking, adobe was the black clay found in deposits throughout the coastal region which bonded well when wet. Similar soils used in building had to be fortified with chopped weeds and other suitable materials.

An enormous mud pie concocted in a pit dug for the purpose provided the mixture which was then cast in molds about 11 by 22 inches and 2 to 5 inches thick. The sun-dried bricks, which weighed from 20 to 40 pounds, were laid both with and without adobe mortar. The walls, several feet thick at the base, tapered toward the top. Lime, commonly obtained by burning enormous quantities of seashells, was used to plaster the walls. This coating, along with a field-stone foundation, protected the adobe from seasonal dampness. Openings for windows and doors were braced with wooden lintels. In the churches, fired bricks called *ladrillos,* about 8 by 10 inches and 2 to 4 inches thick, served both as flooring and to strengthen the walls, which rose no higher than about 35 feet.

Stone construction was not attempted until 1790 when the fifty-odd artisans whom Fr. Lasuén had requested from Mexico to train the Indian neophytes arrived in California. Besides instruction in wood carving and leather working, weaving, blacksmithing, and firing clay for pots, bricks, and roof tiles, master masons taught the methods of quarrying and working stone.

Limestone and sandstone were not difficult to quarry; granite boulders came from river beds and washes, loose volcanic stone and schist from the foothills. But because skilled masons and high-quality stone remained in short supply, rubblework and adobe bricks rather than stones laid in courses were the typical masonry.

Various structural systems were used to build the mission churches. But attempts to build large masonry structures were frustrated by earthquakes which occurred with some regularity from the beginning of the mission building campaign. In 1812, after a severe earthquake toppled the bell tower and some of domed nave bays of the church at San Juan Capistrano, the Franciscans abandoned their attempts to emulate the domed Mexican churches.

The question of who designed the churches is difficult to answer. Although the master masons contributed their skills, the monks in charge of the planning and building of the missions also influenced their design. Master mason José Antonio Ramirez supervised construction at San Gabriel Arcángel under Frs. Antonio Cruzado and José María Zalvidea, at San Luís Rey de Francia under Fr. Antonio Peyrí, and at Santa Barbara under Fr. Antonio Ripoll. Master mason Manuel Ruíz worked on the Capilla Real in Monterey and for Fr. Juan Crespí at San Carlos Borroméo in Carmel. Isidoro Aguilar supervised the work at San Juan Capistrano for Frs. Vicente Fuster and Juan José Santiago, but died before it was finished.

Of the twenty-one Franciscan mission churches finally built under Spanish rule, fifteen had single naves with a choir loft over the entrance or narthex bay. At the other end was the sanctuary, usually raised a step or two, containing the altar and reredos. The sacristy was located off the sanctuary. Since baptism was the rite of entry into the church, the baptistry was placed near the entrance, in the base of the bell tower, if one existed. Only San Juan Capistrano and San Luís Rey were built with transepts to make their plans cruciform. San Luís Rey has an impressive domed mortuary chapel while the baptistry at San Gabriel is now in what was probably also a mortuary chapel. San Juan Bautista originally had aisles flanking the nave, but these were later closed in, perhaps for structural reasons.

Church naves were typically narrow, between twenty-five and thirty feet. (The Spanish unit of measurement, the *vara,* was thirty-three inches. Translating the *vara* into feet produces the odd span of about twenty-nine feet.) Beams, or *vigas,* of pine, Monterey cypress, or redwood, spanned the naves. The tree trunks used for the *vigas* had to be carried, often many miles, and placed by hand. Roof trusses lashed with rawhide thongs carried the roof timbers while, above, heavy corbels reinforced the beams at their ends. The thick adobe walls helped to hold the beams in place.

Roof eaves usually extended well beyond the walls to protect them from rain. Tiles, which may first have been made in about 1780 at San Antonio, were manufactured in 1790 at San Luís Obispo as replacements for flammable, thatched roofs. Roof tiles were

Mission Santa Barbara, Santa Barbara. Books were important sources for the design of the mission churches. The builders of the 1815 church at Mission Santa Barbara derived the central temple-front portion of the facade from Plate X of a 1787 Spanish edition of Vitruvius, still in the mission library.

about twenty-two inches long and tapered from nine to five inches in width. Tule matting was used beneath the tiles for insulation. Floors of tamped earth were either coated with tar, or *brea,* or covered with tiles about eleven to fifteen inches square.

Since the carved stone ornament of the Mexican churches was beyond their means, the Franciscans improvised impressive architectural settings by substituting painting for sculpture. For the now destroyed church at Mission Santa Clara, Augustin Davila, a Mexican artisan, supervised Indian apprentices who painted an architectural composition on the facade. Statues of saints between pilasters that supported sections of cornice topped by festooned cartouches were painted with red and yellow pigment applied in coats of plaster over the adobe. Even the Vitruvian facade of the Santa Bar-

bara church was rendered with polychromed, tinted plaster.

The interior walls of several churches were draped with painted fabric and given simulated marble base sections. Repeated patterns were made with rawhide stencils cut with geometric or foliate motifs. The colors used to pigment the plaster were obtained from plants and then mixed with cactus juice. One exception to the typical practice of simulating architectural elements directly on the walls is the elaborate painted wood and canvas reredos sent up from Mexico to the church at the Mission San Francisco de Asís, commonly called the Mission Dolores.

Most of the literature on the stylistic origins of the mission churches is speculative. Although the churches show an awareness of architectural style, the other

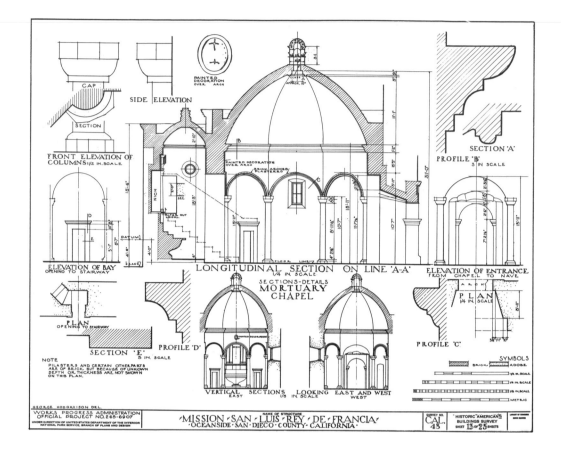

Mission church of San Luís Rey de Francia, near Oceanside. In spite of many earthquakes, the church retains its domed transcept and mortuary chapel; the painted interior has been restored.

buildings in a typical mission complex have a plain, residential character and a kinship with the traditional adobe and rubble-stone structures introduced into Spain by the Moors centuries earlier.

While the Neoclassicism that influenced eighteenth-century European architecture affected the designs of California's mission churches—Santa Barbara's, for example— other styles such as the popular Plateresque and the Baroque found their way north from Mexico. The Mission San Carlos Borromeo de Carmelo, built about the same time as the Monterey presidio's Capilla Real and supervised by the same master mason, combines Baroque with Moorish elements such as the ovoid dome and starlike window in the curved gable. Pyramidal finials accent the tower and entrance architrave, which are otherwise in the Baroque tradition. San Buenaventura, Santa Barbara, San Luís Rey, San Juan Bautista, and San Gabriel also have Mudejar elements freely interpolated into Classical and Baroque features. In general, this lack of stylistic coherence reflected the decline of Spain. Nothing comparable to the churches of the earlier Spanish missionary period in Texas and New Mexico was realized in Alta California.

The soldiers who accompanied the monks were quartered in forts (presidios) established at San Diego (1769), Monterey (1770), San Francisco (1776), and Santa Barbara (1782). The plan of the presidios, like that of the missions, featured a square or plaza, ideally of 480 *varas* and walled on three sides. Four bulwarks marked the corners. Both the presidios and the pueblos were entitled to four square leagues of land measured out from the plaza.

From the beginning, the presidios had served more as residential compounds than as forts. Although they were sited to protect major harbors, their capability for defense was derided by foreign visitors. Following his exploratory voyages along the coast in 1792 and 1793, Captain George Vancouver reported, "If these establishments are intended as a barrier against foreign intruders, the object in view has been greatly mistaken, and the most ready means have been adopted to allure other powers by the defenseless state of what the Spanish consider as their fortresses and strongholds." In 1796, the Spanish Engineer Extraordinary

Mission San Diego de Alacalá, San Diego. The stumpy pilasters on the church facade of this first mission are representative of the use of slightly projecting, linear motifs, sometimes polychromed, to convey architectural style.

Alberto de Córdoba inspected the presidios and found them virtually useless. By 1800, there were fewer than one hundred soldiers to protect the eighteen missions with their thousands of neophytes and the pueblos. The main communications line between the settlements was a rough trail over five hundred miles long, euphemistically called El Camino Real (The Royal Road).

The history of the San Francisco presidio is similar to that of the others. A contingent of soldiers and colonists with cattle established the presidio in July 1776. They came by land from Monterey while equipment came by sea on the ship *San Carlos*. By September, the settlers had built a small village of flat-roofed, log houses. The presidio complex also included lots for the church, royal offices, warehouses, a guardhouse, and houses for the soldier-settlers. The first buildings constructed were a chapel, a

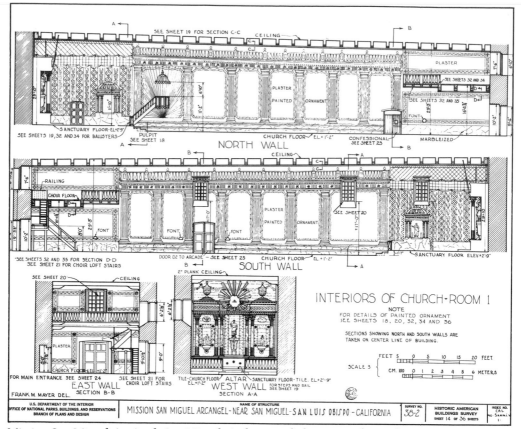

Mission San Miguel Arcángel, San Miguel. Architectural elements such as pilasters, cornices, friezes, and balustrades were simulated in polychromed murals as shown here in the church of San Miguel Arcangel, which preserves its original decoration of 1821, composed from books by Estevan Munras.

house for the *comandante,* and a warehouse for supplies. The soldiers built their own dwellings. The presidio plaza, which measured ninety-two *varas* in each direction, was considerably smaller than the ideal.

By 1825, the presidio population stood at about 500 with 120 buildings. By 1834, the Mexican government officially converted the presidio into a pueblo, presided over by an *ayuntamiento,* or town council. In 1835, the pueblo moved from the original presidio site on the inhospitable table land near the ocean to the bayside cove sheltered by Telegraph Hill where the village of Yerba Buena, "the good herb," was growing. The village lay within the presidio's four square leagues of land, as measured from the center of the plaza.

Like the presidios, the soldiers themselves presented a weak and degraded image

of the Spanish military. Low pay and the requirement for retirement with pay of at least ten years of service on the frontier—with a total of eighteen for retirement—did not attract ambitious men. To make matters worse, the authorities in Mexico used the army as a means of disposing of criminals and other undesirables. Although the soldiers' destructive and immoral habits distressed the mission authorities, they could take no direct action against the military.

Guardianship was the only role clearly assigned to the soldiers. The presidios were sustained and supplied with food and other necessaries by the missions. The soldiers believed that they would lose caste with the Indians if they raised food or provided for themselves in other ways. In an effort to find other methods to increase the food supply and supplement the province's defense force, three pueblos were founded: San José (1777), Nuestra Señora la Reina de Los Angeles de Porciúncula (1781), and Villa de Branciforte (1797).

Progress toward building up the pueblos was halting. Both the San José and the Los Angeles pueblos were sited on rivers that flooded annually. In 1797 San José was removed from the Guadalupe River to a site now in the heart of the present-day city. Los Angeles also had to be relocated to higher ground.

By 1784, the Spanish crown yielded to the petitions of the soldier-settlers who wished to retire and settle on land in the Los Angeles Basin. As many as thirty concessions to graze cattle and to farm were granted outside the Los Angeles pueblo's four square leagues before 1822. Vigorously opposing this secularization of the settlement plan, the mission authorities engaged

in lengthy boundary disputes with the *rancheros*. After 1812, increasing revolutionary activity in Mexico so distracted the Spanish government that the soldiers in Alta California no longer received their pay. This final negligence doomed the presidios to a rapid decline. At Santa Barbara and Los Angeles the soldiers broke through walls to build houses that formed a chaotic but vital urban pattern.

The Los Angeles pueblo began with eleven families, a total of forty-four mestizos of Spanish, Indian, and Negro blood from Sonora. The families were paid to settle there, an indication that California was still a hardship post. The pueblo land was distributed by a lottery. City lots were divided into *peonías,* fifty feet wide and one hundred feet deep, and *caballerías,* one hundred feet wide and two hundred feet deep; settlers could have five of the former

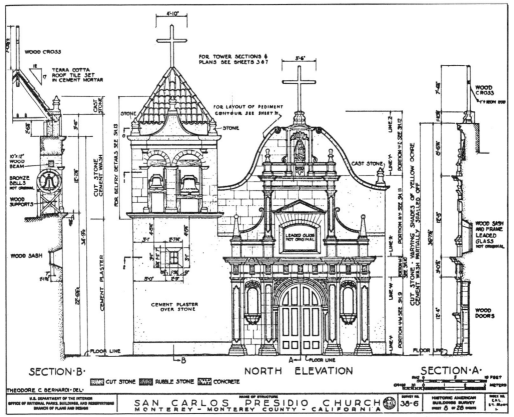

Monterey Presidio church, Monterey. The Capilla Royal or royal chapel is a simplified example of the ornate style called "plateresque" because it was derived from the work of silversmiths.

*Mission San Carlos Borroméo de Carmelo,
Carmel. The interior of this church was the
only one to use stone arches to vault the nave.
In the present restoration, the ceiling intercepts
the wall at the springing of the arches obscur-
ing their form and making the pilasters appear to defy structural principles by bending
inward.*

*Mission San Antonio del Padua near King City. Eccentricities that reveal the pragmatic process of
their design characterize the mission churches. At this church a monumental campanario, which
appears as a kind of billboard, was used instead of the more typical bell tower flanking the
facade.*

THE PRESIDIO

The San Francisco Presidio as drawn in the late 1840s showing the comandante's house and barracks in the center and the storehouse to the right.

and three of the latter. Those who accepted the lots were obliged to build a house, farm the land, and acquire herds and grasslands within a stated period of time. Grains, seeds, and cereals were dispensed free, along with two dry and two irrigable fields.

The siting of the Los Angeles pueblo adhered to the instructions in the Laws of the Indies. The location was healthful, the land fertile, and the pueblo was on the land of the Indian village, or *ranchería,* of Yabit. The one flaw was that the nearby river flooded each year, destroying the settlement.

When the pueblo was relocated in 1815, the town-planning rules were modified. The plaza, measuring 206 by 275 feet, was smaller than standard; instead of four main streets running out from it, there were three. The plaza's corners were set at the cardinal points of the compass, but the prescription for two streets to enter it at each point was not followed. A chapel and other municipal buildings were located on the plaza. Early views show the required covered walks, or *corredores,* lining the streets that lead to the plaza, itself a barren plot much trampled by horses.

Unoccupied land was held by the Spanish crown and let upon petition. Land could be inherited but not sold or mortgaged. In any case, no accurate maps or clear titles existed. The redistribution of land following the relocation of the pueblo in 1815 further confused the ownership.

The first families were entitled *hijosdalgo,* meaning "illustrious men of known ancestry." The Del Valles, the Lugos, the Carillos, and the Ávilas all had houses on the plaza, none of which remain today. An adobe that belonged to the Ávilas still stands on Olvera Street, which leads north from the middle of the plaza. The only other colonial monument is the Church of Nuestra Señora la Reina de Los Angeles, begun in 1818 and dedicated in 1822.

◇ ◇ ◇ ◇ ◇

Just as the Spanish settlement campaign began to achieve a modest success, the dreaded Russians gained their first foothold on the northern coast. In 1812, Fort Rossiya—later shortened to Ross—was established. Settled by ninety-five Russians and

Fort Ross chapel, Sonoma County, 1934 photograph showing the structure as rebuilt in 1915–17 with four bays; it has since been reconstructed twice with three bays. The chapel was last reconstructed after a fire in 1970.

eighty Aleuts, the fort contained the commanders' quarters, a chapel, and seven other sturdily built timber structures within a palisade of redwood timbers. Two blockhouses, one octagonal and the other heptagonal, surmounted the palisade on the side facing the sea. Outside the walls were some fifty other buildings including picturesque dwellings and a barn for two hundred cows. Although the threat posed by Fort Ross outlasted the Spanish rule and even influenced the United States' Monroe Doctrine of

1823, the decline of the sea otter population left the Russians without a source of trade. In 1841, they sold the property to Johann August Sutter of Sacramento and departed.

Sutter also planned to build an empire in northern California. Born in Germany, Sutter had settled in Switzerland, where business failure caused his flight to the New World. He arrived in California in 1839 and became a Mexican citizen. Governor Alvarado gave him the maximum grant of eleven square leagues, or 48,400 acres, located at

Sutter's Fort in Sacramento, as reconstructed in 1891–93 following its acquisition by the state.

the junction of the Sacramento and American rivers. The rancho was adjacent to that of Alvarado's uncle and political rival, General Mariano Vallejo, on whom the governor wished to keep a watchful eye.

Sutter was a quasi-government official with power to enforce the laws. With his great number of Indian serfs, he cultivated a portion of his vast holdings in wheat, orchards, and vineyards. His fiefdom, Nueva Helvetia, was headquartered in a fort of timber and adobe with walls three feet thick and fifteen feet high. Inside the walls was the two-and-one-half story headquarters from which he administered the ranch and a prosperous trading post. By 1844, Nueva Helvetia was a stable trading post, the only place, in fact, where foreigners could take refuge in Alta California.

Sutter never intended to maintain Fort Ross. Instead, he stripped it of artillery and other equipment, and of the horses and cattle. Ironically, his own fort and other lands were despoiled by squatters during the ensuing chaotic periods of the American accession of California. The discovery of gold at his sawmill on the American River in Coloma brought him nothing but ruin. He passed the last years of his life in impoverished obscurity.

Neglect and fires—the last one in the 1970s—also took their toll on Fort Ross's structures. Fortunately, several have been reconstructed and, like Sutter's Fort, offer visitors a view of the fitful and fragmentary course of the settlement of California.

In 1833, the final order for secularization of the missions came from Mexico City. (Spain had issued decrees of secularization in 1813 and 1820, to no effect.) In August 1834, Governor Figueroa issued a proclamation ordering ten missions to be secularized that year, six in 1835, and the last five in 1836. Officials, mostly powerful *rancheros,* were appointed to administer the mission land, half of which was to be given to the neophytes. The Franciscans were to continue at the churches until curates arrived to replace them.

The operation did not proceed as planned. Because ownership entailed cultivating the land and building a house on it within one year, most of the neophytes refused the offer of land. The Indians' refusal, interpreted as a sign of laziness, was more likely caused by their dependency on the mission system, carefully nurtured by the friars, which made the concept of secularization incomprehensible to them. As a result, the mission properties passed into private, non-Indian hands during the settlement process, which lasted until the mid-1840s. (The U.S. Land Commission reduced the mission properties to their present minimal acreage in 1853. Carmel mission, for example, retained only nine acres; San Francisco's Mission San Francisco de Asís only 8.54 acres.)

The mission authorities' antisettlement policy did not inspire reverence for their

Mission church of San Carlos Borroméo de Carmelo in ruins, ca. 1860.

buildings. Used indifferently for a variety of secular purposes, the structures were plundered for building materials, particularly roof tiles. Without their protecting roofs, the adobe walls rapidly fell into ruins. The churches' survival was fortuitous; those not returned to religious use became increasingly ruinous as the decades passed.

As the world of the padres crumbled, town and country life thrived in the increasingly secular society that emerged under Mexican rule. More women arrived to elevate the social tone. The pre-Mexican settlers, who had intermarried, formed great clans. To distinguish themselves from the newcomers, they adopted the unofficial title of "Don." Included in their numbers were Americans who had arrived early, embraced the Catholic faith, married into the families of the so-called Californios, and become naturalized citizens.

For their dwellings, these settlers followed the Laws of the Indies' directions, building domiciles with courtyards where a kitchen garden could be planted and horses and other animals kept in a corral. The Mediterranean climate along the coast made adobe buildings practical. The use of *brea,* or tar, to seal flat-roofed adobes was adapted from the Indians' use of it to caulk boats. Flat roofs were more common in the south,

where there was less rainfall and heavy fog than in the coastlands from Monterey north. Simple adobe boxes such as the San Luís Gonzaga house near Los Baños were the most typical building form. Even the relatively grand houses of the ranchos and haciendas lacked the amenities familiar to Americans. Subsequent alterations to adapt adobes to modern living have altogether obscured the utter simplicity of these domestic settings.

The Casa Estudillo in San Diego exemplifies a form of dwelling that functioned as a *casa del poblador,* or town house. José Antonio Estudillo, a son of José María, who came to California as a soldier in 1806, owned vast ranchos in present-day Riverside and San Diego counties. The main family residence, on the plaza, had twelve rooms disposed around three sides of a walled courtyard, away from the noisy, dusty street. The courtyard, the focus of family life, contained the well, the main water source, and the garden. The latter was planted with fruit trees, herbal plants, and flowers, mostly introduced into California from Spain, Mexico, and South America. Unplanted areas had a surface of rammed earth or *terre pisé.* Many domestic chores were done in a vine-covered arbor called a *ramada.*

The ca. 1843 San Luís Gonzaga adobe near Los Banos reveals the utter simplicity of most adobe ranch houses. Even the larger and grand houses lacked the amenities familiar to Americans.

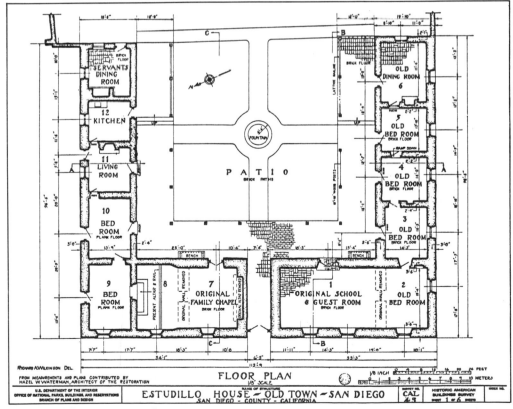

Casa Estudillo, San Diego, plan.

The house's thick walls of plastered adobe brick laid on rubble-stone foundations were punctured with small, wood-braced windows barred by stakes of wood or metal. Shed roofs, an alternative to the gable form, were constructed of wood beams lashed together with leather straps and covered with tule mats, then with tiles. On the court side, a *corredor,* or covered porch, provided a semiprotected circulation area. A family chapel and a kitchen were part of the structure of the Estudillo house; usually the kitchen was detached to lessen the risk of fire.

José Antonio Julián de la Guerra y Noriega, *comandante* of the Santa Barbara presidio from 1815 to 1839, began his house in 1819. Like the Casa Estudillo, the de la Guerra adobe formed three sides of a court. Between the late 1820s and 1850, a two-story addition was built at the rear northeast corner of the house. The upper floor

was allegedly used as an office and housed a library. The possession of enough books to call a library was unusual, not only because literacy was uncommon, but also because the religious authorities opposed private ownership of books. The de la Guerras were known as the royal family; their house was the most important residence of the period in Santa Barbara. Its 111-foot street facade was longer than those of many public buildings of the period.

The life-style of the times made up for the lack of architectural style. Defiantly archaic, the dons refined and elaborated the accoutrements of the lengthy social rituals and celebrations that punctuated their lives. Even the casual attire of Don Tomás Yorba, for example, included velvet knee breeches, white stockings, silver-buckled shoes, a hat trimmed in silver lace with silver and gold ornaments, silver spurs, and a saddle of carved leather inlaid with silver. Pío Pico,

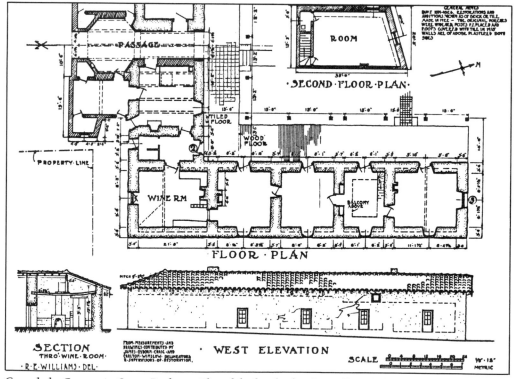

Casa de la Guerra in Santa Barbara. The adobe bricks for the walls and the sycamore timbers for the roof beams, rafters, and lintels of the doors and windows of this important house were obtained locally. The largest beam, of redwood, was imported from northern California and delivered by ship in 1827 about a year after most of the house was completed.

Thomas Larkin house in Monterey, 1936 photograph.

twice governor of California and owner of a forty-room house called El Ranchito, wore gold chains and jewels.

Women also wore silver and gold lace, elaborate mantillas, and velvet vests. Ruffled silk skirts and petticoats swirled over white stockings and high-heeled silk shoes with buckles. Their long hair was pinned up with tortoise shell or ivory combs. That such outfits were no longer stylish in Mexico City hardly mattered. The Californios' personal display of wealth stemmed in part from a barter-based economy. The "California bank note," as the steer hides were called, was neither portable nor easily displayed.

Whereas, under Spain, trade with foreigners had been illegal, Mexico legalized trade, which was concentrated in hides and tallow, materials that the Yankee sea traders conveyed to Boston manufactories. Although this trade gave the Californians a market, it prolonged their dependency on foreigners. Charles Dana's much quoted statement, "The Californians are an idle, thriftless people, and can make nothing for themselves," was true, if tinged with the Protestant ethic.

The ranchos, which swelled to hundreds of thousands of acres during the Mexican period, produced little besides the cattle that furnished the hides. Gathering the shipload of thirty to sixty thousand hides took about a year. Although home uses for leather were many—hides were scraped thin and oiled for window shades, and leather thongs substituted for nails—manu-

factured products such as shoes were imported from Boston. China, flatware, and other household items, and even mill work and window sash were shipped around the Horn. Astonished visitors to the dons' houses reported seeing fine carpets, procured through the Boston-China trade, laid on earth floors.

Most of the buildings associated with this society date from the 1840s. The degree of Yankee influence on these structures is difficult to determine. In Monterey, for example, Thomas O. Larkin built a two-story house, the first of its kind there, which was influential in the area. The first and only American consul, from 1844 to 1848, he was one of the most enterprising merchants and builders in Alta California. By his account, Larkin acquired the property in April 1835, roofed the house in September of that year, and made the final payments on materials in 1838.

When the building assumed the form it has today is unclear. At first, Larkin operated a store that probably occupied the whole ground floor; the family lived on the upper floor. The load-bearing, interior adobe walls are original, but the interior staircase may date from the time when the ground floor was converted to living quarters. Typically, the upper floors of Hispanic colonial dwellings were accessible only by exterior stairs; interior stairs were a sign of American influence. Other features associated with Yankee influence were the glazed window sash and the fireplaces. The Hispanic settlers usually heated their rooms with braziers of charcoal, provided by a source of fire outside the house. But in coastal Monterey, where the damp, fog-cooled climate made the thick-walled adobe houses miserable to live in for much of the year, fireplaces became common earlier than in the south.

Larkin and his house were much visited and widely known. Unfortunately, contemporary comments about the house have not survived to determine its effect on fashion. Other houses echo its form—the José Castro house in San Juan Bautista, 1840–41; the Vicente Lugo house in Bell, 1844; the Casa Los Cerritos, 1844; and the Vincente Martínez house in Martinez, 1849—and may reflect its influence. But, since the style of these buildings has a strong kinship with the architecture that developed in the Southwest, in Texas, Arizona, and New Mexico, following annexation in 1848, a more descriptive name for it would be "Territorial."

Two other notable houses of this type that also survive as museums are General Mariano Vallejo's Petaluma ranch headquarters, the largest adobe structure built in northern California, and the Rancho Los Cerritos hacienda in present-day Long Beach, reputed to be the largest adobe built in the southern part of the state.

Vallejo played a pivotal role in the transition from Mexican to American control. Under Governor Figueroa, he was made

comandante of the northern frontier. He was also in charge of the secularization of Mission Solano in Sonoma. In 1835, he laid out the pueblo of Sonoma adjacent to the mission. Vallejo's town house, the Casa Grande, dominated the plaza, which served as a drilling ground for the general's troops from 1835 to 1846.

All of the activities associated with raising cattle and sheep were conducted at the Petaluma ranch headquarters along with the more domestic activities of weaving wool, drying plants, and curing hides for leather. The solidly built structure had three-foot-thick walls of adobe bricks. Timbers for the roof beams and porch columns were imported from farther north; the roof was shingled, not tiled. All members were bound with rawhide thongs that tightened as they cured, creating joints as strong as nails could have made. Iron grilles and solid wooden shutters secured openings. The rhythms of beam-ends, columns, and railings against the plain wall surfaces conveyed the kind of structural honesty and truth in materials that became important to Modern architects a century later.

A comparison between Vallejo's Petaluma ranch headquarters and that built by Don Juan Temple on his Rancho Los Cerritos in 1844 reveals much about the evolution of such buildings over time. Recurring financial problems caused Vallejo to sell his Petaluma adobe in 1857. Subsequent owners

José Castro house in San Juan Bautista, 1934 photograph.

General Mariano Vallejo's Petaluma ranch headquarters. Built between 1834 and 1844, this was the largest adobe structure in northern California. The main section, about 200 feet long, has two stories; double verandas encircle the building. Although quarters for the family were included, a mayordomo was in residence to manage the ranch and the one thousand or so Indian laborers.

never occupied the building, and after a long period of neglect, it was given to the Native Sons of the Golden West who deeded it to the state in 1951. Now a state park, the restored buildings and some of the ranch site are accessible to the public, who are able to view it as it was during its active period as a ranch headquarters.

By contrast, the Rancho Los Cerritos headquarters, built by Don Juan (Jonathan) Temple in 1844 as the center for his 27,000-acre ranch, continued in use under the ownership of two families until the mid-twentieth century. Originally the ranch was part of the 167,000-acre Spanish grant made to Manuel Nieto in 1784. In 1843 Don Juan Temple bought the property from the Nieto heirs. Don Juan, one of the successful early Yankee traders, married into the Cota family and became a naturalized Mexican citizen. He built the first general store and, later, the first office building in Los Angeles.

The two-story ranch house Temple built in 1844 had a foundation of brick shipped around the horn, walls of adobe brick made on the property, and hand-hewn redwood beams obtained from forests north of Monterey. The main part of the building, where the family lived, had two stories wrapped with a double veranda. One-story wings on the north and south sides housed the ranch operations. The enclosed court, walled on the west side and barren in Temple's day, was used as a corral for animals and equipment. The original roofs were flat and made

of redwood planks covered with a layer of gravel and sealed with molten *brea.*

A planter as well as a rancher, Temple grew the first pepper trees in the Los Angeles pueblo in front of his store. At Rancho Los Cerritos he laid out the so-called Italian gardens that were famous in their time but vanished in the disastrous droughts of the early 1860s which ruined the cattle ranchers and forced Don Juan to sell the ranch to Jotham Bixby in 1866.

Under the Bixby family ownership, the gardens became even more extensive. In her *Adobe Days,* Sarah Bixby Smith, a niece, described the gardens in spring:

. . . spreading beds of iris were purple with a hundred blossoms . . . while later in the year there were masses of blue agapanthus with pink amaryllis. . . . There were no single specimens of flowers, but always enough for us to pick. . . . The garden did not contain even one palm tree or a bit of cactus, nor do I remember a eucalyptus tree. There were two large bunches of pampas grass and two old century plants. . . . Orange blossoms, honey suckle, lilac, and lemon verbena, roses, oleander and heliotrope made a heaven of fragrance.

After the Jotham Bixbys left the ranch in 1881, the building was occupied intermittently until 1930, when Llewellyn Bixby, a nephew who had acquired the house and grounds in 1929, finished restoring and remodeling the house for his family's use. In 1955, the Long Beach City Council purchased the building and grounds. A National Historic Landmark since 1970, the

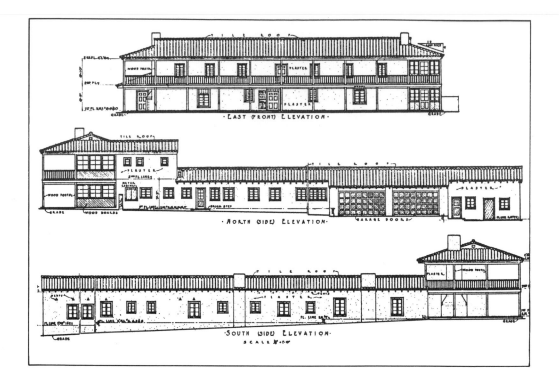

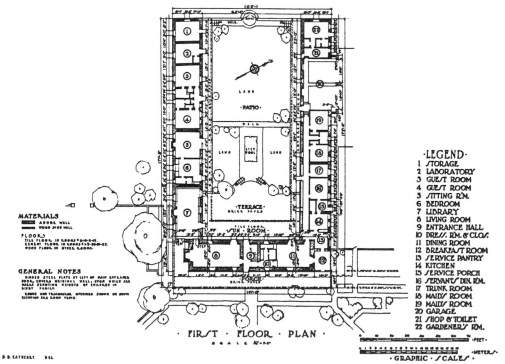

La Casa de Los Cerritos in Long Beach, plans and elevations drawn in the 1930s.

site is open to the public. While the Petaluma ranch offers a window on the vanished past, Rancho Los Cerritos presents a
theme of continuity. The visitor to Los Cerritos senses the past through accumulated
layers that convey an image of timelessness.

One of the most exemplary ranch compounds, the Sherwood ranch near Salinas
belonged for most of its existence to Eugene
Sherwood, who acquired it in 1860 from Jacob Leese. The oldest building, a modest
adobe that stood in the center of the courtyard, was allegedly built in 1823 by a member of the Soberanes family. The later
buildings, which enclosed the courtyard,
were an eclectic mixture of wood plank,
rubble-stone, and adobe construction. Two
were two-story, precut frames shipped from
New England and purchased by Jacob
Leese. This eclectic mixture of structures,
introduced by a monumental wooden gateway, chronicled central California ranch life
with remarkable continuity from colonial
times. The destruction of the compound in
the 1960s robbed the state of a significant
link to the past.

*Sherwood Ranch near Salinas, 1934 photo-
graphs of the entrance and part of the ranch
compound.*

❖   ❖   ❖   ❖   ❖

Adobe buildings did not become extinct
with statehood. Particularly in the south,
where timber was scarce, adobe continued
as a preferred material for nonurban dwellings well into the 1850s. In the Mother
Lode mining country to the north before
lumber mills were common, adobe buildings were erected by newcomers familiar
with adobe construction.

The first civic buildings constructed after
California obtained statehood are a good example of the Americanization of the state's
architecture. In Monterey, Colton Hall, site
of the first state constitutional convention,
was built on speculation by Walter Colton, a
Yale University-educated, American clergy-
man. Commodore Stockton, commander of
the American military forces in California,
appointed Colton mayor of the town in
1846. Although Monterey had been the colonial capital, it lacked a building suitable
for either a town hall or a school. Nor was
there any money in the treasury to con-
struct one. The resourceful Colton financed

the construction of a new building by fining
gamblers, drunkards, and roadhouse pro
prietors. To cut costs even more, he employed convict labor. Work began in 1847;
the building was completed in 1848 and
dedicated in March of 1849, in time for the
convention.

Any hopes for continuity in the evolution
of the new state from Hispanic to American
culture vanished during the Gold Rush.
This massive migration to California had
the disruptive effect of a wartime invasion.
The cultural transformation underway at
the time of the 1849 constitutional convention ceased. In 1842 Sir George Simpson,
Governor General of Her Majesty's Hudson's
Bay Territories, had appraised the California
economy as, "Nature doing everything; man
doing nothing." Ten years later, the situation
was completely reversed.

Evidence of the cataclysmic impact of
tens of thousands of newcomers—mostly
young, Anglo-Saxon and male—has all but
vanished in the state's major cities. San

Colton Hall in Monterey. In March 1849, Mayor Colton wrote a description of the building, which is accurate except that the portico he mentions acquired the branching stair visible in this 1936 photograph from the 1880s: "The town hall on which I have been at work for more than a year, is at last finished. It is built of white stone, quarried from a neighboring hail which is easily carved into the shape you desire. The lower apartments are for schools; the hall over them—seventy feet by thirty—is for public assemblies. The front is ornamented by a portico, which you enter from the hall. It is not an edifice which would attract any attention among public buildings in the United States, but in California it is without rival."

The Clark-Humphrey house, a San Francisco mansion of 1852, had prefabricated Federal style elements topped with a crenellated parapet of Gothic persuasion. This photograph dates from ca. 1880.

Francisco, Sacramento, and Stockton, the principal supply ports, have lost almost all their pioneer building stock. Fortunately, pride in their rapid growth inspired extensive photography, which now must substitute for the actual buildings.

The first waves of gold-seekers took shelter in makeshift tents and hovels made from refuse of wood, paper, and cloth. By the fall of 1849, buildings were rising rapidly on the blocks around San Francisco's center, Portsmouth Square. The few adobe frame buildings that had composed the Mexican port town of Yerba Buena (San Francisco's name until January 1847) were absorbed by the rows of wood frame and later—as a result of disastrous fires—brick buildings.

The departure of workers for the gold country crippled industry, including lumbering and building. A brisk trade in prefabricated buildings filled the gap until late 1850, when local construction resumed. In November 1849, the *San Francisco Chronicle* reported that more than six hundred frames had arrived that year. The final tally on imported buildings remains a matter of dispute; some accounts state that five thousand came from New York and even more from Massachusetts and Maine. While most of the precut frames were American-made, customhouse records give an international provenance for many of the imports. England, Australia, and China provided buildings of both wood and cast iron in a range of styles.

The general use of prefabricated frames exemplifies both the expedient and the egalitarian nature of life during the peak years of the Gold Rush. Even celebrities such as John Charles and Jessie Frémont lived in a prefabricated house from China in San Francisco's so-called Happy Valley, which was mostly a tent encampment. Jessie Frémont wrote of the house: "It was put up without nails except the shingling on the roof, all the rest fitting in together like a puzzle, and was of pretty smooth wood, making a very good temporary lodging. . . . Our little house had but two rooms, but they were large and clean. . . . " Although she did not mention whether the house came with doors and windows, some of those imported from Hong Kong did. A firm in Liverpool, England, offered a small,

furnished two-room iron cottage for $150, provided with five plate glass windows, two beds, one table, one chest of drawers, two chairs, and kitchen apparatus. The iron buildings may have been simple to assemble, "for every piece is marked, every bolt-hole made, and every bolt and nut provided," but they were uninhabitable in hot weather and, as the San Francisco fire of 1851 revealed, deformed and collapsed under extreme heat.

Such prefabricated structures should not be confused with today's standardized products. The buildings were assembled first and then knocked down and packaged. Although they should have been easy to reassemble, enough accounts testify to the contrary to show why they failed to compete with local industry when it got started.

The majority of prefabs were probably small, even miniature by today's norms. Yet, reports exist of two-and-one-half-story structures suitable for warehouses and stores and even large enough for hotels. One example, the Parker House, was a famous hostelry on Portsmouth Square. It consisted of several frames spliced together and was given a modicum of stylistic respectability by the pioneer architect, Levi Goodrich.

Lachryma Montis, the last residence of General Mariano Vallejo in Sonoma, is dramatic evidence of the transition from Hispanic to American architecture. A wealth of Gothic-style detail in lacy bargeboards, porch brackets, and window architraves with pointed arches adorns this two-story house with one-story porches. According to shipping records, this was one of three frames imported by Vallejo in 1849.

Another one was put up in San Francisco by a Mr. Burritt at the corner of Sutter and Stockton streets. In *Men and Memories of San Francisco*, published in the spring of 1850, T. Z. Barry and B. A. Patten described it as, "nestling among the cheerless sandhills like a sweet bit of our old home spirited across the continent by fairies." This house was gone by 1900, but the third frame still stands in Benicia, where it was put up by John Frisbie, a son-in-law of Vallejo. It is better known as the house of Captain Walsh, a sea captain who occupied it from 1849 until his death in 1884.

In 1851, Dr. Benjamin Shurtleff had this pre-fabricated, two-story house with a double portico in the Classical Revival style shipped up to Shasta City in Trinity, photograph from 1934.

Lachryma Montis, General Mariano Vallejo's prefabricated house in Sonoma, as photographed in 1934 before restoration by the state.

Whether in the Mother Lode region of the Sierra foothills or in the northern mining country near the Trinity Alps, the early American towns in California reveal the differences between Hispanic and North American culture. No longer were public and private buildings grouped around a square with land reserved for public use and future growth. In the American towns, buildings lined the main streets in a first-come, first-served order. Towns were incorporated after unplanned development had taken place; public parks followed but were often located away from the valuable commercial property in the center of town.

Nearly every town of consequence had a Wells Fargo Company and an Independent Order of Odd Fellows building. The I.O.O.F., a benevolent society that originated in Manchester, England, was devoted to offering social asylum to strangers, or odd fellows. The organization was enormously popular on the mining frontier, where virtually everyone was a stranger. The familiar logo of the linked chain above or below the acronym identifies, typically, a two- to three-story building which may still be found on the main street of Gold Rush towns. The ground floor was leased for commercial space; the upper floor was a meeting hall. If the importance of the town justified it, other floors were added and leased as office space.

Like San Francisco, the mining towns burned so frequently that the masonry buildings lining the main street are usually the second or third generation. Except for minimal Classical detail such as a cornice molding and dentil course marking the roofline, the buildings lack a strong stylistic imprint. Raised parapets on the facades exaggerated the buildings' height by concealing the gable roof behind them. The as-

William Heath Davis, a real estate developer, had ten frames shipped from Portland, Maine to San Francisco, which arrived in late 1850. By that time, the market for them had declined. To avoid selling them at a loss, he shipped them down to the "new town" he was creating in San Diego. One survives, though moved to another location; its minimal Federal Revival style conveys the Yankee demeanor of many pioneer settlements.

Downieville photographed in 1934. Observers of the mining-era boom towns generally found them evocative of New England. This impression—still strong today—reflected the source of both the architectural imagery and the population.

pirations toward eastern urbanity expressed by these "false fronts" were furthered by wooden canopies built out over the board sidewalks. Merchants hung them with canvas awnings to block the dust from unpaved streets teeming with horses and vehicles. The windows and doors were typically set in deep reveals and protected from fire and theft by cast-iron shutters. Where masonry walls were built, cast-iron plates anchoring the tie-rods used to stabilize the walls con-

tribute a decorative pattern.

Although brick was cheaper than cut stone, thin schist fieldstone was readily available in the mining country. Laid up in rubble form, it was used for embankments and walls of all kinds; its richly colored texture is part of the palette of materials of every Mother Lode town. Building facades were more formally treated with a cut-stone facing or a plaster surface scored to mimic stone. High-quality granite from the Folsom

Wells Fargo building in Columbia, 1934 photograph.

Rivett-Fuller building in Sacramento, photograph 1965. A simplified Classical Revival style was typically used for mining-era commercial buildings.

quarries was used for ashlar masonry. The mighty walls of the Sierra notwithstanding, granite was too expensive to quarry and transport from that far away. Time was of the essence, and even the locally made brick was often too low-fired to weather well.

Like Colton Hall in Monterey, the first building associated with statehood, the post-Gold Rush capital building in Benicia, dated 1853, was in the Classical Revival style. The temple-front building with two

columns in antis also got its start as part of a speculative venture, this time to build a new capital city. The founders, Thomas O. Larkin and Robert Semple, the Kentucky-born printer from Monterey who had presided over the state constitutional convention there, convinced the legislature to move from its inadequate quarters in San Jose to Benicia, a city they promised would exist within a year. The township land was leased from Mariano Vallejo's vast Solano rancho in 1847. Benicia was Señora Vallejo's second name; her first, Francisca, had been chosen and then abandoned when Yerba Buena renamed itself San Francisco the same year.

When the legislators arrived in 1853, they found an assembly building waiting for them, but nothing in the way of an infrastructure. Accommodations were nearly as bad as in San Jose; in the rainy season the streets were rivers of mud. Yet, the capitol had been erected in record time. The San Francisco contracting firm of Rider and Houghton had prepared the plans, probably from a pattern book, and constructed the building in about three months, from late September 1852 to early January 1853. Such speed reveals the transformation of the construction industry during the Gold Rush years. As for the building's architectural image, it would have been familiar to settlers coming from the Atlantic seaboard across the midwestern regions. Even today the building looks more like a transplant than a homegrown product.

A different kind of official architecture was represented by early American military bases. The U.S. Army established itself on Angel Island in 1853, the U.S. Navy on Mare Island in 1854. The Benicia Arsenal, established in 1852 by Captain Charles P. Stone, head of U.S. Army Ordinance for the Pacific Coast, was built at the same time. Captain Stone had come from Virginia in 1851 to choose a site for the arsenal. He considered San Francisco but found the climate too damp for storing powder and weapons. He turned to Benicia, where Larkin and Semple had deeded 345 acres to the U.S. Army for a reservation in 1849. The arsenal was sited east of the army's barracks and north of the quartermaster's depot. Although the climate was favorable, the site lacked water. This situation plagued the commanders until 1889, when an artificial lake fed by water from Suisun Bay was made.

In spite of the urgency of housing weapons and gunpowder, the U.S. Army was no more successful than civilians had been in obtaining materials and skilled labor for construction in the early years. Fortunately, good local sandstone was available for the first storehouses erected from official plans between 1853 and 1856. Although the buildings are known as the Camel barns, it is unlikely that they ever housed the benighted beasts that were purchased by the government in 1855 for military use in the Southwest. When the camels proved to be too exotic and ill-tempered for American handlers, they were driven north through California, arriving in Benicia in February 1864, where they were sold at auction at the end of the month.

Three of the arsenal buildings were

The first State Capitol in Benicia, photographs taken before and after the 1955–57 restoration.

structurally ambitious. Two of them were powder magazines entirely of stone with double aisles and handsome vaults supported on columns with capitals that had original designs with leaf and shell motifs. The third building was the Main Arsenal Storehouse (Building No. 29), the compound's most ambitious structure. The plan of ca. 1858 by J. Fuss, master builder, directed by commanding officer Franklin D. Callender, was not carried out as drawn; only one corner tower was constructed. The most daring aspect of the structure was the interior framing. Supported from below by columns, the second floor was free of columns because the third floor was suspended from the roof trusses.

Except for the Benicia capitol, few government buildings of architectural distinction went up during the first decade of statehood. The 1854 Mariposa County courthouse is a well-proportioned Neo-Georgian building which, like the Benicia capitol, bows to the eastern part of the country for its architectural inspiration. In 1855–56 the now-destroyed state courthouse, an impressive Classical Revival building with a projecting Ionic portico, was completed in Sacramento. As in Benicia, the prospect of occupying a stately structure persuaded the legislature to move to Sacramento, which finally became the official state capital in 1854.

Since the courthouse could not house both the state supreme court and the legislature, the question of a new capitol arose shortly. The legislature approved a bond issue in 1856, chose the plans of architect Reuben Clark, and awarded the contract to Joseph Nougues as builder. But work ceased within two weeks of the December groundbreaking. An uncertain economy postponed the project for four years; by September 1860, a new site was cleared and another appropriation made. Despite the earlier award to Reuben Clark, a new architectural competition was held. M. F. Butler won first place with a design that strongly resembled Clark's. The cornerstone for the new building was laid on May 15, 1861.

As it turned out, the timing of the second building campaign was no better than that of the first. Shortages of materials and other construction problems caused by the Civil War delayed the completion of the

Benicia Arsenal, the interior of Powder Magazine #2, built in 1857. U.S. Army photograph taken ca. 1940.

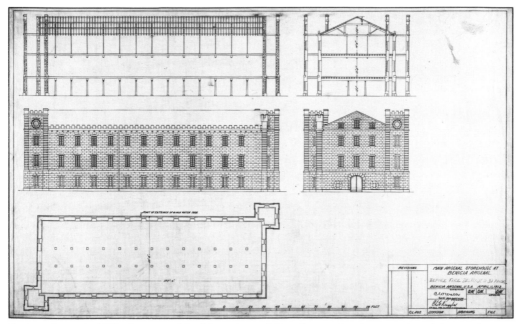

Benicia Arsenal, 1859 drawing of the Main Arsenal Storehouse, showing its original innovative structural system. After an explosion and fire in 1912, the storehouse was rebuilt with two stories instead of three, resulting in the present, awkward proportions.

capitol until February 1874. The final cost was said to be $2,600,000, a staggering sum for the times.

⬦ ⬦ ⬦ ⬦ ⬦

Although the construction of churches lagged in the miner's free-wheeling, secular society, in the mid-1850s miniaturized Georgian and Gothic Revival churches began to punctuate the skylines of towns in the mining regions. The typical source of designs for the churches was pattern books or plans supplied by the eastern parishes from which the clergy or members of the congregation came. The plans were often adapted by carpenter-builders and, therefore, do not appear standardized. St. James Episcopal Church in Sonora, built in 1859, is a fine example of the Gothic Revival style adapted to the frontier.

If the settlers of the mining towns attempted to recreate the familiar context of home with minimal stylistic means, San Franciscans were more ambitious in their emulation of eastern architecture. In 1853 Montgomery Block, located at Washington, Montgomery, and Merchant streets, was designed in a restrained but sophisticated Classical style that reflected the English background of its architect, George P. Cummings. The brick walls were plastered to mimic stone; the ground-floor arcade had twenty-eight shops with entrances set between square stone piers. The four entrances to the building pierced the second-floor cornice with triangular, broken pediments on round columns with Tuscan capitals.

Initially, financiers and lawyers occupied the offices in the four-story building. Even the developer, Henry W. Halleck, was a member of a law firm, Peachy, Billings and Halleck, which had offices on the second floor. The Bank Exchange Saloon, located in one ground-floor corner of the building, served the famed Pisco Punch, which eased many a transaction.

Halleck had been trained in civil engineering at the United States Military Academy at West Point and held the rank of captain. The innovative foundation he designed for the Montgomery Block—a raft-

The 1854 Mariposa County courthouse is a well-proportioned, Neo-Georgian building which, like the Benicia Capitol, reflects eastern influence. This photograph was taken in 1936.

like structure of redwood timbers—allowed it to adjust to the earth's violent movement in 1906 and survive undamaged. Diagonal tie-rods also provided an early version of X-bracing against the shear stress of the quake.

As the financial district moved down Montgomery toward Market Street, the "Monkey Block," as it came to be called, was no longer a prestigious address. Instead, it housed the city's writers and artists. But neither its architectural significance nor its roster of famous tenants saved it from the wrecking ball. A bigger blockbuster, the Transamerica Building, occupies its place.

The Gold Rush attracted architects, as all boom times do. For a while in the 1850s, architecture in San Francisco, and to some extent in Sacramento, emulated international fashions. Unfortunately, none of the work in the early Renaissance Revival style by such architects as the Belgian Peter Portois or the German Victor Hoffman exists except in photographs.

Sacramento boasted one of the state's most elegant Italianate mansions. Shelton C. Fogus, the original owner and builder, was a pioneer merchant in the capital. In 1857 he

Bodie, Mono County. Mining towns in remote areas that had no other raison d'être were usually abandoned, as Bodie was, when the ore ran out or the industry slumped badly. The northern section of the high Sierra in Mono County had its first gold rush in the 1850s. The town of Bodie, named —with a slight change in spelling—for the ore's discoverer, W. S. Bodey, prospered in the 1870s, when the population rose to over ten thousand. The town life thundered on until about 1880, when the mines shut down except for sporadic activity later on. Completely deserted, Bodie, the state's emblematic ghost town, became a state historic park in 1964.

St. James Episcopal Church in Sonora, 1934 photograph. This wooden Gothic Revival style church, probably built by a "carpetect" in 1859, was painted a brick red to suggest masonry.

The 1860 school house in Murphys exemplifies frontier efforts to build in the Georgian Revival mode.

Until its demolition in 1959, the 1853 Montgomery Block, forerunner of today's block-busting office buildings, was the major landmark of post-Gold Rush San Francisco.

commissioned a fine house of brick and plaster from architect Seth Babson, who had come from Maine to San Francisco in 1850. The residence consisted of a main block, 46 by 40 feet, and a rear wing, 20 by 31 feet. Its brick walls were plastered in a buff color and scored to mimic stone. The quoins were real stone; the ornament on the window architraves and frieze panels of the entablature was cast iron painted a darker color for contrast. The Corinthian columns of the portico supported a full entablature with a cornice bearing modillions surmounted by a balustrade with turned finials atop the corner posts.

In 1861, when Leland Stanford purchased the Fogus house for his gubernatorial residence, the *Sacramento Union* alleged that it was "the most perfect specimen of a residence in the state." On January 10, 1862, the rising waters of the Sacramento River forced the governor to return home unceremoniously in a rowboat. Repairs were made, and in 1863 the Stanfords leased the

house to the new governor, F. F. Low. In 1868, when Leland, Jr., was born, they reoccupied it.

In 1871–72 a major remodeling took place which may have combined the talents of Babson and another local architect, Nathaniel Goodell. A new section was added to the house, which was raised a full story to accommodate a ballroom in the basement. Mansard roofs crowned the whole, and a curved and branching stairway was created for the entrance portico. While the mansard roof and its generously scaled dormers reflect the later, Second Empire style, the design is complementary to the original Italianate.

Although most commercial buildings from this time were Italianate in style, few were built in real stone. One famous exception was John Parrott's 1852 business block in San Francisco. A quarry on Goat Island, as Yerba Buena Island was then called, furnished the stone for the basement story. But the building was more famous for having its

The Montgomery Block's cast-stone keystones bore portrait heads of national figures such as Henry Jackson and George Washington, as well as those of its builders, Halleck and Cummings.

This 1960 photograph of the Adams & Company Express building in Sacramento shows its condition prior to renovation following the demolition of most of the original city center for a freeway in the 1960s. The remaining blocks of buildings, now called Old Town, have had their buildings renovated on the exterior and, in most cases, given contemporary interiors.

upper stories of twenty-inch-thick brick walls clad in precut granite blocks shipped from China.

In the southern part of the state, Los Angeles' downtown moved south of the pueblo in the American era. One of its surviving blocks has Italianate buildings ranging in time from the Merced Theater of 1868 to the Garnier Block of 1890. Also in this block is Pico House, designed by Keysor & Morgan, and built on the pueblo plaza in 1869 by the last Mexican governor, Pío Pico.

The state's most typical commercial structures had heavy timber floors supported on cast-iron columns and brick walls; they were faced on the street side with elaborate cast-iron or cast-stone facades. Although their architectural detail was locally manufactured, they took their stylistic cues from eastern prototypes in St. Louis, Chicago, and New York.

Sizable country houses of stone and brick from the 1850s were rare. A modified Italianate villa with a castellated tower, designed by Thomas Boyd for the pseudophysician John Marsh, was built in 1856 on his Mount Diablo ranch. The stone was quarried and the brick fired on the ranch property. Marsh's great wealth and eccentricity (his vast herds of cattle were collected as payments for his medical advice) as well as his choice of a Boston designer may explain such an ambitious structure.

The most exemplary rural Italianate villa of the period belonged to John Bidwell, leader of the first overland immigrant party to California. After twenty-four gruelling weeks the settlers arrived in November 1841 at John Marsh's ranch. Subsequent hard work and success brought Bidwell a twenty-two-thousand acre ranch of his own in Chico, located in the central valley north of Sacramento. In 1865, he built the towered mansion designed by Henry Cleaveland, which still stands on the grounds of Chico State University. Cleaveland, also a pioneer, arrived in California in 1850 from Massachusetts. His popular pattern book, *Village and Farm Cottages* was published in 1856 and reflects the influence of his good friend, Alexander Jackson Downing, the most famous of the American pattern book authors.

By the time the towered Italianate villa

Stanford-Lathrop house in Sacramento. Two views of the house originally built for Shelton C. Fogus in 1857, and sold to Leland Stanford in 1861. The lower photograph, taken in the 1880s, shows the extensive remodeling Stanford commissioned in the 1870s.

Built by former governor Pío Pico in 1869 as a grand hotel, Pico House was the first three-story building in Los Angeles and one of the largest masonry structures of its time.

The 1866 Hotaling Building is the most elaborate of the stand of commercial buildings on Jackson Street in San Francisco that comprise the only surviving remnant of the pre-1906 downtown.

John Marsh's house, near the present-day city of Brentwood, lost its sixty-five foot tower in the 1868 earthquake.

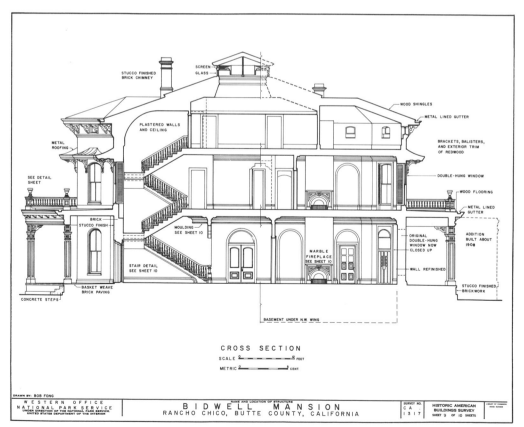

The John Bidwell mansion, built in 1865 in Chico, was designed by a famous pioneer architect, Henry Cleaveland. This sectional drawing of the house shows how the third-floor receives daylight through the monitor centered in the roof.

arrived in California, it was no longer on the cusp of fashion. The lag in styles, typical of the frontier, was greater in the prerailroad days and varied in different parts of the state. The training and background of the pioneer architects, most of whom were "carpetects," was an important factor in the way styles were chosen and built.

While Cleaveland had a sophisticated architectural background, Peter J. Barber, a cabinetmaker turned builder, who came to San Francisco from Ohio in 1852 at the age of twenty-two, was more typical. Within three years of his arrival—and perhaps after apprenticing with Reuben Clark, who later won the Sacramento State Capitol competition—he began taking contracts for buildings. From 1858 to 1869 he practiced architecture in San Francisco but later moved to Santa Barbara for his health. Whatever troubled him seems to have been cured by the famous climate because he ended his career as the designer of several important public buildings in Santa Barbara and served two terms as mayor.

Although the Gothic Revival style was highly popular for houses, few intact examples survive, probably because of the fragility of the ornamental detail. One significant example is the Oakland home of J. Mora Moss. In 1864, ten years after his arrival in California, Moss had Stephen H. Williams design his house. Williams, the architect of Parrott's granite block, is thought to have had extensive architectural experience in the East.

Styles were easier to import than building types that used particular construction techniques. The New England "salt box" was generally built with a heavy timber frame joined by the mortise-and-tenon method. Time-consuming and labor-intensive, this construction method was rare in California, where there was a chronic labor shortage at midcentury.

One of the few salt-box houses survives, now restored, on the shore of Half Moon Bay in San Mateo County. Called James Johnston's White House, it may have been built in 1853, though Johnston recalled moving into it in 1855 or 1856. Although by San Francisco standards the heavy-timber-framed salt box was an anachronism, Johnston may have chosen this type of construction both to recall an earlier family

The Hunt-Stambach house in Santa Barbara, designed and built by Peter J. Barber in 1879–80, has a wood frame, 36'-5" by 29'-6", clad in channeled siding and set on a cut-stone foundation. The decorative detail on both the exterior and the interior, as shown in these two photographs, is well executed and reveals Barber's early training as a cabinet-maker.

J. Mora Moss' house, built in 1864 in Oakland, was much admired for its fine Gothic detail on both exterior and interior.

James Johnston's house in Half Moon Bay is shown here as it looked after long years of neglect and before it was restored in the 1970s. Malcolm Watkins documented its history in The White House of Half Moon Bay, James Johnston's Homestead, 1853.

house in Gallipolis, Ohio, and to show his neighbors in this isolated area what a proper eastern farmhouse was like. Because of the lack of roads over the coastal hills to the bayside lumber mills, the timbers were allegedly sent up the coast by sea and floated ashore.

Another imported building type, the octagonal house, was conceived and publicized by Orson Fowler in his book, *A House for All,* first published in 1849. Fowler's prescription for healthful living called for maximum ventilation and sunlight, hence the many sides of the house. Even the walls should breathe, he insisted, and gave out a recipe for a gravelly mixture that would ensure this healthful feature.

Only two of the seven or so octagonal houses built in San Francisco survive. The former William G. McElroy home, built in 1853 on Union Street, was damaged in the 1906 earthquake and restored. The house is in a Classical Revival mode with a cupola, bracketed cornice, and quoins to accentuate its angled walls. The other octagon, built in 1857 for the Feusiers, was given a mansard roof and other details in the 1870s in emulation of the fashionable Second Empire style.

As the nineteenth century wore on, churches were increasingly designed by architects knowledgeable in the Gothic style that most religious denominations favored. Builders on the frontier had made stylistic compromises, but, in time, expedient measures yielded to more sophistication in form and detail. The alterations that the early churches needed to accommodate larger congregations often made them more elaborate and stylish.

The evolution of St. Paul's Episcopal Church in Benicia was typical of many early churches. St. Paul's was a pet project of Colonel Julian McAllister, commander of the Benicia Arsenal from 1860 to 1886. McAllister came from a prominent southern family; his brother, Hall McAllister, was a noted San Francisco lawyer. Julian's involvement in Benicia's social life led him to play a major role in the Episcopal parish and probably to design its church.

Constructed between November 1859 and February 1860, this building appears to have been small and boxlike with a low

The McElroy Octagon, built in San Francisco in 1853, was moved across the street from its original location on Union Street in the 1950s and remodeled as a museum for the Colonial Dames of America. Its condition after the 1906 earthquake is shown in this dramatic photograph of refugees dividing up clothing from a cart, taken by Arnold Genthe in 1906.

WEST ELEVATION

MATERIALS·
FOUNDATION · CONCRETE
EXTERIOR WALLS·WOOD CLAPBOARD
ROOF · ASPHALT SHINGLES

St. Paul's Episcopal Church in Benicia, west elevation.

tower over the entrance. In 1863 the chancel was moved back and a transept added; in 1873 a choir was added and the nave extended so close to the street that the tower had to be shifted to one side; in 1880 the whole church was moved back to its present location; and, finally, in 1886 a new chancel replaced the old one, which was moved and became the vestry. This last campaign was the occasion for the redecoration of the whole interior. The refinement of the trussed wood ceiling and the richly carved ornament attests to the high level of technology in wood construction at that time.

Romanesque Revival enjoyed a considerable vogue in California, as it did elsewhere in the country in the 1880s and 1890s. While there was a long tradition of adapting stone construction to wood in the Gothic style, the Romanesque was more identified with rugged stone forms and detail. In Cali-

fornia, the much greater expense of stone construction relative to wood meant that the Romanesque tended to be used more for monumental institutions than the smaller community buildings often found in the Midwest and the East. Earthquakes and the processes of urban rebuilding have taken their toll of California's stand of Romanesque Revival structures. Today it is hard to believe that the style contributed so much to the architectural vitality of its cities.

The greatest example of the Romanesque Revival, Stanford University, was created as a memorial to Leland, Jr., the Stanfords' only child, who died of typhoid fever in Italy in 1884 at the age of sixteen. For his father this was the great tragedy in a life otherwise filled with spectacular good fortune.

A New Yorker, trained in the law, Stanford came to California in 1852 to join his brothers in what became a highly profitable mercantile operation in Sacramento and the mining region. However, Stanford's most significant association was with Mark Hopkins, Charles Crocker, and Collis P. Huntington, who were known, collectively, as the Big Four. Having masterminded the building of the western part of the transcontinental railroad, the Big Four extended their transportation and real-estate operations into virtually every corner of the state. Stanford's stellar career culminated in the presidency of the Central Pacific and the Southern Pacific Railroad companies. He also served one term as governor and one-and-a-half terms as U.S. senator (he died in 1893 in the middle of his second term).

Among his land holdings were ranches in Palo Alto that he had developed as a farm for thoroughbred horses. Stanford chose this site for the Leland Stanford Junior University, founded in November 1886. Additional purchases of adjoining land increased the university holdings to more than nine thousand acres.

Accustomed to having the best of everything, Stanford thought to hire Francis Walker, President of the Massachusetts Institute of Technology, to head his university. Walker declined the offer but agreed to be a

planning consultant. At his suggestion Stanford hired landscape architect Frederick Law Olmsted to create the master plan. In 1886 these two men spent several months with Stanford in Palo Alto in a planning session. Although the three agreed that the campus would be composed of stone buildings connected by arcades, Stanford and Olmsted disagreed on the location. Olmsted favored the foothills; Stanford insisted on the plain. Besides revealing their aesthetic biases, the conflict also indicated that Stanford did not intend to be a passive client. He insisted on the flatland site and paid no attention to Olmsted's assertion that the eastern-style landscaping with sweeping lawns that Stanford wanted would be impractical in the semiarid climate.

Stanford also favored a formal plan, a parallelogram, as he described it in a press release. A plausible, but unexpressed, reason for this preference may have been Stanford's long experience with the linear organization of railroad lines.

Stanford also acquired his Boston architects, Shepley, Rutan & Coolidge, at Walker's suggestion. This was a major commission for the young men who had inherited Henry Hobsen Richardson's practice

The decorative detail carved on the arches at Stanford University in Palo Alto was derived from French Romanesque architecture; the arcaded courts and tiled roofs recall the Spanish missions.

upon his death in 1886. At age twenty-eight, Charles A. Coolidge became Stanford's principal designer.

Despite the strong eastern influences at work in the design process, Stanford wanted a California identity for his institution. In April 1887, he told reporters from the *San Francisco Examiner,* "I suggested to Mr. Olmsted an adaptation of the adobe buildings of California with some higher form of architecture, . . . and my Boston architects have skillfully carried out the idea, really creating for the first time an architecture distinctly Californian in character."

The "higher form of architecture" Stanford had in mind was Romanesque à la Richardson. Not only was the style at the height of fashion, but it also lent itself to the general format of the Spanish colonial missions through the use of courtyards, round-arched arcades, and tile roofs. Since the missions were then largely in ruins, most Californians had no idea what they had originally looked like. The Stanfords themselves used such vague terms as "Spanish" and "Moorish," which were duly reported without explanation in the press. In truth, the whole Spanish colonial period had become mythical and was therefore ripe for use as propaganda.

Certainly none of the missions had employed the system of interlocking quadrangles and biaxial orientation of the university plan. What the poor padres and their Indian laborers had lacked in skill, technology, and money was supplied a hundred years later by masons brought over from Italy and supported by Stanford's vast fortune. Rock-faced ashlar masonry of sandstone replaced rubble-stone and adobe walls; carved capitals and other detail drawn from the Richardson-Romanesque vocabulary graced column capitals and friezes. A triumphal entrance arch marked the approach to a monumental church.

The wealthy continued to hire eastern talent. Darius Ogden Mills, another New Yorker, started his banking empire in Sacramento in 1859. In 1864 he joined William Ralston and others in founding the Bank of California. As the city's most flamboyant merchant prince, Ralston commissioned a banking hall with solid granite walls from

the Scottish architect David Farquaharson. Built in 1866, it was modeled after Sansovino's Library of St. Mark in Venice. It was the city's last large building of pure masonry construction, and was razed shortly before the 1906 earthquake.

By contrast, the ten-story business block commissioned by D. O. Mills in 1891 from the Chicago firm of Burnham and Root survived, though fire-damaged, to demonstrate the superiority of the new steel frame construction. Because of the one-hundred-foot height limit in downtown San Francisco, the Mills Building could not compete with the skyscrapers in Chicago. But for many years it was the tallest building in San Fran-

The Mills Building in San Francisco was designed in the columnar format with a tripart division of base, shaft, and capital. Belt cornices marked the horizontal divisions of the base and attic floor; an arched colonnade was stretched vertically to span the office floors of the shaft.

The Hibernia Bank building in San Francisco, built in 1892, signaled the advent of Beaux Arts Classicism that would later dominate the Civic Center.

cisco. Its finely wrought Romanesque ornament in white Inyo County marble on the ground floor and in terra-cotta above was unsurpassed by later buildings. Today, the Mills Building stands as the city's lone example of this pioneering period in the evolution of the tall building.

In 1892 Albert Pissis designed the Hibernia Bank on Market Street well away from the traditional financial district along Montgomery Street. Although the design was a return to the Classical mode, it was a departure from previous interpretation in that it reflected the French Classical tradition that Pissis had absorbed in his two years at the École des Beaux Arts in Paris. The building's copper-domed entrance rotunda strikes a rich Baroque note and anchors the structure firmly to its corner location. Originally, corner pavilions terminated the wings, which had five bays. In 1905 the wings were extended for two more bays; in 1906 the building was damaged but restored. Not until the city hall was designed in 1913 by two former École des Beaux Arts students, Ar

thur Brown, Jr., and John Bakewell, would the style recur with such panache.

The Chicago School's influence on the design of tall buildings also reached downtown Los Angeles. In 1893 Louis Bradbury's commercial block was built on Broadway in the heart of the city's post-railroad-boom downtown. Bradbury originally commissioned the design from Sumner P. Hunt but, for unknown reasons, was not happy with it. He then hired a draftsman in Hunt's office, George H. Wyman, to modify it. Since Hunt's scheme has vanished, its influence on Wyman is unknown. The vaguely Romanesque exterior was not distinguished. Never again did Wyman design such a powerful interior, but neither did Hunt.

One source for the design was probably Edward Bellamy's utopian novel, *Looking Backward, 2000–1887,* which Wyman had read. In it, the author describes a commercial building as a "vast hall full of light, received not alone from the windows on all sides but from the dome, the point of which was a hundred feet above. . . . " Instead of a

The atrium of the Bradbury Building in Los Angeles is enlivened with a skeletal cage of metal and wood that catches the light descending from the glazed roof. Even in today's "atrium age" with its more advanced technology, this 1893 hall is sensational.

The former James Flood mansion on Nob Hill in San Francisco was given a more horizontal and spreading character when Willis Polk remodeled its top and gave it rounded wings after the 1906 earthquake.

dome, which would not have suited the style, Wyman's atrium has a glazed, pitched roof. The brick walls, shading from dark to light yellow at the top, seem to dissolve into light as they rise.

◇ ◇ ◇ ◇ ◇

Grand houses from the closing decades of the nineteenth century also registered changes in style and technology. Mechanized transportation made it possible for the affluent to reside on previously inaccessible heights adjacent to downtown such as Nob Hill in San Francisco and Bunker Hill in Los Angeles. The former became the West Coast's most exclusive residential precinct after 1873, when the newly invented cable car conquered the steep slopes.

The California Street cable line ran from the heart of San Francisco's financial district straight up to the homes of those who ruled it. The Stanfords and the Crockers, along with the rest of the city's high society, built homes on the hilltop, which was shaved flat to receive the stand of proud mansions. After 1906 the James Flood house—the

only one with stone walls—stood alone. The other pretentious mansions were made of wood masquerading as stone; their stylistic claims to equality with the solid residences of eastern capitalists were useless in the raging fire that followed the earthquake.

By 1906 Flood had died, having lived only three years after the completion of his Nob Hill house in 1886. His architect, Augustus Laver, an Englishman with several large architectural commissions to his credit, designed the mansion in a severe Classical Revival mode. The costly exterior cladding of somber brownstone was shipped out from Connecticut. The original building took two years to build and cost $1.5 million. The $30,000 bronze fence was polished every day. Still, in its pre-1906 photographs, the building looks pinched and parsimonious. When it became the Pacific Union Club after the 1906 disaster, Willis Polk's addition of an attic story and hemispherical wings softened its uprightness and made it truly grand.

Another imposing stone mansion, completed a decade after Flood's, was built in the fashionable new district of Pacific

The Whittier mansion in Pacific Heights, now the northern headquarters of the California Historical Society, reflects the eastern influence of the Classical Queen Anne mode favored by McKim, Mead & White.

Heights by William F. Whittier, whose wealth came principally from the manufacture of paint (his company evolved into W. P. Fuller & Co.). Arizona sandstone—kin to brownstone—was used to clad the steel-reinforced brick structure, which survived the 1906 trauma virtually undamaged. Edward R. Swain designed the house in a Queen Anne format with a strong Classical emphasis. The dramatic roofscape, so typical of the Queen Anne style in California, has been tamed despite the use of separate roofs for gabled sections and towers. Inside, the lavish use of exotic woods—Guatamalan primavera, tamano, Honduran mahogany, bird's-eye maple, and cherry—makes a rich contrast with the somber exterior.

Stony monumentality was not characteristic of the homes of well-to-do Californians in the 1880s and the 1890s. Grand houses there were, from one end of the state to the other, but most were built in an exuberant Queen Anne style that translated well into the preferred material of redwood. One of the grandest of these was constructed, appropriately, by a lumber baron of Eureka, William McKendrie Carson.

Designed in 1885 by California's premier architects of the picturesque, Samuel Newsom and Joseph Cather Newsom, the house was built on the site of Carson's first lumber mill in Eureka. After coming to California in 1849, Carson owned a flour mill before going into lumbering in Eureka, a major center of the northern California redwood empire. Carson's partner, John Dolbeer, invented the steam-powered "donkey engine," which revolutionized the lumber industry.

In the 1870s, Carson and Dolbeer was the area's third largest exporter of lumber.

A mixture of paternalism and pride apparently motivated the building of the Carson house. Business was slack, and to keep his men active, Carson employed them to build his house. Though the principal material was, predictably, redwood, Carson sent one of his ships to South America to fetch a shipload of primavera wood. This light-toned wood was used mainly in the great entrance hall and staircase.

The basic form of the house is gaunt and northern, particularly in respect to the brooding, steep-roofed tower. This tumultuous roofscape rests heavily on the lower part of the building, which is skirted on one side by a broad veranda. The full range of the Newsom brother's talent was unleashed in the composition of the flamboyant exterior and interior decorative detail.

Attempts to designate a style for the Carson house are likely to result in a string of stylistic terms—Queen Anne-Stick-Eastlake.

Although scarcely precise, this composite description is helpful because it suggests the general interest in medieval European architecture revealed in the fashionable styles of the period. Not that the exotic possibilities of oriental architecture were neglected; both onion domes and horseshoe arches were incorporated.

The appetite for the exotic, whether in built forms or in landscaping, was insatiable. Never mind that real medieval castles were not set in greenswards dotted with specimen trees from topical places. By virtue of the Mediterranean climate enjoyed along the California coast, the nineteenth-century barons could luxuriate in man-made gardens of Eden.

Although the Carson house seems a leap into the absurd compared with the Italian-ate villas of the previous decade, it is more a high moment in the evolution of the towered villa form than a departure from previous norms. In its format, the house is not so far removed from the 1877 Sacramento

The 1885 Carson house in Eureka, the state's most flamboyant residence in the Queen Anne style.

villa designed for Albert Gallatin by Nathaniel Goodell, and used from 1903 to 1966 as the governor's mansion.

The ceaseless agitation of the surface of the Carson house with both linear and sculptural ornament makes it appear more frenetic than some other examples of the Queen Anne villa. Yet, the obsessiveness that seems a hallmark of California's composite "surface style" was also an indication of the opportunity it offered for idiosyncratic design. Steam-powered milling machinery made possible a never-ending medley of sawed and cast foliate and geometric motifs, cut shingles, spools, and spindles that could be applied at will to angled and undulating surfaces. Whereas the parent Queen Anne style, originally associated with the work of Richard Norman Shaw and others in England, had employed a varied palette of materials—stone, tile, cast terra-cotta, brick, and slate—most of these could be imitated in wood and therefore made cheaper and more generally available.

The expressive powers of the Queen Anne style are well illustrated by the Villa Montezuma, built in San Diego in 1887 for Jesse Shepard. Designed by the prominent local firm of Comstock and Trotsche, the house is a highly picturesque assemblage of fanciful elements conceived by Shepard.

Depending on which account of Shepard and the villa one reads, he was either a gifted musician, mystic, and writer or a talented charlatan who swept into town on the wave of prosperity following the arrival of the railroad. His musical evenings, during which he sang and played the piano, were enthusiastically attended by members of San Diego society. So were his seances. Some years after he left town, rumors spread that Shepard's motives had more to do with personal gain in this world than in the realm of the occult.

Whether or not the villa was a "Temple of Art and Occultism," as one newspaper account put it, the many symbols incorporated into the fabric of the house confirm Shepard's love of art and music. Stained glass windows with portraits of Beethoven and Mozart and other musical motifs in a variety of materials turn relatively modest rooms, such as the music room, into jewel boxes.

The Newsom brothers used horseshoe arches in the upper hall of the Carson house to enliven an otherwise static space.

The interior of the Governor's Mansion is enriched with a variety of ornaments in cast and painted detail.

For the Governor's Mansion in Sacramento, Nathaniel Goodell combined elements of the late Italianate villa style with the mansard roofs of the Second Empire mode.

Shepard had traveled extensively in Europe, even to Russia, where he enjoyed success both with musical performances of his own compositions and with his critical essays. Whatever his motives, the cultural excitement he brought to San Diego was tangible. His sale of the house and departure for Europe in 1889 marked the end of a brief but colorful period in the city's cultural life.

The Queen Anne-Stick-Eastlake style did not match all personalities so well. Yet a real affinity exists between this style and the idiosyncratic structure of Sarah Winchester's 160-room house with its multiple gables, chateauesque towers, skylit cupolas, porches galore, and forty stairways with two thousand doors which often lead nowhere. Myth has it that spirits informed the reclusive heiress to the Winchester Rifle fortune that her life would last as long as construction on her house continued. She began to build in 1884, and although she kept her carpenters at work until her death in 1922, the sources of her architectural ideas are unknown. In any case, she applied the same

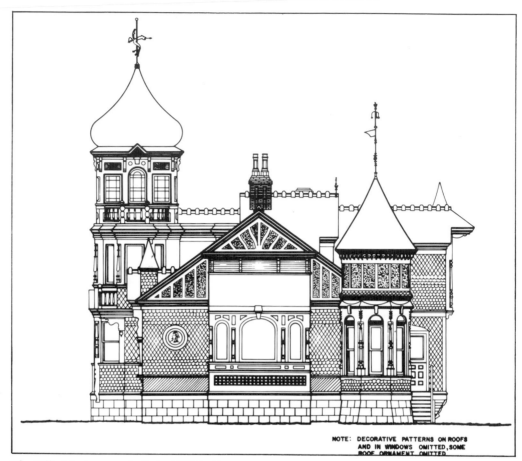

NOTE: DECORATIVE PATTERNS ON ROOFS
AND IN WINDOWS OMITTED, SOME
ROOF ORNAMENT OMITTED

The Villa Montezuma, built in 1887 in San Diego, for the musician, medium, and world traveler, Jesse Shepard, suggests a fanciful music box.

Interiors of the Villa Montezuma display a range of paneled woodwork, coffered ceilings with lincrusta surfaces, and mantelpieces allegedly designed by Shepard himself.

Sarah Winchester never wrote an explanation of her endless house in San Jose. Nor did she stop building to dismantle parts that failed, such as the section in the right of this photograph that she closed after it was damaged in the 1906 earthquake.

passion to building her house that she brought to her extensive agricultural activities. The only consistent aspect of the house is its allegiance to the open-ended, picturesque mode that flowered so freely in California.

In San Francisco, the Queen Anne-Eastlake houses that lined the blocks of the streetcar suburbs were considered beneath contempt by architectural critics. The array of mechanically produced ornament that covered their facades was erroneously attributed to the English designer, Charles Eastlake, whose relatively chaste furniture was inspired by medieval examples. The notched and chamfered treatment of wood members carved with linear motifs, which Eastlake considered an honest approach, was subjected to reworking on the newfangled lathes so that the products could be applied anywhere at any scale.

Although Eastlake lost no time in repudiating any association with the products advertised in his name, no one paid attention. Ironically, his name has been wedded forever to a style he found an insult to his talents. As for the Eastlake-style houses, described as collections of bird cages, vegetable cartons, dog kennels, sewing baskets, and wedding cakes, they have survived opprobrium to become the treasured reminders of a time of unblushing ostentation.

By the 1890s, the frenzied, linear versions of the picturesque began to lose momentum. Towers, rounded bays, and deep-set balconies and porches were given a shingled skin that enhanced their sculptural qualities. Interpenetrating spaces, at least on the ground floor, were typical of the suburban house on a generous lot. The use of wall-size sliding doors to expand ground floor space stemmed from the development of central heating. Although the fireplace remained as a strong symbol, it was ineffective in heating large spaces.

The Hotel Del Coronado on Coronado Island off the San Diego Coast is the lone survivor of the stand of late nineteenth century resort hotels built in the Queen Anne style. Completed in 1888 and designed by the Reid Brothers of San Francisco, its billowing form still seems the perfect expression of the pleasures of a seaside holiday.

As in any style, standard plans were developed and widely used. But outside the mass market for housing, gifted designers created unusual, often unique solutions. One great example is the double house Willis Polk designed in 1892 for his family and the widow of Virgil Williams, founder of the California Institute of Design. Located on the brow of Russian Hill, one of San Francisco's Bohemian enclaves, the house stood

opposite three starkly simple, unpainted, shingled houses. Their owner, a Mrs. David Marshall, had them built on speculation. She gave the end lot to Joseph Worcester, minister of the Swedenborgian church to which she belonged. Worcester, a Bostonian who had considered becoming an architect, was influential in aesthetic as well as spiritual matters. The cultivated rusticity of the hilltop was in part a result of his vision of design in harmony with nature—a vision epitomized in the modest, shingled cottage he built on Mrs. Marshall's lot.

Among the creative individuals Worcester counted as parishioners or friends was Willis Polk. Possessed of a brilliant talent and a self-destructive nature, Polk had a stellar career. The Polk-Williams house was one of the early works that bolstered his reputation.

A modified rusticity suited both the aesthetics and the modest budget for the house. Polk's parents purchased the eastern twenty feet of the lot from Mrs. Williams. A fee was not charged for the design, and construction costs were probably also shared within the family.

From the front, or hilltop, side, the house has a two-story facade composed of two projecting and separately roofed bays of varied composition, which indicate the double occupancy. The two parts are tied together with bands of casement windows set in white painted frames on two levels. The

entrances, one of which is in a porch on the west side, are understated.

If the street facade had a studied informality, the six-story rear portion echoed the helter-skelter quality of familiar building forms that staggered down the backs of San Francisco's hills. If ever a house could be said to have a Queen Anne front and a Mary Ann back, this is it. Inside, the rooms with adjacent outdoor areas gave their occupants panoramic views of the city—including Nob Hill with its mansions to the south—and the bay. Both dwellings were packed with interlocking spaces, particularly on the Polks' side where the living areas on the three floors were alternately expanded and contracted to create both grandeur and intimacy.

To the west, the new San Francisco suburb of Pacific Heights was being developed. Improved municipal transportation made this long ridge stretching out toward the ocean a desirable area. Around the turn of the century, it was built up with both grand

The Polk-Williams house on Russian Hill in San Francisco, 1892, Willis Polk, architect.

and modest houses, for the most part on standard-size city lots. In the inner or eastern part of the area, Polk's 1895 mansion for the mining millionaire William B. Bourn II, offers an interesting comparison with the Russian Hill house.

At the time it was built, the house—which virtually fills the lot—was visible on three sides. Polk articulated the back part as a succession of separate, gable-roofed sections. The now invisible side elevation has a picturesque medieval aspect that reverses the Classical formality of the front.

Polk's design gave the street facade monumentality both by raising the piano nobile a floor above the street level and by overscaling the roof cornice, dormer windows, and chimneys. Instead of a central entrance sequence with a grand stair, a window set in a boldly scaled architrave provides the main

focus. Below the balustrade, an unassuming passage cut through the rusticated basement wall leads to the entrance. In another departure from the academic Georgian Revival style, Polk enlivened the texture of the walls by combining Classical detail in sandstone with clinker brick.

Bernard Maybeck also had a free-wheeling attitude toward style. In 1904, he designed a house in San Jose for Doctor Howard Gates which has certain affinities with the Bourn house. Here the plain entrance door, though graced with an elegant set of elliptical steps, yields its importance to a monumental tripartite window recessed behind a cavernous opening in the middle of the wall. The opening's elliptical arch springs from a belt cornice, the broken edges of which are supported on overscaled consoles. A projecting balustrade that ex-

The William Bourn house in San Francisco, 1895, designed by Willis Polk in a loose Neo-Georgian style that manages to be both formal and picturesque.

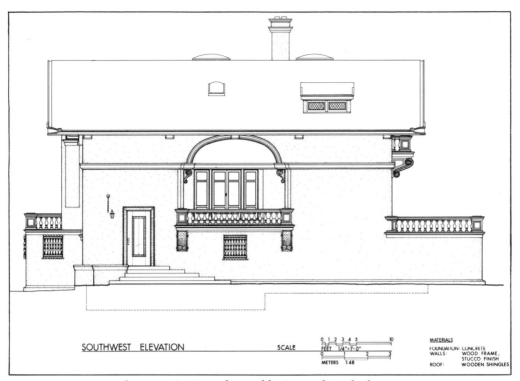

SOUTHWEST ELEVATION

SCALE

FEET 1/4"=1'-0"

METERS 1:48

MATERIALS
FOUNDATION: CONCRETE
WALLS: WOOD FRAME,
              STUCCO FINISH
ROOF: WOODEN SHINGLES

The Howard G. Gates house in San Jose, designed by Bernard Maybeck in 1904.

ceeds the width of the balcony is supported on even larger consoles. All of this sculptural movement takes place beneath the broadly overhanging eaves of a gable roof that masks the presence of a third floor. The stuccoed, wood-frame walls are detailed as though they were masonry, reinforcing the feeling of a Mediterranean villa.

The excitement of San Francisco's topography may have partly inspired the tensions created by changes in scale and the play between formal and informal or urban and rustic elements of the generation of Bay Area architects who began practicing in the 1890s. These tensions were not echoed in southern California, where the vast plain of the Los Angeles Basin, backed by mountains instead of hills, encouraged generally larger lot sizes and a horizontal emphasis for houses.

◇ ◇ ◇ ◇ ◇

Charles Sumner Greene and Henry Mather Greene, whose consummate craftsmanship in wood is unsurpassed in the long history of the material's use in California, arrived in Pasadena in 1893. Their education at the Manual Training School of Washington University in St. Louis, followed by two years in the architectural program at the Massachusetts Institute of Technology, had given the brothers a strong sense of the craft of architecture. Stopping on their way to California at the Columbian Exposition in Chicago, they were powerfully struck by Japan's official exhibit, a reconstruction of the Ho-o-do of Byodo-in, a Buddhist temple of the Fujiwara period. Though they never went to Japan, the Greenes assimilated the spirit of its buildings and gardens through books and prints. Nowhere was the tradition of oriental architecture so alive as in Pasadena in the early decades of the twentieth century.

The Greenes' approach to domestic design was ostensibly practical. In answering a questionnaire sent him in 1906 by Charles Lummis from the Los Angeles Public Library Department of West History, Charles wrote that their efforts were threefold. They attempted "1st to understand as many

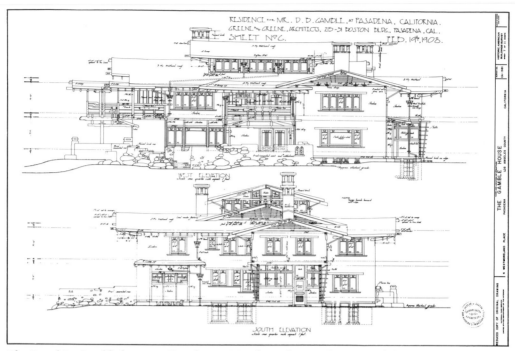

The David B. Gamble house in Pasadena, 1908, the architect's drawings of the west and south elevations.

phases of human life as possible; 2nd to provide for its individual requirements in the most practical and useful way; 3rd to make these necessary and useful things pleasurable." The words evoke the code of plain living and high thinking that ruled the Arts and Crafts Movement, but the concern for refinement that the Greenes lavished on the smallest necessity turned the best known of their houses into aesthetic tours de force well beyond the practical needs of their clients.

The hallmarks of their work were a bold and direct use of structure; the buildup of separate parts with wood members of different dimensions; exposed joinery; the projection of roof beams and even of pegs and other structurally integrated ornament to invite the play of light and shade; and the wedding of structure to site by means of graded terraces and tiered roofs with overlapping gables. These features were well assimilated by some of the contractor/builders of the times, whose houses are sometimes taken for the Greenes' work.

Although the Greenes' convictions about the moral worth of the arts and crafts came from an international movement, the forms

they used were perfectly suited to the life, times, and landscape of southern California. Today, the houses appear to have grown there. That only the affluent could afford the painstakingly crafted stained glass, pegged furniture, and "peanut brittle" walls of rounded boulders set with clinker brick does not diminish their indigenous quality. In this respect, the Greenes' bungalows are kin to Frank Lloyd Wright's prairie houses in suburban Chicago.

The Gamble house, best known and preserved of the "ultimate bungalows," shows the Greenes' efforts to counter the effect of the house as a man-made container of spaces by a gently descending series of horizontal roofs extended well beyond the wall planes. One end of the house fractures into a cagelike sleeping porch on the upper floor.

The 1906 house for Theodore H. Irwin, illustrated here in a plan of the first floor and drawings of the north and west elevations, was an extensive remodeling of a previous Greene and Greene house. The original house was built around a court which became a two-story space when the upper floor was added.

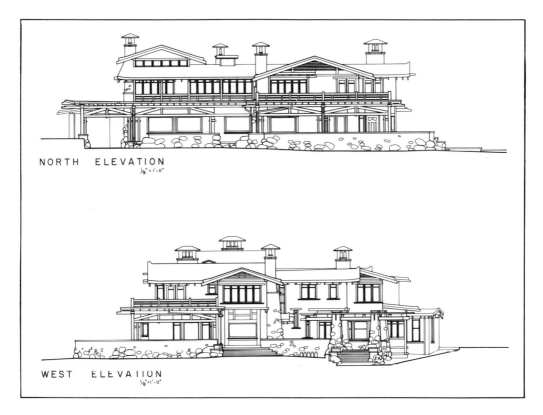

NORTH ELEVATION
1/8" = 1'-0"

WEST ELEVATION
1/8" = 1'-0"

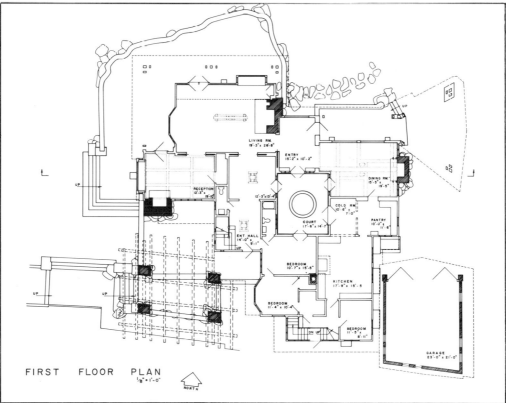

FIRST FLOOR PLAN
1/8" = 1'-0"

NORTH

The Hanchett Residence Park in San Jose was planned by the prominent nurseryman, John Mc-Claren, and built from 1907 to 1911. Architects Wolfe and McKenzie designed many of the houses in the woodsy Craftsman style.

The Peter Col house, designed by Wolfe and McKenzie in Hanchett Park, reflects the influence of Frank Lloyd Wright and the Prairie style.

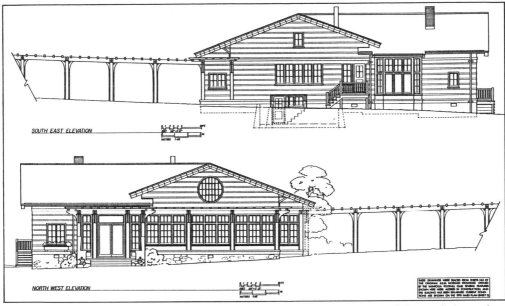

The Foothill Club in Saratoga, designed in 1916 by Julia Morgan, drawings of the southeast and northwest elevations.

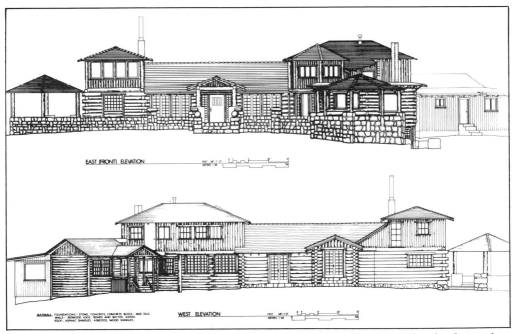

Welch-Hurst was built about 1913 in Saratoga by Judge and Mrs. James R. Welch, who designed it themselves. This rustic retreat shows one pole of the development of the informal woodsy style in California. The rambling, two-storied structure of halved redwood logs, set horizontally on the first floor and vertically on the second, has a dramatic interior stairhall with a balustrade of crooked saplings careening around two sides.

Projecting roof and floor beams reinforce the effect of a skeletal structure bursting through its shingled skin.

As it turned out, Maybeck's work defied imitation, while the Greenes' spawned California's first architectural export, the bungalow. Much has been written in praise of the firmness, commodity and delight to be found in this modest dwelling type. Inexpensive materials, compact, yet open floor plans frequently uniting living-dining spaces and eliminating hallways, an aesthetic of structural honesty, an intimation of the natural life—all these attributes combined to make the bungalow the heir to the workingman's cottage of the nineteenth century.

The western brown-shingle aesthetic spread to other building types whose functions suggested a domestic scale. Julia Morgan, onetime student of Maybeck and the first woman to be admitted to the École des Beaux Arts, designed several women's clubhouses, such as the 1916 Foothill Club in Saratoga, in this informal mode. Morgan

created simple, hearth-centered interiors with adjacent outdoor terraces and wisteria-covered pergolas on woodsy suburban sites. Such settings served well for discussions of the progressive ideals in education and reform which were women's special province.

Others may have been called "Mr. California," but no one deserved the title more than Charles Fletcher Lummis. Though the Santa Fe Railroad and Lummis both reached Los Angeles in 1885, Lummis walked from Cincinnati, Ohio. His report of the trip was such a success that he became the first city editor of the *Los Angeles Times*. For two years, he worked hard at journalism, so hard, in fact, that he had a stroke. Undaunted, Lummis went to New Mexico to recover and live with Indian friends whom he had met on his way to the coast.

Upon his return to Los Angeles, he founded the popular magazine, *Land of Sunshine* (called *Out West* after 1902), which he edited from 1894 until 1910. As director of the Los Angeles Public Library from 1905

El Alisal, Los Angles home of Charles Lummis, incorporates a round tower as if to signal that Lummis' home was his castle. A mission bell in a niche beneath the curving gable speaks of Lummis' devotion to the state's early landmarks.

to 1910, he created an important collection of Southwest material, and in 1914 he founded the Southwest Museum. Lummis's passion for the history of his adopted state led him to found the Landmarks Club in 1897 to raise money to restore the missions and other historic buildings. But no project engaged his attention more than his own house, which he built with the part-time help of Indian youths from 1897 to 1920.

Lummis named his house El Alisal, for the sycamore tree that stood in the patio. Lummis designed and built most of the L-shaped house, which was about 91 feet long and 60 feet wide. The walls were made with rounded boulders set in concrete, the doors of hand-hewn timbers, the built-in cabinetry of different woods with hinges and locks from Lummis' collection of artifacts, and the beams of used telegraph poles. No one described it better than its owner:

It should be good architecture, honest construction, comfortable, convenient, fire-proof, burglar proof, time-proof; a possession, not a taskmaster. Something at least of the owner's individuality . . . should inform it. Some activity of his head, heart, and hands should make it really his. . . . The creative thrill is so fine and keen; it is sheer pitiful to see a man get a home off the bargain counter and miss nearly all the joy he might just as well have of it.

The house recalls the openhanded life of its owner who hosted a wide circle of friends, from national leaders such as Teddy Roosevelt to artists such as Maynard Dixon, who made some of the furnishings.

While fin de siècle residential architecture was dominated, on the one hand, by a riotous display of ornament and, on the other, by the craftsmanly concerns of "the simple life," public buildings led the return to Classicism. The 1893 Columbian Exposition in Chicago had broadcast the seeds of academic Classicism sown earlier in the work of such firms as McKim, Mead & White.

An alumnus of that firm, A. Page Brown, had come to San Francisco in 1889 to design a mausoleum for the Crocker family. Finding that eastern-trained architects commanded great respect among wealthy potential clients, Brown stayed on to establish the local equivalent of McKim, Mead & White's office. Many of the profession's ris-

Both the Campanile in the Piazza San Marco in Venice and the Giralda tower of the cathedral in Seville, Spain, inspired the tower of the Ferry Building at the foot of Market Street in San Francisco.

ing young stars, Willis Polk, Bernard Maybeck, A. C. Schweinfurth, to name a few, worked in the office. Schweinfurth appears to have been the main designer on the restrained but exemplary Ferry Building (officially called the Union Depot and Ferry House), designed and built between 1894 and 1903. (Edward R. Swain supervised the construction after Brown's death in 1896.)

The new building replaced the utilitarian facility of 1877. The site at the foot of Market Street was the major gateway to the city. Ferry passengers from across the bay and railroad passengers who came from the transcontinental terminal in Oakland entered San Francisco through its portals. Toward the west, Market Street stretched as far as the eye could see. Street railways took up much of the street, and municipal streetcars ended their runs on the loop in front of the building. The design from Brown's office showed an educated awareness of the past. The facade's central block was modeled after Charles Atwood's railroad station at the Columbian Exposition.

The steel-frame structure had a foundation of 111 reinforced concrete piers, each 16 by 28 feet at the base, fused together by concrete arches into a single unit, 670 by

160 feet. This adaptation of the innovative principles of the Montgomery Block's raft-like foundation enabled the building to withstand the 1906 earthquake with damage to the tower only.

The twentieth century began auspiciously with the resumption of good times in San Francisco after the depressed 1890s. Building contracts and real-estate sales had increased dramatically. Anticipation of greater boom times to come with the construction of the Panama Canal created an expansive mood. When James D. Phelan, the reform-minded mayor who had served two terms, was defeated for reelection in 1901, he directed all his energies to the cause of city planning, or civic design, as it was then called.

While in office, Phelan had encouraged architect B. J. S. Cahill to prepare a civic center scheme to improve the area around the City Hall. He had also advocated extension of the so-called Panhandle section of Golden Gate Park to Van Ness Avenue and persuaded Phoebe A. Hearst to fund a master plan for the city. None of these plans had produced results. But in January 1904, a group of civic leaders chose Phelan to preside over the Association for the Improvement and Adornment of San Francisco. The association's stated goal was to achieve a plan that would create "a more desirable city in which to live." Phelan was familiar with Daniel H. Burnham's plans for Cleveland, Ohio, of 1900, and Washington, D. C., of 1901–02. In May 1905, Burnham came out from Chicago to address the association membership and was invited to prepare a master plan, which he lost no time in starting.

Described by the press as "a locomotive in full steam holding the right-of-way," Burnham demonstrated great energy and command of the issues. His solicitation of citizen participation in the planning process won wide acceptance of his proposals. From his aerie on Twin Peaks, a small studio designed for the purpose by Willis Polk, Burnham and his associate, Edward H. Bennett, had a suitably lofty view of their subject.

By September 1905, the plan was finished. A significant part of it addressed "street improvements" that would restructure traffic circulation in concentric rings of streets intersected by diagonals—on which rapid transit would run—radiating from a central loop or, in the language of the plan, "a perimeter of distribution." The civic center, located around the intersection of Market Street and Van Ness Avenue (then the geographic heart of the city) would be the core area. Parks and boulevards, including the extension of the Panhandle and a thirty-mile system of boulevards around the bay to the ocean beaches, played major roles. Community centers and athletic facilities were not forgotten.

The plan was praised, Burnham was toasted at its presentation, and the city's board of supervisors appropriated $3,000 to have it printed and distributed as a municipal document. In mid-April 1906, bound copies were delivered to City Hall. A few were given to members of the association, but distribution of the rest was halted on April 18—like everything else—by the earthquake.

While the question of how to rebuild the city's four square miles strewn with ash and rubble engaged everyone's attention in the postquake period, the future of Burnham's plan dimmed. M. H. de Young, publisher of the *San Francisco Chronicle* warned against letting "visions of the beautiful" dictate actions. He also argued that because the practical men of London had not approved Sir Christopher Wren's plan for rebuilding after the great fire of 1666, business had proceeded undisturbed to everyone's advantage. What better precedent was there for San Francisco?

There were more immediate, practical arguments against the plan. Because property lines and building footprints were confused by wreckage, insurance payments were at risk. People feared that a radical program of changes to street and property lines would further jeopardize their claims. Mayor Eugene Schmitz told the Committee for Reconstruction that the city was less able to build in accordance with the plan after the disaster than it would have been a month before.

Burnham himself rushed to the scene and met tirelessly with committees, a tactic that appeared to work. The reconstruction committee, followed by the board of supervisors, adopted his plan. But the reformer's jubilation was short-lived. A political embroilment of unprecedented dimensions not only discredited and jailed top city officials, including the mayor, but succeeded in impugning the motives of the reconstruction committee members. Buffeted about by such strong political currents, the plan once again sank from view. In the meantime, reconstruction proceeded at a whirlwind pace. Within three years, 20,500 buildings were finished. In 1909 San Francisco had built more than half the steel-frame and concrete buildings in the whole country.

Missing from the list of new structures was a city hall to replace the previous graft-riddled building which had taken more than twenty years to build only to collapse in seconds during the quake. The need for a new city hall and civic center strengthened the city's resolve to hold a great exposition to honor both the opening of the Panama Canal and the city's phoenixlike rise from the ashes of 1906.

Between 1909 and 1912, two bond issues were submitted to the voters for a civic center at Market Street and Van Ness Avenue. The last one approved the sale of bonds for land acquisition and a city hall. Appointees to the Civic Center Advisory Board—architects John Galen Howard, Frederick H. Meyer, and John Reid, Jr.—produced a plan in 1913, in the tradition of the City Beautiful Movement.

The plan was close to the previous one developed by B. J. S. Cahill. The City Hall, Civic Auditorium, State Building, Public Library, and Opera House were sited on major streets between Van Ness Avenue and Market Street, Hayes Street and Golden Gate Avenue, facing each other across a

The interior of the San Francisco City Hall was not finished in time for the Panama-Pacific International Exposition (the offices were occupied in 1916), but the building stood for all to see and admire. Architects Bakewell and Brown received national recognition for their design and were much honored in France, where both had attended the École des Beaux Arts in Paris.

great open plaza. To the west of City Hall, Fulton Street led to Golden Gate Park. Though the library site was shifted and the construction of the Opera House delayed until 1931–32 and relocated west of City Hall on Van Ness, the rest of the original plan held. None of the other City Beautiful Movement civic centers around the country achieved such success.

In 1912 the firm of Bakewell and Brown won the competition to design the new City Hall. John Bakewell and Arthur Brown, Jr., had attended the University of California in the 1890s where they were much influenced by Bernard Maybeck. After graduation, the two young men went to Paris to the École des Beaux Arts in 1895 and in 1897, and gained diplomas after spending five and four years there, respectively. (Though more than thirty architects practicing in San Francisco after 1900 had attended the école, only eleven completed the full course of study and passed the necessary examinations to receive a diploma.)

The architects designed the City Hall to stretch across Fulton Street and to be visible at the head of a long axis from Market Street. The dome, a skillful amalgam of memorable European domes from the churches of St. Peter's in Rome, Les Invalides and Val de Grace in Paris, and St. Paul's in London, was scaled to be seen from various vantage points around the city. From the opposite side of the plaza, the dome's massive base and drum somewhat overpower the office wings extending to either side of the central pavilion. Yet, from close up, the building's facade provides a strong, rhythmic base compatible with the scale of the dome. In plan, the Fulton Street axis continues through the building, where space is focused and recirculated in the monumental public lobby commanded by the inner, coffered dome. Through its oculus, the intermediary shell with a cartouche bearing a ship is visible.

The influence of French Classicism is particularly strong in the monochromatic treatment of materials on both exterior and interior. The tone of the granite-clad exterior, enriched with blue and gold metalwork and a copper-covered dome, carries through the interior with variations. Jean Louis

Bourgeois, who designed the interiors, and Henri Crenier, who carved the pediment sculptures, were also trained at the École des Beaux Arts.

◇ ◇ ◇ ◇ ◇

The only building completed for the opening of the Panama-Pacific International Exposition in January 1915 was the Civic Auditorium, designed by the advisory committee architects with John Galen Howard in charge. The Exposition Company, formed in 1910 to plan the 1915 event, paid for the building, which functioned importantly as a reception center and in-town location for exposition activities. Three great arched openings on the facade expressed the auditorium's large interior hall and its public function. The other Civic Center buildings indicated on the plan, the Public Library and State Building, were finished in 1916 and 1926. They were designed by George Kelham and Bliss & Faville, respectively, who won the limited competitions held for the commissions.

The P.P.I.E. Exposition was, in its own way, as innovative as the 1893 Columbian Exposition in Chicago had been. Edward Bennett planned the site, which was located near the terminus of Van Ness Avenue between the U.S. Army reservations of Fort Mason and the Presidio. Called Harbor View after the amusement park located there, the site was completely transformed. Buildings were razed; a cove and a lagoon were filled. In all, 635 acres and two and one-half miles of bayshore land were created. A walled city of interconnecting courts incorporated eleven main palaces. For their design, prominent local architects such as Arthur Brown, Jr., Louis C. Mullgardt, George Kelham, and William B. Faville were joined by easterners Thomas Hastings, Henry Bacon, and McKim, Mead & White.

The exposition's walled city with domed and towered buildings suited the Mediterranean image so carefully cultivated in California. The courts also offered protection from the wind and fog that diminished the sun-splashed image. Jules Guerin's color scheme of blue domes, terra-cotta tiled roofs, and buff-tinted, imitation travertine

Mysterious female figures contemplate the invisible contents of tomblike boxes Maybeck intended as planters atop the colonnades of the Palace of Fine Arts, the lone survivor of the 1915 exposition in San Francisco

plaster added immeasurably to the evocative power of the compound. Ironically, the fair's nostalgic aspect was heightened by its timing. With the world at war, many European countries canceled their buildings. Still, as Chester Rowell put it in the April 15 issue of *California Outlook,* "The spirit that made San Francisco dare to invite the world to an institution of international rejoicing in this year of international chaos is merely the expansion of the spirit in which San Francisco met her own calamity. . . . "

Of all the exposition buildings, the Palace of Fine Arts was the resounding public success. This important commission was originally intended for Willis Polk, who chaired the fair's Architectural Commission. Polk decided to hold a competition for the building. Bernard Maybeck, whom Polk had temporarily employed to work on the expo-

sition, submitted a powerful charcoal sketch that won everyone's unanimous approval. In a magnanimous gesture, Polk gave the commission to Maybeck. The result was a monument of such importance to the city that it survived, perilously, into the 1960s, when a successful bond issue matched donated funds to reconstruct the crumbling structure in concrete.

Maybeck, who was not given to expressing himself in words, wrote an eloquent text for the Palace of Fine Arts. "I find," he wrote, "that the keynote of a Fine Arts Palace should be that of sadness, modified by the feeling that beauty has a soothing influence." Not only is the lost Classical world evoked, but the emphasis is on the late antique world of the provincial temple of Venus at Baalbek, a haunting ruin of exaggerated, baroque forms.

The director of the fine arts exhibition apparently worried that visitors would come into the galleries with their vision still full of the fair's excitement. According to Maybeck's account, the director wanted a "frontispiece" that would induce the appropriate reflective mood for viewing the works of art. Maybeck was frank about his methods:

The process is similar to that of matching the color of ribbons. You pick up a blue ribbon, hold it alongside the sample in your hand and at a glance you know if it matches or not. You do the same with architecture; you examine a historic form and see whether the effect it produced on your mind matches the feeling you are trying to portray—a modified sadness or a sentiment in a minor key. An old Roman ruin, away from civilization, which two thousand years before was the center of action and full of life, and now is partly overgrown with bushes and trees. There seems to be no other works of the builder, neither Gothic, nor Moorish, nor Egyptian, that gives us just this note of vanished grandeur."

The empty rotunda embraced by a colonnade, the bare-backed ladies brooding into tomblike planters, the funerary urns, the stairways leading nowhere, the seemingly inaccessible shrine reflected in the lagoon (walkways were supposed to cross it, but Maybeck had them removed)—all contributed to a magical piece of scenography that has kept its appeal. Maybeck never discussed the architecture per se; it was not admired by the academically inclined, but such criticism amounted to minor carping in view of the building's emotional appeal.

Few examples of Classicism in the grand manner were built in the economic slump following World War I. Contrary to expectations, traffic through the Panama Canal was light. Even the wealthy who could afford to build faced a shortage of materials. Among the palatial residences that were constructed was the 1913 San Francisco mansion of Adolph and Alma de Bretteville Spreckels. The architect, George Applegarth, made good use of his training at the École des Beaux Arts in the design, which applied rich ornamental detail to an orderly arrangement of forms derived from eighteenth-century prototypes.

Most of the Classical manor houses were

The lavishly ornamented white limestone that covers the concrete structure of the 1913 Spreckels mansion in San Francisco's Pacific Heights is an unintended reminder that the family fortune came from importing sugar.

The entrance court and grand stair hall of Fil-oli, the country mansion of William Bourn in Woodside.

built outside San Francisco where large par-cels of land were acquired for country es-tates. In 1912 Louis Hobart designed the Villa Rose for Joseph D. Grant on a terraced site beside a wooded canyon in Hillsbor-ough. In 1914, James D. Phelan's Villa Mon-talvo, designed by William Curlett, was completed in Saratoga. Montalvo was the name of the Spanish author whose six-teenth-century novel first linked California to a terrestrial paradise. The great nursery-man, John McLaren, did his best to make the grounds worthy of the name.

In 1915 Willis Polk designed the man-sion at Filoli, the peninsula estate of Wil-liam Bourn, in a more conventional Georgian Revival style than their 1895 town house discussed previously. Sited on the San Andreas Fault (the source of the 1906 earthquake), the house is near the head of the lakes created by the earth's movement over centuries. These lakes were also the reservoirs of Bourn's Spring Valley Water Company. Polk was to have designed the rest of the estate, but Bourn ended the friendship, and with it Polk's involvement, when he decided that the boisterous archi-tect's extravagant habits would lead to Polk's ruin, and put his commission into a trust for his wife.

Arthur Brown, Jr., succeeded Polk and designed the detached service building at Filoli in 1918. Bruce Porter, San Francisco's most successful dilettante designer and

Polk's old friend, created the gardens, which are Filoli's glory. Since Bourn wished to maintain the seven hundred acres as a game preserve, the formal gardens had to be en-closed to keep them from being consumed by deer. Each garden has a theme and bor-rows a scenic backdrop from the distant

The Andrew S. Hallidie Building, named for the inventor of the cable car and designed in 1917 by Willis Polk, boasts the world's first "curtain wall" facade.

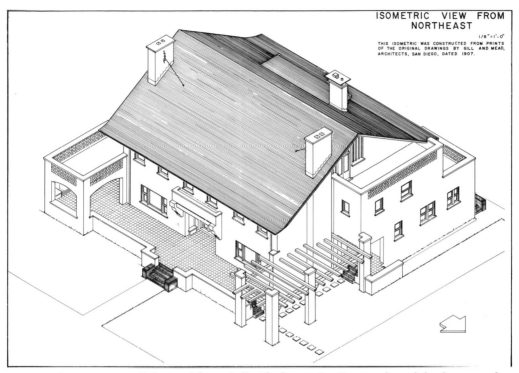

ISOMETRIC VIEW FROM
NORTHEAST
1/8"=1'-0"
THIS ISOMETRIC WAS CONSTRUCTED FROM PRINTS
OF THE ORIGINAL DRAWINGS BY GILL AND MEAD,
ARCHITECTS, SAN DIEGO, DATED 1907.

The 1907 house Irving Gill designed for Melville Klauber in San Diego indicated the direction of his later residential work in the use of strong, simple masonry forms. The construction was unusual in its use of stuccoed hollow tile over wood framing.

hills. The hallway running through the house integrates grounds and building by continuing the main north-south axis of the gardens.

As Polk's checkered career continued, his designs became less inventive and settled more into the mainstream. However, he scored one clear triumph before his untimely death in 1924: the Hallidie Building of 1917. This speculative office building was commissioned by the University of California Regents, owners of the site on lower Sutter Street in San Francisco. At the time of the design, glass was increasingly used in office building facades. But this trend still does not explain what inspired Polk to make a whole facade of glass and to hang it, like a curtain, in front of the structural columns from an elaborate cast-iron cornice. The delicate fire escapes on either side of the facade even suggest pull cords. Alas, Polk left no statement about this first "curtain-wall" design, as it would be called in modern times, making the above explanation mere conjecture.

If Polk was unpredictable, Irving John Gill—who, like Polk, Maybeck, and the Greenes, arrived in California in the 1890s—had the kind of inner direction that gave his career the quality of a narrative unfolding from one building to the next. On the way to California, Gill spent about two years in Chicago where he worked for Adler and Sullivan. As the son of a building contractor in Syracuse, New York, Gill had no formal architectural training and no interest in issues of style. In Sullivan's drafting room he met Frank Lloyd Wright, who was working on the Transportation Building for the 1893 exposition. But before the exposition opened, poor health prompted Gill to go to San Diego. Thus his exposure to Sullivan's principles rather than to the Classicism of the "white city," as the Columbian Exposition was called, shaped his approach to architecture.

Sullivan's "luminous idea of simplicity" gradually molded Gill's work. Later in his career he wrote, "If the cost of unimportant ornamentation were put into construction, then we would have a more lasting and a more dignified architecture." Gill's early buildings, designed during his partnership with W. S. Hebbard from 1898 to 1906, have strong ties to the East. But in 1904, he designed a portentous house for George W. Marston, one of San Diego's most committed civic leaders. In its lack of ornament and use of slab doors and flat board moldings set flush with the walls, the design pointed to his future work.

In 1912 Gill purchased, unwisely as it turned out, some equipment from the U.S. government used to fabricate tilt-slab concrete walls. He invested in the rig because he hoped to reduce construction costs and thereby build low-cost housing projects. Had the work he anticipated materialized, things might have been different. But the volume was never large enough, and the rig also had to be transported from site to site at great expense.

In 1913 Gill used his equipment to build the La Jolla Women's Club. Here, pure rectangular forms were punctured by crisp, arched openings. Space extended into the landscape in an outdoor living court defined by pergolas, or "green rooms," as Gill called them. In the construction, the forms for the concrete were laid on a platform tilted at an angle of fifteen degrees. Concrete was then poured into a form in which the metal window and door frames and reinforcement had been laid. After the concrete set, a finishing coat of fine cement was applied. The wall thickness was 13 to 13¾ inches; the color was white.

Ellen Browning Scripps, Gill's client, donated the building to the community. Born in England in 1836, she came with her family to Illinois in 1844 and then to California in 1891, where she helped her brothers build their newspaper empire and wrote a popular feature called "Miss Ellen's Miscellany." For ninety-six years Miss Scripps led a busy life. Like other progressive women of her time, she chose to serve society. In 1914 Scripps transferred ownership of the property to the club she had organized and presided over earlier. The club's and Scripps's goals were the same: "progress toward higher citizenship, spreading the gospel and the fact of fraternity, of mutual helpfulness." In their wish to leave the world a better place than they found it, Scripps and her architect were well matched.

The Walter L. Dodge house, Gill's acknowledged masterwork, was designed in 1914 and finished two years later. The plan spread across the generous lot in West Hollywood. The importance of indoor-outdoor spaces is clear from the fact that they accounted for 1,100 of the 6,500 square feet of the plan. The balanced masses and the counterpoint of window and wall conveyed a feeling of serenity.

Inside, the entrance hall, which gave cross-axial views of the living and dining rooms, was a perfectly composed space framed with walls of Honduras mahogany

The La Jolla Women's Club beautifully expresses the restful and satisfying qualities Gill ascribed to sheer and plain walls rising boldly into the sky.

The Walter P. Dodge house, built in Los Angeles in 1916 and demolished in 1970.

The stick railing in the upper level of the stair hall permitted light to diffuse from ten-foot-high windows on the north wall into the space below.

without baseboard or ceiling molding. On other interior surfaces, Gill used a white paint with an admixture of primary colors designed to pick up and subliminally reflect the tones of the natural landscape outside. Sadly, the Dodge house was demolished in 1970 after a long battle. It remains one of the most lamented of California's lost architectural monuments.

Although San Francisco's 1915 fair was designated as the official international exposition, San Diego also celebrated the opening of the Panama Canal with an exposition. George Marston, Gill's client, chaired the building committee. In 1910 Marsten underwrote the expense of having the firm of Olmsted and Olmsted lay out the park. Gill was the likely choice for the fair's chief architect. But by the time the political dust settled, Gill was replaced with a dashing outsider, Bertram G. Goodhue, as the fair's designer. Both Gill and the Olmsteds exited, but Gill's departure was apparently more influenced by his discovery of graft related to the purchase of materials for the buildings than by Goodhue's appointment. In

The California State Building from the San Diego Panama-Pacific Exposition, 1913–15, not only introduced visitors to the exposition grounds, but it also brought a revival of the Spanish Churrigueresque style to California.

any case, Goodhue brought out his supporting staff from New York.

Unlike the tightly organized system of courts created for the San Francisco exposition, the buildings in San Diego's Balboa Park were spaced on either side of a main axis, called El Prado. The California Quadrangle, designed by Goodhue, climaxed in a grand building with a tower, the only one constructed of permanent materials (concrete and stone from Mexico). Goodhue chose the lavishly ornamented Churrigueresque style for the California Building because he thought it more appropriate for an exposition than the less festive California Mission Revival mode, which had spawned a large number of buildings around the state. Moreover, mission imagery was not new to fairs, having been used both for the California Building at the 1893 Columbian Exposition in Chicago and for buildings in San Francisco's 1894 Mid-Winter Exposition in Golden Gate Park.

The exposition grounds in Balboa Park

came closer to creating the Garden of Eden in California than any other comparable attempt. The park had existed since 1868. Though many people, including the Olmsteds, had a hand in its development, horticulturist Kate Sessions was one of the most important contributors. Her thirty-six-acre nursery in the northwest corner of the park furnished countless trees and plants, many of them tropical, to the park.

The public reaction to Goodhue's work was enthusiastic. Almost immediately, imported Spanish styles replaced the homegrown Mission Revival. Yet, Gill's work, like the Greenes', continued to influence local building contractors as well as other designers. Goodhue himself acknowledged that Gill's was "some of the most thoughtful

work done in the California of today" and "far safer" for "the average architect" to emulate than his own.

If Goodhue seemed to favor confection over purity for the fair buildings, his Los Angeles Public Library of 1924 reflected his subsequent search for a modern style free of historical reference. Unfortunately, the library grounds have been eroded over time by encroaching new development in downtown Los Angeles. The former west entrance from Flower Street was once approached by paths flanked by Italian cypresses on each side of three long pools. Sad as this is, the grounds still provide a parklike open space—the only one besides Pershing Square—in downtown Los Angeles.

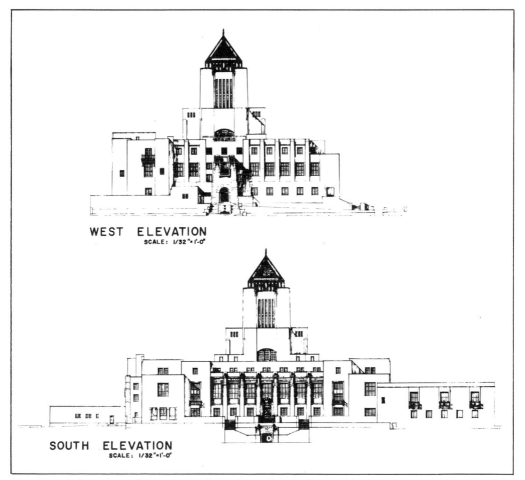

WEST ELEVATION
SCALE: 1/32"= 1'-0"

SOUTH ELEVATION
SCALE: 1/32"=1'-0"

The simplified massing of the Los Angeles Public Library, designed by Bertram Grosvenor Goodhue in 1924, was strengthened by Beaux-Arts planning principles of axiality and spatial hierarchy. These drawings were reproduced from the architect's originals of 1924.

⬦ ⬦ ⬦ ⬦ ⬦

Of all the architects who perceived the Edenic possibilities of California, none capitalized on them with more sensitivity and assurance than Frank Lloyd Wright. His first Los Angeles client, Aline Barnsdall, gave him a notable piece of Hollywood real estate called Olive Hill to work on. The daughter of a Pennsylvania oil millionaire, Barnsdall led what she herself called a vagabond life. Besides travel, she was interested in theater and the arts. Though she met Wright in Chicago and commissioned a theater design from him, she was inspired to move the location to California after a trip there in 1915. She came to California imbued with socialist ideals to build a live/work community for the theater arts.

Barnsdall bought a thirty-six-acre hillock in Hollywood covered with an olive grove planted as part of an aborted real-estate venture in the 1890s. In 1917 she hired Wright to make a master plan for the hill. In 1919 work began on her own residence, Hollyhock House, named for her favorite flower, which grew wild on the site. Wright's oldest son, Lloyd, supervised the construction until the work was halted by one of the many disagreements between the parties involved, who included Barnsdall's business manager. In December of 1920, Rudolph Schindler, who had been producing the drawings for the house in Wright's Midwest office, arrived to assume the supervision. Hollyhock House was finished in 1921.

Wright called the design his "California Romanza," but was at pains to distinguish it

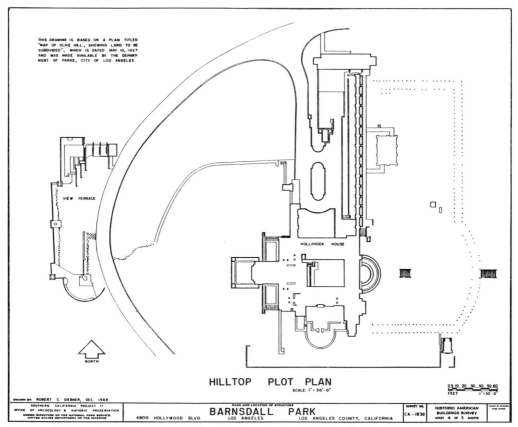

Hollyhock House in Barnsdall Park, Los Angeles, designed by Frank Lloyd Wright. The house faces west with the main axis running eastward through the living room, the interior court, and out to a water course leading to the theater, which was to be built on the east side of the hill. The composition extends to the north by means of the long, low entrance passage. Retaining walls define other minor axes and courts.

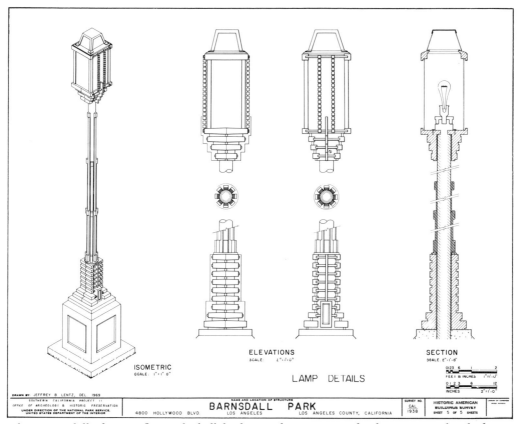

ELEVATIONS
SCALE: ⅛"=1'-0"

SECTION
SCALE: ⅛"=1'-0"

ISOMETRIC
SCALE: 1"=1'-0"

LAMP DETAILS

DRAWN BY: JEFFREY B. LENTZ, DEL. 1969

SOUTHERN CALIFORNIA PROJECT 11
OFFICE OF ARCHEOLOGY & HISTORIC PRESERVATION
UNDER DIRECTION OF THE NATIONAL PARK SERVICE,
UNITED STATES DEPARTMENT OF THE INTERIOR

NAME AND LOCATION OF STRUCTURE

BARNSDALL PARK
4800 HOLLYWOOD BLVD.   LOS ANGELES   LOS ANGELES COUNTY, CALIFORNIA

SURVEY NO.
CAL
1938

HISTORIC AMERICAN
BUILDINGS SURVEY
SHEET 5 OF 5 SHEETS

Aline Barnsdall's favorite flower, the hollyhock, was the inspiration for the geometric detail of these light standards for Hollyhock House.

from what he considered the sentimentalism of the Spanish Mediterranean vogue. Ever loathe to acknowledge sources, he preferred "native" or "primitive" architecture as a better description. Knowledgeable observers generally attributed the source of the design to the Mayan temples that Wright admired in exhibits at the 1893 Columbian Exposition in Chicago.

The plan of the house, though quite formal and balanced in its parts, is full of asymmetries and changing levels, making any path through it a dramatic sequence of indoor and outdoor spaces. The massive block of the house dominates the west side of the site like a temple on an acropolis. A frieze of stylized hollyhocks accents the blank walls. Above the frieze rise slightly battered parapet walls. Although the monolithic composition suggests solid masonry, the structure combines different materials and construction methods. Although

Wright would have preferred to use poured concrete exclusively, a lack of laborers skilled in the technology limited its use to the water table and the belt cornice. The walls above the water table that extend to the floor level are of hollow tile, stuccoed on the exterior and plastered on the interior. The battered parapet is stucco on a wood frame.

Intended for Aline and her daughter plus a staff of servants, the house had seventeen living and sleeping rooms and seven bathrooms. The several wings housed the separate public, private, and service functions. The centerpiece of the composition is the interior garden court, designed as a patio theater. The space, a masterpiece of spatial flexibility, contains alternate stages, seating for audiences, and rooftop promenades. Although many kinds of performances are easy to imagine here, it is difficult to conceive of the house as a domestic setting.

Even the living-room hearth, a monumental sculpture with a skylight above it, is separated like a stage from the seating area by a moat.

In addition to the theater, other residences and buildings, including a row of studio-shops along Hollywood Boulevard, were part of the master plan. Relatively little of the great complex, which was altered several times by both Wright and Schindler, was built. While Wright crisscrossed the ocean to Japan to supervise the Imperial Hotel, Barnsdall also traveled constantly. Her life-style was hardly compatible with that of the director of a resident community devoted to the arts. By the mid-1920s, personal factors combined to end her interest in the project and her residence in the city. By 1926, the process of deeding the hill to the city for a park was accomplished. The city then leased the complex to the California Art Club, which retained it until 1942 when it reverted to municipal ownership. Although it is always tempting to lament what might have been, it is difficult to state with assurance that any of the several proposals for Olive Hill would have been the definitive one. The site seems rather to have served as a screen onto which several directors projected grand scenarios.

In 1923–24 Wright built his famous series of "textile block" houses: La Miniatura in Pasadena and the Storer, Freeman, and Ennis houses in Los Angeles. The eight-inch-thick walls of these structures were made of textured, perforated, and plain concrete blocks, threaded through with reinforcing rods and cemented together. Wright's intention was to combine structure and finished surface into one system. Although the general effect of the cubistic, textured masses is exotic, the houses differ in their compositional character. La Miniatura and the Freeman house convey the feeling of ruins half hidden in a jungle; the Ennis house is a fortress.

Wright's son, Lloyd, began a career in landscape design and came to California in the employ of Olmsted and Olmsted to work on the San Diego exposition. He changed to architecture in the course of supervising his father's work and established himself in practice in Los Angeles.

Lloyd's approach to design was more freely theatrical than his father's, as illustrated by the Sowden house of 1926. Perhaps his best-known work, the house owes much of its fame to the dramatic facade, which is quite visible from the street. Like his father, Lloyd Wright was interested in concrete. Through the use of blocks cast with geometric motifs, he also satisfied his wish to give the building a primitive quality. He first used steel rods in the block system in his Bollman house of 1922 and commented later that it was this use that prompted his father to develop the knit block system used the following year in the Storer house.

The 1920s were to Los Angeles what the decade following the 1906 earthquake was to San Francisco, a boom building period in which the city acquired a new downtown. Except that in L.A. (the only U.S. city to be known by its initials), the new downtown was not confined to its previous location, as it had been in San Francisco. Instead, a whole new linear downtown rose along Wilshire Boulevard, an arterial of such widespread fame and prestige that, ultimately, over two hundred enterprises incorporated Wilshire into their names.

H. Gaylord Wilshire died in 1927 before the decade was out, but not before he had lived over four decades to the fullest in his adopted city. He seemed the right kind of millionaire for L.A. Arriving in California in 1884 at the age of twenty-three, Wilshire proceeded to lose the fortune he had inherited in Cincinnati, Ohio. Then he went on to make and lose several more in such far-flung ventures as orange groves, banks, billboards, and a therapeutic electric belt of his own invention. The bust after the 1888 railroad boom converted him to socialism. He became the first socialist to run for Congress, edited a popular radical journal, *Wilshire's Magazine,* and lived for a time in England where he was a friend of George Bernard Shaw's and other Fabian socialists.

In the 1880s, while still a confirmed capitalist, Wilshire developed the Wilshire Tract through which he laid a 120-foot-wide boulevard bearing his name. The tract lay to the west of Westlake (now McArthur) Park. Though the boulevard did not cut through this park until 1934, it ran, with this brief interruption, from downtown to

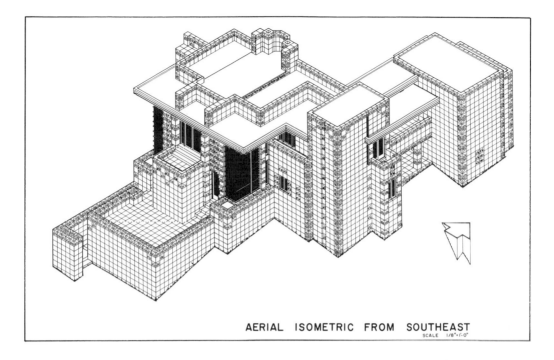

AERIAL ISOMETRIC FROM SOUTHEAST
SCALE 1/8"=1'-0"

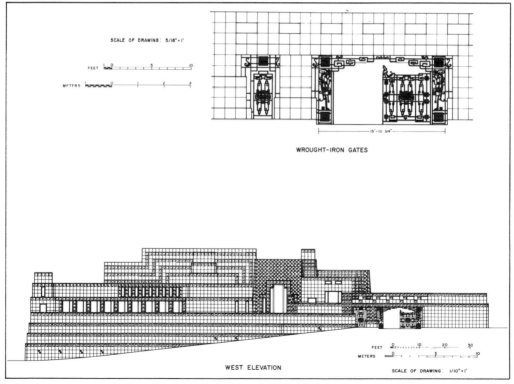

SCALE OF DRAWING: 5/16"=1'

FEET

METERS

WROUGHT-IRON GATES

15'-10 3/4"

FEET

METERS

WEST ELEVATION

SCALE OF DRAWING: 1/10"=1'

These drawings of two of Frank Lloyd Wright's textile block houses in Los Angeles, the Freeman house and the Ennis House, show the tapestrylike effect that the patterned and perforated concrete blocks give to the walls.

Lloyd Wright also used textured concrete blocks for the Sowden house in Los Angeles, but gave them a softer surface than those that his father used. The cavernous entrance to the house contrasts with the plain walls that define the sequence of rooms ranged around a central court. The same jagged, pyramidal forms of the entrance are used at the other end of the court and on the interior with maximum effect.

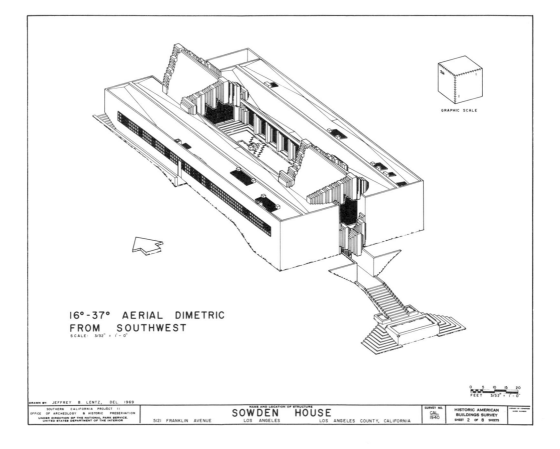

16°-37° AERIAL DIMETRIC
FROM SOUTHWEST
SCALE: 3/32" = 1'-0"

GRAPHIC SCALE

0 5 10 15 20
FEET 3/32" = 1'-0"

DRAWN BY: JEFFREY B. LENTZ, DEL 1969

SOUTHERN CALIFORNIA PROJECT II
OFFICE OF ARCHEOLOGY & HISTORIC PRESERVATION
UNDER DIRECTION OF THE NATIONAL PARK SERVICE,
UNITED STATES DEPARTMENT OF THE INTERIOR

NAME AND LOCATION OF STRUCTURE
SOWDEN HOUSE
5121 FRANKLIN AVENUE   LOS ANGELES   LOS ANGELES COUNTY, CALIFORNIA

SURVEY NO.
CAL
1940

HISTORIC AMERICAN
BUILDINGS SURVEY
SHEET 2 OF 8 SHEETS

the ocean. In the 1920s, real-estate entrepreneur A. W. Ross created a linear shopping district along Wilshire which he called The Miracle Mile. Its extravagant theme expressed L.A.'s unblushing boosterism.

Mobility became a key—indeed, a driving force—in the city's development. As oil strikes stretched from Huntington Beach as far north as Beverly Hills, and the automobile began to vanquish mechanized transit, a new style, now called Art Deco or Streamlined Moderne, replaced the historical revival styles, particularly for tall buildings. New approaches to massing, an emphasis on verticality, and a different vocabulary of ornament, often expressing mobility, characterized the commercial buildings of the 1920s and 1930s.

No example of the decade's architectural and commercial aspirations surpasses Bullock's Wilshire, the great department store designed by John and Donald Parkinson and built in 1928–29. The inscription over

the Wilshire entrance, "To Build a Business that will never know completion," could easily have been applied to the aggressively sprawling city itself. (Mercifully, this symbol of the consumer society's expressive individualism rose on the socialist Wilshire's tract the year after he departed this world.)

The automobile was welcomed by Bullock's, as it was by other buildings on the boulevard, with a generous parking lot behind the store. Shoppers alighting from their cars passed under a monumental *porte cochere* with a ceiling fresco by Herman Sachs featuring the latest modes of transportation.

The building was originally L-shaped in plan, but was filled in by a 1953 addition. Five stories served the store area, a sixth the mechanical equipment, and a 241-foot tower rose east of center on the north facade. The walls were clad in buff-colored terra-cotta above a black marble base. The copper spandrels between the terra-cotta

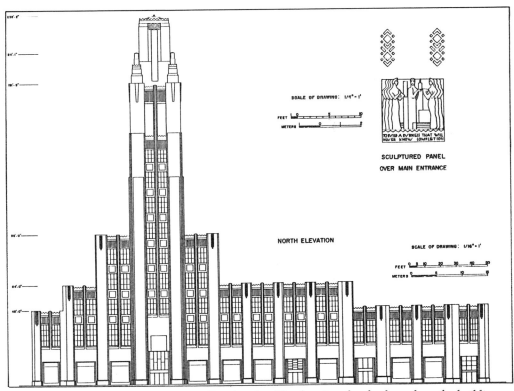

Bullocks-Wilshire Department Store in Los Angeles. The drawing clearly shows how the building steps upward to climax in the slender tower.

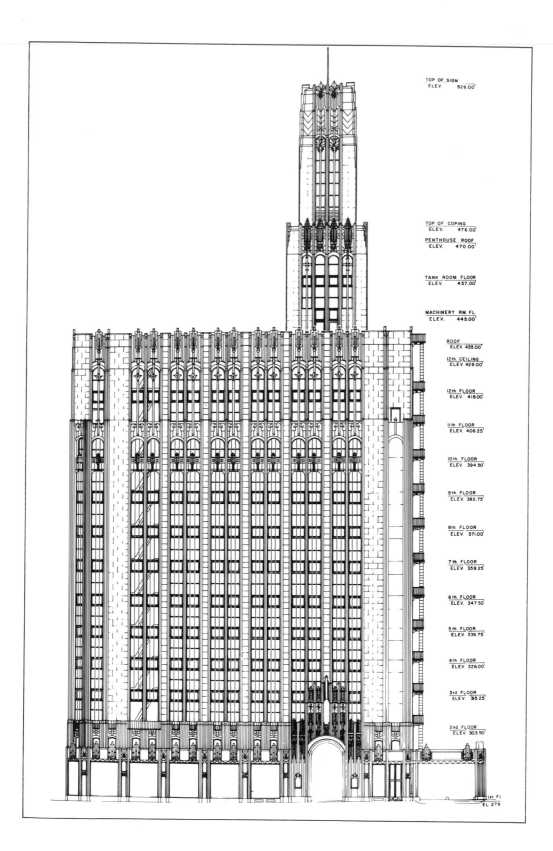

TOP OF SIGN
ELEV.   526.00'

TOP OF COPING
ELEV.   476.00'

PENTHOUSE ROOF
ELEV.   470.00'

TANK ROOM FLOOR
ELEV.   457.00'

MACHINERY RM. FL.
ELEV.   445.00'

ROOF
ELEV. 435.00'

12th CEILING
ELEV. 429.00'

12th FLOOR
ELEV. 418.00'

11th FLOOR
ELEV. 406.25'

10th FLOOR
ELEV. 394.50'

9th FLOOR
ELEV. 382.75'

8th FLOOR
ELEV. 371.00'

7th FLOOR
ELEV. 359.25'

6th FLOOR
ELEV. 347.50'

5th FLOOR
ELEV. 336.75'

4th FLOOR
ELEV. 326.00'

3rd FLOOR
ELEV. 315.25'

2nd FLOOR
ELEV. 303.50'

1st Fl.
EL 279

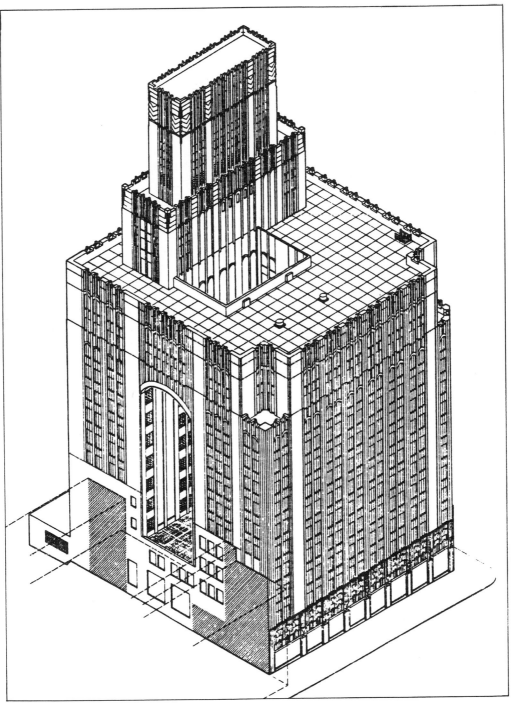

*The Richfield Oil Building in Los Angeles,
truly a jewel in the crown of the early automobile age, was demolished in 1968. The two
black, high-rise towers of Arco Plaza now
stand on the site, but not with the same
pizazz.*

piers above the second story were embossed with eight-pointed stars. Chevrons, a favorite motif, were used on other copper panels. The green hue of the oxidized copper, which was also used on the tower, complemented the tan color of the terra-cotta.

The ultimate architectural statement about mobility and modernism was the Richfield Oil Building, designed by Morgan, Walls and Clements in 1928 and completed in 1929 in downtown Los Angeles. The design owed much to Raymond Hood's 1924 American Radiator Building in New York City. Both buildings were black with gold used for accent; both emphasized vertical lines though the Richfield Building was more squat and square because of the height limit. Designed as freestanding towers, both buildings read as three-dimensional forms, not simply facades.

The colors of the Richfield Building were appropriate to the corporate image: black for oil, accented by blue and gold, the company's service colors. Dramatic night lighting converted the building into a jewel box glowing with energy and also advertised the company, particularly on a sign in the shape of an oil derrick which rose from the penthouse tower to a height of sixty feet and carried the company name on its four sides.

Haig Patigian, a San Francisco sculptor, created the winged guardian angels of mobility that capped the secondary piers on the parapet. He also sculpted the four figures personifying aviation, the postal service, industry, and navigation, which stood like Gothic saints in their niches above the entrance.

A comparison of the Richfield Building in Los Angeles and the Medical-Dental Building at 450 Sutter Street in San Francisco points up some differences between the two cities. The Richfield's scintillating qualities of color and light were not employed by Timothy Pflueger in the 1929 design for 450 Sutter. The beige terra-cotta cladding, enriched by a large-scale, Mayan-esque motif in low relief, suggested masonry. The building's faceted T-form rises cleanly to its parapeted, squared-off top in the most modern manner. Though enriched with additional ornament around the entrance and in the lobby, the building generally expressed the more restricted budget of

For the Medical-Dental office building at 450 Sutter Street in San Francisco the architects in the firm of Miller and Pflueger used a vocabulary of ornament loosely derived from the Mayan calendar symbols, which had been well published in the 1920s.

a speculative office building as opposed to the more generous funds available for a corporate headquarters. The contrast also revealed the more staid character of San Francisco, which had outgrown its brash adolescence and was now the center of old money and traditions.

However, across the bay in Oakland, Pflueger's office designed a movie palace as rich as any in the southland movie capital of L.A. The Paramount Theatre, built in the depths of the Great Depression, broke ground on December 11, 1930, and was completed a year later. The first client was the Paramount-Famous Players-Lasky Corporation, but before construction ended, Paramount went bankrupt and was taken over by the Fox-West Coast theater chain. However, before the name Fox could be emblazoned on the giant sign projecting from the facade, Paramount was bailed out—just in time.

The Paramount's facade on Broadway, a fifty-foot-wide and one hundred-foot-high wall—really a billboard on end, was intended as an advertisement, a poster for the performing arts. Stretching the length of the facade are male and female puppeteers, rendered in tile mosaic and set in a red tile frame. Dressed in robes that hint of Byzantine and Peruvian origin, they dangle from their fingers marionette figures personifying drama and showmanship. The present marquee is a replacement for the original which had to be removed when the street was widened.

The grand lobby is a rectangular box rising to the height of eighty feet. The scale reflects the more public nature of movies in the 1930s when intermissions between features gave lobbies a spectatorship function.

Like many of his contemporaries, Pflueger used light as a material in its own right, and it plays a major role in the Paramount interior. The canopies of light—one in the lobby, the other in the auditorium—were among the most innovative elements devised to enliven and dematerialize hard surfaces. Relatively inexpensive in terms of materials, the ceilings are grilles of galvanized tin strips set on end and welded together in geometric patterns, then hung by chains about five feet below the actual ceiling. The intervening space is filled with

clear or colored light. Depending on the viewer's position, the depth of the linear pattern changes from pencil-thin to crayon-thick.

The most spectacular feature of the lobby is the "Fountain of Life," which is a fountain of light. Set on a platform above the lobby entrance, this monumental composition in receding frosted glass planes with thin metal seams is backlit from sources between the vertical planes. The ripples and billows of light burst into luminous plumes which rise nearly to the ceiling.

The Paramount Theater in Oakland was remodeled in the 1970s by the San Francisco office of Skidmore, Owings and Merrill. Because Broadway was widened, the original marquee had to be replaced with one that did not extend over the narrower sidewalk. The inner vestibule was also removed and a ticket booth designed for the new entrance area.

The auditorium of the Paramount seats about 3,000 people in the orchestra and 300 in the balcony. The "canopy of light," a suspended ceiling made of metal strips which the designers called a giant cookie cutter, covers more than half of its width with a pattern of pointed leaves and flowers.

The south-seas ambiance of the lobby expands in the auditorium where the walls are covered with a relief depicting dense tropical foliage through which Gauguinesque maidens peer out. One inspiration for these scenes came, not from the movies, but from William H. Hudson's *Green Mansions: A Romance of the Tropical Forest,* which was in its fifth edition by 1931. Its heroine, Rima, lived only in the trees and epitomized the forest nymph.

Robert Howard designed the reliefs in part to enhance the acoustical properties of the hall, which was intended for stage and opera performances as well as movies. A statuary group with a central, winged male figure flanked by horses, created by sculptor Ralph Stackpole, dominates the proscenium arch.

A thorough inventory of all the theater's custom-designed features, down to furniture and lighting fixtures, and their probable sources would run several more pages. This

Gesamtkunstwerk was not typical of theater design. Typically, specialists designed the interiors of theaters, leaving the architects only the envelope. Pflueger's team of architects, artists, and craftsmen prefigured Works Progress Administration and Public Works Administration endeavors, where interdisciplinary collaboration was part of the program.

Relatively few buildings were built by private sources during the Great Depression and World War II. Following the war, shortages of materials and government-mandated

The V. C. Morris Store on Maiden Lane in San Francisco was designed by Frank Lloyd Wright with a nearly blank facade. The entrance is a glazed tunnel extending into the building that permitted passersby to glimpse the dramatic interior filled with sparkling objects.

priorities for housing for returning veterans retarded the construction of nondomestic building types.

An early postwar commercial building of note in California was Frank Lloyd Wright's Morris Store of 1948–49. Designed for the sale of fine crystal and china, the building was actually a remodeling of a small warehouse of 1911, all vestiges of which have been concealed. Located just off Union Square on Maiden Lane, this store for Mr. V. C. Morris considerably raised the tone of the alley which, over time, had evolved from a street of ill repute to a service street for major stores on Sutter and Geary streets to the north and south. Wright gave the building a windowless facade punctured at one corner by a round-arched entrance recessed slightly from the sidewalk.

The facade has been interpreted as a translation of Richardson's or Sullivan's mighty masonry into Wright's favored Roman brick. The tapestry of long, thin bricks strikes the right note of sophisticated elegance on a small scale. Inside, however, the only precedent is Wright's own design for the Guggenheim Museum in New York (published in 1946 but not completed until 1959). A two-story, spiraling ramp nearly fills the space. The circle motif is everywhere—in furniture, lighting fixtures, hanging planters, and the translucent bowls that compose the suspended ceiling. Ironically, this dazzling interior did not make an effective background for merchandise. Its present use as an art gallery is an ex post facto link between it and the Guggenheim.

◇   ◇   ◇   ◇   ◇

Wright's genius was the magnet that drew two European architects, Rudolph Schindler and Richard Neutra, from Vienna, Austria, to California. Schindler arrived in 1920 after a stay of six years in Chicago. He had come to the United States in 1914 at the age of twenty-seven in answer to an ad for a draftsman placed by the Chicago firm of Ottenheimer, Stern & Reichert. In 1917 Schindler realized a major goal of his stay when, after repeated pleas, Wright hired him. In an article titled "Space Architecture," published in *Dune Forum* in 1934, Schindler related that a librarian in Vienna

introduced him to Wright in about 1911 with a copy of the Wasmuth portfolio. "Immediately I realized—here was a man who had taken hold of this new medium. Here was space architecture."

After two years at Wright's Taliesin studio in Wisconsin, Schindler came to Los Angeles to supervise construction of Aline Barnsdall's Olive Hill project. Since Wright was occupied with the Imperial Hotel in Tokyo, Schindler not only had to manage the building operation, but also had to placate Barnsdall, who was miffed at Wright's absence. Schindler performed well enough in the perilous role of mediator to go on to largely design two additional Olive Hill buildings, the director's house and the Oleander house. Drawings for both buildings were sent to Japan for Wright's approval; they were built in 1921.

The next year Schindler decided to continue his career in California rather than return to Vienna. The "cooperative house" that he designed for himself and his wife and artist friends, Clyde and Marion Chase, was one result of this decision. Its inspiration was the kind of experience that had moved nineteenth-century newcomers to California to embrace the simple life. The Schindlers had vacationed in Yosemite where Rudolph was particularly captivated by a simple camp structure with solid walls on three sides and a lightweight screen at the front. After their return home, they bought land in what was then a sparsely built area of Hollywood. The Chases, also newcomers, became collaborators in building the Kings Road house.

The Schindlers had made a friend of Dr. Phillip Lovell whose widely read column in the *Los Angeles Times,* "Care of the Body," had made him a local celebrity. Lovell's passion for the natural life lived as much and as strenuously as possible out-of-doors appealed to Schindler, who wrote a series of articles on architecture and health for Lovell's column in 1926. In them Schindler reiterated ideas basic to the earlier Arts and Crafts Movement:

Our rooms will descend close to the ground and the garden will become an integral part of the house. . . . Our house will lose its front-and-back-door aspect. . . . It will cease being a group of dens, some larger ones for social effect and a

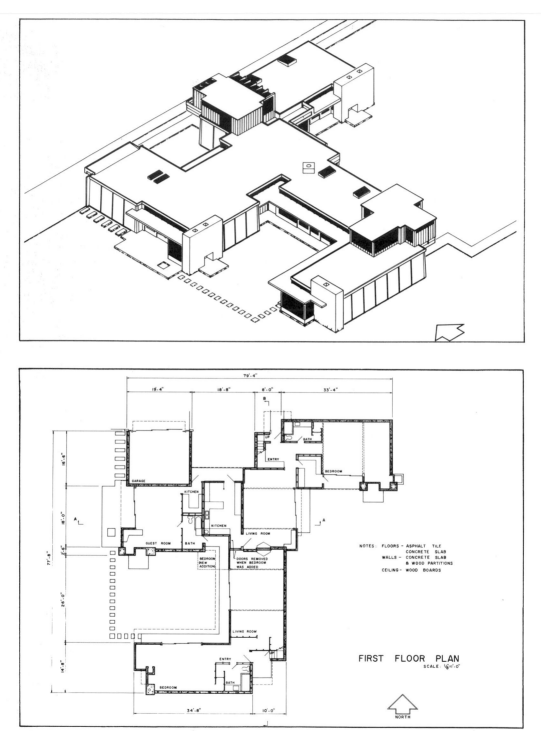

The Schindler house on Kings Road in Los Angeles, now restored as a museum. Schindler treated the 100- by 200-foot lot as a contained environment. Outdoor living zones, gardens and patios with fireplaces were spatially integrated into the irregular plan. Indoor rooms included a pair of private studios for each family. These retreats were separated by service spaces set in L-shaped angles so that the patios were framed on three sides and opened to gardens on the fourth. The so-called sleeping baskets over the two entrances suggested tree houses.

few smaller ones in which to herd the family. Each individual will want a private room to gain a background for his life. He will sleep in the open. A work-and-playroom, together with the garden, will satisfy the group needs.

Schindler shunned conventional technology in building the Kings Road house. His use of the tilt-slab method of making concrete walls was inspired by Irving Gill and passed on to him by Lloyd Wright. The four-foot-wide, one-story high, tapered panels were poured on the concrete slab floor and tilted upright at its edge. The three-inch slits between them, glazed to admit light, marked off the spatial intervals. Walls were separated from the wood-beam ceilings by narrow clerestory windows. As in Yosemite, the cave merged with the camper's tent.

Schindler's friendship with the Lovells brought him the commission for their beach house in Newport Beach, designed in 1922 and completed in 1925. The best known and most aesthetically daring of his works, the house ranks with Le Corbusier's 1930 Villa Savoye near Paris in signaling a new doctrinal era. At the time nothing like it had been built in the United States.

The Lovell Beach House was avowedly experimental in its response to the conditions of the site. For one thing, the structure had to be solid and yet flexible enough to withstand seismic stress. Another factor to consider was the public path to the beach that ran by the property. Schindler gained privacy for the living quarters by raising them to the upper level where there was also a good view of the ocean. Unlike the contemporary work of Europeans such as Le Corbusier and Mies van der Rohe, in which the structural system was internal and minimal, the beach house structure was external and expressive.

The walls of the Lovell house were of solid plaster two inches thick; windows and doors were wooden, premilled units hung by steel rods from the concrete frames; ceilings were wood with exposed beams. The bedrooms were off a balcony running alongside the two-story living room and sandwiched between it and the sleeping porches on the front of the house.

Schindler maintained the campsite image of the cave lightly screened in front. But when wind blew rain into the porches and voices from passersby below (whom the Lovells heard talking about the upside-down house) invaded their privacy, the Lovells asked Schindler to close in the porches. He did this by removing the wood and glass screens that divided the porches from the bedrooms and cutting them down to fit above the balcony railings. Although this solution weakened the effect of complementary voids on both levels, it showed Schindler to be more of a pragmatist than a dogmatist.

Sadly, the cost of the house was more fitting for a castle than a beach cabana. The remote site increased the costs of materials and construction, both of which produced continuous problems. Dr. Lovell judged that the final cost was thirty percent above the estimate, a setback that strained the friendship.

Richard and Dione Neutra were staying with the Schindlers. Richard was a friend from student years at the Vienna Academy; he and Rudolph corresponded during the years after Schindler came to this country. Neutra had also wanted to come to the U.S. and to work for Wright. But for many reasons related to World War I and the ensuing unsettled times, it took Neutra until 1923 to obtain a visa and enough money to come to this country.

After a stay in New York, Neutra went to Chicago in 1924 where he worked for Holabird & Roche for some months. Neutra met Wright at Louis Sullivan's funeral in 1924. Later, at Schindler's urging, Wright invited Neutra to Taliesin. Like the Schindlers, the Neutras reveled in the life and work there with Wright. Sensing, however, that a more productive future awaited them in California, they left for Los Angeles, arriving at the Kings Road house in 1926.

Whether or not the Schindlers actually expected them is unclear. Schindler had little work to share, but Neutra's entrepreneurial instincts guided him into activities that brought him notice. While biding his time, he did small tasks for Schindler such as the minimal landscaping on the Lovell beach house.

The conflicting accounts of how Neutra gained the commission for the Lovell town house are too lengthy to be presented here.

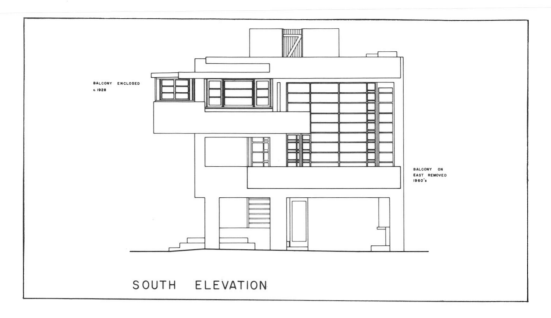

BALCONY ENCLOSED
c 1928

BALCONY ON
EAST REMOVED
1960's

SOUTH   ELEVATION

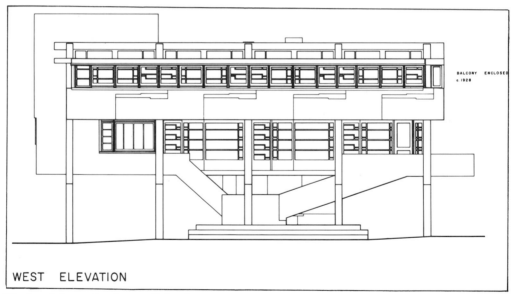

BALCONY ENCLOSED
c 1928

WEST   ELEVATION

The beach house for the Lovell family in Newport Beach was constructed with five free-standing concrete frames cast in the form of stacked, open squares that held the living spaces aloft. The recessed ground area brought the beach home, so to speak, as a playground for the children. Two stairways, one to the kitchen and the other to the living room, introduced strong diagonals into the composition.

(For a thorough account see Esther McCoy's *Vienna to Los Angeles: Two Journeys*.) The friendship between the Schindlers and the Lovells had cooled. The Lovells had planned a town house that they thought Schindler would design. Disgruntled perhaps by the expense and problems of the beach house, but undaunted in his pursuit of Modernism, Dr. Lovell no doubt listened sympathetically to Neutra's talk of the cost control that was possible in an industrial building process. Neutra was desperate to be on his own. Whatever the details, the upshot was that Lovell gave the commission for his Los Angeles house, later called the Health House, to Richard Neutra.

As in the case of the beach house, the site posed problems. As Neutra recalled it, the site in the Hollywood hills adjacent to Griffith Park was an "inclined piece of rugged nature." Cuts had to be made in the hillside to create a base for the massive concrete foundation and the ground floor which had the laundry, utility, recreation, and dressing rooms opening to the pool. The main living floor was also set into a cut in the steep slope. The upper level containing bedrooms and sleeping porches was connected to the entrance bridge leading from the street.

For this first totally steel-frame residence in the United States, Bethlehem Steel reduced the cost of the material and even sent representatives to supervise the construction. Prefabricated pieces of the frame were transported to the site, and in less than forty work hours, the steel cage was assembled and bolted together. Standard casement window sections were clamped on the frame. Gunite was sprayed on wire lath from hoses leading from mixers out on the street. The finished product, a three-dimensional composition in asymmetrical planes, appeared to float effortlessly against the green backdrop.

Neutra's idealism about the cost effectiveness of the industrial process proved to be naive. Even with the reduced cost of the steel, the total cost, as Lovell later recalled, was nearly one hundred percent over the budget. He ran out of money. Since avantgarde Modernism carried no brief with financial institutions, Lovell was forced to turn to Harry Chandler, publisher of the *Los Angeles Times,* for a loan to finish the house. Chandler lent him money for friendship's sake, but said he wouldn't give him a nickel for the house. Not that Chandler's attitude meant that the house was inconsequential. Quite the reverse: it was a high-tech sensation in the city, providing the flamboyant doctor with some theatrical occasions that he thoroughly enjoyed.

Lovell's column carried news of the house which, he said, would "introduce a modern type of architecture and establish it

in California, where new and individualistic architecture is necessary." Lovell invited his readers to see the house on four successive Sunday afternoons on tours that he and Neutra led. About 15,000 people came. Although in 1929 the house no doubt seemed prophetic, it remains unique in respect to its technology and has become a splendid period piece.

Flux and change are forever renewing the fabric of our environment and altering our perception of its history. Proud monuments and humble artifacts come and go. Yet, this process is more a challenge than a cause for despair. As one of California's most illustrious natives put it:

The composition is the thing seen by everyone living in the doing. They are the composing of the composition that at the time they are living is the composition of the time in which they are living. It is that that makes living a thing they are doing.

Getrude Stein,
Four Saints in Three Acts

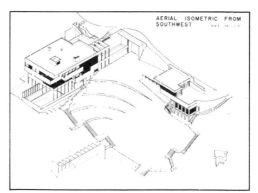

AERIAL ISOMETRIC FROM SOUTHWEST

The Lovell Health House in the Hollywood hills of Los Angeles was sited on a shelf cut from the hillside in order to make a base for the massive concrete foundation. A pool extended from the ground floor, which also contained the laundry, utility, recreation, and dressing rooms. The main living floor was also set into the slope. The upper level, accessible from an entrance bridge leading from the street, contained bedrooms and sleeping porches. Guest quarters and the garage were at the other end of the site.

Lumber Mill, Albion (CA-1469).

The Catalogue of Buildings
Included in the
Historic American Buildings
Survey for California

❖

In accordance with HABS policy, buildings included in the catalogue are listed alphabetically by town or city, or by their vicinity to the nearest town or city in the county in which they are located. The buildings themselves are catalogued according to the name of the building or according to the name of the first owner. If the building is better known by the name of a later owner, both names are listed. Public buildings are listed by their official names.

Following the name of the building is the HABS number, e.g., CA-1555. These numbers should be used when inquiring about a property or when ordering reproductions from the Library of Congress.

Descriptions follow the standard HABS format, listing the building materials, the dimensions or shape of the building, the number of front bays, the number of stories, the type of roof, the position and number of chimneys, notable exterior details, notable interior details, outbuildings and dependencies, the chronology of the building, the architect or builder, if known, alterations, the present condition if different from the original, and, if relevant, a statement of the particular architectural or historic significance of the property. The initials NR, NHL, and SHL at the end of the descriptions stand for National Register of Historic Places, National Historic Landmark, and State Historic Landmark, respectively.

The HABS records for properties include exterior and interior photographs, sheets of measured drawings of plans, sections, elevations and details, and data pages, which give the historical and architectural information in written form. These records may be consulted in the Prints and Photographs Reading Room at the Library of Congress. They may also be purchased by writing to the Library of Congress, Prints and Photographs Division, Washington, D.C. 20540.

Agua Fria   □   Mariposa County

Agua Fria—General (CA-154). Small town of small gable-roofed buildings. Now ruinous. 1 photocopy of 1904 photo.

Alamo   □   Contra Costa County

Henry Hotel (CA-1657). Wood frame with clapboards, five-bay front in gable end, two stories, gable roof intersected by false front, one-story porch across front surmounted by X-braced balcony railing. Built 1854; probably demolished. 1 photocopy of 1940 photo.

Alba   □   San Joaquin County

Farm House (CA-12). Wood frame with channeled siding, five-bay front, two stories, gable roof with cornice returns, two interior brick chimneys, one-story polygonal bays on gable ends, one-story rear wing. Built late 19th c. Not located. 2 ext. photos (1934).

Albany Flats   □   Calaveras County

Romaggi, James, Fandango House (CA-1204). *Hwy. 49, south of Angels Camp*. Rubble stone, slabs of amphibolite schist, two-story central block with metal hipped roof, side and rear one-story wings with gable roofs; irregular plan. Built ca. 1856 and assessed to Andrew Lee & Co.; building associated with Jerome Romaggi as agent for Andrew Lee 1861, and as owner 1879; erroneously called a fandango house; ruinous. 4 ext. photos (1934).

Albion   □   Mendocino County

Albion—General (CA-1468). Wood-framed, gable-roofed houses on bluff overlooking river. 2 ext. photos (1934).

Lumber Mill (CA-1469). *Near mouth of Albion R.* Large complex of wooden buildings: houses, warehouses, sheds. Built mid to late 19th c.; demolished. 1 photo (1934).

Almaden   □   Santa Clara County

See New Almaden.

Altaville   □   Calaveras County

Prince and Garibardi Store (P.F. Pache & Co.) (CA-1205). *Junction Hwys. 4 and 49*. Stone, dressed ashlar, four-bay front, two stories, flat roof, second-floor balcony with decorative cast-iron balustrade, two front entrances with iron doors, iron shutters on windows. Built 1852 for B. R. Prince and G. Garibardi, second floor with living quarters added 1857; a good example of a commercial Gold Rush building in excellent condition. 1 ext. photo (1934), 1 photocopy of 1920s photo.

Alvarado   □   Alameda County

Smith, Henry C., House (CA-1659). Wood frame with drop siding and cut shingles, two-story central section with one-story flanking wings; central-hall plan. Built 1852 by Henry C. Smith, who came to California with John Frémont in 1846, founded town of New Haven, and introduced the bill in the state legislature creating Alameda County in 1853. Demolished. 1 ext. photo (1940).

Amador City   □   Amador County

Amador Hotel (CA-1346). *Hwy. 49*. Wood frame with clapboards, seven-bay front by three bays deep, two stories, gable roof with central cross gable, cornice molding, two-story veranda with second-floor balustrade. Built 1850s–1860s; restored. 1 ext. photo (1934).

"False Front" Buildings (CA-1349). *Hwy. 49*. Three stores with gable roofs and false fronts, one brick, one rough-cut stone, one wood frame with channeled siding, latter two stories, others one story, stone and wood ones with shed-roofed porch across front. Stone store built 1860s; brick 1879; wood frame one demolished. 1 ext. photo (1934).

House and Mine (CA-1350). *Hwy. 49*. Brick, two stories, gable roof, porches front and back, turned balustrade second-level front; wood-framed mine buildings in background. Built 1881; restored as Mine House Inn; foundations of Keystone Mine mill across street and remains of iron mine headframe on slope above. 1 ext. photo (1934).

Imperial Hotel (CA-1348). *Water St. and Hwy. 49*. Brick, three-bay front, two stories, flat roof, high

Imperial Hotel, Amador City (CA-1348).

brick false front in stepped gable form with decorative inset pointed arches, second-floor cantilevered balcony with Chippendale balustrade, segmental-arched ground-floor openings, iron shutters. Built 1879. 1 ext. photo (1934).

Anaheim □ Orange County

Pioneer House (Pioneer House of the Mother Colony) (CA-320). 414 N. West St. Wood frame with horizontal siding, 36' (four-bay front) × 28', one story, gable roof pitches out over porch across front. Built 1857 for George Hansen, originally stood on N. Los Angeles St. between Chartres and Cypress Sts. 2 sheets (1934, including plan, elevations, details); 2 ext. photos (1934); 1 data page (1936). SHL

Sheffield House (Old German House) (CA-37). 506 Los Angeles St. Brick first story, wood-framed second story, one-and-a-half stories, five-bay front, mansard roof with gabled dormers, one-story porch across front with balustrade above, polygonal bays on one side. Built 1886, Chris Stappenback, architect and builder. 10 sheets (1934, including plans, elevations, details); 5 ext. photos (1934); 1 data page (1936).

Angel Island □ Marin County

Fort McDowell (CA-1841). Brick and wood frame, one-, two-, and three-story gable-roofed buildings on leeward side of island. Island deeded to U. S. government 1852–53, served as detention center for immigrants until 1940. Now being restored. 1 photocopy of undated photo. NR

Angels Camp □ Calaveras County

Fox House (CA-1493). Wood frame with horizontal siding, four-bay front, one story with raised basement on hillside site, gable roof, shed-roofed porch across front wraps around. Built 1860s; name "Fox" erroneous. 1 photocopy of 1925 photo.

Hotel Angels (CA-1547). W. side Main St. Stone, plastered, seven-bay front, two stories, low gable roof, two-story veranda across front with turned balustrade and bracketed caps. Original canvas hotel built on site 1851, replaced by one-story wooden structure, rebuilt in stone 1855, second story added 1857; now retail stores with altered street-level display windows and doors, new sec-

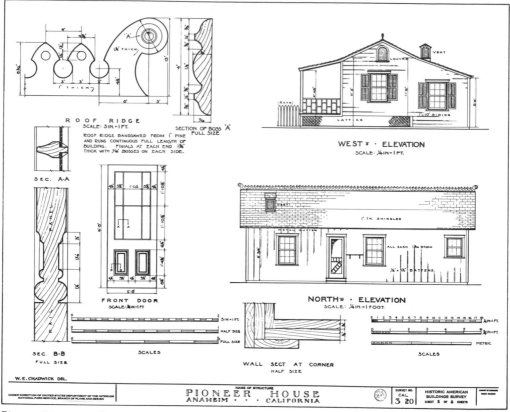

Pioneer House, Anaheim (CA-320).

Angels Camp continued

ond-floor balcony; believed to be the spot where Mark Twain heard about the celebrated jumping frog of Calaveras County. 1 photocopy of undated photo. SHL

House (CA-1275). E. side Main St., N. end of town. Wood frame with clapboards, three-bay front in gable end, two stories on raised basement, gable roof, one-story veranda across front wraps around, balustrade above, fanlight in gable. Built either 1856 or 1872 for Joseph Pierano; new windows and door added to lower level, railing added to veranda and south bay enclosed; fine example of the Classic Revival style; 1 ext. photo (1934).

Main Street Buildings (CA-1499). Buildings primarily two stories of stone or frame construction, porches and canopies. Most structures intact, some alterations to shop windows and second-floor balconies. 3 photocopies of photos (1923, undated).

Pierano, Joseph, House and Store (CA-1276). E. side Main St. Plastered masonry, three-bay front,

one story, corrugated metal gable roof, metal shed-roofed porch across front, iron shutters. Built 1859–60. 1 ext. photo (1934).

Joseph Pierano House and Store, Angels Camp (CA-1276).

Scribner's Store (CA-1491). Stone, three-bay front, at least two stories all that is ascertainable. Built 1856, burned 1941. 1 photocopy of 1925 photo.

Theater (CA-1482). Wood frame with clapboards on front and board-and-batten siding on sides, three-bay front, one-and-a-half stories, gable roof with cornice moldings and returns, frieze board across gable front; single-hall plan with vestibule. Built early 1850s; demolished. Many famous actors of the day, including Edwin Booth, played here. 1 photocopy of 1925 photo.

Utica Mine (CA-1492). Stone ruins; no remains by 1983. 1 photocopy of undated photo.

Angels Camp vicinity □ Calaveras County

Burch, John, House (CA-1278). Half plastered, half with horizontal siding, six-bay front by three bays, shingled hipped roof, one-story porch across front. Built 1860s; not located; may be erroneously named. 1 ext. photo (1934).

Arcata □ Humboldt County

House (CA-1457). 14th and J Streets. Wood frame with horizontal siding, L-shape, one-and-a-half stories with one-story wing, gable roof, scroll-bracketed entrance porches. Built 1860s; remodeled to include shutters with pine tree cut-outs, scroll brackets removed, asphalt shingle exterior. 1 ext. photo (1934).

Nixon House (CA-1458). 1022 10th St. Wood frame with clapboards, three-bay front, T-shaped, two story main unit, steep gable roof, cross gable with quatrefoils pierced in bargeboards, diamond-paned casement windows, polygonal bay window at first-floor side, front entrance porch with balustraded second-floor balcony, rear service wing with full-length veranda. Built 1860s. 2 ext. photos (1934).

Atherton □ San Mateo County

Linden Towers Gates (CA-2118). Middlefield Rd. at James Pl. Brick piers with stone quoins, triglyphs on frieze, cast-iron gates with cartouche above center, adjoining pedestrian entranceway has stone quoins and keystone. Built 1904 for James L. Flood to enhance his father's, James C. Flood's, elaborate estate which included multiple-towered and -gabled mansion; house demol-

Nixon House, Arcata (CA-1458).

ished 1936, gates are all that remain. 9 ext. photos (1975).

Watkins-Cartan House (CA-1990). 25 Isabella Ave. Wood frame with horizontal siding, 46' (three-bay front) × 49', one-and-a-half stories, gable roof with cross gables, gable wall dormers, paired brackets at cornice, one-story porch, partially enclosed, on three sides, hoodmolds on openings, extensive gardens, L-plan, marble mantelpieces. Built 1866; moved in 1903 six blocks to present site; spiral staircase modified. 7 sheets (1974, including site plan, plans, elevations, section); 4 ext. photos (1975); 4 data pages (1974). NR

□ *Carriage House (CA-1990 A).* Wood frame with horizontal siding, 56' (five-bay front) × 29', one-and-a-half stories, gable roof with cross gable; carriageway and work rooms first level, apartments second level. Built early 20th c. 1 sheet (1974, including plans, elevation).

Auburn □ Placer County

Town of Auburn. Founded 1849 as prosperous mining town, became county seat 1850. When surveyed in the 1930s, the Old Town of Auburn contained a number of 1850s and '60s commercial buildings, all brick, one or two stories, flat roofs with parapets and dentils, built on hillsides, usually three-bay fronts, iron shutters. Many of these have been demolished or altered. Distinctive firehouse built 1891 remains: wood frame, two-and-a-half stories, steep-pitched hip roof, belvedere on top. The following entries are general views of the town with nondescriptive names.

□ *Brick Row in Chinese Section (CA-1388).* 1 ext. photo (1934).

WEST ELEVATION

SCALE : 3/16" = 1'-0"

DRAWN BY: STEPHEN FARNETH 1974

SAN MATEO COUNTY PROJECT 1974
OFFICE OF ARCHEOLOGY & HISTORIC PRESERVATION
UNDER DIRECTION OF THE NATIONAL PARK SERVICE,
UNITED STATES DEPARTMENT OF THE INTERIOR | 25 ISABELLA AVENUE | NAME AND LOCATION OF STRUCTURE
WATKINS - CARTAN HOUSE
ATHERTON   SAN MATEO COUNTY   CALIFORNIA | SURVEY NO.
CAL
1990 | HISTORIC AMERICAN
BUILDINGS SURVEY
SHEET 5 OF 7 OF 8 SHEETS |

Watkins-Cartan House, Atherton (CA-1990).

Auburn continued

□ *Group of Buildings in Old Town (CA-1385).* 2 ext. photos (1934).

□ *Buildings in Old Town (CA-1387).* 1 ext. photo (1934).

□ *Buildings in Old Town (CA-1386).* Lincoln Way and Maple St. 1 ext. photo.

□ *Firehouse and Commercial Buildings (CA-1384).* 1 ext. photo (1934).

Ruins of Old Town City Hall (CA-1390). 2 ext. photos (1934) of pilasters, wall.

Stone, Henry, House (CA-1389). Nevada St. Wood frame with clapboards, two stories, three-bay front in gable end, recessed front porch. Built ca. 1856; demolished by 1960. 1 ext. photo (1934).

Bagby   □   Mariposa County

Railroad Station (CA-1650). Near Hwy. 49. Wood frame with drop siding, 40′ × 16′, two stories with raised freight platform on one side, shingled hip roof, variety of wood-framed windows and doors; ground floor with office in center flanked by freight room and waiting room, second floor with living quarters for stationmaster. Built 1904 for Yosemite Valley Railroad; last surviving station house on line; moved to Yosemite National Park late 1960s. 3 sheets (1960s, including plans, elevations, sections).

Town of Bagby (CA-1703). Town on Merced River with one- and two-story wood-framed buildings of typical mid 19th c. vernacular types. First called Benton Mills by John C. Frémont for his father-in-law, renamed Bagby, now submerged under reservoir. 1 photocopy of 1934 photo.

Baldwin Park   □   Los Angeles County

Central School (Baldwin Park City Hall) (CA-2016). 14403 E. Pacific Ave. Stuccoed brick, one story, flat roof with scrolled gable end, low belfry towers with hip roof, main entrance of triple-arched loggia with hip roof, porches and stoops on other elevations, symmetrical arrangement of two wings flanking main block, Spanish Mission Revival style details. Built 1913; additions of similar design, 1918 and 1928; converted to City Hall, 1958; porch filled in, doorway remodeled, n.d.; interior completely remodeled, 1958 and 1972. 12 ext. photos (1978), 1 int. photo (1978).

Bear River □ Yuba County

Bear River Hotel and Wells Fargo Office (CA-1689). Ashlar masonry, hotel two-stories, four-bay front, gable roof, office, one story, two-bay front, hip roof, wooden front porch supporting a balustraded open balcony. Built 1850s; demolished. 1 photocopy of ext. photo (1850s).

Frémont Cottage (CA-1861). Wood frame with clapboards, one story, shingled gable roof pitches out over rear addition, shed-roofed front porch. Built 1858 for John C. Frémont; demolished before 1932. 1 photocopy of undated photo.

Oso House Hotel (CA-1106). Wood frame with clapboards, six-bay front, shingled gable roof, shed-roofed two-story porch around two sides with box columns, stick railing on second level. Built 1851 for John C. Frémont near his Mariposa Mining Co.; also housed Wells Fargo & Co. offices; destroyed by fire ca. 1938. 1 ext. photo (1936), 1 photocopy of 1850s photo.

Wells Fargo Building (CA-1704). Brick ruins. 1 photocopy of 1930s photo also shows the main street, part of Oso House Hotel (CA-1106), car in foreground.

Bell □ Los Angeles County

Casa del Rancho San Antonio (Lugo House) (CA-36). *6360 E. Gage at Garfield*. Plastered adobe and wood frame, stone foundations, approx. 44' × 21' with 8' wide porches all around, two stories, one-story rear addition, hip roof pitches out to cover porches, west porch enclosed with board-and-batten siding, doors have slightly triangulated lintels, both casement and double-hung windows in wood frames, exterior stairway to upper floor; two-room plan, fireplace with wood mantel and plate rail, interior stair. Built 1844 for Vicente Lugo on a ranch originally containing 29,513 acres; good example of the two-story adobe with porches called the Monterey style. 4 sheets (1934, including plans, elevations,

details); 3 ext. photos (1937); 1 data page (1937).

Belmont □ San Mateo County

Ralston-Sharon House (CA-1674). *Ralston Ave. on grounds of College of Notre Dame*. Stuccoed wood frame, large rambling structure, three-and-a-half stories, hipped roof with cross gables and hipped dormers, four-story tower, one-story enclosed porches, porte-cochere; rich interior, stairhall has opera boxes at mezzanine level, skylight above, generous use of etched glass and mirrors. Built 1853, heavily remodeled and enlarged 1864 by John P. Gaynor, for William Chapman Ralston, San Francisco financier; now serves as college of Sisters of Notre Dame de Namur. 6 ext. photos (1975), 7 int. photos (1975), 3 photocopies of ext. photos (ca. 1880, ca. 1930), 3 photocopies of int. photos (ca. 1875, ca. 1885); 10 data pages (1966). NHL

Benicia □ Solano County

Benicia Arsenal (CA-1773). Established 1851, abandoned 1964, now Benicia Industrial Park. Includes site of Benicia Barracks, one of first military posts in state, established 1849. Most impressive buildings built 1853–1863. 1 sheet (1976, including Arsenal map); 4 photocopies of ca. 1856 photos, 4 photocopies of maps (1856, 1863, 1868, 1894), 2 photocopies of drawings (ca. 1860s, 1878); NR, SHL

□ *Barracks (CA-1774)*. Six small frame buildings used as barracks. Built 1849 and after; destroyed by fire 1922. 6 photocopies of ext. photos (ca. 1915 and undated), 1 photocopy of architectural drawings (1877); 1 data page (1981).

□ *Barracks (Building No. 45) (CA-1826)*. Brick, seventeen-bay front, two stories, gable roof, stone quoins, one-story porch across front with modillioned cornice and Corinthian columns. Built 1872 with nine-bay front; enlarged to seventeen-bay front between 1915 and World War II. 1 ext. photo (1977), 2 photocopies of ca. 1915 ext. photos, 1 photocopy of undated architectural drawing; 5 data pages (1976).

□ *Building (Building No. 74) (CA-1775)*. Stuccoed brick, one story, one-bay front. Built 1921. 1 ext. photo (1977).

□ *Commanding Officers' Quarters (Quarters No. 1, Building No. 28) (CA-1843)*. Stuccoed brick,

Benicia Arsenal continued

three-bay front, two stories, low hip roof, one-story porch across front with modillioned cornice and Corinthian capitals, polygonal bay in center of second story. Built 1860; alterations after 1876 include changing entrance from south side to east, replacing Doric-columned porch, adding two polygonal bays. 3 ext. photos (1977), 3 int. photos (1977), 2 photocopies of ext. photos from ca. 1915, ca. 1956. 1 photocopy of original plans: 4 data pages (1976).

□ *Dock (CA-1834).* 1 photocopy of undated photo.

□ *Duplex Officers' Quarters (Officers' Quarters No. 3, 4; Building No. 25–26) (CA-1947).* Stuccoed brick, four-bay front, two stories, low hip roof, stone quoins and belt courses, projecting center pavilion has two doorways, one-story porch with modillioned cornice and Corinthian columns. Built 1874. 3 photocopies of ext. photos (ca. 1890s, 1944), 2 photocopies of architectural drawings (1973); 2 data pages (1981).

□ *Enlisted Men's Quarters (Buildings Nos. 33, 34, 35) (CA-1949).* Each building wood frame with clapboards, five-bay front, one-and-a-half stories, gable roof extended to cover front porch and rear lean-to, decorative jigsawn bargeboard. Built 1870. 3 photocopies of undated photos; 1 data page (1981).

□ *Guard and Engine House (Building No. 39) (CA-1832).* Stuccoed brick, three-bay front, one story, low hip roof; T-shaped plan, with guard house in front and engine house across rear. Built 1872. 4 ext. photos (1977), 1 photocopy of 1915 photo, 1 photocopy of original 1871 plans; 6 data pages (1976).

□ *Gun Yard (CA-1842).* 1 photocopy of undated photo.

□ *Hospital (Building No. 1) (CA-1945).* Sandstone ashlar, T-shaped, 72' (seven-bay front) × 24', rear wing 45' × 36', one-and-a-half stories, gable roof, one-story porch across front, cupola. Built 1854, only remnant of Benicia Barracks (see CA-1774). 3 ext. photos (1977), 1 photocopy of ext. 1944 photo, 1 photocopy of original 1854 plans; 6 data pages (1976).

□ *Lieutenants' Quarters (Officers' Quarters No. 2, Building No. 27) (CA-1825).* Stuccoed brick, two stories, one-story porch with Doric columns. Built 1861. 1 photocopy of 1915 photo; 2 data pages (1981).

□ *Main Gateway (CA-1844).* Brick piers, iron

fence. Demolished. 2 photocopies of photos (early 1900s and ca. 1915).

□ *Office Building (Building No. 47) (CA-1827).* Brick with stone quoins, three-bay front, two stories, hip roof, one-bay front porch with modillioned cornice and paired composite columns. Built 1870. 2 photocopies of 1915 photos, 1 photocopy of architectural drawings (1869); 1 data page (1981).

□ *Powder Magazine No. 2 (Building No. 10) (CA-1948).* Sandstone ashlar, one story, hip roof, few openings, sculpted eagle and cannon over door; groin vaulting, interior stone columns have carved foliate capitals. Built 1857 as copy of first magazine which also survives; sculpture allegedly by stonemason John Gomo. 5 sheets (1976, including site plan, plan, elevations, sections, and isometric of interior vaulting); 2 ext. photos (1977), 5 int. photos (1977), 1 photocopy of ext. undated photo, 1 photocopy of 1944 int. photo, 1 photocopy of undated architectural drawing; 6 data pages (1976).

□ *Powder Magazine No. 5 (Building No. 14) (CA-1839).* Brick, three-bay front by four bays, bays delineated by pilasters and corbeling, gable roof with vents. Built 1903, identical to Building No. 13. 2 photocopies of ext. photos (1915 and undated); 1 data page (1981).

□ *Shop Buildings (Buildings Nos. 55, 56, 57) (CA-1833).* Complex of three brick buildings, gable roofs, round-arched windows separated by pilasters. Building No. 55, one-story blacksmith shop, built 1876; Building No. 56, two-story machine shop, built 1884; Building No. 57, two-story carpenter shop, built 1877. 3 ext. photos (1977), 2 photocopies of undated photos, 10 photocopies of original architectural drawings; 8 data pages (1976).

□ *Shops-Storehouse (Building No. 49) (CA-1838).* Stuccoed brick, fifteen-bay front, two stories, hip roof, pedimented center pavilion five bays wide has bull's-eye window in pediment, belt course between floors; interior has large open spaces due to suspension of second floor from roof trusses. Built 1862; demolished mid-20th c. 3 photocopies of undated photos; 2 data pages (1981).

□ *Stables (Building No. 51) (CA-1979).* Brick with wooden lean-to, three-bay front by six bays, one-and-a-half stories, gable roof with monitors. Built 1909. 1 photocopy of undated photo, which also shows original frame chapel, now demolished.

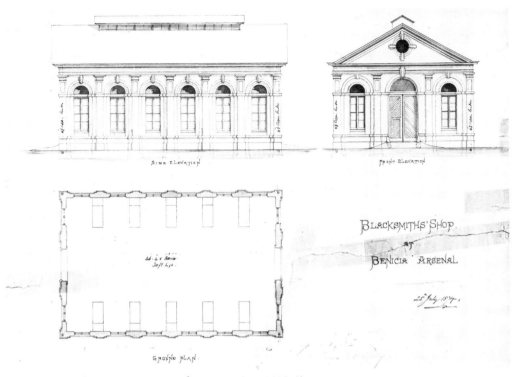

Blacksmith's Shop, Benicia Arsenal, Benicia (CA-1833-8).

□ *Storehouse (Clocktower, Building No. 29) (CA-1828).* Sandstone ashlar, three-bay front by thirteen bays, two-and-a-half stories, gable roof, four-story square tower with crenellations and clock, two-story square tower on opposite corner. Built 1859 as three-story structure with two square towers on opposite corners with turrets on remaining corners, designed by Commander F. D. Callender and master builder J. Fuss; rebuilt as two-story building after explosion and fire in 1912. 6 sheets (1976, including site plan, plans, elevations, plans and elevations of cannon ports and windows); 1 ext. photo (1977), 3 int. photos (1977), 6 photocopies of photos before and after 1912, 1 photocopy of ca. 1908–12 postcard, 6 photocopies of architect's drawings; 12 data pages (1976).

□ *Storehouses (Camel Barns) and Engine House (Buildings Nos. 7, 8, 9) (CA-1946).* Complex of three buildings, sandstone ashlar, gable roof. Building No. 8, the Engine House, one-story, three-bay front, round-arched windows; situated between Buildings Nos. 7 and 9, the Storehouses, each two stories, seven-bay front, round-arched windows first level, flat-arched windows on second level only on rear. Building No. 7 built 1853; No. 8, 1855; No. 9, 1854. 4 sheets (1976, including site plan, elevations); 4 ext. photos (1977), 2 int. photos (1977), 1 photocopy of undated photo, 1 photocopy of architectural drawing (1855); 9 data pages (1976).

⊔ *Storehouse (Building No. 48) (CA-1978).* Brick, one story, gable roof, broad segmentally arched openings. Built 1911. 1 photocopy of undated photo.

Benicia State Capitol (California State Capitol) (CA-1188). NW corner of First and G Sts. Brick, 45'-0" (three-bay front) × 87'-10", two stories, gable roof with modillioned cornice, distyle Greek temple with portico in antis, bull's-eye window in pediment, plastered and fluted brick Doric columns, brick, pilasters with sandstone Doric capitals. Built 1852–53, S. A. Rider and J. Franklin Houghton, architects; used as state capitol for one year, then county courthouse, school, city hall; restored 1955–57 by State Parks and Recreation Department, now museum. 5 sheets (1976, including site plan, plans, elevations, section, detail); 4 ext. photos (undated, ca. 1936, 1977), 1 int. photo (1977), 1 photocopy of undated photo, 6 photocopies of architectural drawings (1956) 15 data pages (1976). SHL

Benicia continued

California Hotel (California House) (CA-1187).
SW corner First and H Streets. First two stories
adobe, third story wood frame with clapboards,
gable roof, second-story veranda over closed-in
ground floor. Built 1847 for Major Stephen
Cooper; one of first hotels in California; converted to brewery, 1854; destroyed by fire. 1 ext.
photo (1930s).

California State Capitol. See Benicia State Capitol (CA-1188).

Carr House (CA-2052). *165 East D St.* Brick,
three-bay front, one-and-a-half stories, gable
roof, decorative bargeboards. Probably built
1870s; one of few remaining early masonry private buildings in Benicia. 7 sheets (1976, including site plan, plans, elevations, section); 2 ext.
photos (1977), 1 int. photo (1977). 1 photocopy
of ca. 1900 photo; 7 data pages (1976); field records. NR

City Hotel (Golden Horseshoe) (CA-2080). *415
First St.* Wood frame with channeled siding, 50'
(six-bay front) × 50', two stories, twin gable
roofs with gable end fronts. Built mid 19th c.;
moved and reassembled differently. 1 ext. photo
(1977), 2 int. photos (1977); 1 data page (1981).

City of Benicia (CA-2079). 2 photocopies of
1878, 1885 lithographs; 4 photocopies of undated, ca. 1908–16, and 1937 photos; 40 ext.
photos (1977).

Crooks House (CA-2081). *285 West G St.* Wood
frame with channeled siding, 50' (four-bay
front) × 60', two-and-a-half stories, gable roof
intersecting with hip roof, belt courses, corner
boards, brackets supporting wide eaves. An imposing house in the Stick style. Built late 1880s.
3 ext. photos (1977), 2 int. photos (1977), 2
photocopies of ext. photos (ca. 1908–16, 1913),
4 photocopies of 1970 architectural drawings; 9
data pages (1976).

**Fairview Hotel (Washington House Hotel) (CA-
2088).** *333 First St.* Wood frame with channeled
siding, 72' (nine-bay front) × 30', two stories,
gable roof. Built mid 19th c.; moved from Fifth
St. 1 ext. photo (1977); 1 data page (1981).

Fischer-Hanlon House (CA-1889). *135 West G St.*
Wood frame with clapboards, six-bay front, two
stories, gable roof, one-story one-bay entrance
porch. Built ca. 1840s as hotel on lower First St.;
moved to present site after fire, by Joseph
Fischer, a butcher, in 1858; restored by State
Parks and Recreation Department in 1976–77;
now a museum. 2 ext. photos (1960, 1977), 1
int. photo (1960); 1 data page (1981). NR, SHL

Fish House. See Riddell Fish House (CA-2082).

Frisbie-Walsh House (CA-2087). *235 East L St.*
Wood frame with horizontal siding, two stories,
T-shaped with one-story porches filling out the
T, high-pitched gable roofs, gable wall dormers,
decorative bargeboards, finials and pendants,
pointed-arch window in one gable, polygonal bay
window at first level. Built ca. 1850 for John
Frisbie, son-in-law of General Vallejo, associated
with two other nearly identical houses of well-
known pioneers; the demolished Judge Burritt
House in San Francisco and General Vallejo's
Lachryma Montis near Sonoma; all three houses
had pre-cut frames shipped from east coast. 3
ext. photos (1977), 2 int. photos (1977); 1 data
page (1981).

Golden Horseshoe. See City Hotel (CA-2080).

Hanlon House. See Fischer-Hanlon House (CA-
1889).

Masonic Temple (CA-1887). *110 West J St.* Wood
frame with clapboards, approx. 30' (three-bay
front) × 60', two stories, gable roof with entrance in gable end, semicircular window in pediment, pilasters at corners. Built 1850; new
front, late 19th c. First hall built by Masons in
California; good example of the simplified Greek
Revival style in wood. 4 ext. photos (1960,
1977), 1 int. photo (1960); 6 data pages (1976).
NR

Riddell Fish House (CA-2082). *245 West K St.*
Wood frame with horizontal siding, fish-scale
and other patterns of shingles, two-and-a-half
stories, hipped roof with gable dormers, round
tower with conical roof, brick exterior chimneys;
interior has elaborate wainscot with copper
panels, fireplaces with tile surrounds and spindled overmantels. Built ca. 1890 for artist Hen-
rietta Riddell Fish. Good example of towered
Queen Anne style villa. 5 ext. photos (1977), 6
int. photos (1977), 4 photocopies of ext. photos
(ca. 1890 and later), 1 photocopy of int. photo, 5
photocopies of ca. 1890 architectural drawings; 8
data pages (1976).

St. Catherine's Academy (CA-1542). *Solano
Square.* Brick and frame, two- and three-story
buildings of simple Classic design. Built 1854
and after, founded by Mother Mary Gomaere,
Dominican nun from Monterey; became coedu-
cational boarding school in 1889; demolished
1970. 1 photocopy of ca. 1920 ext. photo.

St. Dominic's Catholic Church (CA-2083). *475
East I St.* Brick, five-bay front, one story with
clerestory, two square domed towers with pediments, engaged columns and pilasters, belfries,

center entrance framed by Corinthian columns, denticulated cornice with swags and garlands. Built 1890, replacing original church built in 1854. 4 ext. photos (1977), 2 int. photos (1977), 2 photocopies of ext. photos (ca. 1900 and undated), 1 photocopy of int. photo (ca. 1908–16); 1 data page (1981).

St. Paul's Episcopal Church (CA-2053). 120 East J St. Wood frame with clapboards, 51'-8" × 87'8", one story, square tower with corner buttresses and octagonal spire, gable roof, pointed-arch windows; interior paneled wood with bands of tiles and wallpaper, exposed rafters and braces; one-story parish hall attached. Built 1859, designed by Col. Julian McAllister of Benicia Arsenal; major alterations 1863, 1873, 1879, 1882, and 1885–86, when interior took present appearance. 6 sheets (1976, including site plan, plans, elevations, section, schematic diagram of building campaigns, and pew detail); 2 ext. photos (1976), 7 int. photos (1976), 1 photocopy of undated lithograph, 3 photocopies of photos (1886, 1906); 14 data pages (1976). SHL

St. Paul's Episcopal Church Rectory (CA-2084). 122 East J St. Wood frame with clapboards, 42' × 42', one-and-a-half stories, gable roof with saltbox rear addition, center brick chimney. Built 1790s in Torrington, Conn.; brought to Benicia in 1868 by Col. Julian McAllister to serve as rectory. 2 ext. photos (1977); 1 data page (1981).

Semple-von Pfister Store (CA-1912). Foot of D St. Adobe with clapboards, 25' × 40', gable roof, entrance in gable end. Built ca. 1847 by Benjamin MacDonald, builder. 1 ext. photo (1960); 1 data page (1981).

Solano House. See Union Hotel (CA-2086).

Southern Pacific Passenger Depot (CA-2085). SE corner First and A Sts. Wood frame with horizontal siding on first floor and cut wood shingles on second floor, 25' × 112', two stories with one-story freight room, gable roof and pent roof over first floor have bracketed eaves, clerestory over one-story portion. Built late 19th c. in Banta, Calif.; moved to present site ca. 1900. Similar to many other stations on Southern Pacific line. 3 ext. photos (1977); 1 data page (1981).

Union Hotel (Solano House) (CA-2086). 401-05 First St. Heavy timber frame with horizontal siding, six-bay front, three stories, hip roof. Built mid 19th c. 2 ext. photos (1977), 1 int. photo (1977); 1 data page (1981).

von Pfister Store. See Semple-von Pfister Store (CA-1912).

Walsh House. See Frisbie-Walsh House (CA-2087).

Washington House Hotel. See Fairview Hotel (CA-2088).

Wingfield, Bishop J. H. D., House (CA-2089). 36 Wingfield Way. Wood frame with channeled siding, approx. 36' (three-bay front) × 54', two stories, gable roof with cross gable, bracketed cornice, one-story porch across front, polygonal bay on end. Built ca. 1876 for Bishop J. H. D. Wingfield, president of St. Augustine's College and rector of St. Paul's Episcopal Church; only remaining structure in St. Augustine's complex. 2 ext. photos (1977), 1 int. photo (1977), 2 photocopies of 1878 and ca. 1882 drawings; 1 data page (1981).

Berkeley □ Alameda County

Peralta Hall (St. Joseph's Academy) (CA-1655). Wood frame with variety of board siding and shingles, four to six stories, multiple gable roof with cross gables, towers, profusions of detail. Built 1882 as a retreat for actors, served a variety of uses until 1903 when the Christian Brothers used it as a boarding school. An eclectic architectural tour de force. Demolished 1959. 1 ext. photo (1929).

St. Joseph's Academy. See Peralta Hall (CA-1655).

Big Oak Flat □ Tuolumne County

I.O.O.F. Hall (CA-1578). Rubble stone, five-bay front, one-and-a-half stories, gable roof, five pairs of eight-panel iron double doors with brick surrounds, gable end window with iron shutters, boxed cornice. Built 1850s; second-story hip-roofed addition in rear; demolished. 1 photocopy of undated photo.

Bodie □ Mono County

Bodie—General (CA-1918). State Historic Park. Mining town that reached its peak 1879–80 with population of 10–12,000; now a ghost town of wood frame buildings with gable roofs and false fronts; designated State Historic Park in 1962. 12 ext. photos (1962), 1 photocopy of ca. 1928 photo, 1 photocopy of 1880 plat; 7 data pages (1962). NHL, SHL

Bodie Bank (CA-1926). Main St. between King and

Bodie continued

Union Sts. Brick, one-room ruin, one story, no roof, elaborate iron door with panels and hood-mold. Built ca. 1890; burned 1932. 3 photos (1962).

Bodie Jail (CA-1925). Wood frame with clapboards over vertical planks, one story, two-bay front in gable end with lean-to on one side, gable roof. Built mid-19th c. 3 ext. photos (1962).

Bodie Railroad Station (CA-1928). *E of town.* Wood frame with shingles, two stories, gable roof, various one-story additions. Built mid-19th c. 1 ext. photo (1962).

Bodie Schoolhouse (CA-1934). *Green and Mono Sts.* Wood frame with channeled siding, five-bay front, two stories, hipped roof with square cupola with flagpole, all windows double windows. Built 1879. 1 ext. photo (1962), 1 int. photo (1962).

Boone Store (CA-1932). *Main and Green Sts.* Wood frame with horizontal siding, one story, gable roof behind parapet, store section has show windows and recessed entry, warehouse has two sets of double glazed doors flanked by wood pilasters. 1 ext. photo (1962).

Cain, D. V., Residence (CA-1921). *Green and Fuller Sts.* Wood frame with channeled siding, L-shaped plan, 42′ (two-bay front) × 25′, one-and-a-half stories, gable roof, shed-roofed porch in ell. Built 1873; James Stuart Cain came to Bodie and lived here 1879; his son David Victor born here 1880, lived here after his marriage in 1904, until 1920s when moved in with father. 9 sheets (1962, including plans, elevations, section, details); 1 ext. photo (1962), 1 int. photo (1962); 4 data pages (1962).

Cain, J. S., Residence (CA-1920). *Green St.* Wood frame with channeled siding, 32′ (three-bay front) × 36′, one-and-a-half stories, gable roof with cornice returns on gables, entrance in gabled projecting bay, glassed-in porch to one side. Built late 19th c. for Mr. McGrath, moved to present site ca. 1904 for James Stuart Cain, owner of most of Bodie in 20th c.; later additions. 9 sheets (1962, including plans, elevations, section, details); 4 ext. photos (1962), 1 int. photo (1962); 4 data pages (1962).

Johl Residence (CA-1922). *Main St.* Wood frame with channeled siding, 23′ (three-bay front) × 44′, one story, gable roof, hoodmold with consoles over door, piecework bargeboard. Built 1870s, owned ca. 1879 by H. C. Osborne, newspaper publisher; moved to east side Main St. 1892; home of Eli Johl, butcher; later moved to present site and served as last post office in Bodie. 6 sheets (1962, including plans, elevations, details); 1 ext. photo, detail of door (1962); 5 data pages (1962).

Methodist Church (CA-1924). *Green and Fuller Sts.* Wood frame with channeled siding, 28′ (three-bay front) × 40′, one story, gable roof, square belfry, pointed-arch windows; interior has tongue-and-groove siding. Built 1878 for Nevada State Methodist Mission; restored 1928 by E. J. Clinton; only church remaining in Bodie. 5 sheets (1962, including plans, elevations, section, details); 2 ext. photos (1962), 1 int. photo (1962); 3 data pages (1962).

Miners' Union Hall (CA-1919). *Main St.* Museum. Wood frame with channeled siding on front, board-and-batten siding on sides and rear, 30′ (three-bay front) × 96′, one story, gable roof with false front. Built 1878, center of social life in Bodie, contained first electric motor ever to be turned by long distance power. 5 sheets (1962, including plans, elevations, section, details); 2 ext. photos (1962), 1 photo of stove (1962); 3 data pages (1962).

Murphy House (CA-1935). *NW corner Prospect and Union Sts.* Wood frame with clapboards, bay window in gable end. 1 ext. photo, detail of window (1962).

Parr House (CA-1931). *Main St.* Wood frame with clapboard siding, three-bay front, one story, gable roof, lean-to on one side, bracketed hoods over openings. Built 1870s. 1 ext. photo (1962).

U.S. Land Office Building (Wheaton and Hollis Hotel and Bodie Store) (CA-1933). *NE corner Main and Green Sts.* Wood frame with horizontal siding, two stories with one-story addition, flat roof with paired brackets at cornice, storefront at first level; pressed tin walls on interior. Built mid to late 19th c. 1 ext photo (1962), 1 int. photo (1962).

Bolinas   □   Marin County

Booth, F.E., Company, Pier (CA-2073). *Point Reyes National Seashore.* Wood frame pier with one-story, gable-roofed, superstructure. Built ca. 1919; demolished. 7 ext. photos (1977), 8 int. photos (1977); 2 data pages (1980).

Brentwood vicinity □ Contra Costa County

Marsh, Dr. John, House (CA-1500). *Hwy. 21, 4*

mis. SW of Brentwood. Rubble sandstone with ashlar quoining, five-bay front, two-and-a-half stories, gable roof with three cross gables, off-center square tower, fourth story of wood frame, one-story wrap-around veranda with flattened Tudor arches supported by box columns, surmounted by turned wood balustrade, openings on first and second floors segmentally arched, windows in gables pointed arched. Built 1853–56, Thomas Boyd, architect; tower, originally all stone with crenellations, destroyed in 1868 earthquake and rebuilt in simpler form; this combination Italianate and Gothic villa was built for Dr. John Marsh, a self-educated physician murdered by Indians shortly after the house was completed. 5 photocopies of photos (late 1850s, ca. 1870, ca. 1920, 1921, 1925); 10 data pages (1966).

Bridgeport   □   Nevada County

Covered Bridge (CA-1401). Pleasant Valley Rd. over Yuba R., W. of Hwy. 49. Heavy timber covered bridge with round arches on either side and interior wood truss, a combination of truss and arch construction. Built 1862 by John Wood with lumber from his mill in Sierra County; as part of the Virginia Turnpike Company toll road that served the northern mines and the Nevada Comstock Lode, the bridge is one of the oldest housed spans in the west and the longest covered bridge in the U.S. 1 ext. photo (1934). SHL

Bridgeville   □   Humboldt County

Bridgeville-General (CA-1456). Valley, buildings barely visible. 1 photo from a great distance (1934).

Brown's Valley vicinity   □   Yuba County

Oregon House (CA-1428). Wood frame with channeled siding, five-bay front, two stories, gable roof, boxed cornice, two-story front veranda with X-railing on second level, one-story porch in rear. Built ca. 1850; demolished. 1 ext. photo (1934).

Buellton   □   Santa Barbara County

La Casa de Eduardo de la Cuesta (CA-27). Hwy. 101. Adobe, partially covered with clapboards,

54' (five-bay front) × 86', one story, gable roof pitches out to cover porch on three sides, triangulated window heads. Built 1856 for Ramundo de la Cuesta. 3 sheets (1936, including plan, elevations, section, details); 2 ext. photos (1936); 1 data page (1937).

Buellton vicinity   □   Santa Barbara County

La Casa de Cota de la Cuesta (CA-28). Lompoc Rd., 6 mis. W of Buellton. Adobe, 44' (six-bay front) × 46', U-shaped, one story, hipped roof extends to cover porch across front, porches on sides partially enclosed with board-and-batten siding. Built ca. 1840 for Francisco Cota. 3 sheets (1936, including plan, elevations, section, details); 2 ext. photos (1936); 1 data page (1937).

Buena Vista   □   Amador County

Stone Store (CA-1508). NE corner Lancha Plana and Jackson-Stockton Rds. Stone, two-bay front, two stories, gable roof with stepped false front, iron doors, canopy across front. Built 1850s, the first store in Buena Vista; it had been built in Lancha Plana and moved stone by stone in 1876 to Buena Vista by Chinese miners who received land under old store for their effort. 1 photocopy of undated photo.

Burlingame   □   San Mateo County

Southern Pacific Railroad Station (CA-2120). Burlingame Ave. and California Dr. Stuccoed frame, 61' × 25', one story with two-story pyramidal-roofed tower, gable roof with tiles, arcades on both sides reminiscent of *corredors,* false-front gable end on track side reminiscent of *espadaña;* baggage room at one end, waiting room at other, stationmaster's quarters in attached building. Built 1894, George H. Howard, Jr., and J. B. Mathison, architects; fine example of Mission Revival style, reflecting popularity of California Building at Columbian Exposition of 1893, A. Page Brown, architect; 14 ext. photos (1971, 1975), 5 int. photos (1971). NR

Butte City   □   Amador County

Benoist-Ginocchio Store (Butte Store) (CA-1506). Hwy. 49, 2.5 mis. S. of Jackson. Rubble stone,

Butte City continued

three-bay front in gable end, one story with raised basement, gable roof, only pediment remains, brick framing for doors and windows, cornice moldings, iron doors. Built 1857 for Xavier Benoist, only structure remaining of this once-prosperous mining town; ruinous. 1 photocopy of undated photo. SHL

Calabasas   □   Los Angeles County

Leonis, Miguel, Adobe (CA-342). 23537 Calabasas Road. Museum. Adobe and wood, approx. 29' × 65' with 10' wide porches, main two-story section with wood-framed one-story section sheathed with board-and-batten siding, one side in tongue-and-groove siding, hip roof originally extended over two-story porch on three sides, chamfered box columns, second-floor jigsawn balustrade, brick chimney; L-shaped plan, large living room in adobe section. Built ca. 1875, possibly an earlier one-story building remodeled by Miguel Leonis, called the "King of Calabasas" because of his extensive land holdings; after his accidental death in 1889, building passed through a succession of owners and alterations, saved from demolition by the L.A. Cultural Heritage Board and restored after 1963 by the Leonis Adobe Association. 5 ext. photos (1960); 12 data pages, including sketch plans (1963).

Calabasas vicinity   □   Los Angeles County

Reyes Adobe (CA-329). Plastered adobe, wood frame with board-and-batten siding, approx. 61' × 28', five-bay front, one-and-a-half stories, lean-to kitchen sheathed in board-and-batten siding, gable roof with shakes, porches in front center and on one end, variety of wood-framed openings; hall-less plan with interior stair. Built ca. 1836 by Jacinto Reyes on what later became Los Virgenes Rancho, 26,000 acres; demolished. 3 sheets (1935, including plan, elevations, details); 3 ext. photos (1937); 1 data page (1937).

Calistoga vicinity   □   Napa County

Bale, Dr. E. T., Grist Mill (CA-166). Hwy. 29, 3 mis. N. of St. Helena. State Historic Park. Grist mill with waterwheel and granary. Wood frame with channeled siding and clapboards, three-bay front, two stories on raised basement, gable roof with high wood parapet, wooden 45' wheel fed by water brought through a hollow log aqueduct

from a stream at the rear of the site; L-shaped plan with single large main space with two millstones imported from France in 1847. Built 1846 for Dr. Edward Turner Bale, grantee of the Carne Humana Rancho; deeded to Native Sons of Golden West and subsequently restored as State Historic Park. 2 ext. photos (1937), 2 photocopies of ext. photos (ca. 1930, ca. 1934).

Callahan   □   Siskiyou County

Callahan Ranch Hotel and Farrington Hotel (CA-1189). Callahan Ranch Hotel is wood frame with clapboarding, seven-bay front, two stories, shingled gable roof with cornice returns on gable end; Farrington Hotel is rubble stone, plastered, two stories, shingled gable roof, front porch. Both built 1850s; demolished, town gone. 1 ext. photo (1937).

Campo Seco   □   Calaveras County

Eproson, Robert, Building (CA-1115). Main St. Rough stone, adobe and frame, eight-bay front, mostly one story with two-story section, flat roof, two-story veranda and exterior staircase on two-story portion. Built 1864; one-story portions served as stores; ruinous, second story gone. 1 ext. photo (1936).

Messenger, Captain, House (CA-1206). Wood frame with clapboards, one story, low gable roof, central front porch. Built 1860s; demolished. 1 ext. photo (1936).

Carlsbad vicinity   □   San Diego County

Casa del Rancho Agua Hedionda (CA-410). E. San Marcos Rd. Plastered adobe and wood frame, L-shape, 73' × 26', one story, gable roof extended over porch on one side, wood-framed openings; hall-less plan. Built ca. 1850 as four-room house with flat roof, enlarged and roof altered 1870s and '90s, rancho was a Mexican grant of 13,311 acres made to Juan María Marrón in 1842. 4 sheets (1937, including plan, elevations, section, details; plan, elevation, details of milk house); 5 ext. photos (1937), 1 int. photo (1937); 2 data pages (1937).

Carmel   □   Monterey County

Mission San Carlos Borroméo del Carmelo (CA-136). SW corner Rio Rd. and Lawsen Dr. Sand-

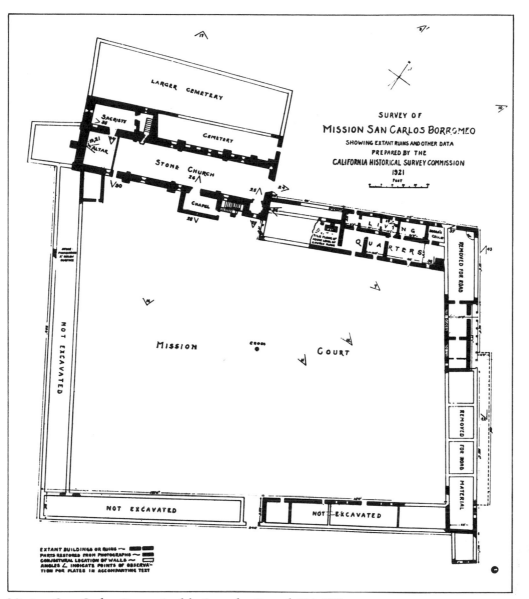

Mission San Carlos Borroméo del Carmelo, Carmel (CA-136).

stone, one story, gable roof, two square towers on front, one on south with two round-arched openings at belfry and dome, smaller one on north with single round-arched opening at belfry, round-arched entrance with pilasters, star window above set in round-arched *espadaña*. Building begun 1793, dedicated 1797, headquarters for Fr. Junípero Serra as Father-President of all missions in California; Serra's burial place; in ruins after secularization in 1836; partially restored 1882; restoration begun again 1924; became parish church 1933. 6 ext. photos (1936),

11 int. photos (1936, 1937), 17 photocopies of ext. photos (ca. 1860, before 1860, ca. 1870, 1876, 1880, ca. 1909, 1921, 1928, 1929, n.d.), 12 photocopies of int. photos (1860s, before 1880, ca. 1880, 1924, 1934, n.d.), 10 photocopies of photos of quadrangle (1908, 1920, 1921, n.d.), 6 photocopies of drawings (ca. 1790, before 1835, 1839, ca. 1870, n.d.), 1 photocopy of plat (1854), 2 photocopies of site plan (1921), 1 photocopy of plan of church (1918), 1 photocopy of section of church. (1918). SHL

Carrville vicinity   □   Trinity County

Gold Dredge (CA-1186). Wood frame with vertical wood plank siding, metal and wood machinery. Abandoned by 1937; demolished. 1 ext. photo (1937).

Carson Hill   □   Calaveras County

Frame and Stone Stores (CA-1490). Three adjoining structures of same size, wood frame with channeled siding and rubble stone, gable roofs with gable ends toward street, canopies over wooden sidewalks. Built 1850s; demolished. 1 photocopy of undated photo.

House (CA-1273). Wood frame with clapboards, one-and-a-half stories, two-sectioned gable roof with cornice returns on gable ends, wrap-around porch, rear lean-to. Built ca. 1850; only foundations remain. 1 ext. photo (1934).

Cherokee   □   Butte County

Brewery (CA-1702). Rubble stone, a portion with gable roof and vertical board siding in gable end. Built 1850s; ruinous. 1 photocopy of 1932 photo.

Wells Fargo & Co. Vault (CA-1680). Concrete vault abutted by rubble-stone walls. Built 1850s for Wells Fargo Express Co. to store diamonds from Cherokee mine. 1 photocopy of undated photo.

Chico   □   Butte County

Bidwell Mansion (CA-1317). *525 Esplanade, grounds of Chico State Univ.* Open to the public. Stuccoed brick, 71′ (three-bay front) × 94′, irregular shape, hip roof with central monitor, central tower in front with hip roof and balustrade with corner newels, molded cornice with scroll brackets, modillions and architrave, segmental-arched second-floor windows with large bracketed hoods, tall round-arched ground-floor windows, wrap-around front one-story veranda with turned balustrade and ornate newels supported by square paneled columns with caps and scroll-sawn brackets, two-story polygonal bay on side plus one-story wings; central-hall plan, marble mantels and interior detail. Built 1865–67, Henry W. Cleaveland, architect, for John Bidwell, pioneer settler, prominent state citizen and senator; the large estate included outbuildings, exper-

imental orchards and vineyards. 10 sheets (1960s, including plans, elevations, section, details); 9 data pages (1966).

Chinese Camp   □   Tuolumne County

Bruschi Store (CA-1569). Brick, one story. Built 1850s; ruinous or gone, not located. 1 photocopy of undated photo.

Chino vicinity   □   San Bernardino County

Slaughter House (CA-333). *Prado Rd.* Adobe with wood-frame additions, one-and-a-half stories, 101′ (seven-bay front) × 42′, hipped roof pitches out to cover porch across front, gable dormers. Built ca. 1853 for Antonio Yorba. 3 sheets (1936, including plans, elevations, section, details); 2 ext. photos (1936); 1 data page (1937). NR, SHL

Coloma   □   El Dorado County

Barn (CA-1377). Wood frame with clapboards, two stories, gable roof, large lean-to addition with scalloped barge board. Built 1860, demolished. 1 ext. photo (1934).

Chinese Bank (CA-1379). *S. side Main St.* Stone, ashlar on front, cobblestone on sides, three-bay front, one story, hipped roof, iron doors and barred windows. Built 1858–59 by Jonas Wilder for Chinese merchant Wah Hop; restored in State Park. 1 ext. photo (1940).

Chinese Store (CA-1380). *S. side Main St.* Stone, ashlar on front, cobblestone on sides, one story, two-bay front, hipped roof, iron doors. Built 1858–59 by Jonas Wilder; restored in State Park. 1 ext. photo (1934).

House (CA-1378). Wood frame with clapboards, one-and-a-half stories, three-bay front, gable roof, hip-roofed entrance porch. Built ca. 1860; demolished. 1 ext. photo. (1934).

Marshall, James W., Cabin (CA-1309). *Marshall Monument Rd.* Museum. Wood frame with board-and-batten siding, one story, gable roof. Built 1856 by discoverer of gold at Sutter's Mill; burned 1862; rebuilt soon after and occupied by Marshall for several years; demolished, replica marks site in State Park. 3 photocopies of photos (1926, 1928, undated).

Meyer's Dance Hall and Saloon (CA-1381). *Shin-*

gle *Spring Rd.* Stone, ashlar quoining and sur-rounds, rubble elsewhere, two stories, three-bay front, no roof. Built 1858–59 by Jonas Wilder; ruins. 2 ext. photos (1934).

Sierra Nevada Hotel (Meyer Hotel) (CA-1503). Wood frame with clapboards, two stories, six-bay front, gable roof, two-story porch across front. Built 1851 for Philip Schell, one of few temper-ance hotels in mining region; destroyed by fire, 1902, rebuilt 1903, demolished. 1 photocopy of undated photo.

U. S. Post Office (Orleans Hotel) (CA-1376). Main St. Wood frame with channeled siding, five-bay front, one-and-a-half stories, gable roof. Built ca. 1855, post office after 1935; extensively remodeled. 1 ext. photo (1934).

Sutter's Mill (CA-1301). Marshall Gold Discovery State Historic Park. Mill foundations heavy split pine, structure 70′ × 60′ laid on bedrock, super-structure of heavy hand-hewn pine timbers set in decomposed granite bedrock 15′ apart, forming main cross supports of the two-story mill, main lengthwise supports were hand-hewn 60′ plates set in notches of cross supports, 20′ apart and running full length of building, timbers fastened together with oak pins. Built 1847, gold discov-ered by James W. Marshall, January, 1848; mill torn down 1853; site submerged by American River 1862; monument in river stones erected 1924; replica of mill built 1965–66. 2 photo-copies of drawings (1851, undated), 1 photocopy of ca. 1850 photo of mill, 2 photocopies of pho-tos of monument (before 1940). SHL

Columbia □ Tuolumne County

Brick Building (CA-1695). Brick, three-bay front, roof and rest of building not ascertainable. 1 photocopy of 1937 photo.

City Hotel (CA-1146). Main St., Columbia State Historic Park. Brick, seven-bay front, two stories, low gable roof, brick dentil course, second-floor balcony across front with shed roof, ornate cast-iron balustrade, iron double doors on ground floor, metal canopy over street. Built 1850s; re-stored by state, gable roof and small side balcony removed. 2 ext. photos (1934).

Commercial Buildings (CA-1299). Main St. Brick and wood frame, one-story with canopies over sidewalk. 7 photocopies of photos (1930s, n.d.).

I.O.O.F. Buildings (CA-1693). State and Broadway Sts., Columbia State Historic Park. Brick, three-bay front, two stories, gable roof, iron doors on both floors, second-floor center door bricked in. Built 1850s; restored after 1937, gable roof re-moved, wrought-iron balcony added. 4 ext. pho-tocopies of ext. photos (1937).

Livery Stable (CA-1872). State and Columbia Sts. Wood frame with board-and-batten siding, one story with loft, gable roof, lean-to addition on side. Built 1850s as Dondero Stable. 4 photo-copies of ext. photos (1937).

Mills, D. O., Building (CA-1573). Main and Ful-ton Sts. Brick, one story, parapeted roof with brick dentil course, three front doors with paneled iron shutters. 2 photocopies of undated photos.

Mountain View Cemetery (Public Cemetery) (CA-38-11). School House Rd. Simple vertical grave-stones, round-arched and rectangular, with carv-ings. Stones date from 1852–53, several carved by Hugh Coyle. 1 sheet (1934, including eleva-tions and details of five gravestones in this ceme-tery, one in St. Anne's Churchyard in Columbia, and one in Jewish Cemetery, Sonora); 9 photos (1934).

Old Trading Post (Tonle-Leavitt Building) (CA-1143). Main and State Streets, Columbia State His-toric Park. Brick, four-bay front, one story, para-peted roof with brick dentils and moldings, rounded corner at street intersection, iron doors, continuous wood canopy below cornice sup-ported on brackets. Built 1850s; canopy brackets replaced with wood posts. 1 ext. photo (1934), 1 photocopy of 1934 photo.

Pioneer Saloon (CA-1145). (Charles St.) Brick, three-bay front, one story, with raised basement parapeted roof with coffered frieze and brick moldings, high ground-floor openings with iron shutters, shake-roofed metal sidewalk canopy. Built before 1854 and reconstructed after 1857 fire. 3 photocopies of 1930s photos.

St. Anne's Church (CA-1142). Church St. Brick, 41′ (three-bay front) × 70′, one story, central three-story tower with entrance in base, gable roof, two-stage buttresses at corners and on sides, lancet windows, one ogee-arched window in tower, louvered lancets in belfry, pointed-arch entrance with double wood-paneled doors; single nave plan, altar reredos triptych with paintings by James Fallon. Built 1856 with funds donated by miners, John Wallace, architect; belfry added 1857; major repairs 1926, minor alterations to interior; fragments of cemetery in front. 5 sheets (1965, including plan, elevations, sections, de-tails); 3 ext. photos (1934), 3 int. photos (1934), 1 photo of gravestone (1934; for elevations and

Columbia continued

details of this gravestone see drawing for Mountain View Cemetery, CA-38-11).

Solari's Building (CA-1144). Main and Jackson Sts., Columbia State Historic Park. Brick, two-bay front, one story, parapeted roof, brick cornice molding, high openings with iron shutters, metal frames of sidewalk canopy. Built 1856 for V. E. Magendie, many later owners including Solari family (1928). 3 ext. photos (1934); 1 photocopy of 1930s photo.

Store (CA-1147). Main St. between Fulton and State Sts., Columbia State Historic Park. Brick, nine-bay front, one story, parapeted roof with dentil course, canopy hung over sidewalk, iron doors. Built 1954 as four buildings known as Levy, Brainard, Franklin, Schwartz Block; partially restored with shops, only front facade remains on southernmost building. 1 ext. photo (1934).

Sun Ling Store (CA-2000). N. Main St., Columbia State Historic Park. Brick, one story, flat roof, brick dentil course on cornice, two sets of iron doors. Built 1850s; stabilized ruin, roof gone. 4 photocopies of 1937 photos.

Springfield Brewery. See Tuolumne Engine House No. 1 (CA-1871).

Town of Columbia (CA-1873). Columbia State Historic Park. Wood frame, one story, gable-roofed buildings. 2 photocopies of lithographs (1852, 1854). NHL

Tuolumne Engine House No. 1 and Office of Duchow Building, Springfield Brewery (CA-1871). Columbia State Historic Park. Firehouse: brick, one story, flat roof with parapet, brick dentil course, large wood door, bracketed hood. Brewery: brick, two stories, gable roof, brick dentil course, three pairs of iron doors on first floor, two sets of smaller iron doors on second, wrought-iron balcony, Classical Revival detailing. Built 1856; restored. 3 photocopies of 1930s photos.

Wells Fargo & Co. Building (CA-174). Main St. at Washington St., Columbia State Historic Park. Brick, 38' (three-bay front) × 76', two stories, flat roof, balcony across front, ornamental cast-iron railing, three sets of iron doors on each floor. Built 1858; restored. 11 sheets (1936, including plans, elevations, details); 1 ext. photo (1934).

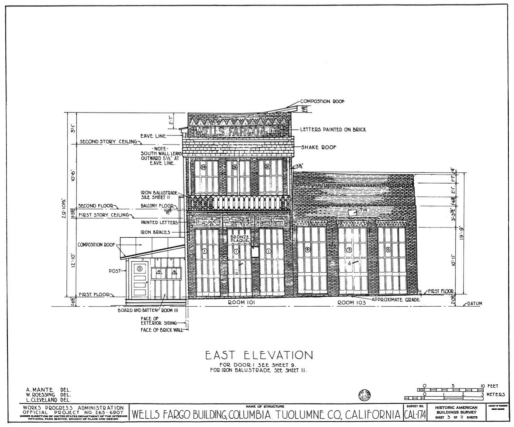

Wells Fargo & Co. Building, Columbia (CA-174).

Colusa □ Colusa County

Colusa County Courthouse (CA-1806). Stuccoed brick, 56' (three-bay front) × 65', two stories, gabled roof with polygonal cupola, pediment over a two-story portico supported by paired Tuscan columns, entablature with raking molded cornice and dentil course. Built 1860–61, Vincent Brown, architect. 1 photocopy of ca. 1908 photo.

Hall of Records and County Jail (CA-1807). Jail. Stuccoed, two stories, three-bay front, parapeted roof with fortified corners, windows with hoodmolds, belt course. Hall of Records: octagonal, brick and concrete, no wood used in construction. Jail built 1878; Hall of Records built 1882–83. 1 photocopy of ca. 1908 photo.

Concord □ Contra Costa County

Pacheco, Fernando, Adobe (CA-173). 3119 Grant St. Adobe, five-bay front, one-and-a-half stories, gable roof, shed-roofed porch across front, woodframe lean-to addition in rear. Built 1843; restored 1941 by California Horseman's Association, county-owned. 1 ext. photo (1930s), 2 photocopies of undated photos. SHL

Pacheco, Salvio, Adobe (CA-1847). Central Plaza. Adobe with clapboard siding, two stories, hip roof, two-story shed-roofed porch across front. Built 1853 for Captain Salvio Pacheco, grantee of the Rancho Monte del Diablo in 1835; much altered with lean-tos on either side. 2 photocopies of photos (n.d., ca. 1918).

Congregational Church (I.O.O.F. Hall) (CA-1123). Main St. Brick, three-bay front by three bays, one story, gable roof, slightly projecting entrance bay rising to square tower with pronounced corners, pointed-arched windows, decorative bargeboard. Built 1862, simplified Gothic Revival style; now community center. 1 ext. photo (1936).

Copperopolis vicinity □ Calaveras County

Stage Station (CA-1480). Wood frame with vertical and horizontal siding, five-bay front, one story, shingled gable roof. Built 1850s; now under Tulloch Reservoir. 1 photocopy of undated photo.

Coronado □ San Diego County

Hotel del Coronado (CA-1958). 1500 Orange Ave.

Hotel del Coronado, interior detail, Coronado (CA-1958).

Wood frame with horizontal siding and shingles, concrete foundations, approx. 250' × 440', four and five stories, gable roof with dormers, cross gables, hip roofs, conical roofs and semi-flat section, exposed rafter ends and outriggers, multiple towers and chimneys; courtyard plan with open and closed verandas on all levels, guest rooms on all five levels, main level has public rooms including round ballroom, 120' in diameter and 30' high; the oval dining room, 156' × 62' × 33' high with arched ceiling, set at 45 degrees to the building mass; the Coronet or Breakfast Room which is half of the oval dining room and joined to it at mid-point; interior corridors of upper floors run parallel to court wall, major public rooms have sugarpine paneling, iron cage elevator, coffered ceilings in lobby. Built 1887, Reid Bros., architects, constructed by the Coronado Beach Company, headed by E. H. Babcock and H. L. Story, which built its own lumber-planing mill on the premises, labor by Chinese Seven Companies of San Francisco; allegedly first hotel to use electric lighting throughout; many historic events and persons associated with hotel, which is the last remaining 19th c. luxury resort hotel on the Pacific coast. 8 sheets (1971, including site plan, plans, section, section/elevation of ballroom, plans and int. elevation of main lobby); 13 ext. photos (1971), 3 int. photos (1971), 1 ext. photo of boathouse (1971), 4 photocopies of architects' plans (ca. 1888), 1 photocopy of bird's-eye view (1888); 14 data pages (1971). NHL, SHL

Corral Hollow □ San Joaquin County

Frame House (CA-1619). Wood frame with clapboard siding, five-bay front, two stories, gable roof, one-story porch across front, rear lean-to. Built 1853, a typical vernacular dwelling of the period; demolished. 1 ext. photo (n.d.)

Corral Hollow continued
Outbuilding *(CA-1613).* Rubble stone with heavy timber corner posts, small one-story structure, roof demolished, may have been a smokehouse; also, a wood frame house with clapboard siding, four-bay front by two bays with front one-story lean-to, gable roof. Built ca. 1860, two vernacular structures. Not located. 1 ext. photo (n.d.)

Coulterville   □   Mariposa County

Bruschi Building *(CA-1531).* Adobe, plastered and painted to imitate brick, three-bay front, one story, gable roof, wood canopy in front over sidewalk with six turned posts, paneled iron shutters in front of glazed doors. Built 1857, now a firehouse. 1 photocopy of photo (n.d.), detail of doorway.

Bruschi Store *(CA-1532).* Ruins of walls of schist and brick. Built 1851 with brick imported from Stockton by Francisco Bruschi, who built three stores and a warehouse here. 1 photocopy of 1920s photo.

Buildings—Main St. *(CA-1107).* Typical vernacular brick, stone, and wood-frame buildings, one and two stories, some with simple front porches. George Coulter opened a tent trading post here in 1850, changed name from Banderita in 1853. 1 photo (1936).

Coulterville—General *(CA-1336).* Two streets and one cross street lined with one-, two- and three-story brick and wood-frame gable- and parapeted flat-roofed buildings typical of the vernacular types of mid 19th c. Gold Rush towns. 1 photo (1930s).

Coulter's Hotel and Wagoners' Store *(CA-1533).* Stone hotel, brick store, three-bay fronts, one story, gable end on store, parapet front on hotel, shed-roofed front porch. Built 1850s and used by town founder, George Coulter, after first hotel burned; Wagoners' Store had the Wells Fargo & Co. office; buildings ruinous. 1 photocopy of 1920s photo.

Coyote   □   Santa Clara County

Laguna Seca Rancho (Rancho del Refugio de la Laguna Seca) *(CA-2003). NE of U.S. Hwy. 101.* House: wood frame, two stories, hipped roof with hipped dormer, porch across front. House built 1894 on site of earlier adobe house; ranch with grist mill first operated by Juan Alvírez; acquired in 1845 by William Fisher. 1 sheet (1980,

site plan); 3 ext. photos (1980); 8 data pages (1977, 1979, 1980, 1981).

□ *Stone Building.* Rubble stone, two stories, approx. 21' × 23', hipped roof. Built between 1823 and 1845 as grist mill. 3 sheets (1977, including plans and elevations); 5 ext. photos (1980).

□ *Barn.* Wood frame with vertical plank siding, approx. 64' × 80', T-shaped, two-and-a-half stories, hipped roof with cross gables. Built ca. 1845. 2 sheets (1977, including plan, elevations); 2 ext. photos (1980).

□ *Office.* Wood frame with channeled siding, one story, approx. 20' × 31', T-shaped, one story, hipped roof with gabled projection in front which extends to cover front porch. Built late 19th c. 1 sheet (1977, including plan, elevation, detail).

Coyote vicinity   □   Santa Clara County

Stevens Ranch Complex *(CA-2018). approx. 1 mi. W of St. Rte. 101 off E. Emado La.* Fruit orchards and drying plant comprised of eighteen structures including two residences, numerous outbuildings and drying equipment, built between 1856 and 1920, most outbuildings ca. 1890–1920, by Orvis Stevens and Sons, early and prominent orchardists. Early 20th c. tram tracks connect drying buildings. Ranch continues to grow and dry fruit; several buildings and tram tracks removed 1979 due to freeway improvements. 23 ext. photos (1978), 1 photocopy of 1977 site plan; 9 data pages (1979).

Twin Oaks Dairy *(CA-2017). Metcalfe Rd. off St. Rte. 101.* Complex comprised of eight frame structures built ca. 1910–15 and residence built ca. 1905. Structures are typical of early 20th c. dairies in the county. Operated as a dairy until 1930 by tenant families of Italian-Swiss and Portuguese descent, ethnic groups most often involved in California dairy industry. Most structures dismantled 1979 due to freeway construction. 22 ext. photos (1978), 8 data pages (1979).

Cupertino   □   Santa Clara County

Collins School (Cupertino de Oro Club) *(CA-2091). 20441 Homestead Ave.* Wood frame with clapboards, one-and-a-half stories, irregular shape, gable roof, square tower with shingled siding and pyramidal roof. Built 1889 as one-room schoolhouse; added to in 1908 and 1914,

*Maryknoll Seminary, Cupertino
(CA-2092).*

Wolfe and McKenzie, architects. 6 ext. photos
(1980); 1 data page (1981).

*Maryknoll Seminary (CA-2092). 23000 Cristo
Rey Dr.* Concrete, two stories, tiled gable roof,
large square corner tower with pagoda-style roof,
arcaded cloister walk along main flank of building. Built 1926, Maginnis and Walsh, architects;
chapel added 1935. 3 ext. photos (1980); 1 data
page (1981).

*Picchetti Winery (CA-2012). 13100 Montebello
Rd., Midpeninsula Regional Open Space Park District.* Complex of buildings including large rectangular brick winery, pressing house, two wood
frame houses, and other outbuildings. Old house
built ca. 1882, main house built 1886, winery
built 1896, outbuildings built 1900–1922. 4
sheets (1978, including site plan, site sections,
detail); 6 ext. photos (1980); 7 data pages
(1978). NR

*Woodhills (Older House) (CA-2007). End of Pros-
pect Rd., Midpeninsula Regional Openspace Park.*
Wood frame with cedar shingles, 64′ × 64′, L-
shaped, one story, flat roof with parapets, multi-
paned doors and windows; landscaped hillside
setting. Built 1913–14, Wolfe and Wolfe and
Charles W. McKenzie, architects, for Fremont
and Cora Older, journalist social reformers. 5
sheets (1977, including site plan, plans, elevations, section); 10 ext. photos (1980), 3 int. photos (1980), 4 photocopies of 1914 and ca. 1955
photos; 15 data pages (1976, 1977). NR

Danville vicinity □ Contra Costa County

*O'Neill, Eugene, House (Tao House) (CA-2078).
End of Kuss Rd. off Bradford Pl.* Concrete and
wood, two stories, L-shaped, tiled gable roof extends to cover two-story porch across front. Built
1937, Carlotta Monterey O'Neill and Frederick
Confer, architects, house where playwright Eu-

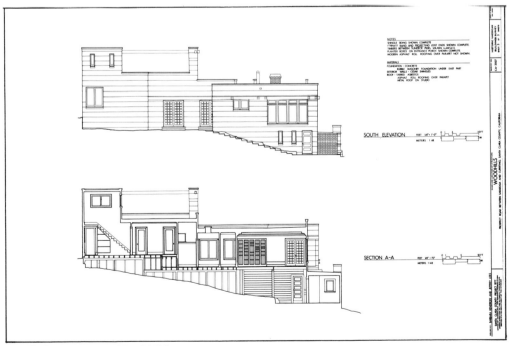

Woodhills, Cupertino (CA-2007).

Danville vicinity continued
gene O'Neill lived until 1944 and wrote some of his greatest works. 3 ext. photos (1975).

Dobbins   □   Yuba County

Hotel (CA-1477). Wood frame, nine bays by five bays, two-and-a-half stories, gable roof, two-story porch partially enclosed and partially with X-railing on second level. Built ca. 1850; demolished. 2 ext. photos (1934).

Downieville   □   Sierra County

Catholic Church (CA-1405). Wood frame with horizontal siding, one-bay front by four bays deep, gable roof, square tower set against gable front has two stages with paired louvered opening and a bell-shaped roof, entrance is on one side of the tower. Built ca. 1858. 1 ext. photo (1934).

Commercial Buildings—Courthouse (CA-1402). Wood frame and horizontal siding, three-bay front, one-and-a-half stories on raised basement, gable roof, rectangular belfry with molded cornice and louvered sides, lunette with fan tracery in pediment in gable, dentil course and blank frieze, fenestrated basement. Built 1854, burned 1947; fine example of an early, small public building in a simplified Georgian Revival style. 1 ext. photo (1934).

Downie, Major, House (CA-1407). Sierra City Rd. Wood frame with horizontal siding, four-bay front, two stories, gable roof, first-floor room projected on one side and front, and roof extended over front door, two-bay one-story wing. Built 1850s or '60s; called Major Downie's House but never owned or occupied by him. 2 ext. photos (1934).

Elmwood Cottage. Included with Houses on Sierra City Rd. (CA-1408).

Frame Houses and Church (CA-1410). N side Sierra City Rd. Two wood frame houses and a church, all with horizontal siding: first house two-bay front in gable end, two stories, gable roof with entablature and raking cornice, one-story wrap-around porch with turned balustrade; second house has five-bay front, one story, hip roof, front porch; church gable-roofed with square front belfry. Row built 1860s; altered. 1 ext. photo (1934).

House behind Courthouse (CA-1417). Wood frame with channeled siding, one story, gable

I.O.O.F. Hall, Downieville (CA-1403).

roof extends over porch across gable end, lattice encloses porch. Built mid-19th c. 1 ext. photo (1934).

Houses on Sierra City Rd. (CA-1408). Group of six houses, all wood frame with horizontal siding, one-and-a-half and two stories, some with three-bay fronts in gable ends, gable roofs, one- and two-story porches across fronts, some decorative bargeboards. Built 1850s and '60s. 4 ext. photos (1934).

Hydraulic Mine (CA-1420). Washed-down embankment showing effects of hydraulic mining. 1 photo of general view, no structures (1934).

I.O.O.F. Hall (CA-1403). Wood frame with clapboards, three-bay front in gable end, one-and-a-half stories, gable roof with cornice molding and returns, corner boards, louvered lunette in gable. Built 1852; this may be a prefabricated building shipped around the Horn; fine example of the simplified Classic Revival style with a strong New England influence frequently found in the Gold Rush country. 1 ext. photo (1934).

Main Street (CA-1290). Wood frame buildings with horizontal siding, one and two stories, gable roofs with ends towards street, sidewalk canopies. Built 1850s and '60s. 4 ext. photos (1934), 3 photocopies of 1930s photos.

Methodist-Episcopal Church (CA-1404). Sierra City Rd. Wood frame with clapboards, three-bay front, one-and-a-half stories, gable roof, pediment in gable end supported by four pilasters, two at the corners, with molded caps, square, two-stage belfry with spire and louvered openings on one side. Built ca. 1856, a good example of a pioneer Classic Revival church, recalling the New England meeting house. 1 ext. photo (1934).

Pioneer Museum Building (CA-1687). Rubble stone and brick, three-bay front, roof missing, paneled iron shutters on windows and door. Built 1850s; converted to museum. 1 photocopy of ca. 1850 undated photo showing building in ruinous state.

St. Charles Hotel (CA-1406). Wood frame with clapboarding, two-and-a-half stories, gable roof, three-bay front in gable end, sidewalk canopy. Built ca. 1855; burned 1947. 3 ext. photos, 1 also shows Wells Fargo Express Bldg. (CA-1292), and 1 shows neighboring building (1934).

Town of Downieville (CA-1291). Wood frame buildings on the river banks. 3 photos (1934), 2 photocopies of photos (ca. 1865 and undated).

Wells Fargo Building (Miner's Drug Store) (CA-1292). Brick, three-bay front, one story, hip roof, inset panels and brick stringcourses, round-headed pronounced arches with keystones, iron paneled shutters. Built ca. 1850; demolished in 1937 flood. 1 ext. photo (1934).

Dragon Gulch   □   Tuolumne County

Gilman, Tom, Cabin (CA-1200). Wood frame, vertical board siding, one story, gable roof, massive rubble-stone and brick chimney on front corner. Built 1852 by slave from Mt. Pleasant, Tennessee; demolished. 1 photocopy of undated photo.

Drytown   □   Amador County

Drytown Hall (CA-1155). Brick, two-bay front in gable end, four bays deep, one story, gable roof, iron-shuttered doors. Built 1858; demolished. 1 photocopy of ca. 1925 photo.

Masonic Lodge (CA-1515). Brick, two-bay front in gable end, two stories, gable roof, one-story porch across front. Built ca. 1855; demolished. 1 photocopy of 1920 photo.

El Dorado   □   El Dorado County

False Front Buildings (CA-1355). Main St. Wood frame with clapboards on front, vertical board siding on sides, rubble-stone base plastered on front, multi-story, gable and shed roofs, imposing stepped false front with shed-roofed sections, tall central opening flanked by double-hung windows, openings of different sizes on ground floor, some with paneled iron shutters, one-bay entry

porch with hipped roof and chamfered columns. Built 1860s; unusual large barn-like structure built into hillside with false front perhaps added later. 1 ext. photo (1934).

Ruined Store (CA-1367). Main St. Stone, ashlar front, rubble sides, six-bay front, two stories, first-story segmentally arched openings in stuccoed and scored wall, second-story windows flat-arched, no roof; other one- and two-story buildings with brick fronts, equally ruinous. Built ca. 1855; town declined 1870s; 1923 fire reduced buildings to ruinous state; removed by 1957. 1 photo (1934).

Eldoradotown (now Mountain Ranch)   □   Calaveras County

Raggio Adobe (Bartolomeo Dughi Building) (CA-1587). Washington St. Adobe, plastered, square, two stories, shingled hip roof, iron-shuttered openings. Built 1850s; addition 1862. 1 photo (1936) of the building's side, also showing Rodesino Adobe (CA-1586).

Rodesino House (CA-1586). Garibaldi St. Plastered stone, four-bay front, square, two stories with one-story rear wing, shingled hip roof, iron-shuttered openings. Built 1850s as a trading post; burned 1969. 1 photo, a distant view showing rear of building (1936).

Elizabeth Lake vicinity   □   Los Angeles County

Gorman, Major, Stage Station (CA-330). San Francisquito Rd. Plastered adobe, stone foundations and wood, one story, gable roof with shakes, wood-framed openings; four rooms, no hall, adobe fireplace with two hearths. Built 1859 for Major Gorman, ruinous condition in 1937. 4 sheets (1936, including plans, elevations, details); 3 ext. photos (1936); 1 data page (1937).

Elk   □   Mendocino County

Elk—General (CA-1471). Rugged coast line and straggling line of wood frame buildings. 1 photo of general view (1934).

Escalon   □   San Joaquin County

Jones House (CA-117). Brick, five-bay front, two stories, hip roof with deck and balustrade, two brick chimneys, one-story porch three bays wide

Carson House, detail, Eureka (CA-1911).

Escalon continued

with box columns and balustrade above. Built mid 19th c.; not located. 2 ext. photos (1934); 1 photocopy of undated ext. photo.

Eureka □ Humboldt County

Carson House (CA-1911). Second and M Streets. The Ingomar Club (private). Redwood frame with a variety of surface treatments, fish-scale and other cut shingles, vertical strips, horizontal siding and other decorative detail, irregular shape, two-and-a-half stories, multi-gable roof with several finialed tower elements including a four-story off-center main tower with high peaked roof, decorative gable forms, balconies and a wealth of detail, one-story veranda wraps around with unusual spindled columns with out-sized bulbous forms in their centers, variety of openings in elaborate architraves usually with transoms; central-hall plan with vestibule and main rooms opening off central hall, lavish interior of carved wood, both redwood and South American Primavera, with much idiosyncratic detail typical of the Newsom Brothers as well as typical period detail, wooden horseshoe arches along second-floor hallway, Mexican onyx mantels, stained glass, some original furnishings,

ballroom and billiard room on third floor. Built 1884–85, Samuel and Joseph Cather Newsom, architects; minor alterations. One of the most flamboyant late 19th c. residences combining the Stick-Eastlake and Queen Anne styles, the Carson House sums up the Victorian fantasy expressed in the motto, "A Man's Home is His Castle;" the architects were among the country's most prolific designers with a practice that stretched from 1879 to about 1908 and encompassed several hundred projects. 14 ext. photos (1960), 13 int. photos (1960), 1 photocopy of 1902 photo, 1 photocopy of architect's drawing (1885, elevation); 7 data pages (1964). NR

Fort Humboldt (CA-1643). One- and two-story wood-frame structures with gable roofs pitching out to cover front porches. Fort established in 1853, abandoned in 1870s, now gone; sites of fort buildings marked with plaques. 1 photocopy of undated drawing, 1 photocopy of 1925 photo of building in state of collapse. SHL

House—314 H Street (CA-1461). Wood frame, four-bay front, T-shaped, one-and-a-half stories, steep gable roof, gabled dormers, bargeboard scrollwork on gable ends of house and dormers, rectangular drip molds over most windows, side porch with pierced columns. Built 1860s; demolished. 3 ext. photos (1934).

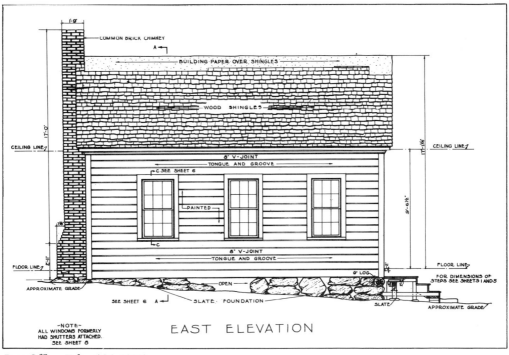

Post Office, Felix (CA-1118).

Eureka continued

Hustes House (Hanna House) (CA-1462). 916 2nd St. Wood frame with clapboards, five-bay front, square, one story, hipped roof, three-bay front porch, denticulated cornice. Built 1860s; demolished. 1 ext. photo (1934).

Lindsay House (CA-1459). Wood frame with clapboards, three-bay front, two stories, gable roof, one-story porch across front, paired brackets supporting plain cornice, one-and-a-half story rear wing. Built 1850s; demolished. 1 ext. photo (1934).

Stokes House (CA-1460). Wood frame with clapboards, three-bay front, T-shape, two-story main unit, steep gable roof with boxed cornice and returns, front entrance porch, corner pilasters. Built 1850s; demolished. 3 ext. photos (1934).

Felix   □   Calaveras County

Pedroli Ranch House (Andrew Williams Ranch) (CA-1208). Plastered stone, two stories, three-bay front, hipped roof, one-story wing. Built mid-19th c. Ruinous. 1 ext. photo (1936).

Post Office and School (CA-1118). Tower Ranch. Wood frame with channeled siding, 18′ (one-bay front) × 24′, one story, gable roof, one room. Built 1869 as community schoolhouse, moved to present site shortly after construction, used as post office and meeting house. 8 sheets (1936, including plan, elevations, section, details); 1 ext. photo (1936); 2 data pages (1937).

Felix vicinity   □   Calaveras County

House Ruins (CA-1122). Stone Creek, Bear Creek, or Dry Creek Settlement. Ruins of stone houses and mine, laid schist slabs. Settlement by Frenchmen begun 1850s. House built by Eugene Barbé 1877–1895; burned 1914. Settlement also called Lost City. 1 ext. photo (1936).

Mine Building (Andrew Williams or Tower Ranch) (CA-1209). Stone rubble, rough-hewn schist, three-bay front by one bay, one story, gable roof. Built ca. 1870; ruinous, roof gone. 1 ext. photo (1936).

Tower Ranch Barn (CA-1207). Wood frame, stone foundation, two-and-a-half story bank barn, gable roof extended over rear section. Built 1850s, 1 ext. photo (1936).

Tower Ranch House (CA-1117). Wood frame with clapboards, five-bay front, L-shaped, two stories,

gable roof, two one-story wings, one-story porch across front, wood balustrades on second floor. Built ca. 1861; burned 1973. 2 ext. photos (1936).

Fiddletown   □   Amador County

St. Charles Hotel (CA-1154). Wood frame with channeled siding, two stories, five-bay front in gable end, gable roof, two-story porch across front. Built 1850s; demolished. 1 photocopy of 1926 photo.

Folsom   □   Sacramento County

House (CA-1361). Wood frame, horizontal siding, three-bay front in gable end, two stories, gable roof, diamond-shaped attic vent, flat-arched windows, wrap-around one-story porch with columns. Built 1860s. 1 ext. photo (1934).

Methodist Episcopal Church (CA-1359). Brick, three-bay front by six bays, one story, bracketed gable roof, three-stage central front tower with open belfry supported by oblique square shingled columns that appear above roof line capped with balls, second stage has diamond-shaped window with twelve lights, ground floor of tower has paired round-arched windows with rondel set in round-arched architrave with pronounced

Methodist Episcopal Church, Folsom (CA-1359).

Trinity Episcopal Church, Folsom (CA-1360).

headmolding of bricks, tower has three-stage buttresses, side walls have two-stage buttresses double wood-paneled doors set in round-arched architraves on both sides; single nave plan. Built 1860s; belfry altered. 1 ext. photo (1934).

Trinity Episcopal Church (CA-1360). Wood frame with clapboards, three-bay front, one story, gable roof with central section raised, corner boards, diamond-shaped window over pointed-arch entrance. Built 1860s, a good example of a variation on the Carpenter Gothic theme. 1 ext. photo (1934).

Wells Fargo & Co. (Assay Office) (CA-1358). Ashlar stone front on brick, three-bay front, one-and-a-half stories, parapeted gable roof, raised center block with "1860" inscribed, stone pilasters with molded caps, double glazed doors, paneled iron shutters. Built 1860; demolished 1960. 2 ext. photos (1934) also showing one-story brick building next door.

Fort Bragg vicinity   □   Mendocino County

Abandoned School (CA-1465). Wood frame with channeled siding, five-bay front by three bays, one-and-a-half story, gable roof with square louvered cupola, narrow triangular wood buttresses along walls, two entrance doors. Built 1860s. 1 ext. photo (1934).

Buildings—Main St. (CA-1467). Wood frame, various sidings, one and two stories, gable roofs with false fronts, some bay windows, Masonic Temple (CA-1801) in foreground. 1 photo of general view (1934).

Fort Ross   □   Sonoma County

Fort Ross (CA-120). State Historic Park. Complex of wood frame buildings surrounded by a stockade. Founded 1812 by Russians from Alaska; abandoned and sold to Captain Sutter in 1841; acquired by state 1906 and partially restored. For plot plan, see drawings of Russians Chapel (CA-110). 2 photos (1934), 3 photocopies of photos (late 19th c., late 1880s, ca. 1915), 3 photocopies of drawings (before 1840, ca. 1843, ca. 1870). NHL, SHL

□ *Russian Chapel (CA-110).* Heavy timber frame with vertical board siding, 24' (one-bay front) × 31', one story, gable roof, polygonal cupola with peaked roof at front, round cupola with round window; single nave with X-braced framing expressed on interior. Build ca. 1828; rebuilt 1915–17, four bays long instead of three; rebuilt 1955–57, three bays long; rebuilt after 1970 fire. 6 sheets (1934, including plot plan, elevations, sections, details), 8 ext. photos (1934, 1930s, 1960), 3 int. photos (1934), 8 photocopies of photos (1880s, ca. 1900, ca. 1907, ca. 1910, ca. 1920, ca. 1968).

□ *Russian Barracks (Commandant's House) (CA-1315).* Heavy timber frame with horizontal siding, seven-bay front, approx. 48' × 36', one story, hip roof extended over porch across front; two-room plan. Built ca. 1812 as gable-roofed structure with ten-bay front and two-story building with six-bay front, built in two sections, attached to one end; altered between ca. 1915 and early 1930s. 1 ext. photo (1934), 2 int. photos (1934), 2 photocopies of photos (ca. 1860, undated but before alteration).

□ *Russian Blockhouse (CA-1314).* Square hewn log construction, eight-sided with peaked roof, two stories, built into corner of stockade. Built ca. 1812; ruins. 1 ext. photo (1934).

Fort Yuma   □   Imperial County

Fort Yuma (CA-415). Adobe, one-story, hip-roofed structures. Founded as American military post in 1849 at the lower crossing of the Colorado River; buildings built 1852–55 and later;

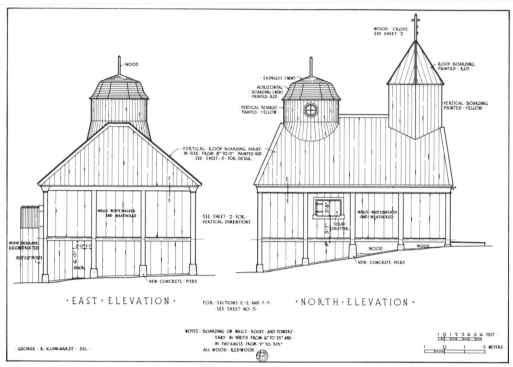

Russian Chapel, Fort Ross (CA-110).

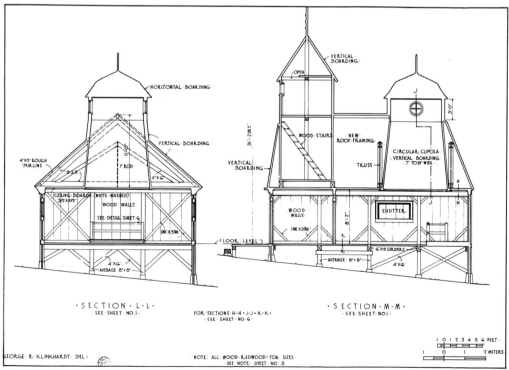

Russian Chapel, Fort Ross (CA-110).

Fort Yuma continued
used by Army until 1885; buildings assigned to Yuma Indian Reservation in 1892. Building exteriors have been plastered; roofs replaced. 5 data pages (1960s). SHL

□ *Old Officers Quarters (CA-412)*. 3 sheets (1960s, including plan, elevations, section, details).

□ *Cottage—Old Officers Kitchen (CA-413)*. 3 sheets (1960s, including plan, elevations, section, detail).

□ *Old Barracks (CA-414)*. 3 sheets (1960s, including plan, elevations, section).

□ *Old Indian Girls Dormitory (CA-416)*. Wood frame with clapboard siding, two-and-a-half stories, hipped roof with hipped dormers. Built 1892. 2 sheets (1960s, including plans, elevations, detail).

Fourth Crossing □ Calaveras County

Reddick, John, House (Foreman's Ranch) (CA-1129). Wood frame with clapboards, two buildings at right angles, one seven-bay front, one three-bay front in gable end, two-and-a-half stories, gable roofs with cornice moldings, one-story front porches on both buildings with openwork balustrades, attic of one building has louvered lunette. Built 1850s as Foreman's Ranch Hotel, stage station on Stockton Road officially called Fourth Crossing, sold 1858 to John Reddick; building now in two sections. 2 ext. photos (1934, n.d.), 2 photocopies of photos (after 1934).

Fremont □ Alameda County

Indian Cemetery (CA-1658). *Mission San Jose-Irvington Road, 1 mi. from Mission San José*. Burial ground for Indians converted at mission from 1797–1836. Granite marker erected in 1915 memorializes 4,000 of the Ohlone tribe buried here. 1 photo (1940).

Mission San José de Guadalupe (CA-1132). *Mission Blvd. at Washington Blvd*. Museum. Restored remains of fourteenth establishment in the mission chain. Adobe, plastered, and wood, eight-bay porch across front, rectangular, approx. 40′ × 175′, one story, tiled gable roof; six rooms and hallways remain of the original monastery wing; northernmost room, 36′ × 16′, is thought to have been the padres' *comedor*. Mission estab-

lished 1797, second, permanent church begun 1805 from designs by Padre Felipe de la Cuesta of San Juan Bautista, earthquake of 1808 damaged the incomplete structure, mission secularized in 1836, church destroyed by earthquake in 1868, restoration begun 1915 by Native Sons and Daughters. Mission: 3 drawings (early 1860s, 1866, 1881), 1 painting (1868); 4 ext. photos (early 1860s, after 1868, 1936). Convent: 10 ext. photos (1850s, 1860s, ca. 1870, ca. 1928, 1932, 1934, 1937). Misc. mission buildings: 2 plot plans (1854, 1868); 2 ext. photos (1850s, 1860s); 17 data pages (1960). SHL

Vallejo, José de Jesus, Adobe (CA-1194). *Niles Blvd. at Nursery Ave*. Hospitality House of the California Nursery. Adobe, plastered, and wood, rectangular, one story, shingled gable roof; one room plan. Built after 1842 by José de Jesus Vallejo, appointed manager of Mission San Jose (CA-1132) after secularization. Interior altered. 1 ext. photo (1937), 1 int. photo (1937).

Vallejo Mills (CA-1660). Two mills built 1842 and 1853, the first of adobe and stone, one-story rectangular block, the second of wood frame and stone with board siding, four stories. Demolished. 2 ext. photos (1940).

French Camp □ San Joaquin County

Noble, Colonel, Store (CA-1617). Wood frame with clapboard siding, seven-bay front, two-and-a-half stories, gable roof, paneled corner pilasters and simple entablature, second-story porch supported by single chamfered posts, side wing stylistically later, perhaps a store. Built ca. 1855, a good example of the vernacular version of the Greek Revival house; demolished. 1 ext. photo (n.d.).

Gilroy □ Santa Clara County

Christian Church (Latin American Assemblies of God) (CA-2060). *160 Fifth St*. Wood frame with horizontal siding, 32′ (three-bay front) × 60′, one-and-a-half stories, gable roof with cornice returns on gable end, square entrance tower with corner pilasters, belfry, flat roof. Built 1857. 3 sheets (1978, including plan, elevations, sections); 4 ext. photos (1980); 10 data pages (1979).

Eschenburg-Silva Cow Barn (CA-2096). *3665 Pacheco Pass Rd*. Heavy timber frame with vertical board siding, approx. 85′ (three-bay front) ×

Eschenburg-Silva Cow Bar, Gilroy (CA-2096).

Gilroy continued
100', gable roof pitches out to cover wings, two hip-roofed cupolas. Built before 1889. 4 sheets (1980, including site plan, plan, elevations); 5 ext. photos (1980); 6 data pages (1980).

Gilroy Free Public Library (Gilroy Historical Museum) (CA-2093). *195 Fifth St.* Brick with stone trim, one story, three-bay front, flat roof with parapet, denticulated cornice, Roman Doric entrance portico with pediment. Built 1910, William H. Weeks, architect. 4 ext. photos (1980); 1 data page (1981).

Hoenck House (CA-2095). *9480 Murray Ave.* Wood frame with drop siding on first floor, decorative shingles on second floor, approx. 30' (four-bay front) × 45', two stories, hipped roof with cross gables, round corner tower with conical roof, one-story front porch with spindles and fan brackets. Built ca. 1895–1900. 8 ext photos (1980); 6 data pages (1980).

Lilly's Auto Camp (CA-2094). *8877 Monterey Hwy.* Office and ten of original fifteen cabins, all wood frame with horizontal siding, one story, gable roofs; office approx. 30' (five-bay front in gable end) × 65'; typical cabin approx. 12' (two-bay front in gable end) × 14', shed roof across front, carports between cabins. Built ca. 1927. 2 sheets (1980, including site plan, plan, elevations); 6 ext. photos (1980); 9 data pages (1980).

Live Oak Creamery (CA-2065). *88 Martin St.* Brick, 37' (four-bay front) × 96', one story, gable roof on original portion, flat parapeted roof on additions. Built 1908 as first butter factory in Gilroy. 3 sheets (1979, including plan, elevations, section); 7 ext. photos (1980); 9 data pages (1979).

Willson House (CA-2097). *1980 Pacheco Pass Rd.* Brick, approx. 40' (five-bay front) × 30', two stories, gable roof with cross gable, cornice returns on gables, one-story porch on all four sides, balustrade above, pointed-arch window in front gable. Built 1859 by brickmason Horace Willson, first brick house in Santa Clara Valley. 10 ext. photos (1980); 5 data pages (1980).

Gilroy vicinity   □   Santa Clara County

Norris, Frank, Memorial (CA-1544). *Near Redwood Retreat Rd.* Part of a rubble-stone wall surmounted with a cross and with a plaque commemorating the California writer, Frank Norris, author of *The Octopus*. Erected ca. 1902 at the behest of Mrs. Robert Louis Stevenson. 1 photocopy of 1910 photo.

Stevenson, Mrs. Robert Louis, House (CA-1545). *Redwood Retreat Rd.* Wood frame with narrow horizontal siding, one-and-a-half stories, low-pitched gable roof extended over front porch partially wrapping around one side, shed-roofed dormers, exposed rafter ends, projecting boxed bay window with small-paned lights. Built 1902 for the widow of Robert Louis Stevenson as a summer home called Vanumanutangi; a fine example of a rustic country lodge with a bungalow form highly popular in the state from the turn of the century to World War I. 1 photocopy of 1910 photo.

Glen Canyon   □   Santa Cruz County

Covered Bridge (CA-1551). Wood frame, gable roof, vertical planking in gable. Built 1892, since moved, location unknown. 1 photocopy of ca. 1936 photo.

Lilly's Auto Camp, Gilroy (CA-2094).

Glencoe   □   Calaveras County

Frame Store (CA-1488). Wood frame, board-and-batten siding, three-bay front, two stories, gable roof with false front, two-story front veranda exterior wood staircase with zig-zag diagonal patterned balustrade to second floor. Built 1860s; demolished, town gone. 1 photocopy of 1925 photo.

Glendale   □   Los Angeles County

Casa Adobe de San Rafael (CA-323). 1340 Dorothy Dr. Plastered adobe with board-and-batten siding on gable ends, stone foundations, approx. 57′ × 35′, shingled gable roof extended over eight-bay porch or corredor on two sides. Built 1860s for Tomás Sanchez, Sheriff of Los Angeles County, on part of the first colonial land grant made in 1784 to José María Verdugo, called Rancho San Rafael, purchased by City of Glendale and restored 1934–35. 3 sheets (1935, including plans, elevations, detail); 5 ext. photos (1936); 1 data page (1937). SHL

Goodyear's Bar   □   Sierra County

Town of Goodyear's Bar (CA-1679). Small town of one- and two-story buildings set in valley. 1 photocopy of ca. 1850 drawing.

Grass Valley   □   Nevada County

Brick Stores A and B (CA-1692). Mill St. Brick, three-bay fronts, flat roofs with parapets, cornice moldings, cast-iron paneled doors. Built ca. 1855 in Boston Ravine by William Campbell and Alex Stoddard as general supply stores for miners; typical Gold Rush vernacular commercial structures; demolished 1929. 1 ext. photo (1934).

Frame Farm House (Taylor-Barker House) (CA-1392). 653 Linden St. Wood frame with clapboards, three-bay front, one-and-a-half stories, high-pitched gable roof with central cross gable, one-bay front entrance porch with columns and molded caps surmounted by a balustrade, pointed-arch casement window in cross-gable. Built 1860s, a good example of the pattern book Gothic Revival or Downingesque cottage. 2 ext. photos (1934).

House (Thomas House) (CA-1393). 220 N. School St. at Linden St. Wood frame with clapboards, five-bay front, shed-roofed rear extension, two stories, gable roof with plain entablature and raking molded cornice on gable ends, porch

Thomas House, Grass Valley (CA-1393).

Grass Valley continued

across front with turned columns and balustrade, columns have fan brackets supporting bands of spindles, second-floor balustrade has ornate, flat-sawn balusters. Built 1860s, a fine example of the Greek Revival or late Federal style wood frame farmhouse. 1 ext. photo (1934).

Iron Stove (CA-1667). Cast-iron wood-burning stove, narrow deep fire box with hinged door, sides corrugated and fluted with cast-in ribbon design. Made in 1839 and shipped around the Horn. 1 photocopy of undated photo.

Montez, Lola, House (CA-1642). *248 Mill St.* Wood frame with drop siding, three-bay front, two stories, gable roof with central cross gable, boxed cornice, one-story porch across front, quoins, round-arched window in second-floor central bay. Built ca. 1852 when actress Lola Montez came to Grass Valley from Europe where she was the Countess of Landsfelt; house originally one-story schoolhouse remodeled by Montez; restored late 1970s. 2 photocopies of 1930s ext. photos. SHL

Morateur's Store and Hotel (CA-1539). *Boston Ravine, S. end of Mill St.* Wood frame with channeled siding, six-bay front, one-and-a-half stories, shingled gable roof with one gabled dormer, roof extended over the front porch. Built by pioneers Adolf and Paul Morateur in Boston Ravine; demolished 1929. 1 photocopy of undated photo.

Mount St. Mary's Academy (CA-1799). *Church and Chapel Sts.* Brick with stone foundation, eleven-bay front, two stories, gable roof, two paneled brick chimneys, octagonal cupola with onion dome and cross (removed), central projecting bay with cross gable, quoins on all corners, one-story entrance portico with columns and entablature surmounted by balustrade reached by two-stage grand staircase with turned balustrade; central-hall plan with double-loaded corridors to either side, high ceilings, hardwood interior trim, paneled folding doors. Built 1863–64 for Father Thomas Dalton who brought the Sisters of Mercy from Ireland to San Francisco and thence to Grass Valley in 1863, founded Grass Valley Orphan Asylum at same time as St. Mary's, a girls' academy and boarding school; building enlarged by two bays ca. 1890 about the same time St. Joseph's Church was built adjoining it; roof pitch raised ca. 1900, cupola removed. 1 photocopy of drawing (1880s), 1 photocopy of photo (ca. 1895) also showing Gothic Revival church of St. Joseph. SHL

Watt House (Finney-Watt House) (CA-1391). *506*

Linden St. Wood frame with clapboards, two-bay front in gable end, two-and-a-half stories, gable roof with boxed cornice, corner boards, L-shaped porch with turned posts, one-story gable-roof addition across rear; L-plan. Built 1860s, a good example of a farmhouse probably built from carpenter-builder's patternbooks widely disseminated in the West. 2 ext. photos (1934).

Groveland vicinity   □   Tuolumne County

Harte, Bret, House ("Tennessee's Cabin") (CA-1568). Wood frame with clapboards, rectangular, two stories, gable roof extended over side wing, balcony on side with stairway. Built 1850s; demolished. 1 photocopy of undated photo.

Guadalupe   □   Santa Barbara County

Guadalupe Rancho Adobes (CA-29). *114 and 120 Third Ave.* Built 1840s. 1 ext. photo (1936); 1 data page (1937).

□ *Adobe #1 (CA-29 A)*. Adobe, 57' (five-bay front) × 33', one-and-a-half stories, hipped roof pitches out to cover porch on all sides, one gable dormer. 3 sheets (1937, including plan, elevations, details); 2 ext. photos (1936).

□ *Adobe #2 (CA-29 B)*. Adobe, 70' (six-bay front) × 25', one-and-a-half stories, hipped roof extends to cover porch on three sides, gable on fourth side, gable dormers; building originally longer. 3 sheets (1937, including plans, elevations, section, details); 3 ext. photos (1936).

Half Moon Bay   □   San Mateo County

Community Methodist Church (CA-2121). *Johnston and Miramontes Sts.* Wood frame with channeled siding, three-bay front in gable end, gable roof with octagonal open belfry, double doors and fanlight set in striking ogival arch, round-arched windows with hoodmolds. Built 1872, Charles Geddes, architect. 6 ext. photos (1975), 2 int. photos (1975). NR

Johnston, James, House (CA-2122). *Higgins Rd.* Wood frame with clapboards, mortise-and-tenon construction, five-bay front, two stories, gable roof, salt-box form. Built ca. 1853, restoration in progress. 9 ext. photos (1971, 1975), 5 int. photos (1971), 1 photocopy of ext. photo (ca. 1908). NR

Johnston, William, House (CA-2123). *306 Higgins*

Rd. Wood frame with channeled siding, mortise-and-tenon construction, T-shape, two stories with one-story wing, gable roof, bracketed cornice. Built ca. 1854. 4 ext. photos (1975).

Vásquez, Pablo, House (CA-2124). 270 N. Main St. Wood frame with clapboards, three-bay front in gable end, one story, T-shape, gable roof, portico at entrance, pedimented openings. Built 1869 for Pablo Vásquez, livery stable owner. 4 ext. photos (1975).

□ *Stables (CA-2124 A).* 200 N. Main St. Wood frame with channeled siding, two stories, gable roof with cross gables, different sidings indicate built in stages. Built before 1872, additions. 3 ext. photos (1975).

Happy Valley   □   Calaveras County

Stone Building and North Star Mine Building (CA-1497). Rough ashlar masonry with finished stone at corners, one-and-a-half stories, gable roof; mine building; wood frame, board-and-batten siding, one story, gable roof, rear secondary gable over back room. Built 1850s; mine 1890s; demolished, town gone. 1 photocopy of undated photo.

Hayward   □   Alameda County

Brewery (CA-1325). Brick and wood, rectangular, three stories with four-story tower, hip roof with tall vent towers. Demolished. 1 ext. photo (1937).

Hillsborough   □   San Mateo County

Villa Rose (Grant-Blyth House) (also called Strawberry Hill) (CA-2125). End of Redington Rd. Reinforced concrete, seven-bay front, two stories, flat roof with parapet, denticulated cornice, quoins, hoodmolds over round-arched windows first floor, segmental-arched windows second floor, elaborate terraced and walled gardens; interior has several rooms and murals imported from England. Built 1912, Lewis Hobart, architect; interior renovated 1936. 9 ext. photos (1975), 3 int. photos (1975).

Clark House ("House on the Hill") (CA-2126). 945 Tournament Drive. Stone, brick in half-timbering on second level of one side, H-plan with service wing, two-and-a-half stories on sloped site, gable roof with three cross gables on one

side, gable wall dormers on other side, massive stone chimneys, leaded-glass casement windows; imported antique paneling and parquet floor, ornamental plaster ceilings. Built 1930–31, David Adler, architect; fine example of Cotswold Tudor style. 12 ext. photos (1975), 3 int. photos (1975); 4 data pages (1974).

Hornitos   □   Mariposa County

Hornitos Hotel (CA-1102). Wood frame with clapboards, seven-bay front, two-and-a-half stories, two chimneys, shingled gable roof extended over two-story porch across front, latticed railing on second level, one-story rear lean-to. Built ca. 1860; representative of the frontier Greek Revival style in a large building; demolished 1939. 1 photo of general view (1936), 1 photocopy of 1925 photo.

Jail (CA-1522). High St. Museum. Random ashlar stone, one-bay wide, one story, gable roof, narrow rectangular entrance with stone lintel, 3' thick stone walls, small window high in one side. Built 1851. 1 photocopy of 1934 photo.

Hornitos Hotel, Hornitos (CA-1102).

Jail, Hornitos (CA-1522).

Hornitos continued

Masonic Hall (CA-1523). *Main St.* Local schist ashlar walls, two-bay front, one story, flat roof, brick parapet with dentiled cornice, iron doors, corrugated metal canopy across front. Built ca. 1852 as a saloon; purchased by Masons in 1860. 1 photocopy of 1925 photo.

Native Sons of the Golden West (CA-1521). Plastered brick, two-bay front, one story, flat roof with brick parapet with brick dentils under cornice, two large openings with iron shutters. Built 1850s as Wells Fargo & Co. building; demolished. 1 photocopy of 1920s photo.

Plaza (CA-1103). Open space surrounded by one story, adobe, brick and stone buildings. Town built in 1850s, first and only incorporated town in county, named for tombs in the form of "little ovens" erected above ground by Mexican settlers. 1 photo (1936).

Principal Street and Plaza (CA-1104). One-story adobe, two-story brick, one-story wood-frame, and other buildings. Built mid-19th c. 1 ext. photo (1936).

Small Adobe House (CA-1101). Adobe, one story, hipped shake roof extending to form porch on both sides, board-and-batten lean-to. Built 1850s, first adobe building in Hornitos; demolished. 1 ext. photo (1936).

Indian Gulch   □   Mariposa County

Fandango Dance Hall (CA-1530). *Main St.* Plastered brick or adobe, two-bay front, one story, flat roof, canopy in front. Built 1850s; demolished. 1 photocopy of 1925 photo.

Ghirardelli Store (CA-1526). *Main St.* Two walls of dressed schist and one adobe wall, two-bay front with simple entablature, roofless, one story, two pairs of paneled iron doors. Built 1855 for pioneer San Francisco chocolate merchant who had several Mother Lode stores in early 1850s. 1 photocopy of 1925 photo of ruins.

Solari Hotel (CA-1525). Wood frame with channeled siding on front and clapboards on other walls, one-and-a-half stories, gable roof, shed-roof porch. Built 1850s, probably demolished. 1 photocopy of 1925 photo.

Inglewood   □   Los Angeles County

Academy Theater (CA-2020). *3141 W. Manchester Blvd.* Reinforced concrete, T-shaped, 94′ × 185′, two stories, flat roof with parapet at front, hip roof over auditorium, projecting semicircular marquee over entrance, tall off-center spiral tower, metal and etched glass doors; lobby, theater, and stage, stuccoed walls and ceiling with polychrome lighting. Built 1939, S. Charles Lee, architect; front ext. walls covered with rubble stone; signs replaced. 2 ext. photos (ca. 1975).

Casa del Rancho Aguaje de la Centinela (CA-312). *7634 Midfield Rd.* Museum and park. Plastered adobe and wood frame, adobe section 69′ × 20′, one story, shingled gable and hip roof (originally flat and tarred), wood additions sheathed in board-and-batten siding, porches on three sides with chamfered box columns; original section had three rooms. Built ca. 1840 on 2220-acre ranch, later frame additions, roof altered. 4 sheets (1934, including plan, elevations, details); 5 ext. photos (1936); 1 data page (1937).

Freeman, Daniel, House (CA-2115). Frame with clapboards first floor, stucco and half-timbering second floor, shingles in gables, two-and-a-half stories, hip roof with cross gable, dormers with hip, gable, and conical roofs, circular and rectangular bays, wide one-story porch on three sides, exterior brick chimney. Built 1889, Curlett, Eisen, Cuthbertson, architects; demolished. 9 ext. photos (ca. 1972).

Jackass Hill   □   Tuolumne County

Twain, Mark, Cabin (Gillis Cabin) (CA-1296). Log, one story, gable roof, massive stone chimney on one end, one plain door. Built 1860s by Gillis brothers, used by Twain 1864–66 while writing *The Celebrated Jumping Frog of Calaveras County;* demolished; replica built 1922 some 200 yds. south of original site. 6 photocopies of photos (late 19th c., 1900, 1923, and undated).

Jackson   □   Amador County

Brick House (Armstead C. Brown House) (CA-1277). *Church St.* Amador County Historical Museum. Brick, four-bay front, two-story main section with one-story rear wing, gable roof with molded cornice and returns, one-story front porch. Built 1859; new roof, grounds restored. 2 ext. photos (1934).

Hotel (CA-1283). *Marcucci Lane and Broadway.* Wood frame with horizontal siding, L-shape, two stories, shingled gable roof with cornice molding and frieze boards, corner boards, triangular lou-

National Hotel, Jackson (CA-1520).

vered attic vent, two-story wrap-around porch with turned balustrade at second level, one-story back porch with X-braced railing. Built 1904. 2 ext. photos (1934).

National Hotel (CA-1520). *Main and Water Sts.* Brick, seven-bay front, two and three stories, gable roof over three-story section, two-story veranda across entire front, elaborate brick entablature above second story, bracketed eaves on gable end. Built 1863; remodeled and severely altered after 1925 in "Spanish Style" with white cement plated exterior and tile roof, balconies rebuilt in heavy dark brown timbers, two-story adjoining section remodeled with rusticated board-and-batten siding. 1 photocopy of 1925 photo.

Native Daughters of the Golden West Building (CA-1509). Brick, one story, six-bay front, parapet with dentil course. Organization founded in this building in 1886; demolished. 1 ext. photo (1930s). SHL

Serbian Church (CA-1870). Stuccoed brick, one-bay front by three bays, central front three-stage tower with round-arched open belfry and peaked roof, star in circle motif on second stage, gable roof, buttresses at tower corners and on sides, round-arched side windows, vestibule entrance with fanlighted double doors, cross above. Built

1894. 1 ext. photo (1934) also showing cemetery.

Toll House (CA-1519). Wood frame with vertical board siding, shake gable roof, lean-to porches, barn-like structure; demolished. 1 photocopy of 1927 photo.

Wells Fargo Express Office (CA-1156). *NE corner Main and Water Sts.* Brick, one story, flat roof, wide entrance facing corner, canopy over sidewalk. Built ca. 1855; served as Wells Fargo Express Office 1857–58. 1 photocopy of 1925 photo.

Jackson Gate □ **Amador County**

Chichizola Store (CA-1513). *Jackson Gate Rd., 1 mi. N of Jackson.* Stone, cement plastered, three-bay front, one-and-a-half stories, gable roof. Built 1853; remodeled for new store, new awning. 1 photocopy of undated photo.

Jesus Maria □ **Calaveras County**

Frame Buildings and Houses (CA-1483). Scattered wooden buildings in rolling landscape. The center of a large placer mining section, town received its name from a Mexican who raised vege-

Jesus Maria continued

tables and melons for the miners; settled in 1850s by Mexicans, French, Chileans, and Italians; ruins of stone foundations remain. 1 photocopy of 1925 photo. SHL

Jolon vicinity   □   Monterey County

Mission San Antonio de Padua (CA-13). Hunter Liggett Military Reservation. Adobe, three-bay front, rectangular, tiled gable roof, church preceded by a free-standing tripartite brick campanario connected to church by one-story entry, curved and stepped gable, brick coping, three openings for bells set in pronounced brick arches, brick belt courses, three wooden entrance doors in round-arched openings; single nave; brick arcade on grounds. San Antonio was the third mission founded by Fr. Junípero Serra, July 14, 1771; present church built 1810–13; *convento* in 1814; quadrangle, living quarters, workshops, walls and some twenty miles of irrigation troughs and ditches built by Fr. Sitjar were finished by 1828; following secularization in 1835, mission fell into ruins; in 1928 the property was returned to the Franciscan Order; complete restoration begun in 1948; church rededicated 1950. 17 sheets (1934, including plot plan, plan, elevations, sections, restored elevations, details, including details of wine vats and vault, mill); 4 ext. photos (1934), 37 photocopies of ext. photos (1850s, ca. 1870, 1870s, ca. 1880, ca. 1885, ca. 1890, 1890s. ca. 1895, early 1900s, ca. 1905, ca. 1910, ca. 1930, ca. 1936, undated), 2 int. photocopies (n.d.), 2 photocopies of drawings (before 1843, 1835), 2 ext. photos of wine vats (1934), 3 ext. photos of water mill (1934), 2 photocopies of photos of aqueduct (1918, n.d.), 3 photocopies of photos of vineyardist's house (ca. 1900, n.d.), 1 photocopy of stone foundations (n.d.); 1 data page (1936). NR, SHL

Roth Ranch (CA-1433). 1 mi. west of Lockwood. Two adobe buildings, one large, one small, rectangular, set at angle to each other, gable roof, one story porch on one side of large adobe. Built 1850s; demolished in bomb target practice ca. 1942. 2 ext. photos (1934), 2 int. photos—details of roof (1934).

Julian   □   San Diego County

Witch Creek Schoolhouse (CA-1972). Fourth and Washington Sts. Wood frame with channeled siding, one story, approx. 34′ × 43′, irregular shape, hip roof with cupola on corner. Built 1889–90 as schoolhouse; moved to present site in 1971, now used as library. 1 photocopy of ext. photo (ca. 1890); 8 data pages (1975).

Keeler   □   Inyo County

Main Street—Commercial Buildings (CA-1678). Wood frame with board-and-batten siding, gable roofs with false fronts, plank sidewalks. Built 1860 town named for Julius M. Keeler, Mills College professor, State Assemblyman and founder of Oregon State U., who came to this mining center in 1883. 1 photocopy of late 19th c. photo.

Kelsey   □   El Dorado County

Marshall, James W., Blacksmith Shop (CA-1696). Stuccoed wood frame, one story, three-bay front, rubble-stone chimney. Built 1870 as blacksmith shop by James Marshall, restored as museum in 1921. 1 photocopy of 1926 photo. SHL

Marshall, James W., House (Tom Allen's Saloon) (CA-1308). Wood frame with clapboards, three-bay front in gable end, one story, gable roof, porch across front. Built 1850s or '60s, home of James W. Marshall after 1868; demolished. 1 photocopy of 1926 photo.

Knights Ferry   □   Stanislaus County

Covered Bridge (CA-158). Tullochs Mill, Stanislaus River. Wood with piers and abutments of local stone, X-braced truss, iron tie rods and bolts, locust wood pins intact, 330′ of planking on three piers, board siding, gable roof. Built 1864 by Schuylkill Bridge Co.; toll bridge until 1884; longest covered bridge remaining in the state. 2 ext. photos (1934), 1 photocopy of bridge and Tullochs Mill complex (n.d.).

Dent House (CA-1193). Ellen St. Wood frame with horizontal siding, eight-bay front, L-shaped, one-and-a-half stories, gable roof, boxed cornice with returns, one-story porch in L with box columns and railing. Built ca. 1852 for Lewis Dent and wife Julia, sister of Ulysses S. Grant; the Dents owned the ferry after William Knight died in 1849. 2 ext. photos (1936).

Fire House (CA-161). Wood frame with horizontal siding on front, vertical siding on sides, one-bay front, one story built into hill, gable roof with high false front, square hose tower vented at top with peaked roof. Built second half 19th c.; demolished in flood. 1 ext. photo (1934).

Jail (CA-164). Main St. Wood frame with iron panel sheathing, two-bay front, one story, corrugated metal gable roof; two cells with one iron door to each. Built 1850s. 1 ext. photo (1934).

Miller's House (CA-18). Sonora Hwy. Stone, rough dressed ashlar, 20' (one-bay front) × 30', one story, shingled gable roof with horizontal siding in gable, front porch with wood posts, wood frame additions on one side. Built 1854; wood frame additions. 3 sheets (1934, including plan, elevations, window details); 3 ext. photos (1934).

Schell House (CA-118). Dressed sandstone blocks, three-bay front in gable end, two stories, gable roof with cornice returns, stone frieze with over-scaled dentils, one-story porch with turned posts across front; side-hall plan. Built 1860s on large cattle ranch, attenuated Greek Revival style. 1 ext. photo (1934).

Town of Knights Ferry (CA-169). One- and two-story wood frame buildings in valley of Stanislaus River. Originally a trading center built around the first ferry on the river between Stockton and the southern mines established by William Knight in 1849; placer deposits nearby turned the town into a gold mining center in the 1850s. 1 photo (1937).

Tulloch Mill (CA-137). Stanislaus River.

□ *Mill and Power House.* Rubble stone, two-and-a-half-story mill and one-story power house adjoining, mill 40' × 45', power house 36' × 27', gable roofs with one dormer in mill, frame one-story lean-to on mill. Mill built 1862 for David Tulloch, T. Vinson, master mason; power house built 1904. 7 sheets (1934, including plot plan, plans, elevations, sections, details of whole complex); 7 ext. photos include general views of complex (1934, 1936), 1 photocopy of undated int. photo.

□ *Warehouses.* Brick and stone, one story, attached to corner of mill; brick warehouse

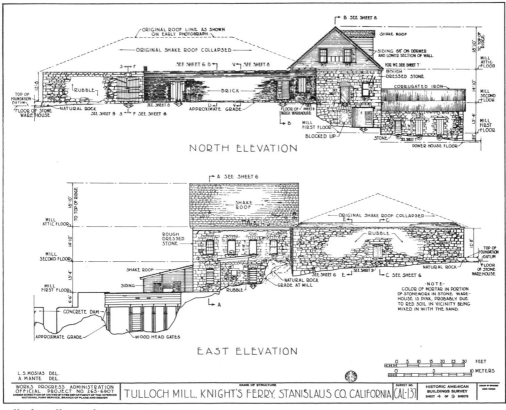

Tulloch Mill, Knights Ferry (CA-137).

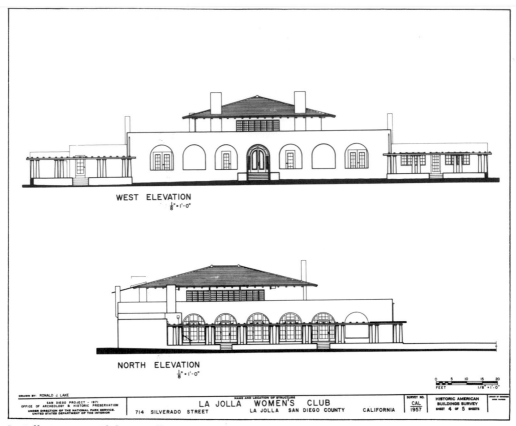

WEST ELEVATION
⅛" = 1'-0"

NORTH ELEVATION
⅛" = 1'-0"

DRAWN BY: RONALD J. LAKE

SAN DIEGO PROJECT - 1971
OFFICE OF ARCHEOLOGY & HISTORIC PRESERVATION
UNDER DIRECTION OF THE NATIONAL PARK SERVICE.
UNITED STATES DEPARTMENT OF THE INTERIOR

714 SILVERADO STREET

NAME AND LOCATION OF STRUCTURE
LA JOLLA   WOMEN'S   CLUB
LA JOLLA   SAN DIEGO COUNTY   CALIFORNIA

SURVEY NO.
CAL
1957

HISTORIC AMERICAN
BUILDINGS SURVEY
SHEET 4 OF 5 SHEETS

La Jolla Women's Club, La Jolla (CA-1957).

Knights Ferry continued
76′ × 74′ shares common wall with stone warehouse 43′ × 74′. Brick warehouse built 1852–58 for Capt. Dent and D. M. Locke; stone warehouse added 1862; now ruinous, roof missing. 2 sheets (1934, details; see also drawings listed above under Mill and Power House); 1 ext. photo (1934), 3 photocopies of int. photos (1934); see also general views listed above under Mill and Power House.

□ *Crib Dam (CA-168).* Apparently horizontal squared logs with stone sluice section to side, approx. 20′ high. Built ca. 1862; demolished. 1 ext. photo (1937).

Kyburz   □   El Dorado County

Kyburz Hotel (CA-1708). Wood frame with channeled siding, two-and-a-half stories, gable roof with cross gable, two-story veranda across front. Built mid 19th c.; destroyed by fire 1956. 1 ext. photo (1934).

La Jolla   □   San Diego County

La Jolla Women's Club (CA-1957). 715 Silverado St. Tilted concrete slab construction, 93′ (seven-bay front) × 86′, one story, flat roof with hip roof in center, pergola extensions both sides, round-arched openings cast into tilt-slab walls. Built 1913, Irving J. Gill, architect; one of an important group of innovative structures designed by Gill which form the community center of La Jolla. 5 sheets (1971, including site plan, plan, elevations, sections); 10 ext. photos (1971), 4 int. photos (1971); 15 data pages (1971).

Bishop's School (CA-1968). 7607 La Jolla Blvd. Grouping of buildings of tilted concrete construction, two stories, corridor-like arcade along first floor, square windows at second floor, a personalized Mission Revival style. Bentham Hall built probably 1912, Irving J. Gill, architect; Gym/Auditorium built 1925, Louis Gill, architect; chapel built 1917, Carleton Winslow, architect. 7 ext. photos (1971), 2 int. photos (1971); 2 data pages (1981).

Pueblo Ribera Courts Apartments (CA-1943).
230-38 Gravilla St. Twelve units grouped to form
patios, each slab-cast concrete, two stories, approx. 36′ × 24′, U-plan around private walled patio, flat roof, board cornice, generous overhang,
concrete roof terrace with fireplace and wood
trellis, wood and glass doors, wood-framed casement windows and fixed sash stacked in vertical
bands. Built 1923, Rudolph M. Schindler, architect, a notable example of this famous Vienna-
born architect's work in innovative construction
and planning for small residential units. 12 ext.
photos (1968); 18 data pages (1969, 1976).

Red Rest and Red Roost (Neptune) Cottages (CA-
1973). *1187 and 1179 Coast Blvd.* Each wood
frame with vertical siding, one-and-a-half stories,
approx. 36′ × 41′, hipped roof with wide eaves,
front porch recessed under roof; interior wood-
paneled, rustic fireplace. Built 1894. 4 photocopies of architectural drawings (no date, including site plan, plans, elevations), 1 photocopy of
1927 photo of beach. NR

Lathrop   □   **San Joaquin County**

Commercial Buildings (CA-1595). *One side of*
Main St. Wood frame, one story, vernacular commercial buildings with false fronts and front
porches. Probably built in third quarter of 19th
c. 1 photocopy of 1928 photo of street scene.

Lebec vicinity   □   **Kern County**

Fort Tejon (CA-39). *Hwy. 99.* Museum. Five
adobe buildings, mostly one story, gable roofs.
Built 1854–57 as headquarters for U.S. Army's
First Dragoons for U.S. Army post established to
protect San Joaquin Valley Indians; post abandoned 1864; restoration in progress since 1947.
1 sheet (1937, plot plan); 2 data pages (1937).
NR

□ *Barracks #1 (CA-39 A).* 2 sheets (1937, including plan, elevations, details of southwest
portion); 3 ext. photos (1937).

□ *Barracks #2 (CA-39 B).* 2 ext. photos (1937).

□ *Officers' Quarters (CA-39 C).* 3 sheets (1937,
including plans, elevations) 3 ext. photos (1937).

□ *Soldiers' Quarters (CA-39 D).* 2 sheets (1937,
including plan, elevations, section, details); 2 ext.
photos (1937).

□ *Smokehouse (CA-39 E).* 1 sheet (1937, including plan, elevations, section); 1 ext. photo
(1937).

Locke   □   **Sacramento County**

Town of Locke (CA-2071). Town of approximately 50 frame structures built for Chinese immigrants between 1915 and 1922. Buildings

Elevation of Main Street, Locke (CA-2071).

Locke continued

generally frame with clapboard and board-and-batten siding, one and two stories, gable roofs with false fronts, one- and two-story porches. 18 sheets (1979, including site plan, elevations, some plans, some sections); 32 data pages of general history (1979), 115 data pages of history and description of 29 individual structures (1979). NR

Lockeford   □   San Joaquin County

Harmony Grove Methodist Church (CA-1614). 1 mi. W of Lockeford on Locke Rd. Brick, approx. 45′ × 31′, three-bay front, one story, gable roof, modified pedimented temple front with four brick pilasters, simplified entablature and dentil course, pointed-arch entrance and side windows. Built 1859–61, one of the extant examples of the fusion of Greek and Gothic Revival styles in California; windows altered to pointed Gothic Revival style at early date; gable roof raised to present height ca. 1915. Said to be oldest church in the Central Valley, site adjacent to old main road from Stockton to Sutter's Fort. 1 photocopy of 1938 photo.

Lodi   □   San Joaquin County

Commercial Buildings (CA-1598). One-story frame commercial buildings with gable roofs, false fronts, and front porches along one side of what was probably main street of Lodi. Probably built during the third quarter of the 19th c. 1 photocopy of ca. 1876 photo of street scene.

Lompoc vicinity   □   Santa Barbara County

Mission La Purísima Concepción (CA-211). Monastery or Residence Building: Adobe with reinforced concrete columns and bond beams, one-and-a-half stories, tiled gable roof extends to cover corredor across front. Founded 1787 as eleventh in chain of 21 missions; after earthquake in 1812 destroyed buildings, mission moved to present site and rebuilt; present buildings date from 1812 to ca. 1830; monastery reconstructed from ruins 1935–37; church reconstructed 1937–41. 1 photo of church ruins (1937), 5 ext. photos of monastery (1937); 2 data pages (1937). NR, SHL

Long Beach   □   Los Angeles County

Casa de los·Cerritos (CA-37-12). 4600 Virginia Rd. Museum. Plastered adobe, 102′ × 172′, five-bay front, U-shape, two stories with one-story wings, tiled gable roof extended over two-story porch around three sides, one-story covered walkway on patio side, high adobe wall on west side, wood posts and railing on upper level; 22 rooms, one room deep. Built 1844 for Don Juan Temple upon a ranch of 27,000 acres; purchased 1866 by Flint, Bixby and Co. who replaced flat tar roof with shakes; renovated 1930 with some alterations by Llewelyn Bixby, a descendent, as his home; purchased by City of Long Beach in 1955 with 4.74 acres. 5 sheets (1934, including plan, elevations, sections, details); 12 ext. photos (1937); 1 data page (1937).

Casa de Rancho los Alamitos (CA-310). 6400 Bixby Hill Rd. Museum. Plastered adobe with wood frame additions, adobe section approx. 60′ × 42′, 4 rooms, two stories, gable roof, vertical plank siding. Built ca. 1834 on land grant of Manuel Nieto, acquired 1842 by Abel Stearns, N. wing added ca. 1845 with board-and-batten siding, property leased to Bixby family 1878 and sold to John W. Bixby in 1881, south wing and other additions including second story over adobe section added between 1878 and 1925, extensive gardens added 1920s, 1930s, now the Rancho Los Alamitos Foundation. 4 sheets (1935, including plans, elevations, detail); 1 data page (1937).

Los Altos   □   Santa Clara County

Christ Episcopal Church (Foothills Congregational Church) (CA-2013). 461 Orange Ave. Heavy timber with stucco, approx. 29′ × 76′, one-and-a-half stories, gable roof with small belfry, pointed-arch openings. Built 1914, Ernest Coxhead, architect; additions in 1926, 1951, 1973, resulted in quadrangle layout. 1 sheet (1978, plan); 5 ext. photos (1980), 5 int. photos (1980); 8 data pages (1979).

Los Altos Hills   □   Santa Clara County

Lynn, Martha, Tank House (CA-2066). 12889 Viscano Pl. Heavy timber with redwood shingles, 17′ square, three stories, hipped roof, third story is cantilevered open belvedere with balustrade, first and second stories have battered walls. Built ca.

Martha Lynn Tank House, Los Altos Hills (CA-2066).

1906. 1 sheet (1979, including plan, elevation, section); 4 ext. photos (1980); 4 data pages (1979).

Los Angeles □ Los Angeles County

Angels Flight (CA-337). SW corner Third and Hill Streets. Two-car funicular or cable railway, trestle built on a 33% grade running from Hill to Clay to Olive Street; Hill Street entry had an arch with metal canopy, Doric columns supporting an entablature with triglyphs, metopes, and cornice molding, below a parapet with ornamental posts flanking a sign inscribed "Angels Flight;" wooden cars named Olivet and Sinai, originally painted white and later black and orange, had seven seats to a side and a rear entry platform; observation tower stood at top of flight. Built 1901 by Col. J. W. Eddy to provide access to Olive Heights, now called Bunker Hill, sold several times and in operation until 1952, demolished by the Community Redevelopment Agency in the late 1960s. 5 ext. photos (1960); 6 data pages (1964).

Apartment Building (CA-2042). 462 South Cochran Avenue and 5515-25 West Sixth Street. Frame covered with stucco with reinforced concrete foundation, irregularly shaped, 54' × 72', two stories, flat roof, wooden floored decks with stuccoed parapets and pipe rails; eight apartments around L-shaped court with entrances.

Built 1938, Milton J. Black, architect. 1 ext. photo (ca. 1975).

Barnsdall, Aline, House. See Hollyhock House (CA-356).

Bolton Hall (CA-340). 10110 Commerce Ave., Tujunga. Wood frame, veneer of stone boulders, approx. 33' × 77' with 14' × 12' jail at east end, 11' × 50' concrete porch at south side, three-bay front, tiled gable roof originally shingled supported by scissor trusses, stone boulder chimney, hip-roofed square tower at north corner open on upper level, main entrance recessed in porch at base, ground floor has two large segmental-arched windows with a stone boulder mullion, upper floor has tripartite window in triangular form; L-plan with lobby preceding main assembly room with massive boulder fireplace 16' wide, offices in southwest corner, rear wing has two-cell jail. Built 1913 as a clubhouse for the "Little Landers," owners of small plots of land in the subdivision, designed by George Harris, craftsman designer of furniture; named after George Bolton, author, reformer, and philosopher; passed through several ownerships and served as Tujunga City Hall, 1928–32; restored. 4 ext. photos (1960); 6 data pages (1963).

Bradbury Building (CA-334). 304 South Broadway. Steel frame, brick and stone, 125' (seven-bay front) × 188', five stories, flat roof with hipped skylight of iron webbing and glass, end bays project slightly, piers express the central bay division, openings in rhythms of three and two with flat-arched windows for middle three stories, paired round-arched openings with running archivolt trim on fifth floor, chamfered corner bay; court plan, glazed skylights, office spaces around open balconies on court, court walls sheathed in warm tones of brick and marble, ornamental relief frieze in terra cotta at top, office wainscoting and balcony ceilings oak-paneled, cast-iron stairway at each end of building extends out into the court, stairway and balcony balustrades have foliated cast-iron arabesques, open cage elevators with ornate ironwork screens serve north and south sides of court. Built 1893 for Louis Bradbury, George H. Wyman, architect; inspiration for the skylit court from Edward Bellamy's *Looking Backward* in which a utopian office building of the year 2000 was depicted as being ". . . a vast hall full of light . . ." 12 sheets (1968, including plans, elevations, section, isometric of central court, railing details); 4 ext. photos (1960, 1971), 10 int. photos (1960, 1971); 7 data pages (1963). NR

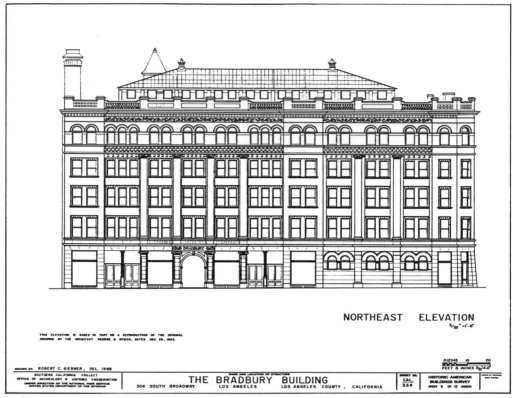

Bradbury Building, Los Angeles (CA-334).

Broadway Department Store. See Coulter's Department Store (CA-2023).

Bullocks-Wilshire Department Store (CA-1941). *3050 Wilshire Blvd.* Brick and terra-cotta over steel frame and concrete, 291′ (thirteen-bay front) by seven bays, two-, three-, and five-story sections, 241′ tower, flat parapeted roof, buff-colored walls rise from a black marble base, expressed piers, copper spandrel panels with relief ornament of concentric eight-pointed figures, chevron motif on top edges of piers, tower steps back in three stages, piers terminate in pyramidal copper finials, top stage of tower sheathed in patterned copper with metal screened openings, pyramidal top, plate-glass show windows on ground floor have projecting black metal canopies, main entrance in tower bay has large, square-headed opening and a recessed doorway, doors are metal and glass with metal grills in a fan pattern; irregular plan with major and minor sales spaces, elevator lobby on west side, interior rich in materials and detail, many artists represented. Built 1928–29, John and Donald Parkinson, architects, fine example of the set-back or stepped form applied to a luxury department store. 1 sheet (1969, elevation, detail); 7 data pages (1969). NR

Bunker Hill District (CA-344). *Temple, Hill, Fifth, and Figueroa Streets.* A residential district on the edge of downtown Los Angeles built up in the late 19th c. first with private homes and later with apartment buildings and hotels; houses were typically wood frame with irregular massing, multiple-gable and hip roofs, and featured cupolas, towers, porches, balconies, and an abundance of decorative detail in porch tracery, panels, cut shingles, art glass and interior decorative detail in plaster ceiling embellishments and woodwork. Following the major building period in the 1880s and '90s the area began to decline and became an urban renewal area in the 1950s, systematically razed in the 1960s and regraded by the L.A. Community Redevelopment Agency. 1 ext. photo (1960); 8 data pages (1963). See also entries listed as Houses on South Bunker Hill Ave.

Carl's Market. See Union Market (CA-2021).

Casa Ávila (CA-37-2). *14 Olvera Street.* Adobe, approx. 36′ × 79′, one story, gable roof extending over front porch with square wood posts, wood railing, shed roof over back rooms, variety of wood-framed windows and doors. Built ca. 1818 by Don Francisco, mayor of the Los Angeles Pueblo, now the oldest house in the city, originally flat-roofed and nearly twice its present length, restored 1930. 3 sheets (1934, including plans, elevations, section, details); 2 ext. photos (1934); 1 data page (1936). SHL

Casa de Vicente Lugo (CA-319). 516-22½ North Los Angeles St. Brick and wood, approx. 68′ (four-bay front) × 62′, two-and-a-half stories, high-pitched hip roof with gable dormers, variety of wood-framed windows and doors, second floor overhangs first and has central three-bay balustraded balcony. Built ca. 1840 by Don Vicente Lugo who gave it to St. Vincent's College (now Loyola) in 1856; original adobe house of two stories had a flat roof and balcony running across the second story; after many alterations structure served as Chinese rooming house with shops; demolished. 1 sheet (1934, including plans, elevation, detail); 1 ext. photo (1936); 1 data page (1937).

Casa Pelanconi (CA-37-3). 33-35 Olvera St. Brick, approx. 38′ (four-bay front) × 33′, two stories, shingled hip roof, corbeled brick cornice, front porch with wood railing on upper story, openings have flat arches, segmental-arched entrance with wood doors, ground-floor windows barred, upper floor has six-light french doors with wood paneled aprons. Built 1855 by Giuseppe Covacichi as a bodega with living quarters upstairs; one of the earliest brick houses in Los Angeles; remodeled into a cafe in 1929. 5 sheets (1934, including plans, elevations, section, details); 2 ext. photos (1934); 1 data page (1936).

Casa Ricardo Vejar (CA-37-10). Diamond Bar Ranch, Valley Blvd. (Originally recorded as being in town of Spadra). Adobe, stone foundations, 51′ (four-bay front) × 18′, two stories, gable roof extended over two-story veranda on three sides of house, chamfered wood posts, railings in X-braced form, exterior stair to second floor, access to all rooms from outside, one-story wing extends from rear; no hall, three rooms. Built 1850 for Ricardo Vejar. 3 sheets (1934, including plans, elevations, section, details); 2 ext. photos (1934); 1 data page (1936).

Cathedral of San Vibiana (CA-343). Second and Main Streets. Brick, limestone, and concrete, 82′ (three-bay front) × 202′, 62′ high, gable-roofed nave double the height of side aisles, tripartite division expressed on limestone-faced facade by paired pilasters at nave-aisles division, horizontal division expressed by a belt cornice, upper pilas-

ters support returns of broken-base pediment, entrance portico architrave has fluted Doric columns on bases supporting entablature with broken-base pediment, aisle doors have segmental pediments on consoles, arched niches with statues above aisle doors and flanking central rose window arch on upper part of nave, narthex section raised above main part of nave, three-tiered squared belfry at east end, side elevations with segmental arches, hoodmolds and label stops, brick buttresses, projecting cornice; interior has three-centered arches supported on wooden Corinthian columns, chancel with communion rail, raised altar. Built 1871–75, Ezra F. Kysor, architect with W. J. Mathews, design freely derived from the church of the Puerto de San Miguel in Barcelona, fresco work by Alex Zins; extensively altered 1922 by John C. Austin, architect, west front extended 24′ to sidewalk and redesigned in limestone; one of the most imposing early buildings in southern California and until 1880s the largest church in Los Angeles. 1 ext. photo (1960), 3 photocopies of ext. photos (ca. 1880, ca. 1885, ca. 1888); 11 data pages (1963).

Coca-Cola Bottling Company (CA-2022). 1334 S. Central Ave. Reinforced concrete, rectangular with rounded corners, 150′ × 200′, two stories with rear four-story section, flat roof with parapet, tower with an open ship bridge, round-arched doorways, porthole windows; corporate office and bottling factory, nautical trimmings; designed to resemble oceanliner. Built by remodeling several existing brick buildings 1936–37, Robert V. Derrah, architect; interior remodeled 1976. 2 ext. photos (ca. 1975).

Coulter's Department Store (Broadway Department Store) (CA-2023). 5600 Wilshire Blvd. Textured reinforced concrete, trapezoidal shape, 146′ × 176′, five stories with basement and mezzanine, flat roof with parapet, rounded picture windows at street level, large areas of glass brick bands at upper levels, main entrance in rear accessible to parking lot; open merchandising spaces punctuated by columns and service areas along perimeter, horizontal cabinets with rounded corners; good example of streamlined commercial building. Built 1937, Stiles O. Clements, architect. 2 ext. photos (ca. 1975).

The Dark Room (CA-2024). 5370 Wilshire Blvd. Reinforced concrete storefront with carrara glass sheathing, 19′ front with projecting bay shaped like a camera, one story, glass brick around entrance, metal bandings; retail area, office and storage. Built 1935, Marcus Miller, architect. 1 ext. photo (ca. 1975).

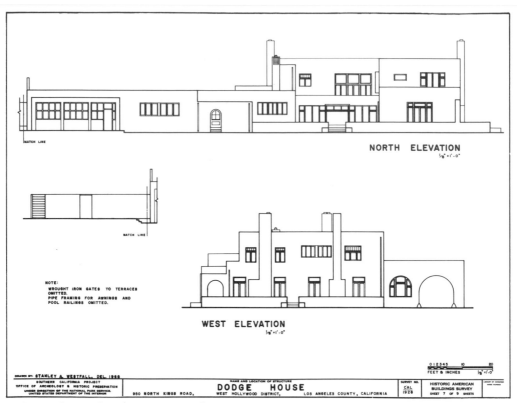

Walter Luther Dodge House, Los Angeles (CA-355).

Dodge, Walter Luther, House (CA-355). *950 North Kings Road.* Reinforced concrete, main two-story block approx. 60' × 60', U-shaped, one-story service wing 24' × 82', four-bay front, flat parapeted roof, no cornice, raised concrete terrace on west and south sides opening into a patio centered in south side, open court in southeast corner, small second-story porches off bedrooms. French doors to porches and terraces, other doors are wood or wood sheathed with sheet metal, casement or fixed-glass windows in wood frames, mullions of thin sheet metal; interior has round-arched entrances to ground-floor rooms, mahogany stair, architect-designed cabinet work, library fireplace tiles, window and door latches. Built 1914–16 for Walter Luther Dodge, retired patent medicine manufacturer, Irving J. Gill, architect; one of the most significant works of this famous and influential architect; demolished 1970. 9 sheets (1968, including aerial isometric, site plan; plans, elevations, sections, stair hall elevations); 22 ext. photos (1965, 1968), 7 int. photos (1965); 9 data pages (1965).

Dominguez-Wilshire Building. See Hiss Tower (CA-2027).

Walter Luther Dodge House, interior detail, Los Angeles (CA-355).

Los Angeles continued

Drum Barracks, Officers' Quarters (CA-353).
1053-55 Cary Ave. (Originally recorded as being in Wilmington). Museum. Wood frame on brick foundations, approx. 60' (six-bay front) × 81', two stories, shingled hip roof, walls sheathed in clapboards with drip boards at base of siding, corner boards, entablature with architrave trim, frieze panels, double-scrolled brackets under wide overhang, molded cornice, 11' × 24' front porch with turned balustrade, posts with open-work bracketed caps, bracketed cornice, surmounted by balustrade with corner posts and ball finials, two brick chimneys, two sets of double front doors on each floor with sidelights and transoms, rear doors have paneled aprons and glazed upper panels, all openings have flat triangular lintels; central-hall plan with rear wings enclosing court, first-floor living rooms have fireplaces, middle rooms were for dining, service rooms in rear wings, second floor had rooms for single officers. Built 1862 as quarters for officers on the Wilmington Federal Army post for the Southwest, mainly a supply post but also the southwest terminus for telegraph line from the east; troops withdrawn in 1868, quarters only remainder of post which had twenty-two structures; a fine and rare example of a transitional design between late Federal and Italianate styles in excellent condition; materials were pre-cut and shipped around the Horn. 10 ext. photos (1965), 2 int. photos (1965); 11 data pages including sketch plans of Barracks and this building (1965). SHL

Eastern Outfitting Company (CA-2025). *849-51 S. Broadway.* Reinforced concrete with brick infill, turquoise terra cotta walls with gold and blue terra cotta ornament, 165' × 115', thirteen stories, flat concrete and composition roof with parapet, top tier faced on all sides with an open terra cotta grille and large clock and the building name, terrazzo public sidewalk in chevron patterns; best extant local example of ziggurat skyscraper clad in polychrome terra cotta. Built 1930, Claude Beelman, architect. 2 ext. photos (ca. 1975).

El Alisal (Charles Lummis House) (CA-339). *200 E. Avenue 43.* Museum. Stone boulders, concrete, and wood, approx. 91' × 60' with 50' × 7' north porch, two-story central section off south side has main entrance with hipped roof, two flanking gable-roofed wings, 30' circular tower off southwest corner, another gable-roofed section north of the tower has a 24' campanile with latticed tile top and scroll-topped *espadaña*, bell in place, handcrafted openings in a variety of sizes and designs; L-plan of eight rooms with patio, cement floors, handmade furniture, several fireplaces, mission-type kitchen with open hearth and ceiling tapering upward to a vent. Built 1896–1910 and left unfinished. Charles F. Lummis, designer, built El Alisal as a home/office/museum combining both castle and mission features, using water-worn boulders from the Arroyo Seco, and wood telephone poles from the Santa Fe Railroad; Lummis had illustrious and varied career as editor of the *Los Angeles Times,* "Land of Sunshine," and "Out West" magazines, and general publicist and preserver of Hispanic-American culture in California and the Southwest. 5 ext. photos (1960); 13 data pages (1964). NR, SHL

El Escorpión Rancho, Adobe Barn (CA-326). *(Originally recorded as being in Owensmouth).* Adobe and wood frame, stone foundations, approx. 32' × 57', two stories with one-story lean-to sheds, shingled hip roof, shed-roofed porch with wood posts on front. Built ca. 1840 on property once owned by San Fernando Mission. 4 sheets (1935, including plan, elevations, details); 3 ext. photos (1936); 1 data page (1937).

Ennis House (CA-1942). *2607 Glendower Ave.* Concrete "textile" blocks, reinforced, two stories, flat parapeted roofs, walls have bands of "textile" blocks defining edges of planes and used as surface pattern on some wall sections, detached garage and servant quarters connected to main house by a bridge, garden terrace with swimming pool along north side, court on west side, several terraces on upper and lower levels, main entrance north side through metal auto gates with Mayanesque motifs, dining and living rooms have large leaded glass openings, also casement windows in teak frames; informal plan, main rooms reached from gallery along large north terrace, beamed teakwood ceilings, teak and marble floors, mosaic fireplace in hall opposite living room, bronze relief on dining room fireplace. Built 1924, Frank Lloyd Wright, architect, largest and most monumental of Wright's "textile" block houses reflecting the influence of Mayan architecture in form and detail. 1 sheet (1969, including elevation and detail); 7 data pages (1969). NR

First Masonic Temple. See Masonic Temple (CA-32).

Freeman, Samuel, House (CA-1935). *1962 Glencoe Way.* Textured concrete block reinforced with steel rods, two-story hillside plan, flat roof,

Los Angeles continued

sometimes with parapet and sometimes with eaves, terraces on both levels, entrance loggia joins detached garage at upper level, typical windows are casement set in concrete block, southeast and southwest corners have stacked vertical glazed bands, "textile" blocks, some pierced to admit light, define edges of wall planes; L-plan with living room and kitchen on street or main level, bedrooms on ground level, walls of exposed block, some "textile," custom lighting fixtures and interior furnishings. Built 1924, Frank Lloyd Wright, architect, assisted by Lloyd Wright; interior alterations 1932, 1940, by Rudolph M. Schindler. 7 sheets (1969, including aerial isometric, plans, elevations, section, detail); 7 photocopies of architect's drawings (1924, including plans, elevations, sections, details); 4 data pages (1969). NR

Garnier Block (CA-321). 415 North Los Angeles St. Brick, 100' (four-bay front) × 80', two stories, flat roof, bays divided by two-story red sandstone pilasters, ground floor has square cast-iron columns and lintels, second floor cast-iron balcony, brick corbeled parapet and cornice with studded brick frieze panel, red sandstone pediment with scroll supports projects above parapet at entrance bay, relief letters at apex say "1890" and "P. Garnier," adjacent posts had torches on top, main entrance has segmental pediment of red sandstone with incised floral motifs over sandstone brackets and pilasters, each bay has three narrow, rectangular windows in redwood casings with sandstone lintels; central-hall plan, mezzanine promenade, skylit ceiling, office/shop units flank halls. Built as rental space for the Philippe Garnier family in 1890; Garnier was one of the organizers of the Farmers and Merchants Bank of Los Angeles, but returned to France in 1891; south end of the building was cut by Santa Ana freeway construction in 1949, the remaining part now restored as part of El Pueblo de Los Angeles State Historic Monument and Park. 1 ext. photo (1960); 6 data pages (1963).

Health House. See Lovell House (CA-1936).

Hiss Tower (Dominguez-Wilshire Building) (CA-2027). 5400-20 Wilshire Blvd. Concrete with cement finish, ten-story tower flanked by two-story wings, 252' × 107', flat roof with parapet, elaborate zigzag and angular motifs; original Moderne style elevator doors. Built 1930, Morgan, Walls & Clements, architects; retail area enlarged 1931. 1 ext. photo (ca. 1975).

Hollyhock House (Aline Barnsdall House) (CA-356). 4800 Hollywood Blvd. City park and museum. Hollow clay tile, stuccoed and plastered, concrete footings and water table, approx. 121' × 99', one and two stories, flat parapeted roof with hollyhock finials, walls battered above projecting concrete belt cornice surmounted by a frieze of stylized hollyhock motifs, roofed entrance gallery extends 68' from auto court to vestibule on north side, semicircular walled terraces on south and east sides, three walled terraces on west side, square reflecting pool, small porch overlooking reflecting pool on east side, second-floor balcony off main bedroom, wood-framed french doors, casement windows, leaded glass in geometric patterns, banded clerestory windows; complex irregular rectangle with inner court, principal space is 44' × 24' high-ceilinged living room on west side, oak wainscoting, moldings, doors, massive concrete living room fireplace with abstract geometric bas-relief and skylight with wood grill above, wealth of built-in cabinet work, unusual lighting fixtures, and other detail. Built 1917–20 for Aline Barnsdall as part of a planned municipal art center and park of originally 36 acres, Frank Lloyd Wright, architect, assisted by Rudolph M. Schindler and Lloyd Wright; buildings reflect influence of Mayan architecture in massing; property deeded to the city in 1926, used by the California Art Club and for official functions; following a long period of neglect the main house was restored in the mid-1970s. 5 sheets of Barnsdall Park (1969, including plot plans, aerial isometric, lamp details); 9 ext. photos (1965), 4 int. photos (1965); 13 data pages (1965). See also residence "A" (CA-357). NR

House (CA-350). 523 East 3rd St. Wood frame, clapboards, approx. 28' × 42', three-bay front, two stories, multiple gable and hip roofs, decorative barge board with pendant and finials, second-floor overhang on paired knee braces, glazed front porch. Built 1893; demolished. 1 ext. photo (1960); 2 data pages (1963).

House (CA-348). 221 South Bunker Hill Ave. Wood frame with clapboards, approx. 42' × 78', four-bay front, one-and-a-half stories on raised basement, hipped roof with symmetrical gabled dormers, front porch with pierced decorative braces, two rear porches; irregular plan, twenty rooms. Built 1895; demolished. 1 ext. photo (1960); 2 data pages (1963).

House (CA-347). 231-41 South Bunker Hill Ave. Wood frame with channeled rustic siding, approx. 38′ × 59′, three-bay front, one-and-a-half stories in front, three in rear, cross gable and hip roof, bracketed cornice, large porch, chamfered box columns with fan braces, enclosed rear porches, hooded bay window; irregular plan. Duplex built 1890; demolished. 1 ext. photo (1960); 2 data pages (1963).

House (CA-352). 238 South Bunker Hill Ave. Wood frame with channeled rustic siding, approx. 41′ × 40′, five-bay front, two stories with three-story tower, gable and hip roofs, bracketed cornice, square tower with bracketed mansard roof and dormers, second-story balcony and elaborate jigsawn balustrade, porch and turned columns and spindlework. Built 1895 for Judge Julius Brousseau; demolished. 1 ext. photo (1960); 2 data pages (1963).

House (CA-351). 251 South Bunker Hill Ave. Wood frame with channeled rustic siding, approx. 24′ × 54′, one-and-a-half stories, cross gable roofs, bell-cast dome on corner turret, porch with turned columns and spindlework. Built 1890; demolished. 1 ext .photo (1960); 2 data pages (1963).

House (CA-349). 245 South Grand Avenue. Wood frame with channeled rustic siding, approx. 38′ × 58′, three-bay front, two stories, hipped roof with cross gables, fish scale shingles in gables, entrance portico with turned columns surmounted by balcony between two two-story polygonal bays; central hall plan. Built 1895; demolished. 1 ext. photo (1960); 2 data pages (1963).

House (CA-346). 221 South Olive St. Wood frame with clapboard siding, approx. 40′ × 84′, three-bay front, one-and-a-half stories on raised basement, hipped roof with gable dormers, front porch with turned columns, spindle work and pierced wood ornament in angles above porch arches; irregular plan. Built 1890; demolished. 1 ext. photo (1960); 2 data pages (1963).

House (CA-345). 605 West 3rd St. Wood frame with channeled rustic siding, 24′ × 26′, three-bay front, two stories, hipped rood, bracketed cornice, porch with turned posts. Built ca. 1875; demolished. 1 ext. photo (1960); 2 data pages (1963).

Kehe Radio Studios (CA-2028). 133-41 N. Vermont Ave Brick reinforced horizontally and vertically with steel, 100′ × 156′, one story, flat roof with parapet, cornice articulated by three projecting bands, central pylon tower displaying station's call letters, ribbon windows; public vestibule and rotunda flanked by offices and broadcasting studios, stuccoed cement walls and ceiling, elaborate Moderne motifs on rotunda walls; good example of small-scaled Streamline Moderne style. Built 1936, Morgan, Walls & Clements, architects. 1 ext. photo (ca. 1975).

Leimert Park Theater (CA-2029). 3341 W. 43rd Pl. Stuccoed concrete, irregular trapezoid, 95′ × 236′, two stories, flat and hip roofs with parapet, central polygonal tower topped by square cagework metal spire, projecting marquee over entrance; wall murals in auditorium by André Durencea, derived from Cubist influence, interior hardware in zigzag motifs. Built 1931, Morgan, Walls & Clements, architects. 1 ext. photo (ca. 1975).

Los Angeles Public Library (CA-1937). 630 West 5th St. Stuccoed, reinforced concrete, stone trim, irregular rectangle, approx. 239′ × 212′, three stories, flat parapeted roof, set-back tower capped with pyramidal roof sheathed in a mosaic pattern of gold suns against blue background with green and white detail, second stage of tower has massive corner piers flanking vertical strip windows, five-bay projecting central section flanked by six-bay sections, monumental round-arched entrances on two elevations, metal sash windows, generous amount of relief sculpture and inscriptions; cross-axial plan with corridors leading to central lobby, rotunda passes through second floor of building which has the main reading rooms in the perimeter, third floor administration, rotunda has painted geometric stencil work on ceiling and murals, history reading room also has murals by Albert Herter depicting California history. Built 1924, Bertram Goodhue, architect, Carleton M. Winslow, supervising architect, an outstanding building in an Hispanic/Modernist mode by a nationally prominent architect. 5 sheets (1969, including plans, elevations); 11 ext. photos (1971), 3 int. photos (1971); 6 data pages (1969).

Lovell House (Health House) (CA-1936). 4616 Dundee Dr. Steel frame sprayed with dense concrete painted white, approx. 78′ (fifteen-bay front) × 42′ (eight bays), three stories, flat roof with parapet, upper-level entrance terrace with patio below, sleeping porch on upper level, large swimming pool and terrace on lowest level, glass-paneled doors to outside levels with side casements; rectangular plan with bedrooms and living room on upper floor, main level one clear space with small library at one end, two-story glazed stair hall, built-in couches, shelves, and

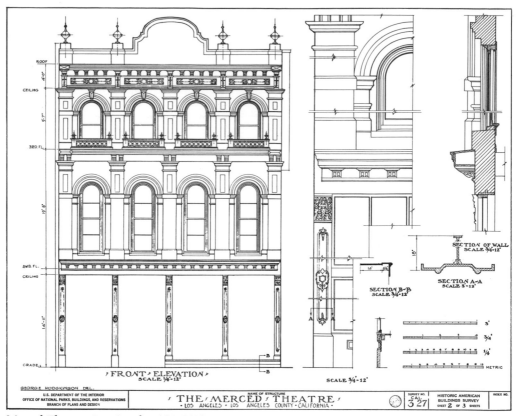

Merced Theatre, Los Angeles (CA-327).

cabinets, two-level garage studio on southeast corner of property follows modular plan of house. Built 1928–29 for Dr. Phillip Lovell, a naturopath and writer on health, Richard J. Neutra, architect; this house is a highly significant example of the European International style in this country by an architect who was a leading figure of the Modern Movement. 9 sheets (1969, including aerial isometric, plans, elevations, sections); 6 data pages (1969). NR

Lummis, Charles, House. See El Alisal (CA-339).

Masonic Temple #42 F. & A. M. (First Masonic Temple) (CA-32). 416½ North Main St. Plastered brick, approx. 24' (three-bay front) × 74', two stories, parapeted flat roof, full entablature with blank frieze panels and paired brackets, elaborate cast-iron balcony railing across arched, glazed french doors at second-floor level, three first-floor openings have segmental arches and transoms. Built 1858 as the first lodge building in southern California and the only one until 1869, now restored as part of El Pueblo de Los Angeles

State Historic Park. 1 sheet (1934, including plans, elevation, section, detail); 1 ext. photo (1934); 1 data page (1936).

May Company Department Store (CA-2031). 6067 Wilshire Blvd. Steel frame, lower story sheathed in black granite, upper walls facing principal streets covered with Texas limestone, 240' × 146', five stories, flat roof with low parapet, tiled balcony extends from roof-top restaurant, round entrance pavilion covered with gold mosaics and punctuated by evenly spaced horizontal bands, flat cantilevered canopy over sidewalk. Built 1939–40, Albert Martin and Assoc., architects. 1 ext. photo (ca. 1975).

Medical Square (CA-2032). 2200 W. 3rd St. Brick over frame, complex of five one-story buildings, each 50' × 100', flat roofs with parapets and projecting secondary roofs, main doorway fronted by four convex fluted shafts; Streamline Moderne details with Spanish Colonial Revival influences. Built 1937, Arthur Heineman, architect. 4 ext. photos (ca. 1975).

Los Angeles continued

Merced Theatre (CA-327). *420-22 North Main St.* Plastered brick, steel girders, approx. 36′ (four-bay front) × 96′, three stories, flat roof with parapet, entablature has ornamented frieze panels, brackets and modillions under molded wood cornice, bay division expressed on upper floors by paneled pilasters, molded belt cornices with consoles mark floor divisions, third-floor windows have ornamental balconies, ground-floor bay divisions marked by paneled cast-iron columns with bosses and modified Classical caps, upper floors have round-arched windows; irregular rectangular plan, auditorium second floor. Built 1869–70 by William Abbot, attrib. to Ezra F. Kysor, architect; first permanent theater in Los Angeles; subsequently altered on the interior and ground-floor exterior for other uses; now restored as part of El Pueblo de Los Angeles State Historic Monument and Park. 3 sheets (1934, including plans, elevations, details); 1 ext. photo (1936); 1 data page (1937). SHL

Merle Norman Building (CA-2043). *2525 Main St.* Painted stucco over frame, 109′ × 96′, two stories, flat roof with one-story parapet, round tower and curved window at corner of parapet, metal three-band streamlining on street-level cornice and entrance, cast stucco Art Deco ornamentation over windows. Built by remodeling existing structure 1935, George Parr, architect; section added 1936. 2 ext. photos (ca. 1975).

Pan Pacific Auditorium (CA-2033). *7600 Beverly Blvd.* Stuccoed wood and steel frame, 368′ × 231′, one story, flat and slightly curved roof, four streamline pylons dominate front elevation, deep cantilevered canopy over main entrance; interior lobby and auditorium, painted stuccoed cement walls and ceiling. Built 1935, Wurdeman and Becket, architects. 5 ext. photos (ca. 1975).

Pico Hotel (CA-317). *430 North Main St.* Plastered brick, U-shaped, 117′ (thirteen-bay front) × 84′ (ten bays), three stories, flat parapeted roof with corner posts and false curved gables inscribed "Old Pico House," full entablature with paired brackets, blank frieze panels and molded cornice with modillions, ground-floor arcade has piers with bases and molded caps supporting round arches, second floor has segmental-arched window heads, third floor round-arched, central bay on upper floors has paired windows; open U-plan with two courts divided by a wall, ground floor commercial space with lobby and stair hall centered on west side, rooms on upper floors. Built 1869 for Don Pío Pico, last Mexican gover-

nor of California, Ezra F. Kysor, architect, Cris Stoffenback of Anaheim, builder; city's first three-story masonry business and hotel block, restored 1976 as part of El Pueblo de Los Angeles Historic Park. 8 sheets (1934, including plans, elevations, details); 1 ext. photo (1936); 1 data page (1937). SHL

Plaza Church (CA-37-1). *535 North Main St.* Adobe and brick, 58′ (three-bay front) × 110′ (five bays), approx. 35′ high, one story, gable roof, one-bay campanario on south side with round window, pierced belfry, three bells, squeezed segmental pediment, facade has three two-stage buttresses with pyramidal caps, two-part elevation with molded belt course and cornice, gable end of church has raking cornice and round window, ornamental iron cross on a molded base caps the ridge, entrance with pronounced archivolt on plain pilasters with reduced caps, wood-paneled doors; central nave and side aisles divided by piers, wood-beamed ceiling, sanctuary with high altar raised three steps, curved altar railing, altars in side aisles. Present church built 1818–22 as the pueblo church largely by Indian labor under the direction of the priests; timber roof framing may have been planned by Joseph Chapman, a Yankee shipbuilder; in 1861 the fallen adobe front was replaced by one of brick; church was renovated and repaired in 1875, 1912, and 1923. 16 sheets (1934, including plans, elevations, sections, details); 2 ext. photos (1934); 2 data pages (1936).

Plaza Firehouse (CA-338). *126 Plaza St.* Museum. Brick, approx. 38′ (three-bay front) × 60′, two stories, flat roof with parapet, brickwork cornice of corbeled arches, wood witch's cap cupola overhanging front, supported on wood brackets, wood shed-roofed balcony on center of second floor, ground-floor vehicular entrance, doors and windows have segmental heads; rectangular plan with engine room on main floor, mezzanine level at rear had hayloft over horses' stalls. Built 1884 as the second firehouse in the city for Volunteer 38's Engine Co. #1, W. A. Boring, architect; in 1897 ceased to be a firehouse; in 1950 acquired by the state and restored as part of El Pueblo de Los Angeles State Historic Monument and Park. 1 ext. photo (1960), 2 int. photos (1960), 3 photocopies of ext. photos (1887, 1894, 1920); 8 data pages (1963). SHL

Rancho La Brea (CA-354). *6301 West 3rd St.* Plastered adobe, approx. 61′ (four-bay front) × 62′, one story, U-shape, original shake gable roof

Los Angeles continued

now tiled, front porch with pitched roof, bracketed wood posts, wood-framed casement windows. Built ca. 1828 by Antonio José Rocha, a Portuguese gun- and blacksmith and prominent early citizen of Los Angeles Pueblo; one of the earliest houses and center of a rancho of 44,000 acres, most of which is now Hollywood with southern border at Wilshire Blvd., site of famous brea (tar) pits and source of roof material for the pueblo; acquired 1883 by Arthur Gilmore who stuck oil here, birthplace of Earl Gilmore, philanthropist and oil industrialist house; little altered except for the addition of two rear wings in 19th c., interior altered. 7 ext. photos (1965); 14 data pages, including sketch plan (1965).

Rees and Wirshing Building (CA-318). 223-27 North Los Angeles St. Plastered brick, rectangular, ten-bay front, flat roof with parapet, brick corbeled cornice, quoins, ground-floor bays divided by cast-iron pilasters, four outer bays have segmental arches, two central bays have flat heads under French doors that indicate former second-floor balcony, second story has alternating triangular and segmental pediments on corbels, third story windows have round-arched architraves with rusticated quoins, ground floor has bi-folding wood-paneled doors. Built 1890 for Rees & Wirshing, purveyors of agricultural implements and wagons, C. U. Kubach, architect; demolished 1962 after a fire. 1 ext. photo (1960); 5 data pages (1964).

Residence "A", Barnsdall Park (CA-357). 4800 Hollywood Blvd. Stuccoed concrete blocks, approx. 67' × 45', two stories, flat roof with broad overhangs, ornamental cast concrete block with hollyhock frieze band under eaves of south wing, around openings, and on tops and ends of auxiliary walls of garden and terrace levels, cantilevered wood balcony on north side, main entrance from west terrace through pair of wood-framed doors with sidelights, French doors on north side from living room to balcony, banded windows with wood sash, glazed clerestory band, and vertical glazed bands on east side; entrance from west terrace leads to low hall, main space is high-ceilinged living room, dining on second floor overlooking living room. Built 1920, Frank Lloyd Wright, architect, construction supervised by Rudolph M. Schindler assisted by Lloyd Wright, for Aline Barnsdall as one of two studio residences in the arts center complex that was the first work of Frank Lloyd Wright in Los Angeles; Residence "A" strongly reflects the Prairie style of Wright's Midwest practice. See Hollyhock House (CA-356) for more information and drawings of site. 6 ext. photos (1965); 9 data pages, including floor plans (1965).

Richfield Oil Building (CA-1933). 555 S. Flower St. Concrete and terra cotta over steel frame, approx. 119' (eight-bay front) × 120', twelve stories, set-back tower 526' high, flat parapeted roof, main elevations have vertical emphasis with piers clad in black terra cotta, recessed spandrels of polished glass against sheet metal, spandrels above eleventh-story windows have pairs of figures facing secondary columns that rise through the upper-story windows and become pedestals for 9' terra cotta figures that project above parapet, tower has a similar decorative treatment with geometric forms and a band of chevrons near the top of the second stage, main east entrance has an elaborate gold terra-cotta architrave with a segmental arch framed by piers and surmounted by four niches which have figures symbolizing Aviation, Postal Service, Industry, and Navigation, crown-like pediment enriched with a variety of geometric ornament, west elevation open to the eleventh floor where segmental arch carries upper floors as a bridge, chevrons, sunbursts, and voluted forms characteristic of Art Deco style; open court plan, elevator lobby off east entrance enriched with bronze, etched stone, marble and glass, decorative detail derived from Art Deco vocabulary of forms: chevrons, sunbursts, volutes. Built 1928–30 for the Richfield Oil Co., Morgan, Walls & Clements, architects, this outstanding example of the set-back skyscraper with Art Deco styling reflected the national trends of the 1920s and specifically the American Radiator Building in New York, 1928, by Raymond Hood; demolished 1968–69. 17 sheets (1969, including aerial isometric, plans, elevations, details); 19 ext. photos (1968), 16 photos of ext. details (1968), 23 int. photos (1968), 10 photocopies of architect's drawings (1928, including plans, elevations, sections, details); 7 data pages (1969).

Rocha, Antonio José, House (CA-311). Cadillac and Shenandoah Sts. Adobe, approx. 35' × 32', three-bay front, one-and-a-half stories, shingled gable roof, shed-roofed porch on four sides enclosing frame kitchen in southeast corner, shiplap siding above porch roof; three rooms with rear interior stair. Built ca. 1872 for José Rocha on the Rancho Rincón de los Bueyes; demolished 1979. 3 sheets (1934, including plans, elevations, section, details); 2 photocopies of 1937 ext. photos; 1 data page (1937).

Sawtelle Veterans' Administration Center. Wilshire and Sawtelle Blvds. The Pacific Branch, National Home for Disabled Volunteers, established 1888 for Civil War veterans on donated ranchland; the most extensive and representative complex of Shingle-style buildings in Los Angeles area, reminiscent of contemporary resort architecture; complex included five domiciliaries, a dining hall, hospital, headquarters building, staff residences, library, street car depot, chapels, and architects' office; only the last three named buildings remain.

□ *Chapels (Catholic-Protestant) (CA-335)*. Back-to-back chapels with cross gables and square towers, wood frame with variety of wood cut shingles and drop siding, 40' and 60' fronts, 126' deep, two different entrance facades with broad gable ends, multiple-gable roof originally shingled, three square towers of varying heights with pyramidal roofs, iron finials and crosses, cornice with bargeboards supported by over-scaled solid, sawn-wood brackets; interiors have proscenium arches with decorative plaster archivolt and painted cornice frieze. Built 1900, J. Lee Burton, architect; interior of Protestant chapel altered after 1955 fire, balcony closed. 3 ext. photos (1960), 2 int. photos (1960); 7 data pages (1963).

□ *Domiciliary #6 (CA-336)*. Wood frame with drop siding and a variety of cut shingles, 188' × 26', three-story central section, two-and-a-half-story flanking wings, high-pitched gable roof with cross-gable and hip-roof dormers, fake half-timbering in gable end, two-story wrap-around porches on wings with stick railings and paired box columns. Built 1893, originally with domed tower, by Peters and Burns, architects from Ohio; demolished 1960. 1 ext. photo (1960), 1 photocopy of 1902 photo of whole complex; 8 data pages (1964).

Schindler, Rudolph M., House (CA-1939). *833 N. Kings Rd*. House Museum. Concrete slab and wood frame, approx. 79' × 78', flat roof with redwood board cornice and soffits, tapering concrete slab walls with glazed slits between slabs and clerestory windows in wood frames, horizontally stacked panels of fixed sash combined with sliding doors form large glazed areas on patios, two main entrances recessed under overhang of two upper sleeping porches, patio/courts on two sides; two L-plans, studio unit projects at northwest corner, concrete walls, wood tongue and groove ceilings, concrete slab floor. Built 1921–22 as a double residence for Rudolph M. Schindler, architect, and Clyde B. Chase; occupied by Rudolph until his death in 1953 and by Pauline Schindler until her death in 1978; one of

the most significant examples of the European-born Modern Movement that flourished in southern California in the 1920s in large part because of the influential work of the Viennese architects Rudolph M. Schindler and Richard J. Neutra. 6 sheets (1969, including aerial isometric, plans, elevations, sections, detail); 5 data pages (1969). NR

Security First National Bank Building (CA-2039). *5207-09 Wilshire Blvd*. Reinforced concrete with black terra cotta finish, 43' (five-bay front) × 95', two stories, flat composition roof with parapet, gold terra cotta ornament; front two-story open banking area, separate stories in rear contain offices and services, painted plaster interior finish with relief ornament. Built 1929, Morgan, Walls & Clements, architects; original tables, counters, and cabinet work removed. Fine example of zigzag Moderne architecture. 3 ext. photos (ca. 1975).

Selig Commercial Building (CA-2041). *269-73 Western Ave*. Reinforced concrete with terra cotta and vitriolite finish, rectangular with notch out of rear and rounded front corner, 141' × 60', one story, flat roof with parapet, rear elevation sheathed in brick, street facades sheathed in ornamental black and gold terra cotta and vitriolite below window level; bank teller counters with frosted glass in chevron pattern added ca. 1938. Built 1931, Arthur E. Harvey, architect, originally as clothing store; remodeled for use as a bank, 1938. 2 ext. photos (ca. 1975).

Skinner House (CA-2035). *1530 Easterly Terrace*. Stuccoed frame, irregular shape, 38' × 39', two stories, flat roof with low parapets and deep horizontal eaves, sliding front door, expansive window areas, numerous decks, exterior staircases; irregular plan; good example of Streamline Moderne in a residential design. Built 1936, William P. Kesling, architect. 1 ext. photo (ca. 1975), 1 int. photo (ca. 1975).

Smith House (CA-2036). *191 S. Hudson Ave*. Steel and frame covered with stucco to simulate stone, rectangular with rear wing, 55' × 109', two stories, flat roof with decorative parapet, enclosed entrance porch, geometric motifs carved into spandrels and window surrounds, art glass windows. Built 1929-30, C. J. Smale, architect; rear wing added 1936. 4 ext. photos (ca. 1975).

Sowden House (CA-1940). *5121 Franklin*. Stuccoed wood frame and concrete, 64' × 125' enclosing a rectangular courtyard, one story with partial front basement, front facade has a cave-like entrance, deeply recessed entrance gate of

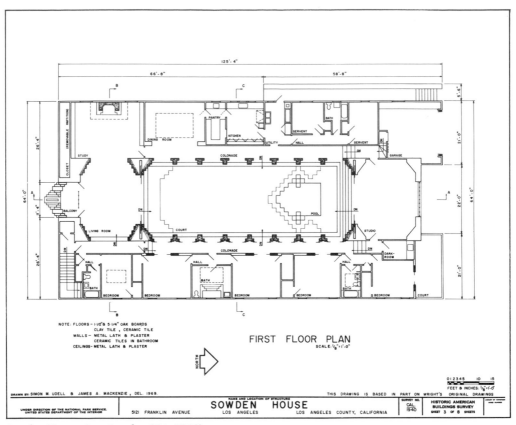

Sowden House, Los Angeles (CA-1940).

copper chevron plates on vertical metal bars, balcony above is preceded by a low concrete block wall with quatrefoil patterns corbeled out in courses to create a pyramidal form in plan and elevation, above balcony is a concrete block hood that echoes the balcony wall form below, north and south walls of the inner court have the same composition; court plan, corridors provide circulation around court, cathedral ceilings in living room and studio, studio wall has decorative metal grill resembling pattern of the blocks, glazed sliding doors to court, casement and hopper windows, skylights, court originally had elaborate fountain with pools, "textile" blocks form major decorative elements on court piers and end walls as well as interior wall sections. Built 1926–28, Lloyd Wright, architect, a remarkable, exotic design by F. L. Wright's son, influenced by Mayan architecture. 8 sheets (1969, including aerial dimetric, plans, elevations, sections, details); 5 ext. photos (1971), 6 photos of courtyard (1971), 8 int. photos (1971); 4 data pages (1969).

Storer House (CA-1944). *8161 Hollywood Blvd.*

Concrete blocks, 49' × 58', irregular shape, five levels, raised terrace with pool, walls sections of "textile" blocks inside and out, some perforated to admit light, flat roofs with parapets, two-story high wood-framed windows stacked vertically between narrow mullions, variety of openings; informal plan with bedrooms on half levels below and above two-story living room, dining room and kitchen on lowest levels. Built 1923, Frank Lloyd Wright, architect, one of Wright's series of "textile" block houses of the early 1920s. 7 sheets (1972, including plans, elevations, sections, details). NR

Story, W. P., Building Garage Entrance (CA-2040). *610 S. Broadway.* Iron and marble sheathed entrance to reinforced concrete structure, 18'-11" wide, elaborate bronze-finished iron gates with stylized geometric and floral motifs, cast bronze letters "SLOW" and "STOP" embedded in pavement; ramp descends from street to basement parking area. Built 1934, Morgan, Walls & Clements, architects; garage added to 1916 building by same architectural firm. 5 ext. photos (ca. 1975).

Los Angeles continued

Sunset Tower Apartments (CA-2037). *8358 Sunset Blvd.* Stuccoed concrete, T-shaped nine-story section, 88′ × 54′, topped by square three-story tower, 46′ × 46′, flat roof with parapet, Art Deco motifs carved into wide stone panels; good example of early Art Deco apartment building. Built 1929–31, Leland A. Bryant, architect. 2 ext. photos (ca. 1975).

Thomas Jefferson High School (CA-2026). *1319 E. 41st St.* Stuccoed concrete, original four sections arranged in open courtyard plan, 81′ × 152′, 91′ × 103′, 65′ × 269′, 75′ × 141′, two stories, flat roofs with parapets, horizontally banded cornices, horizontal ribbing on rounded ext. surfaces, slightly concave central entrance, covered walkways. Auditorium and classrooms built 1936, cafeteria built 1937, Morgan, Walls & Clements, architects. 2 ext. photos (ca. 1975).

Union Market (Carl's Market) (CA-2021). *1530-36 W. 6th St.* Stuccoed concrete, 120′ × 124′, one story, flat roof with front parapet, two pylons shaped in a Moderne motif flank building. Built 1933, Morgan, Walls & Clements, architects; one of a series of commercial markets designed by the architects. 1 ext. photo (ca. 1975).

Val D'Amour Apartments (CA-2038). *854 S. Oxford Ave.* Brick covered with stucco, 68′ × 137′, six stories, flat composition roof with uneven parapet, elaborate cast concrete ornamentation around entrance, along parapet and in spandrels; apartments along either side of a central corridor. Built 1928, G. W. Powers, architect. 2 ext. photos (ca. 1975).

Wilshire Building. See Hiss Tower (CA-2027).

Los Banos vicinity   □   Merced County

San Luis Gonzaga Ranch Adobe (CA-1891). *State Hwy. 152.* Adobe, 46′ (three-bay front) × 20′, gable roof originally shake-covered, some adobe bricks missing in walls at intervals, possibly gun ports. Built ca. 1843 on 48,821-acre land grant to J. P. Pacheco by Governor Micheltorena, on the trail to the Pacheco Pass to the coast; arched porch added on one side, 1930s; moved in 1960s to nearby site. 3 sheets (1960, including plan, elevations, section, details); 5 ext. photos (1960), 1 int. photo (1960), 2 photocopies of undated photos; 6 data pages (1961).

Los Gatos   □   Santa Clara County

Forbes Mill Addition (CA-2062). *1 blk. NW of*

Church and E. Main Sts. Stone, approx. 73′ × 32′, two stories, flat roof. Built 1880 as addition to four-story mill built in 1853–55 and demolished 1915 and 1929; addition in deteriorated condition. 2 sheets (1979, including plot plan, plan, elevation, section); 7 ext. photos (1980), 1 int. photo (1980); 5 data pages (1979).

Yung See San Fong (The Young's Home in the Heart of the Hills) (CA-2070). *16660 Cypress Way.* Wood frame with stucco, board-and-batten siding, and shingles, 27′ × 74′, with 16′ × 30′ addition set at angle, two to four stories, gable roofs with exaggerated splayed overhangs; interior heavily decorated with Chinese motifs. Built 1916–17 for Ruth Comfort Young, a writer, and her husband, Sanborn Young, gentleman farmer and state senator, probably by Leo L. Nichols, builder. 6 sheets (1979, including plans, elevations, sections); 5 ext. photos (1980), 7 int. photos (1980); 15 data pages (1979).

Lynwood   □   Los Angeles County

Lynwood Pacific Electric Railway Depot (CA-2074). *11453 Long Beach Blvd.* Brick, one story, seven-bay front, tiled gable roof, fluted columns separate bays, one hall is open. Built 1917. 8 ext. photos (1980), 1 photocopy of 1919 drawing, 1 photocopy of ca. 1916 photo; 3 data pages (1980).

Mad River vicinity   □   Humboldt County

Erickson Ranch House (CA-1454). Wood frame with horizontal siding, four-bay front in gable end, one-and-a-half stories, gable roof with cornice returns on gable end, two entrance doors on front. Built 1860s; demolished. 1 ext. photo (1934), 1 int. photo (1934), of house in deteriorated state.

Erickson Ranch—Log Cabin (CA-1455). Log construction, saddle-notching, one story, gable roof. Built 1860s; demolished. 1 ext. photo (1934).

Mare Island   □   Solano County

U.S. Naval Buildings (CA-1543). Navy Yard established October 3, 1854, David G. Farragut, Commandant of the Yard; has remained one of most important Naval installations until present time. 1 photocopy of undated lithograph of general view; 1 photocopy of 1890s photo of general

Mare Island continued
view, 1 photo of aerial view. NR

□ *Building No. 47 (CA-1543 A)*. Wood frame with board-and-batten siding, three stories, flat roof, wooden exterior stairway to third floor. 1 ext. photo (1975).

□ *Commandant's Office and Administration Building (CA-1824)*. Brick, two stories, hip roof, pediment over center three bays, round-arched windows first level, segmentally arched windows second level, set in recessed panels. Built ca. 1870. 1 ext. photo (1931).

□ *Magazine A-1 (CA-1543 B)*. Sandstone ashlar with quoining, one story, gable roof, few openings, elaborate sculpture over doorway signed "P. Kennedy." Built 1857. 3 ext. photos (1975).

□ *St. Peter's Chapel (CA-1543 C)*. Wood frame with wood shingles, one story, gable roof with bargeboards on gable end, square tower with pyramidal roof, gable hood over entrance. Built early 20th c. 5 ext. photos (1975).

□ *Smithy (Building No. 46) (CA-1543 D)*. Brick, one story, three-bay front, low-pitched gable roof, round-arched windows paired in round-arched panels. Built late 19th c. 2 ext. photos (1975).

Mariposa   □   Mariposa County

Frémont's Store (CA-1528). Brick, four-bay front, one story, flat roof with brick parapet, denticulated cornice, corrugated metal awning on two sides of building. Built 1850s and alleged to be John C. Frémont's store and assay office for his mining interests in the area. 1 photocopy of 1925 photo.

Gazette Building (CA-1534). Wood frame with clapboards, one bay by about eight bays, one-and-a-half stories, gable roof, one-story shed-roofed porch around two sides, rear part enclosed. Built 1854, moved to county fairgrounds. 1 photocopy of 1925 photo.

Mariposa County Courthouse (CA-1105). *James St. at 10th St.* Mortise-and-tenon wood frame with clapboards, three-bay front, two stories with square two-stage clock tower with crenellated crown, gable roof, raking molded cornice, entablature with blank frieze, round window in gable, corner pilasters, entrance with shouldered architrave; interior somewhat altered, courtroom preserved on upper floor with wooden railings and woodwork. Built 1854, the oldest courthouse in state, fine example of the frontier Greek Revival

style, modern north addition. 2 ext. photos (1936). NR, SHL

Martinez   □   Contra Costa County

Martinez, Vicente, Adobe (CA-1913). *Pleasant Hill and Franklin Canyon Rds*. Adobe, plastered on front, clapboards on sides, 45' (four-bay front) × 19' with wood-frame additions on rear and side, two stories, hip roof, two-story shed-roofed porch across front. Built 1848 or 1849 on a portion of Rancho Pinole, acquired 1874 by Dr. John Strentzel, builder of John Muir House (CA-1890). 3 sheets (1960s, including plans, elevations, section, details); 2 ext. photos (1960), 2 photocopies of photos (1885, n.d.); 4 data pages (1965). NR, SHL

Muir, John, House (CA-1890). *Alhambra Blvd*. Wood frame with channeled siding, 38' (three-bay front) × 77', irregular plan, two stories, hipped roof with cupola, bracketed cornice, polygonal one-story bays, quoining, segmentally arched windows under heavy flat-arched hood-molds, balustraded one-story portico. Built 1880 for Dr. John Strentzel, John Muir married his daughter and occupied this house; John Muir was a botanist and naturalist, known as "Father of the National Park System." 13 sheets (1960s, including plans, elevations, section, details); 6 ext. photos (1960), 6 int. photos (1960), 2 photocopies of photos (1900, ca. 1920); 8 data pages (1961). NR, SHL

John Muir House, Martinez (CA-1890).

Marysville   □   Yuba County

Commercial Buildings (CA-1808). D St. Two- and three-story brick commercial buildings, most parapeted with continuous canopies over sidewalks supported by wood posts. 1 photocopy of 1905 photo.

House (CA-1431). C St. near 6th St. Brick, two-bay front, two stories, high-pitched slate gable roof with cross gable dormers with generous carved foliated bargeboards, wrap-around ground-floor porch on latticed podium has full Classical entablature surmounted by Classical balustrade and supported by Tuscan columns, second-floor windows are narrow and round-arched. Built ca. 1860; demolished; an unusually fine transitional Greek Revival/Gothic Revival cottage. 1 ext. photo (1934).

House (CA-1432). C St. between 5th and 6th Sts. Brick, three-bay front, two stories, flat roof, simple cornice with dentil course, front porch with turned posts, paneled wood railing and steps, entrance with fanlight and sidelights. Built ca. 1860; demolished. 1 ext. photo (1934).

Marysville Grammar School (CA-1812). Plastered brick, three-bay front with projecting entrance block, two stories, parapeted roof, Classical cornice, pediment over entrance block, large square tower with open gallery and pyramidal roof over rear section. Built ca. 1865; demolished. 1 photocopy of 1905 photo.

Marysville High School (CA-1811). Wood frame, three-bay front by two bays deep, two stories, mansard roof with gabled dormers, square central tower with central round-arched window and bowed mansard roof, bracketed cornice with pediment over central projecting bay which has second-floor Palladian window and round-arched entrance doors with hood on consoles, quoins on bay as well as corners. Built 1870s; demolished. 1 photocopy of 1905 photo.

Miller-Aaron House (Mary Aaron Museum) (CA-1113). 704 D St. Museum. Brick, 40′ × 40′, two stories, flat roof with crenellated parapet and crocketed pinnacles over corner buttresses, wood front and side porches with square wood posts, variety of windows with segmental drip molds, French doors, second-floor round-headed casement windows with a molded architrave; L-shaped plan with polygonal bay off living room, some interior doorways have shouldered architraves, marble fireplaces, period furnishings and historical displays. Built 1856, Warren P. Miller, architect from New York; a whimsical Gothic Revival castle with doll house scale; a design

unique to the state and possibly the whole Pacific coast; willed by the last owner, Frank Aaron, to the city as a memorial to his mother. 1 ext. photo before refurbishing (1960).

Presbyterian Church (CA-1429). 5th and D Sts. Brick, three-bay front, one story, high-pitched gable roof with coping and corner pinnacles, central five-stage tower in front with entrance at base, corner buttresses at right angles, last stage terminates in a molded cornice and polygonal wood-shingled spire with clock faces, main door pointed-arch with multi-fasciaed architrave, pointed window arches with Gothic tracery. Built ca. 1860; demolished. 1 ext. photo (1934).

Row Houses (CA-1430). C St. near 6th St. A row of seven, two-bay two-story units with flat or low-pitched roofs divided by party wall and chimney, continuous first-floor porches divided by wood lattice and having bracketed cornices supported by turned columns with decorative bracketed caps, tall rectangular windows with straight cornice heads and wooden shutters, boxed and molded cornice with scroll-shaped brackets and dentil course, entablature not continuous. Built ca. 1860; demolished. 1 ext. photo (1934).

Yuba County Courthouse (CA-1810). 6th and D Sts. Brick, three-bay front, two stories, high crenellated parapet, projecting corner turrets with blind windows and crenellated tops, two polygonal front towers with open belfries and crenellated and molded tops, openings have drip molds, second-floor windows in central bay have pointed arches. Built 1855–56, Warren P. Miller, architect, who practiced in Marysville long enough to design the courthouse and the Mary Aaron House, then disappeared; demolished ca. 1960. 1 photocopy of 1905 photo.

Yuba County Hall of Records (CA-1813). Rusticated stone, three-bay front, two stories, roof has square central tower and castellated parapet, large pointed-arch entranceway. Built 1860s; demolished. 1 photocopy of 1905 photo.

Melones vicinity   □   Calaveras County

Barn (CA-1274). Wood frame with vertical siding, three aisles, central gable-roofed section and shed-roofed lean-tos on each side. Not located; probably inundated by Melones Dam. 1 ext. photo (1934).

Masonic Temple, Mendocino (CA-1801).

Mendocino   □   Mendocino County

Group of Frame Houses (CA-1466). Ukiah St. between Howard and Lansing. Wood frame with channeled siding, one story, L-plans, bay windows with bracketed cornices, cresting and finials. Built 1870s. 1 photo of general view (1934).

Masonic Temple (CA-1801). NE corner Lansing and Ukiah Sts. Wood frame with shiplap siding, three-bay front by four bays, two stories, gable roof with scalloped bargeboards, two-stage belvedere with square base and paneled corner pilasters supporting denticulated cornice, second stage is octagonal drum with engaged Ionic columns and paired brackets, above which is wood sculpture group of Father Time holding the hair of a young woman who holds a wand over a broken column, openings have denticulated cornice heads; highly ornamented interior. Lodge #179 organized Oct. 23, 1865, temple completed 1871 on site donated by William Heeser, building designed by the First Master, Erick Albertson, sculpture carved by him from solid redwood log, interior carvings also his work, brass decorations on interior columns made by George Hagenmeyer, a charter member of lodge. Outstanding example of an early transitional Classic/Gothic

Revival building combining vernacular building practice with individual talent. 5 ext. photos (1960), 4 int. photos (1960), 1 photocopy of undated photo.

Menlo Park   □   San Mateo County

Atalya (J. Henry Meyer House) (CA-2127). 2212 Santa Cruz Ave. Stucco, five-bay front, two stories, tiled hip roof with balustrade, denticulated cornice, iron balconies at second-floor windows. Built 1918, Arthur Brown, Jr., architect. 1 ext. photo (1975), 1 int. photo (1975).

Church of the Nativity (CA-1995). 210 Oak Grove Ave. Redwood frame with horizontal siding, 66' (three-bay front) × 131', Latin cross plan, one story with three-stage square tower with steeple, gable roof, quatrefoil tracery at eaves, two- and three-stage buttresses, pointed-arch windows; exposed hammerbeam truss. Built 1872, James R. Doyle, builder; moved to present site 1878, transept and chancel added 1887, rose window installed 1900; one of earliest Roman Catholic churches in area. 4 sheets (1974, including plan, elevations, sections); 12 ext. photos (1975), 8 int. photos (1975); 4 data pages (1974). NR

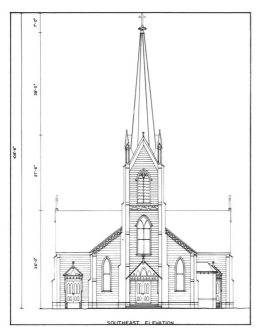

Church of the Nativity, Menlo Park (CA-1995).

Payne-Douglass House (CA-2128). Menlo Park School and College. Reinforced concrete, three-bay front by seven bays, three stories, flat roof, elaborate modillioned cornice between second and third floors, smaller cornice and parapet above third floor, columned porte cochere, concrete balconies at second-floor windows; elaborate interior ornamentation, including coffered ceilings, gold leaf, marble mantels, oak parquet floors. Built 1909–13, William Curlett, architect, for Mary O'Brien Payne, heiress of Comstock Lode fortune; in 1921 acquired by Leon Forrest Douglass, inventor of many items including the Victrola, Technicolor process, and coin-slot pay telephone. 5 ext. photos (1975), 4 int. photos (1975); 4 data pages (1974).

San Francisco and San Jose Railroad Station (Southern Pacific Railroad Station) (CA-1994). 1100 Merrill St. Wood frame with channeled siding, 101′ × 34′, one story, gable roof with cross gable, jigsawn cresting, finials, pendants, and more, pent roofs and hoodmolds over openings. Built 1867, small addition 1870s, larger addition early 1890s, waiting shed addition 1917. 4 sheets (1974, including plan, elevations, sections); 9 ext. photos (1975), 2 int. photos (1975); 4 data pages (1974).

Michigan Bar □ Amador County

Heath's Co. Store (CA-1516). Wood frame with channeled siding, three-bay front with one-bay addition, one story, gable roof with stepped false front, porch across front. Built early 1850s; demolished late 1930s. 1 photocopy of undated photo.

Millbrae □ San Mateo County

Southern Pacific Depot (CA-2059). 21 E. Millbrae Ave. Frame with clapboarding, 65′ × 50′, two stories with one-story wings, hip roofs with brack-

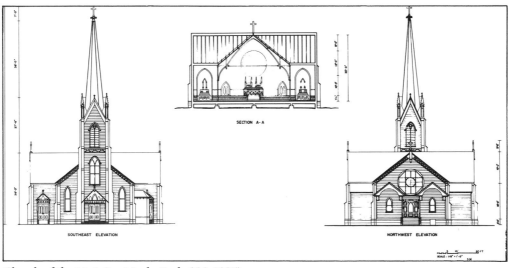

Church of the Nativity, Menlo Park (CA-1995).

Millbrae continued

eted eaves, extended roof supported by columns, semicircular bay on one side. Built 1907 from Southern Pacific stock design; overhanging roofed area on south removed; relocated 1979. 7 ext. photos (1979), 4 int. photos (1979). NR

Millerton vicinity □ Fresno County

Camp Barbour-Blockhouse (CA-1306). Rough-hewn logs, half-dovetail joints, gun ports, one story, dog-trot configuration, gable roof. Military post established 1850 to protect miners from marauding Indians; name changed to Fort Miller 1852, blockhouse removed 1944 because of construction of dam and Millerton Lake; reconstructed in Roeding Park, Fresno, and dedicated 1954 as Fort Miller Blockhouse Museum. 1 photocopy of 1914 photo.

Fort Miller (CA-170). Adobe and rough-hewn log structures with shake roofs. Built 1852 as a temporary headquarters for the Commissioners during the latter part of the Mariposa Indian War and to protect the southern mines from marauding Indians; peace treaty signed here; nearby village of Rootsville grew into the town of Millerton which became the first county seat in 1856; site now inundated by Millerton Lake. 2 photos of general views (1936).

□ *Blockhouse (CA-1324)*. Squared timbers, dovetailed, one story, gable roof. 1 ext. photo of collapsing building (1937).

□ *Officers' Quarters (CA-1326)*. Probably adobe, one story, hipped roof, two brick chimneys. 2 ext. photos (1935–36).

□ *Hospital (CA-1327)*. Adobe, five-bay front, hipped roof. 1 ext. photo (1935–36).

□ *Mess Hall (CA-1328)*. Two adjoining buildings, one stone, one adobe, both one story, both gable roofs but of different pitches. 2 ext. photos (1935–36).

□ *Bakery (CA-1329)*. Adobe, square, hipped roof. 1 ext. photo (1935–36).

□ *Ford (CA-1330)*. Wood construction, truss over deep channel. 1 photocopy of ca. 1934 photo.

Milpitas □ Santa Clara County

Alviso, José María, Adobe (CA-1663). *Piedmont and Calaveras Rds*. Adobe with clapboard siding on second floor, two stories, hip roof extends to cover two-story porch on all sides, X-braced rail-

ing with center diamond on second floor. Built ca. 1837 by the claimant to Rancho Milpitas; one of four original structures, others no longer standing. 2 photocopies of 1940 photos.

Milpitas vicinity □ Santa Clara County

Higuera, José, Adobe (CA-1661). *Rancho Higuera Rd. 3.5 mis. N. of Milpitas*. Adobe and wood frame, two stories, gable roof, exterior stair on side to upper floor. Built ca. 1845 for José Higuera; restored 1979 as part of 20-acre park. 2 photocopies of 1940 photos.

Mineral vicinity □ Shasta County

Lassen Volcanic National Park (CA-2114). Small buildings of logs, wood frame, boulders, and cut stone, with boulder chimneys and generally rustic appearance. Most built after park established 1916 around Lassen Peak, volcano which erupted between 1914 and 1921.

□ *Lost Creek Flume (CA-2114 A)*. 9 ext. photos (1976).

□ *Headquarters (Building #1) (CA-2114 B)*. 4 ext. photos (1976), 6 int. photos (1976).

□ *Service Station (Building #21) (CA-2114 C)*. 4 ext. photos (1976), 2 int. photos (1976).

□ *Summit Lake Ranger Station (Building #37) (CA-2114 D)*. 4 ext. photos (1976), 4 int. photos (1976).

□ *Naturalist's Residence (Building #41) (CA-2114 E)*. 4 ext. photos (1976), 4 int. photos (1976).

□ *Loomis Museum (Building #43) (CA-2114 F)*. 4 ext. photos (1976), 5 int. photos (1976).

□ *Comfort Station (Building #44) (CA-2114 G)*. 4 ext. photos (1976), 4 int. photos (1976).

□ *Manzanita Ranger Residence (Building #49) (CA-2114 H)*. 4 ext. photos (1976), 4 int. photos (1976).

□ *Manzanita Kiosk (Building #50) (CA-2114 I)*. 4 ext. photos (1976), 1 int. photo (1976).

□ *Warner Valley Ranger Residence (Building #58) (CA-2114 J)*. 4 ext. photos (1976), 4 int. photos (1976).

□ *Loomis Seismograph Station (Building #178) (CA-2114 K)*. 4 ext. photos (1976), 2 int. photos (1976).

□ *Warner Valley Hay Barn (Building #284) (CA-*

I.O.O.F. Building, Mokelumne Hill (CA-1281).

2114 L). 4 ext. photos (1976), 4 int. photos (1976).

□ *Warner Valley Cook's Cabin (Building #287) (CA-2114 M).* 4 ext. photos (1976), 2 int. photos (1976).

Mokelumne Hill □ Calaveras County

Frame Church (CA-1282). Main St. Wood frame with board-and-batten siding and horizontal siding, three-bay front, one story, shingled gable roof with raking cornice and central front bell tower with hipped roof, louvered openings with pedimental heads, corner pilasters on building and belfry, closed entrance vestibule with gable roof. Built 1856; restored. 1 ext. photo (1934).

I.O.O.F. Building (CA-1281). N. side Center St. Stone, ashlar, four-bay front, three stories, flat roof with pedimented parapet, raking cornice, "I.O.O.F." in inset plaque, iron shutters on all openings. Original two-story building erected in 1854 for Adams Express Co., third story added 1861 for lodge purposes; front veranda altered to simple one-story porch with shed roof. 1 ext. photo (1934), 1 photocopy of photo (before 1934). SHL

Leger Hotel (CA-1874). S. side Main St. Brick,

plastered, seven-bay front by five bays plus rear ell, two stories in front, three in rear, flat parapeted roof, two-story wrap-around wood veranda. Built 1854, interior little altered; a portion of this building served as county courthouse from 1854–66, George W. Leger later acquired it and made it part of his adjoining hotel; damaged by fire 1874, restored with second story added 1874, remodeled 1973. An outstanding example of a Gold Rush hostel. 1 ext. photo (1934). SHL

Ruined Store (CA-1279). Center St. Stone, dressed ashlar, three-bay front, one story, roof missing, parapeted front with cornice molding. Built 1854; only walls standing. 1 ext. photo (1934), shows also wood-framed, gable-roofed buildings with clapboard siding and front porches.

Stone Ruins (Brewery) (CA-1280). Stone, coursed ashlar, three-bay front, three-and-a-half stories, roof missing, only exterior walls remain, equally ruined one-story addition. Built 1850s; demolished. 1 ext. photo (1934).

Store (Sturges) and Post Office (CA-1875). N. side Center St. Store of finished ashlar, post office wood frame with clapboard, three-bay front on each, both two stories, two-story verandas with balconies across both fronts, store with shingled front gable end and louvered attic window, iron

Mokelumne Hill continued

shutters on doors and windows of store, post office with stepped parapet with massive wood cornice and entablature with side pilasters. Built 1854; both structures now one story due to fire, facades altered considerably, stone building now Calaveras County Branch Library. 1 ext. photo (1934).

Monte Vista vicinity □ Santa Clara County

Woelffel Cannery (CA-2099). 10120 Imperial Ave. Wood frame with horizontal siding, one story, gable roofs, series of clerestories with sawtooth profile. Built 1920s, only cannery in western side of county; roofline changed after 1927. 11 ext. photos (1980); 4 data pages (1980).

Montecito □ Santa Barbara County

Ortega House (CA-314). 29 Sheffield Dr. Adobe, 68' × 22', essentially two adobe buildings separated by alley now enclosed with wood frame, one and two stories, hipped roofs, second-story balconies on one building. Built 1868–69 for Angel Mazzini. 5 sheets (1934, including plans, elevations, wall section, details); 3 ext. photos (1936), 1 ext. photo of adobe barn (1936); 1 data page (1937).

Monterey □ Monterey County

Adobe Wall (rear of Alvarado-La Porte Adobe) (CA-1646). NW corner Alvarado and Pearl Sts. Built ca. 1850 to enclose rear property of Gov. Alvarado's house; demolished. 1 photocopy of ca. 1925 photo.

Alvarado-La Porte Adobe. See Adobe Wall (CA-1646) for rear wall.

Brown-Underwood Adobe (CA-129). NW corner Pacific and Madison Sts. Plastered adobe, five-bay front on Pacific St. by four bays plus rear ell chapel, one story, shingled gable roof, six-bay front wood veranda and chamfered box columns; rear courtyard garden. Built 1843 by Santiago Stokes, Alcalde of Monterey; acquired by city in 1934 and renovated for use as city offices. 1 ext. photo (1936).

Casa Abrego (CA-139). 592 Abrego St., NW corner Webster St. Plastered adobe, eight-bay front on Abrego, one story, gable roof over central

rooms, veranda across front with box columns and balustrade, French doors and six-over-six-light windows open onto veranda, board-and-batten gable end. Built 1835 by Don José Abrego, a Spanish merchant who came to Monterey from Mexico in 1834 on the ship "La Natalie" as one of the colonists under Don José María Hijar; property originally included length of block with several structures, gardens and store; now private women's club. 2 ext. photos (1936, 1960), 1 int. photo (1960), 1 photocopy of 1918 photo.

Casa Adolfo Sambert (CA-1536). Three adobe walls, ruins of house. Original location unknown; demolished. 1 ext. photo (1939).

Casa Alvarado (CA-135). 570 Dutra St., SW corner Jefferson St. Adobe brick with channeled siding, seven-bay front, one story, gable roof extends to cover front veranda which has box columns. Built 1830s by Don Juan Bautista Alvarado, first Monterey-born governor of Alta California, 1836–42. 1 ext. photo (1936), 2 int. photos (1960), 1 photocopy of ca. 1912 photo. SHL

Casa Amesti (CA-143). 516 Polk St. Private club. Plastered adobe, approx. 41' (six-bay front) × 84', two stories, hip roof, second-floor balconies across front and rear under main roof, cantilevered in front, supported by turned wood columns in rear, French doors on second floor, adobe oven in garden. Built ca. 1833 by José Amesti, a Spanish Basque, who came to Monterey in 1822 and married Prudenciana Vallejo, daughter of Don José Vallejo; second story and south part added 1853, restored 1919 as home for Frances Elkins, famous interior decorator; acquired 1953 by National Trust for Historic Preservation; side patio and rear garden designed by David Adler, Elkins' brother. 10 sheets (1958, including site plan, plans, elevations, section, details); 3 ext. photos (1936, 1958), 2 int. photos (1958), 2 photocopies of 1919 photos (including view of adobe oven); 6 data pages (1958).

Casa Bonifacio (Sherman Rose Cottage) (CA-153). 785 Mesa Rd. Plastered adobe, three-bay front by three bays, two stories, tiled gable roof with rear extension. Built 1835 on Alvarado St. by José Rafael Gonzales, a retired cavalryman and then Administrator of the custom house; in 1860 acquired by Carmen Pinto de Bonifacio and passed to her daughter María Ygnacia who never married but was the subject of a legend that she was betrothed to Lt. W. T. Sherman who planted a boutonnier rose in the garden saying that if it took root and grew their love would endure; he never returned but the bush that grew here was known as the Sherman Rose; house moved to present location in 1922. 2 ext. photos (1936), 3 photocopies of ext. photos (1860s, before 1922, ca. 1930).

Casa Boronda (CA-1821). Boronda St. Adobe, three-bay front, one story, gable roof. Built 1817 by Don Manuel de Boronda who came to California as Corporal in early Spanish Army and was first schoolmaster in San Francisco, 1794–97; remains of earliest adobe in Monterey. 2 ext. photos (1936), 1 int. photo (1936). SHL

Casa García (Casa Molera) (CA-148). Van Buren and Jackson Sts. Ashlar chalkstone, six-bay front, two stories, gable roof; adobe lean-to additions. Built 1848–50 for Francisco García, Judge at San Feliciano 1845–46. 6 ext. photos (1936, 1939, undated), 5 int. photos (1939, undated), 1 photocopy of ext. 1916 photo.

Casa Gutiérrez (CA-1201). 590 Calle Principal. Museum. Plastered adobe and frame with channeled siding on gable end, three-bay front by two bays, two stories, gable roof pitches out to cover rear addition. Built after 1841 by Don Joaquín Gutiérrez, Acting Governor of Alta California for three months in 1836. Purchased by Monterey Foundation and given to state, 1953; restored and remodeled. 1 ext. photo (1936). SHL

Casa Jesús Soto (Lara-Soto House) (CA-151). 460 Pierce St. Plastered adobe and frame, four-bay front by one bay, one story, gable roof; two-room interior with chair rail and wood mantel; spectacular cypress trees in front yard, rear garden. Built after 1849 by Feliciana Lara whose family occupied it until 1905; no known association with Jesús Soto; name is in error; restored and remodeled for offices. 1 ext. photo (1936).

Casa Molera. See Casa García (CA-148).

Casa del Oro (CA-132). 200 Oliver St., SW corner Scott St. Museum. Plastered stone rubble and adobe, three-bay front by one bay, two stories, gable roof, central double wood doors flanking barred casement windows, wide overhanging roof; interior restored as general store with wide plank floors and steep stairway to second floor. Built 1845, by Thomas Larkin, property purchased by José Abrego, 1848 and leased to Joseph Boston & Co., 1848–62; purchased by David Jacks, 1862; deeded by Jacks family to state in 1934. 2 ext. photos (1936, 1939). SHL

Casa Pacheco (CA-140). SW corner Abrego and Webster Sts. Plastered adobe, four-bay front on Abrego St. by nine bays, two stories, hip roof, recessed two-story veranda on Abrego St. Built ca.

1840 by Don Francisco Pacheco who came from Mexico in 1819 in the Artillery and became a wealthy landowner; remodeled, 1903, with cross gables, opened as boarding house by Mrs. Glotzbach with 25 rooms; in 1922 purchased by Dr. McAuley and converted to a hospital, gables and Victorian detail removed; remodeled for use as private club, new second-floor front glass doors, new front entrance. 1 ext. photo (1936), 1 photocopy of 1915 ext. photo.

Casa Serrano (CA-152). 412 Pacific St. near Franklin St. Plastered adobe, four-bay front, one story, gable roof extends over veranda, buttressed wall at veranda ends, south extension now shop. Built ca. 1845 and purchased unfinished by Florencio Serrano, a clerk of various offices; Monterey History and Art Association headquarters since 1959; restored. 1 ext. photo (1936).

Casa de la Torre (CA-149). 502 Pierce St., SW corner Jefferson St. Adobe and frame, four-bay front, one story with loft, gable roof, shed roof over front veranda which has brick floor and plain wood posts, frame lean-tos. Built 1851 by Francisco Pico and sold to José de la Torre in 1862. 1 ext. photo (1936).

Casa de la Torre. See First Federal Courthouse (CA-122).

Casa Verde (Stoddard House) (CA-146). 303 Decatur St., SW corner Oliver. Wood frame with channeled siding, two stories, hip roof with cross gables topped by cast-iron cresting, projecting bays, double veranda with turned posts. Built late 19th c.; home of professor and author Charles Warren Stoddard from 1905–08, when he wrote his last works; demolished late 1940s.

Casa de los Vientos. See House of the Four Winds (CA-126).

Castro, General José, Headquarters (CA-142). SW corner of Tyler and Pearl Sts. Adobe and chalkstone, four-bay front, one story, gable roof, end wall faced with horizontal boards. Built ca. 1846; used as headquarters by General José Castro after he succeeded General Vallejo as Commandant; at rear of building were bull and bear pits enclosed by high rock and adobe walls; demolished. 1 ext. photo (1936).

Colton Hall and Jail (CA-130). Pacific St., W. side between Madison and Jefferson Sts. Museum. Hall: plastered stone, approx. 76′ × 26′ (eight-bay front by one bay) with 32′ × 16′ rear wing, two stories, hipped roof, central wood portico with two-story modified Tuscan columns, second-floor balcony and broad flanking stairways with

Monterey continued

turned balusters, pedimented gable with flagpole, two central entrances on first and second floors, flat stone lintels over doors and windows, clapboard exterior on south end; rectangular plan, second floor one large room. Jail: adjoining on south; stone, one-story, 43' × 35'; vaulted granite ceiling. Built 1847–49 by Walter Colton, Alcalde of Monterey, for Town Hall and school; site of the 1849 Constitutional Convention; jail built 1854; two-story portico added to Hall, exterior plastered and scored, 1880s; capitals altered, 20th c., 9 sheets (1961, including plans, elevations, sections, details); 5 ext. photos (1936, 1960), 4 int. photos (1960), 5 photocopies of ext. photos (ca. 1888, ca. 1890, ca. 1913, 1955); 7 data pages (1962). SHL

Convent of St. Catherine at Monterey (CA-1169). Stone foundation with adobe walls plastered on front, eleven-bay front, two stories with rear frame lean-to, gable roof. Built 1850 by Don Manuel Jimeno as a hotel; served as first Dominican convent school in state, 1851–54; demolished after 1885. Photocopy of undated ext. photo.

Cooper House (Molera House) (CA-125). 508 *Munras St.* Museum, Monterey State Historic Park, property of National Trust for Historic Preservation. Plastered adobe, four-bay front, two stories, hipped roof, second floor wood balcony with chamfered box columns under extension of main roof across front and side; extensive walled grounds with barns. Built 1832 by Captain J. N. R. Cooper, half-brother of Thomas O. Larkin, U.S. Consul in Monterey; second story added and building enlarged in 1850s; part of a compound of buildings including barns and servant quarters; remodeled in 1920s; given to state by Frances Molera 1968; restoration in progress. 1 ext. photo (1936), 1 photocopy of late 19th c. photo. See also Stone Wall—Cooper House (CA-1647).

Custom House (CA-133). Alvarado St. north of *Scott St.* Museum. Plastered adobe and stone, 116' (six-bay front) × 21', one-story gable-roofed section four bays long flanked by two-story hip-roofed pavilions, veranda on three sides, tile roofs, barred windows. Northern one-story section built 1827; second story and southern section built by Thomas Larkin, 1841; served as custom house under Mexico ca. 1822–46 and U.S. 1846–68; transferred to state in 1902; restorations in 1903, 1917, and 1929. 10 sheets (1962, including plot plan, plans, elevations, sections, details); 6 ext. photos (1936, 1940) 1 pho-

tocopy of undated drawing, 8 photocopies of photos (1960s, ca. 1920, undated); 10 data pages (1962). NHL, SHL

Díaz Store. See Escolle Store (CA-1185).

Francis Doud House (CA-1648). 177 *Van Buren St. at Scott St.* Wood frame with horizontal tongue-and-groove siding, eleven-bay front by two bays, one story, gable roof, rear five-bay veranda with shed roof and plain chamfered columns, balustrade. Built probably 1860s for Francis Doud, assistant sergeant-at-arms at Colton Hall during Constitutional Convention of 1849; restored and remodeled by Monterey History and Art Association. 1 photocopy of ca. 1920 photo.

El Cuartel (Mexican Army Barracks) (CA-1168). *Munras St.* Adobe, nineteen-bay front, two stories, gable roof extends over two-story veranda, exterior stairway. Built at unknown date; seized 1846 by U.S. forces for offices of military governor; subsequently house of first newspaper, library and school; demolished ca. 1910. 1 photocopy of ca. 1880 photo.

Escolle House. See Stokes House (CA-123).

Escolle Store (Díaz Store) (CA-1185). *Munras St., corner Polk St.* Adobe and frame, one story with wood-frame attic, flat roof. Built at unknown date by Manuel Díaz; name is misnomer; demolished. 1 ext. photo (1936).

Finch-Fleischer House (CA-1893). 410 *Monroe St.* Wood frame with horizontal siding, central block one-and-a-half stories, three-bay front in gable end, one-story wings three bays wide, gable roof with cornice returns, low-pitched gable roof on wings, main block and south wing have one-story porches, balustrade on roof of main porch. Central portion built 1870 by James William Finch for his mother; south wing with bedroom and kitchen added 1881; north wing and kitchen added between 1910 and 1920; dormer windows on main roof, 1910; house still in family. The original house is a good example of provincial Greek Revival design modified by later stylistic influences. 4 ext. photos (1960), 2 int. photos (1960); 7 data pages (1964).

First Brick House (CA-145). 351 *Decatur St.* Brick laid in common bond, one-bay front in gable end by five bays, two stories, gable roof, exterior stairway at north gable end. Built 1847 by Gallant Duncan Dickinson, native of Virginia and survivor of the Donner Party. 1 ext. photo (1936).

First Federal Courthouse (Casa de la Torre) (CA-

122). 599 Polk St., SE corner Hartnell St. Plastered adobe, five-bay front on Polk St. by one bay, one-and-a-half stories. Built ca. 1840 for Gabriel de la Torre; claim to have been first federal courthouse ambiguous and unfounded; one room may have been rented for use as a courtroom; extensive rear and side additions in late 19th c.; restored. 2 ext. photos (1936).

First Frame House (CA-1535). Corner Munras and Webster Sts. Wood frame with clapboards, six-bay front, two stories with one-story wing, gable roof, all joints mortised. Built ca. 1850 by William Bushton from cut and matched boards carried in hold of the ship he and his family took from Australia to Monterey; demolished 1924. 8 photocopies of ext. photos (19th c., ca. 1900, ca. 1906, ca. 1909, ca. 1912, ca. 1920).

First French Consulate (CA-1202). 404 Camino El Estero at Franklin St. Plastered adobe and wood frame, five-bay front by one bay, one story, gable roof extended over front veranda supported by extensions of the side walls, rear veranda with chamfered box columns. Built 1848 at SE corner of Fremont and Abrego Sts. by Jacques Antoine Moerenhaut, French Consul to California in 1848; moved to El Estero Park 1939. 1 ext. photo (1936).

First Theatre in California (CA-131). SW corner Scott and Pacific Sts. Museum. Adobe, eleven-bay front, one story, gable roof, frame section of three bays with veranda at one end. Built ca. 1844 by Jack Swan as saloon and boarding house; converted to a theater 1847–48 by members of Col. Jonathan D. Stevenson's regiment; restored by state ca. 1930s. 1 ext. photo (1936), 7 photocopies of photos (ca. 1910, ca. 1920, 1934, undated). SHL

Fleischer House. See Finch-Fleischer House (CA-1893).

Frémont, General, House (CA-121). 539 Hartnell St. Museum. Adobe and frame, channeled siding, three-bay front, two stories, gable roof, two-tiered front veranda with simple wood posts and balustrade, exterior side stairway to second floor, rear lean-to frame extension. Built 1840; name is a misnomer—Frémont was not a general at this time and memoirs say he camped on a hill near town; restored in 1961 by Monterey History and Art Association. 1 ext. photo (1936).

Gordon House (CA-150). 526 Pierce St., corner King St. Frame with clapboards, five-bay front by four bays, one story, gable roof, veranda across front with chamfered box columns and balustrade. Built 1849 from milled lumber prefabri-

cated and shipped around the Horn for owner Philip Roach, last Alcalde and first Mayor; 1871—1900, property of Samuel B. Gordon, member of the State Legislature; restored. 1 ext. photo (1936).

Hall of Records. See House of the Four Winds (CA-126).

Halleck Headquarters. See Sherman Quarters (CA-127).

House of the Four Winds (La Casa de los Vientos, Hall of Records) (CA-126). 540 Calle Principal. Plastered adobe, one-and-a-half stories, broad low-hipped roof with long lean-to extension, French doors. Built in 1834 as a store for Thomas O. Larkin; name derived from weathervane on roof which was the only one in early Monterey; in 1914 restored as headquarters for Monterey Women's Civic Club. 1 ext. photo (1936), 1 photocopy of late 19th c. photo, 1 photocopy of undated drawing. SHL

Jimeno, Don Manuel, Adobe (CA-1895). Main St. north of Franklin St. Adobe, eight-bay front, two stories, hip roof extends to cover two-story veranda on front, rear lean-to. Built 1851 for Don Manuél Jimeno, Secretary of State under Governors Alvarado and Micheltorena. 1 photocopy of ca. 1880 photo.

Lara-Soto House. See Casa Jesús Soto (CA-151).

Larkin House (CA-128). 464 Calle Principal, corner of Jefferson St. Museum. Plastered adobe, five-bay front by four bays plus rear stone extension, two stories, low-hipped roof, double veranda under main roof on three sides with simple wood posts and balustrade; central hall plan. Built between 1835 and 1837 by Thomas Oliver Larkin, U.S. Consul to California, 1844–46; probably the first two-story adobe structure in Monterey; restored and furnished with many original Larkin items; deeded to state by Alice Larkin Toulenin in 1957. 15 sheets (1959, including site plan, plans, elevations, section, details); 6 ext. photos (1936, 1959), 6 int. photos (1959), 1 photocopy of late 19th c. photo; 6 data pages (1958). SHL

Merritt House (CA-147). 386 Pacific St. Plastered adobe and frame, two-bay front in gable end, two-story main house with newer one-story rear extension, gable roof, double veranda with three two-story paneled box columns, clapboard siding in gable, exterior stair to balcony. Built early 1850s by John Tierny; purchased 1852 by Judge Josiah Merritt, first Judge of Monterey County; house is a fine example of a Greek Revival

Monterey continued

adobe. 1 ext. photo (1936). NR

Mexican Army Barracks. See El Cuartel (CA-1168).

Molera House. See Cooper House (CA-125).

Pacific House (CA-124). *200–222 Calle Principal.* Museum. Plastered stone rubble and adobe, ten-bay front, two stories, hipped roof, cantilevered second story balcony, extensive walled rear garden. Built 1845; added to in 1847 by David Wight for Thomas O. Larkin as a supply depot; became a hotel and saloon in 1850 with arena at rear for bull and bear fights; purchased by David Jacks in 1880; restored after his death in 1909, arena converted to gardens; deeded to state by Margaret Jacks in 1954. 2 ext. photos (1936, 1939). SHL

Royal Presidio Chapel of San Carlos Borromeo (Capilla Royal) (CA-16). *550 Church St.* Plastered stone, single-aisle nave with corner bell tower or campanario, one story, intersecting gable roofs, tripartite facade with raised espadaña in segmental form broken at the top with a niche, scrolled coping, main part of facade has a superimposed Neo-Classic triumphal arch frontispiece with re-cessed segmental-arched window with pediment above the central round-arched entrance door; tower has two stages divided by a cornice molding, second stage has two round-arched openings with bells under a heavy molded cornice with pinnacles surmounted by a pyramidal tiled roof; cruciform plan. Built in 1794 in stone after a fire destroyed most of the presidio buildings of log and adobe, designed by master mason Manuel Ruíz, slightly modified by Antonio Velásquez, Director of the Royal Academy, San Carlos, Mexico; completed by José Santiago Ruíz and Pedro de Alcantara; facade formerly polychromed; transepts added 1858 when the church was restored with money given by Gov. Pacheco; nave lengthened 1865; pyramidal tower roof added 1893; windows and interior have been modernized. 28 sheets (1934, including plot plan, plans, elevations, sections, details); 10 ext. photos (1934), 10 int. photos (1934), 1 photocopy of 1816 drawing, 3 photocopies of photos (1914, ca. 1928, 1930); 1 data page (1936). NHL, SHL

Sherman, General, Quarters (Sherman-Halleck Headquarters) (CA-127). *464 Calle Principal.* Museum. Plastered stone rubble, two-bay front in gable end, one story, gable roof; one room, wood groin-vaulted ceiling. Built in 1834 for

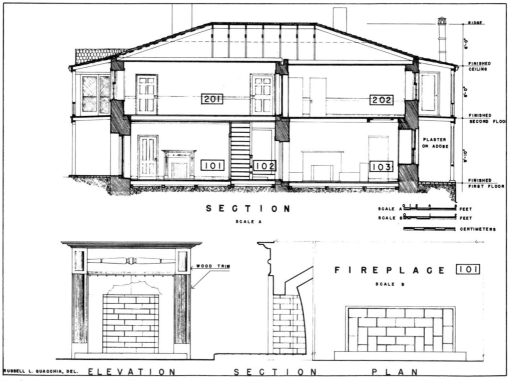

Larkin House, Monterey (CA-128).

Royal Presidio Chapel, detail, Monterey (CA-16).

Thomas Larkin, U.S. Consul during Mexican regime; was occupied during first months of U.S. occupancy of Monterey by Lt. William Tecumseh Sherman and Captain Henry W. Halleck; deeded to the state, 1957 and restored. 1 ext. photo (1936), 2 photocopies of photos (undated, ca. 1925).

Sherman Rose Cottage. See Casa Bonifacio. (CA-153).

Soberanes Adobe (CA-1892). 336 Pacific St. Museum. Adobe and wood, four-bay front, two stories, tiled gable roof extended to cover second-floor balcony. Built ca. 1840 by Jean Rafael Estrada or José Estrada and sold to cousin Feliciano Soberanes in 1860. 4 ext. photos (1960), 8 int. photos (1960), 2 photocopies of undated photos, 1 photocopy of undated architectural drawings; 6 data pages (1964). SHL

Stevenson, Robert Louis, House (CA-141). 530 Houston St. Museum. Adobe and frame, two stories, six-bay front section with flat roof and bracketed wood cornice, set back section with four-bay front and gable roof. Built 1830s for Don Rafael Gonzales; flat-roofed section was where Stevenson stayed for four months during 1879 when it was called French Hotel; in 1941,

restored as house museum in Monterey State Historic Park. 1 ext. photo (1936), 6 photocopies of ext. photos (ca. 1908, ca. 1910, 1931, undated). NR, SHL

Stoddard House. See Casa Verde (CA-146).

Stokes House (Escolle House) (CA-123). 500 Hartnell St. Adobe and stone, three-bay front, two stories, gable roof, two-story veranda with simple box columns and balustrade, lean-to with shed roof and board-and-batten siding. Built ca. 1837 and purchased by James Stokes, consulting physician to Governor Figueroa; sold 1866 to Honore Escolle for a bakery; restored and remodeled for restaurant use. 1 ext. photo (1936).

Stone Wall—Cooper House (CA-1647). 508 Munras St. Ashlar stone with tiled gable coping. Built from 1826 to ca. 1900 to enclose buildings on property of J. B. R. Cooper. 1 photocopy of undated photo. See also Cooper House (CA-125).

Underwood Adobe. See Brown-Underwood Adobe (CA-129).

U.S. Post Office (CA-1203). 497 Alvarado St. Plastered adobe first level, clapboard siding second level, three-bay front, two stories, gable roof. Built mid-19th c.; demolished. 1 ext. photo (1936).

Washington Hotel (CA-1894). NW corner Washington and Pearl Sts. Plastered adobe, 200' × 50' main building, gable roof, five-bay center section has recessed two-level porch with exterior stairways, cornice between second and third stories, rear two-story annex at right angle to main section. Two-story rear wing built 1832 by Don Eugenio Montenegro; front addition built ca. 1849 as hotel and owned by Don Alberto Trescony; demolished 1914. 1 photocopy of undated photo.

Whaling Station (CA-144). 391 Decatur St. Plastered adobe, three-bay front, two stories, gable roof. Built ca. 1850 by David Wight, a Scotsman, for his residence, modeling the interior on plan of his ancestral home; by 1855 headquarters for a Portuguese whaling company; second-floor balcony with simple box columns and balustrade all added 1903; rear frame extension with shed dormers added later; restored 1970s. 1 ext. photo (1936), 1 photocopy of 1879 photo.

Monterey vicinity □ Monterey County

Lighthouse (CA-1264). Point Pinos. Plastered, cylindrical lighthouse, two stories, polygonal lookout tower, balustrade all around. Built mid 19th c. 2 ext. photos (n.d.). NR

Montezuma   □   Tuolumne County

Hotel and Store (CA-1574). Wood frame, two-and-a-half stories, gable roof with cornice returns on gable end, two-story front veranda; attached store, one-and-a-half stories, gable roof, one-story veranda on front and sides. Hotel built ca. 1854, store later. 1 ext. photo (1930s).

Moraga Valley □ Contra Costa County

Moraga, José Joaquin, Adobe (CA-1860). 1½ *miles N. of Moraga*. Adobe, plastered with some clapboarding, one story, hip roof, porch across front. Built 1840; dilapidated by 1922. Restored 1940s by Katherine Brown Whilte Irvine. 2 photocopies of 1922 photos. NR

Morgan Hill □ Santa Clara County

Fountain Oaks (CA-2100). *15835 Carey Ave.* Stuccoed clay tile, two stories, approx. 80′ (four-bay front) × 90′, tiled hip roof, porte cochere on front with two round-arched openings, exterior chimney on front. Built 1927 for Gertrude Strong Achilles, heiress to Kodak fortune, and Charles Kellogg, the "California Nature Singer," her friend and ranch manager. 5 ext. photos (1980), 4 int. photos (1980); 13 data pages (1980).

□ *Guest House (CA-2100 A)*. Stuccoed clay tile, 40′ (five-bay front) × 51′, one-and-a-half stories, tiled gable roof, shed dormer, boulder chimney on exterior. Built 1922 for Gertrude Strong Achilles. 5 ext. photos (1980), 1 int. photo (1980); 5 data pages (1980).

Villa Miramonte (Morgan Hill House) (CA-2101). *17860 N. Monterey Rd.* Wood frame with horizontal siding, one-and-a-half stories, hip roof with cross gables, one-story porch across front wraps around. Built late 19th c. 6 ext. photos (1980). NR

Morgan Hill vicinity □ Santa Clara County

Machado School (CA-2102). *Sycamore Ave.* Wood frame with horizontal siding, one story, gable roof with cross gables, belvedere over pedimented portico. Built 1895. 8 ext. photos (1980).

Malaguerra Winery (CA-2004). *End of Burnett Rd.* Two-story stone block 22′ × 24′; stucco-covered frame addition 14′ × 26′; stone and frame with horizontal siding barn, 31′ × 80′; and frame addition to barn, 12′ × 32′; gable roofs. Winery built 1869, now oldest extant winery in county; barn built ca. 1900. 3 sheets (1977, including plan, elevations, section); 5 ext. photos (1980); 9 data pages (1977, 1979). NR

Mount Bullion □ Mariposa County

Marre Store (CA-1527). Plastered adobe, two-bay front, slightly pitched roof, front porch with turned wood posts. Built 1850s and called La Mineta, this was one of the first trading stores, sold mining supplies and general merchandise purchased in 1860 by Carlos Marre, owned by the Marre family until 1930s; demolished. 1 photocopy of 1926 photo.

Murphys   □   Calaveras County

Compere, Victorene, Store (CA-1108). *570 Main St.* Stone, ashlar on front, rubble on sides, two-bay front, one story, gable roof, two doorways in front with iron doors, shed-roofed porch across front. Built 1858; by Pierre Bonnet as general provision store; gable roof and veranda gone by 1936, restored as residence with windows in place of front doors and new side windows, new second-story addition in rear. 3 ext. photos (1936 and earlier), 1 photocopy of undated photo.

Main Street Buildings (CA-1211). Buildings with shingled, gable roofs, including house of physicist Albert Michelson. Built 1850s. 1 ext. photo (1930s).

Mitchler Hotel (CA-1109). *S. side Main St.* Stone, ashlar, six-bay front, two stories, low gable roof, iron shutters throughout, second-floor front balcony with iron balustrade. Built 1856 for J. L. Sperry of Sperry Flour fame, and his partner John Perry; rebuilt in 1860 after a fire. According to tradition, this hotel is the one referred to in Bret Harte's *Night in Wingdom*; hosted Mark Twain, U. S. Grant, Horatio Alger, Henry Ward Beecher, Black Bart; interior restored. Fine example of mid-19th c. Mother Lode hotel. 1 ext. photo (1936), 2 photocopies of photos (1860s, n.d.), 1 photocopy of 1926 drawing. SHL

St. Patrick's Catholic Church (CA-1112). Brick, one-bay front by three bays, one-and-a-half stories, steep gable roof, small square louvered belfry, pointed-arched windows with tracery divisions, bays separated by small two-stage brick buttresses. Built 1861, John Thompson, builder, dedicated Nov. 1861 by Bishop Alemany; front porch and steps restored. Good example of simplified Gothic Revival of the Mother Lode region. 1 ext. photo (1936).

School (CA-1110). Jones St. Wood frame with clapboards, three-bay front by seven bays, one story, gable roof with entablature and raking cornice on gable end, square belfry over front with round-arched openings, pilasters and hip roof, one-bay central entrance porch with fluted Doric columns, corner pilasters. Built 1860; restored. First public school in state and among oldest west of the Mississippi in continuous use. 1 ext. photo (1936).

Napa   □   Napa County

Behlow Building (CA-1982). NW corner Second and Brown Sts. Ashlar sandstone veneer over steel framing, 111' × 71', two stories, flat roof, department store with mezzanine and second-floor offices. Built 1901–02, Luther Mark Turton, probable architect; interior rebuilt after 1932 fire, entrances and store windows remodeled, E. W. Doughty, contractor; demolished 1974. 8 sheets (1974, including site plan, plans, elevations).

Migliavacca Building (CA-1983). NW corner First and Brown Sts. Coursed ashlar sandstone veneer over steel framing, 150' × 110', two stories, flat roof, department store and bank with second-floor offices. Built 1905, Luther Mark Turton, architect; later alterations; demolished 1973. 6 sheets (1973, including site plan, plans, elevations).

Nashville   □   El Dorado County

House (CA-1353). Wood frame with board-and-batten siding, two-bay front, one story, shingled gable roof pitches out over rear lean-to, three-bay front porch. Built 1860s, vernacular cabin by the highway with picket fence; demolished. 1 ext. photo (1934).

Log Barn (CA-1354). Round log construction, saddle-notching, vertical board siding, one-bay front, one story with hay mow, shingled gable roof extended over rear and side lean-tos. Built 1860s, nearly ruinous in photo, demolished. 1 ext. photo (1934).

National City   □   San Diego County

Granger Music Hall (CA-1998). 1700 E. Fourth St. Wood frame with shingles, one-and-a-half stories, approx. 36' × 101', hipped roof, flared exposed rafter ends, hoods over doorways supported by brackets, hipped-roof diamond-pane dormers on vestibule, oval windows on auditorium; paneled interiors, plaster moldings, painted murals on ceilings. Vestibule built 1896 as music room, Irving J. Gill, architect; auditorium added 1898; known for excellent acoustics; closed 1906, damaged by fires and vandalism, moved to present site 1969. 3 sheets (1975, 1976, including plan, elevations, section, detail); 1 photocopy of ext. photo (ca. 1900), 5 photocopies of int. photos (ca. 1900); 16 data pages (1975). NR

Kimball Block Row Houses (CA-1969). 906-40 A Ave. Brick, ten-unit row 250' × 45' with each house front 25'; units are paired to appear as five houses, two stories, flat roof, sheet metal cornice molding, five false pediments with semicircular louvered vents in center, brick arches and decorative brickwork in pediments, continuous one-story front porch, stickwork railing, turned posts with sawn brackets, spindlework frieze under molded cornice, all openings have segmental hoodmolds; L-plans flipped every other unit to create U-shaped rear service yards. Built 1887–88 for Frank Kimball, constructed according to drawings sent from Philadelphia, the eastern-style row houses are unique in southern California for this period. 4 ext. photos (1971), 3 int. photos (1971), 4 data pages (1971).

Kimball, Frank, House (CA-2166). 21 W. Plaza Blvd. Wood frame with channeled siding, two stories, approx. 51' × 32', hipped roof, paired brackets at cornice, pilasters at corners, one-story porch across front with balustrade above. Built 1868 for Frank Kimball, founder of National City; moved and altered ca. 1910, with porch and pilasters added then. 3 photocopies of ext. photos (ca. 1873, ca. 1906), 2 photocopies of architectural drawings (1974, including plans, elevations, section, details); 13 data pages (1975).

St. Matthew's Episcopal Church (CA-1959). 521 E. 8th St. Wood frame with horizontal siding, brick foundations, 39' × 96', one story, shingled gable roof with cross gables flanking front gable, three-stage tower with tall, tapering polygonal spire with exposed rafter ends, pointed-arch windows of varying sizes on all stages, middle section shingled, decorative half-timbering in gable ends, two-bay shed-roofed entrance porch with pointed arches set in square framed bays, open-

St. Matthew's Episcopal Church, National City (CA-1959).

work corners, square columns; single nave, sanctuary extended from one end divided from nave by wall section with arch spanned by rood screen with cross atop center, exposed roof truss with rafters connected by tie beams reinforced with diagonal braces, tongue-and-groove wainscoting. Built 1887, Henry E. Cooper, architect; a wooden rendition of Gothic Revival style built during National City's boom period in the 1880s. 5 sheets (1971, including plan, elevations, section); 3 ext. photos (1971), 10 int. photos (1971); 8 data pages (1971). NR

Navaro River □ Mendocino County

Fishing Resort (CA-1470). Mouth of Navaro R. Wood frame buildings, most prominent is Navaro Inn: six-bay front, two stories, gable roof. Built mid to late 19th c.; recently remodeled; outbuildings unchanged. 1 photo of general view (1934).

Nevada City   □   Nevada County

Commercial Buildings (CA-1538). A row of wood-frame, one-story commercial buildings with gabled pediments with fan-louvers over bracketed cornices, glazed shop fronts have polygonal bay windows, canopies extend over side-walks. Built 1860s; demolished for Post Office building. 1 photocopy of ca. 1927 photo.

Fire House #2 (CA-1395). Broad St. Brick, two stories, gable roof with boxed cornice and returns, drop siding in gable end, square bell tower at front end with round arches with pronounced keystones, hip roof with finial, two-story front porch. Built 1861, a good example of a frontier fire house, well preserved. 1 ext. photo (1934).

Nevada City (CA-1802). Town founded 1848 upon discovery of gold in Deer Creek, center of a great quartz mining district. 1 photocopy of 1903 photo showing rooftops of wooden buildings.

Nevada County Courthouse (CA-1803). Brick and stone, five-by-five bays, three stories, flat roof with balustraded parapet, pedimented central part of facade slightly expressed by quoins on third floor around arcaded section, pilasters on main floor around round-arched opening, ground floor has rusticated three-bay portico with segmental arches and metal balustrade above. Built 1860s; demolished. 1 photocopy of undated photo.

Store (CA-1394). NW corner Broad and N. Pine Sts. Brick, eight-by-six bays, two stories, flat roof with parapet composed of entablature with bracketed cornice, ornamental wrought-iron balcony at second-floor level around both sides, ground floor has a variety of glazed openings and shop fronts, also iron-shuttered doors. Built ca. 1870, remodeled in the 1930s; a typical commercial block of the second half of the 19th c. in the Mother Lode region. 1 ext. photo (1934).

New Almaden □ Santa Clara County

Town of New Almaden. Named for the famed mercury mines in Spain, New Almaden mining operations began in 1824 during the Spanish-Mexican Colonial period. Because mercury was essential to the reduction process of gold and silver ore, the mines became the largest mercury-producing operation in the country during the Gold Rush era. Mining was carried on in the Cinnabar Hills; the mining community, called the Hacienda, was developed along Alamitas Creek. At its entrance stood the Casa Grande, residence of the General Manager and reception center for the important visitors to the mines. At the other end of the Hacienda were the great furnaces and reduction works. Mining operations were intermittent beginning in the late 1920s. In

1958 the area was designated a National Historic Landmark within which Santa Clara County established the 3,500-acre Quicksilver Park, 1975; a historic district protects the historic character of the Hacienda through design review.

Adobe House (CA-1623). *Almaden Rd.* Adobe, four-bay front, one story, gable roof extended over porch across front. Built ca. 1854 for mine office workers. 1 ext. photo (1936).

El Adobe Viejo (CA-1622). *Almaden Rd.* Adobe, four-bay front, one story, gable roof extended over porch across front, two entrances. Built ca. 1854 for mine office workers; later wood frame additions, somewhat altered. 1 ext. photo (1936).

Carson House (CA-115). *21570 Almaden Rd.* The New Almaden Museum of Mercury Mining. Plastered adobe with wood frame additions with board-and-batten and clapboard siding, 36′ (five-bay front) × 31′ with offset rear wing 29′ × 34′, one story, gable roof extended over front porch, sawn brackets. Built ca. 1845, rear wing added 1850s, occupied by Mr. Carson, Superintendent of the Mine. 11 sheets (1936, including plans, elevations, section, details; elevation of dovecote); 3 ext. photos (1936), 1 ext. photo of dovecote (1936); 2 data pages (1937).

Casa Grande (Almaden Club House) (CA-1116). *21350 Almaden Rd.* Brick, stuccoed on the first floor, eight-bay front, two stories on sloping site, hip roof, one-story porch across front. Built 1854 as residence of general manager of New Almaden Mining Co., Gordon Parker Cummings, architect, and Henry W. Halleck, manager; landscaping by John McLaren. 7 ext. photos (1936, 1980), 2 int. photos (1936), 1 photocopy of undated ext. photo; 12 data pages (1977).

Guadalupe Mine—Church and Schoolhouse (CA-157). Wood frame with channeled siding, three-bay front, one story, gable roof with square open belfry, corner boards, pointed-arched windows, one-bay entrance porch with curved brackets and flat roof. Built 1860s; demolished. 2 ext. photos (1936); 1 int. photo (1936).

Guadalupe Mine—Miner's Cabins (CA-120). Row of three cabins, each wood frame with board-and-batten siding, three-bay front, one story with rear lean-to, shingled gable roofs, front porches. Built 1850s for furnace workers; good examples of the kind of basic vernacular structure that was the typical pioneer shelter. 1 ext. photo (1936).

Laird Adobe (CA-134). *Almaden Rd.* Plastered adobe, two-bay front, one story, shingled gable roof with sawn wood brackets. Built 1854 for mine office workers. 1 ext. photo (1936).

Mine Hill School (CA-1125). *Off Almaden Rd.,*

Casa Grande (Almaden Club House), New Almaden (CA-1116).

New Almaden continued

New Almaden Quicksilver Mine County Park.
Wood frame with channeled siding, 56' (five-bay front) × 78', cross-shaped plan, one story, gable roof with bracketed cornice and cornice returns on gable ends, hoodmolds on windows. Built ca. 1860 by New Almaden Quicksilver Mine as six-bay rectangular structure; additions before 1885, including square belvedere in center, now gone; only company-built school still standing. 3 sheets (1977, including plot plan, plan, elevations); 2 ext. photos (1936), 4 photocopies of photos (ca. 1860, 1862, ca. 1885); 10 data pages (1977). NHL

New Almaden Quicksilver Mine (Almaden Mine, Office and Shop Buildings) (CA-114). Almaden Rd., New Almaden Quicksilver Mine County Park. Office building: Adobe, brick and wood frame, irregularly shaped, 23' front × 195', with another wing 34' × 171', one story, shingled gable roof with some sheet metal, main section has front porch with square louvered cupola and a round-arched colonnaded section on one side. Built according to some accounts under Spanish occupation and named after mines in Spain; completed by the Americans; during the Gold Rush period this was the largest mercury mine in the U.S. 16 sheets (1936, including plot plan, plan, elevations, sections, details); 6 ext. photos (1936), 2 int. photos (1936), 8 photocopies of photos (1876, 1877, 1878, ca. 1885, ca. 1886); 14 data pages (1937, 1977). NHL

Shannon Farmhouse (CA-1124). 14475 Shannon Rd. Wood frame with channeled siding, four-bay front, two stories, hip roof with boxed cornice extends to cover two-story wrap-around veranda, flat-sawn decorative railing at second-floor level. Built 1866 for Thomas Shannon, one of the early settlers of Santa Clara Valley. 1 ext. photo (1936).

West, Dr., House (CA-1183). Adobe, three-bay front, one story, gable roof extended over porch across front. Built ca. 1854; not located. 1 ext. photo (1936).

Newport Beach ◻ Orange County

Lovell Beach House (CA-1986). 1242 W. Ocean Front. Great reinforced concrete frames, exposed, with stuccoed wood-frame superstructure, two raised stories, 57' (four-bay front) × 33', flat roof, house elevated above beach on five huge concrete cradles. Built 1926, Rudolph M. Schindler, architect; sleeping porch on second-story

front enclosed in 1928, Rudolph M. Schindler, architect. 10 sheets (1968, including plans, elevations, sections, details of interior divider); 7 ext. photos (1968), 3 int. photos (1968); 2 data pages (1968). NR

Niles ◻ Alameda County

See entries under Fremont.

Nipomo vicinity ◻ San Luis Obispo County

Dana, William G., House (CA-23). Guadalupe Rd. Adobe, 91' (seven-bay front) × 57', two stories with one-story wings in rear, H-shaped, porch between projections on front, gable roof. Built ca. 1839 as one-story structure, second story added later; restored 1980s. 7 sheets (1936, including plans, elevations, section, details); 8 ext. photos (1936); 1 data page (1937). NR

Norman Bar ◻ Mariposa County

Chinese Adobe Building (CA-1529). Portions of three adobe walls, two openings in one wall. 1 photocopy of 1925 photo.

North Bloomfield ◻ Nevada County

Frame Houses (CA-1537). A row of wood-frame cottages, one-and-a-half stories with gable roofs, shed-roofed porches, largely obscured by a row of mature locust trees planted in front of them. Built early 1850s in a town originally called Humbug that was a gold mining town in the 1850s and later. 1 photocopy of undated photo.

North San Juan ◻ Nevada County

Brick Buildings—Main St. (CA-1398). Brick, one and two stories, flat roofs, denticulated parapets, three-bay fronts, one-story porches. Built ca. 1855, now either destroyed or heavily remodeled. 1 ext. photo (1934).

Brick Store (CA-1397). Main St. Brick, three-bay front by six bays, two stories, parapeted roof with elaborate brickwork entablature, ornamental cast-iron balcony railing around both sides, round-arched openings with pronounced archivolt trim on corbel stops, paneled iron shutters.

Brick Store, North San Juan (CA-1397-1).

Built 1859, allegedly as the Capwell & Furth Store; second floor used as offices of mining companies; good example of Gold Rush era brickwork; demolished 1960s. 2 ext. photos (1934).

Church (Methodist Episcopal Church) (CA-1399). *Flume St.* Wood frame with clapboards, one-bay front by three bays, gable roof with boxed cornice and returns, square open belfry, paneled corner pilasters with molded caps, lunette in gable, enclosed vestibule with shed roof. Built 1857, a modest example of a frontier Georgian-style church. 1 ext. photo (1934).

Frame Buildings—Main St. (CA-1697). Frame with horizontal siding, two stories, gable roofs, porches. Built ca. 1855, now either destroyed or heavily remodeled. 1 ext. photo (1934).

House (CA-1396). Wood frame with clapboards, one story, three-bay front, shingled gable roof extends over front porch with turned posts, rear addition, barn in back. Built mid-19th c. 1 ext. photo (1934).

Masonic Hall and Wells Fargo Building (CA-1698). *Main St.* Brick, three-bay front, two stories, flat roof with parapet and brick cornice on corbeled brackets, two-story shed-roofed porch across front, openings with cast-iron paneled shutters. Built ca. 1850, first brick building in town, meeting hall on second floor, commercial space and post office on first floor, reported to be location of Wells Fargo & Co. office 1860s–1880s; restored 1960s. 1 photocopy of undated ext. photo shows also a brick building next door.

Oak Grove   □   San Diego County

Butterfield Stage Station (CA-49). *State Hwy. 79,* *15 mis. NW of Warner Springs.* Adobe, variety of board siding, one story, gable roof extended over porch with wood posts. Built ca. 1855, trading post and then stage station on Butterfield Stage line operating between San Francisco, Yuma, and St. Louis, 1858–61. 6 ext. photos (1937, 1960); 1 data page (1937). NHL, SHL

Oakland   □   Alameda County

Galinda Hotel (CA-1898). *8th and Franklin Sts.* Brick and stone, seven-bay facade, rectangular, four stories, mansard roof with numerous chimneys, arched windows, patterned brickwork. Built 1877, J. C. Matthews & Sons, architects; one of Oakland's most sumptuous early hotels, converted to apartments during World War II, destroyed by fire 1972. 2 ext. photos (1960).

Greek Orthodox Church of the Assumption (CA-2055). *950 Castro St.* Concrete, three-bay front, one story with gallery, cruciform shape, cross-gable roof with hemispherical dome at intersection, pedimented portico in antis with Ionic columns, double-doored main entrance with transom and denticulated cornice, windows with brackets and denticulated cornices, side entrance emphasized by broken pediment and band containing Greek fret motif; cruciform plan, notable plasterwork; Greek Revival details. Built 1920, Charles Burrell, architect. First permanent structure in Oakland for Greek community. Moved from 920 Brush St. 5 ext. photos (1978), 5 int. photos (1978); 3 data pages (1978, 1979).

House (CA-2058). *716 Castro Street.* Wood frame with novelty siding and plaster cast trim, three-bay front, two stories, gable roof, paneled bargeboards with brackets at either end of gable, one-bay entrance porch with Tuscan columns, three-sided, one-story bay projection with Ionic pilasters between windows, denticulated cornice across top of first story; original cast iron fence around yard. Built 1890. Moved to Heritage Park. 6 ext. photos (1978).

Mahoney, Thomas, House (CA-2056). *18th St. N.* *side between Market and West Sts.* Wood frame with clapboards, three-bay front, one story, gable roof, boxed eaves, one-bay entrance porch with Tuscan columns, windows with double hung sash, six-over-six lights. Built in mid-1850s using clapboarding and window frames produced by California Mills. One of the earliest structures in Oakland, the building dates from the first decade of California's statehood. Moved from 669 8th St. 2 ext. photos (1978).

Galinda Hotel, Oakland (CA-1898).

Moss, J. Mora, House (CA-1897). *Broadway and McArthur Boulevard, Mosswood Park.* Wood frame with ship-lap siding, three-bay front, approx. 63′ × 48′, one-and-a-half stories, hip and gable roof with dormers, polygonal bays; notable interiors with Gothic detail, panelling, marble mantels. Built 1864, S. H. Williams, architect, for J. Mora Moss, who came to California in 1854 and became one of state's leading citizens. One of few remaining examples of important early houses in Gothic Revival style, now offices for City of Oakland Recreation Department. 12 sheets (1960s, including site plan, plans, elevations, section, details); 4 ext. photos (1960), 3 int. photos (1960); 11 data pages (1961).

Paramount Theater (CA-1976). *2025 Broadway.* Built 1929–31, Miller and Pflueger architects. One of most important examples of Art Deco style in California. 8 ext. photos (1972, 1975), 8 int. photos (1972, 1975), 23 photocopies (including 1 ext. 1931 photo, 2 ext. 1932 photos, 11 int. 1932 photos, and 9 architect's drawings of plans, a section, and details); 52 data pages (1976, 1980).

Pardee, Governor, House (CA-1899). *672 Eleventh St.* Wood frame, drop siding scored to imitate stone, three-bay main section of facade projects slightly from south and north wings, corner quoins, two stories on raised brick basement, rectangular central cupola with cross-gabled roof, bracketed cornice. Built 1868 by Dr. Enoch Homer Pardee, pioneer physician, later occupied by his son, Dr. George Cooper Pardee, both of whom were mayors of Oakland. George Pardee was Governor of state from 1903–07, house deeded by family to City of Oakland for a museum; restoration in progress. 3 ext. photos (1960), 3 int. photos (1960), 2 ext. photos of stable (1960); 7 data pages (1966).

Quinn, William H., House (CA-2057). *NW corner 16th and Filbert Sts.* Wood frame with deep V-groove rustic siding, three-bay front, two stories, irregular shape, truncated hip roof, bracketed eaves, parapeted one-story entrance porch with paired square columns and solid railing, three-sided bay projections flank entrance, windows on bay projections have segmental heads with siding cut to imitate masonry voussoirs and keystones, one-story V-shaped bay projection on side elevation; outbuildings include a carriage house. Built c. 1890. Moved from 1425 Castro St. 3 ext. photos (1978), 1 ext. photo of carriage house (1978).

Southern Pacific Oakland Mole and Pier (CA-1888). Foot of 7th St. Iron frame with segmental arched trusses, wood siding. Industrial complex consisting of several hangar-type buildings that served as train and storage sheds. Site developed as ferry landing 1862, became terminus of transcontinental railroads in 1869, developed as Oakland Mole and Pier by Central Pacific and opened to traffic in 1882. Wharf used as shipping terminal until 1919, ferry commuter service until 1939, terminal abandoned in 1960, demolished. 3 drawings. (1878, 1882), 1 painting (1871), 15 ext. photos (1869, 1871, 1887, 1890s, c. 1900, 1909, after 1919); 11 data pages (1960).

White, James, House (CA-2054). S.E. corner 13th and Castro Sts. Wood frame with coved rustic siding, two-bay front, two stories, irregular shape, truncated hip roof, bracketed eaves. Built 1875, home of James White, leader of the Seventh Day Adventists and founder of the Pacific Press. Moved from 702 11th St. 6 ext. photos (1978); 2 data pages (1978, 1979).

Oceanside vicinity □ San Diego County

Casa del Rancho Santa Margarita y Las Flores (CA-48). 10 mis. off U.S. 101. Adobe and wood frame, two stories, tiled gable roof extended over two-story porch with wood posts, recessed openings with wood lintels; rectangular plan with courtyard. Built ca. 1841, part of holdings of Mission San Luís Rey, granted to 1841 to Gov. Pío Pico. 14 ext. photos (1937); 1 data page (1937).

Mission San Luís Rey de Francia (CA-42). Mission Rd., 5 mis. E. of Oceanside. Adobe, fieldstone foundations, Latin cross plan, three-bay facade, tiled gable roof, two-stage polygonal tower rises from square base on one side, domical roof with square lantern, round-arched openings with archivolt molding on intrados, central portion bracketed by pilasters tied to cornice molding, espadaña with central round-arched niche with statue of saint surmounted by small domed lantern with cross, entrance architrave enframed with fluted pilasters, wooden entrance doors set in deep reveal, round-arched opening with flanking pilasters supporting pediment with straight cornice molding, round window above, niches with statues to either side, church attached to corredor of adjacent *convento* with 32 square piers supporting round arches; four-bay nave has choir loft above entrance, low dome of brick at crossing flanked by shallow transept arms with

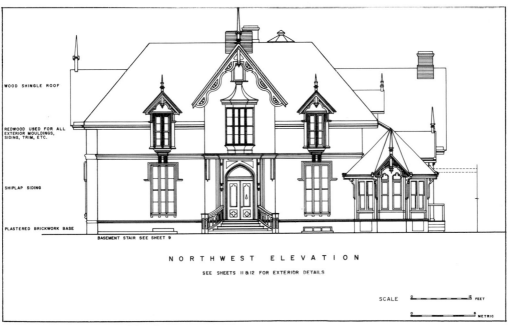

J. Mora Moss House, Oakland (CA-1897).

Paramount Theatre, interior detail, Oakland (CA-1976).

altars, octagonal dome on round arches spanning nave and transepts, arches spring from paneled piers with molded caps and bases decorated with geometric motifs as are nave pilasters, raised sanctuary, wood railing, two-tiered altar reredos polychromed with tripartite division, richly ornamented interior, octagonal mortuary chapel off nave. Founded June 13, 1798, by Father Fermín de Lasuén as the ninth mission; built under the supervision of Father Antonio Peyrí 1811–15, construction of chapels and adjacent structures went on over period of years, building fell into uins after 1834 secularization, mission property restored by President Lincoln 1865, restoration began 1893 under Father Joseph O'Keefe and has continued, dome and lantern over crossing differ from original but restored church is otherwise much the same, outbuildings and *convento* have also been restored. 25 sheets (1936, including plot plan, plans, elevations, sections, details); 14 ext. photos (1936), 4 int. photos (1936), 6 ext. photos of the grounds (1936); 1 data page (1937). NHL, SHL

Olema vicinity   □   Marin County

Lime Kiln (CA-1437). 4 mi. SE of Olema on CA 1. Rubble stone, round-arched opening, ruinous, tree growing on top. 5 photos (1934). NR

Oleta   □   Amador County

Frame Barn (CA-1352). Wood frame with vertical board siding, high-pitched gable roof, shed-roofed open lean-tos on three sides. Built 1850s; not located. 1 ext. photo (1934).

Oroville Dam vicinity ▫ Butte County

Suspension Bridge and Stone Toll House (CA-1476). Suspension bridge shipped around the Horn from Troy, New York, in 1853, and placed in service in 1856, operated as a toll bridge until 1889, when it became a free bridge and was in use until 1954; the bridge with its toll house was moved from its original site, which is now covered with the waters of Lake Oroville, to a site overlooking Oroville Dam. 1 photocopy of 1937 photo of general view.

Owensmouth ▫ Los Angeles County

See entry for El Escorpión under Los Angeles.

Pala ▫ San Diego County

Asistencia San Antonio de Pala (CA-44). Plastered adobe, stone foundations, L-shape, chapel in one ell, living quarters in other, one story, 125′ front, tiled gable roof, plain facade, detached companario originally on boulder and adobe base, two stages with curved top, molded belt cornice, round-arched openings contain two bells; interior has exposed wood timber roof framing, plastered walls with Indian paintings, sanctuary at north end. Built 1816 by Indian labor under supervision of Father Antonio Peyrí of Mission San Luís Rey as dependency of the Mission; building declined to ruinous state, restored after 1901 by Southern California Landmarks Club under Charles Lummis; original campanario destroyed by rains in 1916, restored 1917; building restored again 1957–59 as a school and convent. 7 sheets (1936, including plot plan, plan, elevations, int. elevations, details); 12 ext. photos (1936, 1937), 2 int. photos (1936); 2 data pages (1937). SHL

Palo Alto ▫ Santa Clara County

Courtyard Building (CA-2098). 533-39 Ramona St. Stuccoed, three-bay front, two stories with center bay rising to three stories, tiled roof, arched entrance, balcony above has tiled shed roof, tiled entrance and interior courtyard lavish in Spanish ornament. Built 1927, Birge M. Clark, architect. 6 int. photos (1980).

Emperger Grocery (Channing Market) (CA-2103). 532 Channing Ave. Wood frame with drop siding, 18′ (three-bay front) × 58′, two stories, gable roof with gabled false front, storefront with canopy. Built 1900. 2 sheets (1980, including site plan, plans, elevations); 3 ext. photos (1980); 13 data pages (1980).

Kennedy, John G., House (CA-2076). 423 Chaucer St. Stuccoed wood frame, approx. 60′ (five bay front) × 45′, two stories, tiled hipped roof, prominent exterior chimney on front, round-arched recessed entrance, casement windows. Built 1922, Julia Morgan, architect. 3 ext. photos (1980), 7 int. photos (1980), 8 photocopies of architect's drawings (1921, including plans, elevations, section, details); 6 data pages (1980).

Mission San Luís Rey de Francia, Oceanside vicinity, (CA-42).

Palo Alto continued

Ramona Street Commercial Building (Pedro de Lemos Building) (CA-2067). *520-526 Ramona St.* Stuccoed tile construction, 24' (three-bay front) × 100', L-shaped, one-story front portion, two-and-a-half stories, in rear, tiled hipped and gabled roofs, tiled gable dormers, courtyard with tree in front section, lavish use of Spanish ornament. Built 1925, Pedro de Lemos, graphic artist and director of Stanford Art Museum, designer. 5 sheets (1979, including plans, elevation, sections); 6 ext. photos (1980); 15 data pages (1978, 1981).

Stanford University:

□ **Dunn-Bacon House (CA-2175).** *565 Mayfield Ave.* Wood frame with clapboards, two-and-a-half stories, five-bay front, hipped roof with gable dormers on sides, two-story pedimented portico with paired fluted Ionic columns, wide eaves with extended modillions. Built 1899, Charles Edward Hodges, architect, for the Dunns, who were not connected with Stanford Univ. but who received permission from Mrs. Stanford to build on its property. 4 ext. photos (1975).

□ **Durand-Kirkman House (CA-2176).** *623 Cabrillo Ave.* Wood frame with shingles, two-and-a-half stories, cross gambrel roof, variety of windows, some bay windows, some geometric patterns in lead, one-story porch across front; extensive hand-carving on interior. Built 1904,

John G. Kennedy House, Palo Alto (CA-2076).

Prof. A. B. Clark, architect; first campus house built outside established residential area. 2 ext. photos (1975), 2 int. photos (1975), 2 photocopies of architect's drawings (1904, including elevations and partial section).

□ **Escondite Cottage (CA-2168).** *Escondido Rd.* Wood frame with board-and-batten siding, one story with two-story section, L-shape, gable roof with wide eaves and stick-like brackets, drip moldings on openings. Built 1875 for Jean-Baptiste-Paulin Caperon, a.k.a. Peter Coutts, who returned to France in 1882 and sold his property to Leland Stanford. 5 ext. photos (1975).

□ **Frenchman's Library (CA-2169).** *860 Escondido Rd.* Brick, two stories with three-story square

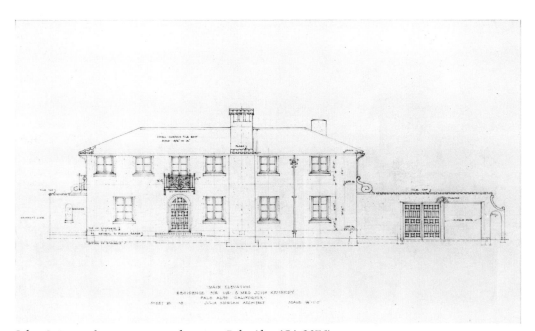

John G. Kennedy House, main elevation, Palo Alto (CA-2076).

tower originally topped with Norman steeple, gable roof with wide eaves, enclosed porches and other additions. Built ca. 1875 for Jean-Baptiste-Paulin Caperon, a.k.a. Peter Coutts; steeple replaced by multi-windowed room and low pyramidal roof. 4 ext. photos (1975), 2 int. photos (1975).

□ *Frenchman's Tower (CA-2170). Old Page Mill Rd.* Brick, round, approx. 50' high, crenellated parapet, bricked-in lancet windows. Built ca. 1875 for Jean-Baptiste-Paulin Caperon, a.k.a. Peter Coutts, with no known function. 3 ext. photos (1975).

□ *Griffin-Drell House (CA-2173). 570 Alvarado Rd.* Wood frame with shingles, two-and-a-half stories, hipped roof, round tower with conical roof at each front corner, two-level porch in between towers. Built ca. 1891 to patternbook design as faculty housing for Stanford Univ. See also its duplicate, Salvatierra Street—House (CA-2174). 3 ext. photos (1975).

□ *Hoover, Lou Henry, House (CA-2177).* Concrete, brick, and hollow tile construction covered with stucco, three stories on sloping site, variety of cubic forms with flat roofs forming terraces, plain surface, rambling quality, outside stairways and fireplaces; interior in Tudor style features

spiral staircase, oak paneling. Completed 1920, Birge Clark and Charles Davis, architects, for Herbert Hoover and his wife Lou Henry, although they lived here only briefly. 12 ext. photos (1975), 4 int. photos (1975), 4 photocopies of architect's drawings (ca. 1918, including elevations, details). NR

□ *House (CA-2174). Salvatierra Street.* Wood frame with shingles, two-and-a-half stories, hipped roof, round tower with conical roof at each front corner, two-level porch in between towers. Built ca. 1891 to patternbook design as faculty housing for Stanford Univ. See also its duplicate, Griffin-Drell House (CA-2173). 4 ext. photos (1975).

□ *Memorial Church (CA-2172 A).* Rough-faced ashlar, three-bay front in gable end, two stories, tiled gable roof, three round-arched entrances on first level, round-arched window on second level flanked by triple round-arched windows, ornate stone carving over openings, mosaic depicting Sermon on the Mount in gable, rounded apse and other rooms protrude from rear. Built 1899–1903, Clinton Day, architect, based on sketch by Charles Allerton Coolidge; memorial to Leland Stanford; damaged in earthquake of 1906, rebuilt 1913. 14 ext. photos (1975), 5 int. photos (1975).

Hoover House, Stanford University, Palo Alto (CA-2177).

Stanford University Quadrangle, Palo Alto (CA-2172).

□ *Palo Alto Winery (CA-2171).* Brick, two-and-a-half stories, L-shaped, gable roof, board-and-batten siding in gables, monitors on roof, segmental-arched openings. Built 1888 for Leland Stanford, served as winery until 1915; then housed dairy until 1958; in 1961 converted to shops and offices. 8 ext. photos (1975).

□ *Stanford University Quad(CA-2172).* Inner and outer quadrangles of collegiate buildings, all rough-faced ashlar, one and two stories, tiled hipped roofs, long arcades along sides of buildings connecting buildings into quadrangles with Romanesque openings, intricate stone carving. Built 1887–93 and 1898–1905, Charles Allerton Coolidge, architect, Frederick Law Olmsted, initial landscaping; outer quadrangle buildings collapsed in 1906 earthquake, reconstructed. 26 ext. photos (1975).

Violet Ray Gasoline Station (General Petroleum Gasoline Station) (CA-2069). 799 *Alma St.* Stuccoed tile construction, gas station $17' \times 17'$ with porte cocheres extending 12', one garage $21' \times 80'$, another garage $25' \times 61'$, one story,

Violet Ray Gas Station, Palo Alto (CA-2069).

tiled gable and flat roofs. Built 1929. 2 sheets (1979, including plan, elevations); 5 ext. photos (1980); 7 data pages (1979).

Y.W.C.A. Hostess House (CA-1670). University Ave. and El Camino Real. Wood frame with board-and-batten siding, one-and-a-half stories, shed-roofed dormers, porch across front has shed roof with exposed rafter ends. Built during World War I, Julia Morgan, architect; originally located on Santa Cruz Ave. in Menlo Park to serve Camp Fremont; moved to present site after War to serve as community center. 2 ext. photos (1975).

Pasadena   □   **Los Angeles County**

El Molino Viejo (CA-34). 1120 Old Mill Rd. Stone, brick, and adobe, plastered inside and out, 23' (two-bay front) × 60', two stories, timber-framed tiled hip roof; L-plan. Built ca. 1816 on property of San Gabriel Mission as first grist mill in California, Claudio López, builder, under supervision of Padre José María Zalvidea; damaged in 1812 earthquake and abandoned as a mill; purchased 1859 by Col. E. J. C. Kewen and converted to a residence; restored 1928 by Mr. and Mrs. James Brehm. 6 sheets (1934, including plans, elevations, sections, details); 4 ext. photos (1935); 1 data page (1937). SHL

Gamble House (CA-1981). 4 Westmoreland Place. House museum. Wood frame with shingles, irregular shape, three stories, rafter ends rounded and sheathed in copper typically extend beyond the cornice, three concrete chimneys with pronounced cornices, terraces with boulder and brick retaining walls, three second-floor sleeping porches above terraces with horizontal board railings and planter boxes with expressive wood joinery, notched beams extend beyond porch floor supported by truss and braces, framing structure expressed on exterior walls, triple main entrance with larger central door, doorway has heavy wood architrave with glazed transoms and corner brackets, varieties of art glass joined by soldered copper; central hall plan with living and dining rooms in back, entry hall and stairwell in mahogany and teak with complicated orientalized joinery, living room inglenook with benches and hearth with decorative tiles, divided from main space by a wood truss, other hearths have decorative tiles, lavish use of exotic wood in oriental motifs used to heighten the structural expression, rich use of materials and custom-designed lighting fixtures throughout, built-in cabinetry and furnishings all architect-designed.

Built 1908 for David B. Gamble, Charles and Henry Greene, architects; a masterpiece of the Craftsman movement. 11 photostats of architect's drawings (1908, including plot plan, plans, elevations, interior elevations, section, details) from the Greene & Greene Library at the Gamble House. NR

Irwin House (CA-1985). 240 N. Grand Ave. Wood frame, shingled, irregular shape with inner court and fountain, two stories, multiple gable roof, rafters with rounded ends extend beyond eaves, four brick chimneys with boulders inset, brick and boulder porch piers support second-story decks off bedrooms, wood posts and trusses with horizontal wood railings set back from supporting structure, variety of wood doors and windows; inner two-story court roofed with trellis, second-floor bedrooms off court with porches, elaborate wood-pegged joinery derived from oriental architecture expressed in interior detail and finishing, rich use of materials, architect-designed lighting fixtures and hardware. Built 1906 for Theodore M. Irwin as a major alteration to a 1900 house with an inner court built for Katherine Duncan, Charles and Henry Greene, architects, complete second floor added along with related ground-floor alterations; the Irwin House is notable in the oeuvre of the Greene brothers for the complexity of its inter-related forms and spaces. 14 sheets (1968, including site plan, plans, elevations, section, interior elevations, details).

Neighborhood Church (CA-2116). S. Pasadena Ave. and W. California Blvd. Frame with shingles, steeply pitched cross gable roofs, square corner tower with spire, entrances in base, large pointed-arch window in one gable end, rose window in other gable end. Built 1887, fine example of Shingle style. Demolished. 5 ext. photos (ca. 1972), 8 int. photos (ca. 1972).

Pescadero   □   **San Mateo County**

Congregational Church (CA-163). San Gregorio St. Wood frame with scored channeled siding, one story, one-bay front by three bays deep with lower wing behind, low-pitched gable roof with cornice returns on gable front, square tower with steeple, entrance at base, round-arched openings, quoining formed by channeled siding. Built 1867; steeple added 1889. 6 ext. photos (ca. 1935, 1975), 2 int. photos (1975). NR

Frame Building (CA-1996). 108-114 San Gregorio St. (CA-1996). Four wood frame late 19th c. structures on east side of San Gregorio St. 1

Pescadero continued

sheet (1974, including site plan, elevations of streetscape); 2 ext. photos of general views (1975); 4 data pages (1974). For individual listings, see Methodist-Episcopal Church (CA-162), I.O.O.F. Hall (CA-2134), Woodhams House (CA-2135), Thomas W. Moore House (CA-2136).

Garretson Schoolhouse (CA-2132). 2307 Pescadero Rd. Wood frame with horizontal siding, one-bay front in gable end by two bays deep, one story, gable roof with curling brackets. Built 1875 as a private school on San Gregorio Rd.; moved to present site in 1885, served as dairy. 2 ext. photos (1975).

Graham, Isaac, House (White House) (CA-2130). Wood frame with channeled siding on gable end, clapboards elsewhere, two stories with one story ell, gable roof, entrance in gable end. Built ca. 1851 on hill where it served as landmark to sailors; moved to present site 1880; destroyed by fire 1976. 6 ext. photos (1975).

I.O.O.F. Hall (CA-2134). 110 San Gregorio St. Wood frame with channeled siding, two stories, three-bay front in gable end, gable roof with bracketed cornice on gable front, porch across front has turned-wood balustrade. Built 1878; porch and brackets added 1890. 2 ext. photos (1975). See 108-114 San Gregorio St. (CA-1996) for elevation drawing and photos of general views.

McCormick, James, House (CA-2131). San Gregorio St. Wood frame with scored channeled siding, two stories, three-bay front in gable end, gable roof, porch across front wraps around, turned balustrade above, doorway has transom and sidelights, square water tower in backyard has bracketed cornice. Built late 1860s. 3 ext. photos (1975), 1 int. photo (1975).

Methodist Episcopal Church (CA-162). 108 San Gregorio St. Wood frame with channeled siding, shingles in gables, vertical boards in gable peaks, one-and-a-half stories, cruciform plan, steeply pitched gable roof, pointed-arch windows, one-story wing in front. Built 1890; by 1905 sold by church; steeple and tower removed after ca. 1935. 9 ext. photos (ca. 1935, 1975); 3 int. photos (1975). See 108-114 San Gregorio St. (CA-1996) for elevation drawing and photos of general views.

Moore, Thomas W., House (CA-2136). 114 San Gregorio St. Wood frame with channeled siding, two stories, three-bay front in gable end, gable roof, porch across front has balustrade above. Built ca. 1863. 2 ext. photos (1975). See 108-114 San Gregorio St. (CA-1996) for elevation drawing and photos of general views.

St. Anthony's Roman Catholic Church (CA-2133). North St. Wood frame with channeled siding, one story, one-bay front by four bays, gable roof with cornice returns on gable end, square tower with pyramidal roof, small rose window in Classical frame over pedimented entrance. Built 1906. 6 ext. photos (1975), 4 int. photos (1975).

Steele Brothers Dairies (CA-2129). Cabrillo Highway. Dairy founded originally in Marin County, expanded to San Mateo County 1862, owned by Rensselaer Steele and his three cousins.

□ *Cascade Ranch Dairy Building (CA-2129 A).* Wood frame with clapboards, two-and-a-half stories, gable roof, brick chimneys. Built 1862, first building at new dairy site. 5 ext. photos (1975).

□ *Cascade Ranch House (Rensselaer Steele House) (CA-2129 B).* Wood frame with clapboards, two stories, five-bay front, gable roof with cornice returns on gable ends, porch on three sides with balustrade on second level and box columns at first level. Built 1862, Isaac Steele, probable architect; wing added 1884; later additions. 3 ext. photos (1975); 4 data pages (1974).

□ *Cloverdale Ranch Barn (CA-2129 C).* Wood frame with vertical planks, pegged mortise-and-tenon construction, gable roof, three aisles wide. Built 1863. 3 ext. photos (1975), 9 int. photos (1975).

□ *Ramsey-Steele House (CA-2129 D).* Wood frame with channeled siding, one-and-a-half stories, L-plan, gable roof with cornice returns on gable ends, quoining effected with channeled siding, one bay window. Built 1873 for William F. Ramsey. 5 ext. photos (1975), 2 int. photos (1975).

□ *Dickerman Barn (CA-2129 E).* Wood frame with vertical planks, mortise-and-tenon construction, gable roof. Built late 19th c. for Edward Dickerman and his wife, Effie, daughter of Isaac Steele. 4 ext. photos (1975), 3 int. photos (1975).

□ *Año Nuevo Ranch House (Horace Steele House) (CA-2129 F).* Wood frame with channeled siding, three-bay front, two stories, gable roof with cornice returns on gable ends, saltbox-style slope to rear, one bay window. Built 1895. 2 ext. photos (1975).

□ *Barn (CA-2129 G).* Wood frame with vertical siding, gable roof. Built late 19th c. 1 ext. photo

(1975), 1 ext. photo of post-and-rail fence (1975).

□ *House (CA-2129 H)*. Wood frame with channeled siding, one story, five-bay front, gable roof, paneled door now boarded, end bay has garage-type opening. Built late 19th c. 2 ext. photos (1975).

□ *House (CA-2129 I)*. Wood frame with channeled siding, three-bay front, one-and-a-half stories, gable roof, paneled wood door. Built late 19th c. 2 ext. photos (1975).

Weeks, Bartlett V., House (CA-2137). *172 Goulson St.* Wood frame with clapboards, one story, three-bay front, L-shape, gable roof, one-story porch with fan brackets wraps around. Built 1885. 4 ext. photos (1975).

Weeks, Braddock, House (CA-2138). *Pescadero Rd.* Wood frame with clapboards, three-bay front, one-and-a-half stories, gable roof with bracketed cornice, one-story porch across front has pierced columns and fan brackets. Built 1860s. 7 ext. photos (1975).

Wells Fargo & Co. Building (CA-1701). Wood frame with channeled siding, two stories, three-bay front, flat roof with parapet, scrolled brackets at cornice, one-story porch with balustrade above wraps around. Built mid to late 19th c., demolished. 1 photocopy of late 19th c. photo.

Woodhums House (CA-2135). *112 San Gregorio St.* Wood frame with channeled siding, one story, three-bay front, L-shaped with front porch in L, hipped roof, fan brackets on porch posts, bay window on front. Built mid-1890s. 4 ext. photos (1975). See 108-114 San Gregorio St. (CA-1996) for elevation drawing and photos of general views.

Pescadero vicinity □ San Mateo County

Pigeon Point Lighthouse (CA-1997). *State Highway 1.* Brick, 110' high cylindrical tower, 23' diameter at base, 16' diameter at gallery, conical roof, iron gallery and brackets; iron spiral staircase, seven landings, French-made lens; one-story watch house attached, brick, 27' × 19', gable roof with brackets, bracketed hood over entrance, segmental-arched openings. Built 1871–72 as earliest lighthouse on West Coast to have First-order lens. 5 sheets (1974, including plans, elevations, section, details); 11 ext. photos (1975), 6 int. photos (1975), 2 photocopies of ca. 1921 ext. photos; 4 data pages (1974). NR

□ *Work Shop (CA-1997 A)*. Wood frame with channeled siding, 40' (three-bay front) × 18', gable roof. 1 sheet (1974, including plan, elevations, section).

Petaluma vicinity □ Sonoma County

Small Vallejo Adobe (CA-19). *Corona Rd., 3 mis. NE of Petaluma.* Plastered adobe, 16' × 24', one story, shingled hip roof with vent at ridge; one-room plan. Built ca. 1834 for General Mariano Vallejo; present condition unknown. 1 sheet (1934, including plan, elevations, section, details); 1 ext. photo (1934).

Vallejo Adobe (Casa Grande) (CA-11). *State Historic Park. 4 mis. E. of Petaluma on Adobe Rd.* Adobe and wood on rubble-stone foundation, F-shape (built around three sides of court with one end extended), 200' (nineteen-bay front) × 93', two stories, hip roof, two-story porch on all sides except ends of court wings, exposed ends of rafters and joists; multi-room interior without halls. Built over about a ten-year period from 1834 as headquarters of General Mariano Vallejo's ranch, originally built around four sides of court, one of the largest adobe structures remaining from the Mexican period; restored. 9 sheets (1934, including plot plan, plans, elevations, section, details); 8 ext. photos (1934), 2 int. photos (1934). SHL

Pilot Hill □ El Dorado County

Hotel (CA-1382). Wood frame with clapboards, five-bay front by three bays, two-and-a-half stories, gable roof with two front gabled dormers, front two-story veranda with box columns, central door at each floor onto veranda. Built 1854, served as post office, store, and service station; demolished. 1 ext. photo (1934). Placerville.

Bayley, A. J., House (CA-1383). Brick, five-bay front, L-shape, three stories, hip roof with modillion cornice, two-story fort veranda with entablature and six giant paneled box columns, second-floor gallery has turned balustrade, rear three-bay ell with shed-roofed porch. Built 1861–62 by Alcander J. Bayley; one of the finest examples of a large Classical Revival building in the Mother Lode area; deteriorated condition. 5 ext. photos (1934). NR

Pine Grove □ Amador County

First House (CA-1514). Wood frame with clapboards, four-bay front, one story, low gable roof.

Pine Grove continued
House not located, perhaps gone. 1 photocopy of
undated photo.

Piru vicinity   □   Ventura County

La Casa Del Rancho Camulos (CA-38). *State
Highway 126, 2 mis. E. of Piru*. Plastered adobe,
110' × 150', L-shaped, one story, hipped roof, recessed porch across front, porch in L. Portion
built 1841, rest of adobe section added 1846; setting for Ramona's home in novel by Helen Hunt
Jackson. 8 sheets (1934, including plans, elevations, sections, details); 11 ext. photos (1934), 2
int. photos (1934); 1 data page (1936). SHL

□ *Chapel*. Wood frame, 12' × 42', one story, gable roof, most of it covered but not enclosed. 3
sheets (1934, including plan, elevations, sections,
details); 2 ext. photos (1934).

□ *Winery*. Brick, 38' × 123', one-and-a-half stories, gable roof. 5 sheets (1934, including plan,
elevations, sections, details); 2 ext. photos
(1934).

Placerville   □   El Dorado County

Bedford Inn (CA-1364). Wood frame with clapboards, five-bay front by two bays, two-and-a-half
stories, gable roof with molded cornice and returns at gable end, two-story front veranda with
box columns and turned balustrade on both
floors; central-hall plan. Built 1850s; rear two-
story, wood frame, shed-roofed addition. 1 ext.
photo (1934).

Brick and Stone House (CA-1373). Brick, four-
bay front by two bays, two stories, gable roof,
two-story veranda on front and one side with
turned columns, fan brackets, balustrade on second floor, stone lintels and sills, rear and side
frame lean-tos. 1 ext. photo (1934).

Brick House (CA-1371). *2934 Bedford St.* Brick
on stone foundation, three-bay front in gable
end, one-and-a-half stories on full raised basement, steep gable roof with molded cornice and
returns on gable end, shed-roofed four-bay veranda on all sides, turned columns with ornate
bracketed caps and closely spaced turned balusters, gable end window with lunette, brick relieving arch, stone sill. Built ca. 1860. 1 ext. photo
(1934).

Building adjoining Federated Church (CA-1366).
Wood frame with clapboards, three-bay front in

Bayley House, Pilot Hill (CA-1383).

gable end, two stories, gable roof with cornice
molding and returns, two-story veranda on two
sides, second-floor railing with flat balusters.
Built ca. 1860. 1 ext. photo (1934).

Commercial Building (CA-1362). *Main St.* Brick,
ten-bay front, one story, low-pitched parapeted
roof with three raised-paneled sections, brick
pilasters divide front into nine bays, some with
round arches, some filled in, tenth bay is curving
arch on corner. Built ca. 1860. 2 ext. photos
(1934).

Commercial Buildings (CA-1673). *Main St.* One-
and two-story wood frame structures. 1 photocopy of ca. 1860 photo of general view in winter
snow.

El Dorado County Courthouse (CA-1675). Two-
story masonry buildings. 1 photocopy of ca.
1939 photo of fire-damaged buildings, one of
which is courthouse, originally a brewery.

El Dorado County Federated Church (CA-1365).
Brick, three-bay front, one story, gable roof, central square tower with angled corner buttresses
and cornice molding, gable-roofed portico on
one side at street level, three round-arched windows with double round-arched sash and rondel
above. Built ca. 1860; demolished 1961. 1 ext.
photo (1934).

Frame House (CA-1370). Bedford St. Wood frame with clapboards, three-bay front by four bays, one story, two parallel gable roofs with a central cross gable with scrolled bargeboards, shed-roofed veranda across two sides. Built ca. 1860; demolished. 2 ext. photos (1934).

Frame House (CA-1374). Coloma Rd. Wood frame with board-and-batten siding, three-bay front in gable end, one-and-a-half stories, gable roof with dormer, scalloped bargeboards, one-story porch across front, eight-light casement windows, contemporary gable-roofed one-room addition with board-and-batten siding. Built ca. 1860; not located. 1 ext. photo (1934).

House (CA-1368). 50 Benham St. Brick, three-bay front in gable end, three bays deep, one-and-a-half stories, gable roof with cornice molding and returns, one-story front porch with box columns, gable end window with lunette, brick relieving arch, stone sill. Built ca. 1860; not located. 2 ext. photos (1934).

House (CA-1372). Main St. Wood frame with clapboards, five-bay front, one story, gable roof with cornice moldings and returns, front porch with four simple turned columns with squared capitals supporting shed roof, four sets of French doors, entrance door with transom, addition on one end. Built ca. 1860; wing and garage added later. 1 ext. photo (1934).

House (CA-1375). Bedford St. Wood frame with clapboards, one-and-a-half stories, gable roof with central cross gable and window in gable end, shed-roofed front veranda. Built ca. 1860; demolished. 1 ext. photo (1934).

Pony Express Courier Building (CA-1707). Wood frame with clapboards, rest of appearance not ascertainable. 1 photocopy of undated photo of strong box and cradle on front porch, 1 photocopy of int. 1937 photo of scales.

Thompson, Judge, House (CA-1369). 32 Cedar Ravine. Wood frame with clapboards, three-bay front, two stories with one-story rear wing, gable roof with central cross gable with round-arched window, shed-roofed veranda wraps around. Built ca. 1860. 1 ext. photo (1934).

Zeisz, J., Building (CA-1363). Stone, exposed rubble on sides and plastered on front, four-bay front, two stories set into hillside, gable roof with clapboards in end and raking cornice, false front with cornice molding intersects gable end midway, wood balcony across front, two-story porch on side; wood frame two-story section meets

Frame House, Placerville (CA-1374).

Placerville continued

stone portion in L-shape. Stone portion built ca. 1860; ruinous condition, few stone walls remain. 2 ext. photos (1934).

Pleasanton   □   Alameda County

Kottinger, John W., Adobe (CA-1859). *Ray St. between Main and 1st Sts.* Adobe, one-and-a-half stories with dormers, rectangular, gable roof extends over porch. Built 1855; ruinous for many years, restored (1980s). 1 ext. photo (n.d.).

Plymouth   □   Amador County

House (CA-1351). Wood frame with clapboards, irregular shape, one story, gable roof, entrance porch with spindlework frieze. Built late 19th c. 1 ext. photo (1934).

Pomona   □   Los Angeles County

Casa de Ygnacio Palomares (CA-37-25). *1569 N. Park Ave.* Adobe, approx. 57' (four-bay front) × 20', wood-frame additions in rear, double-pitched gable roof extended over east corridor, or porch, with wood posts; no hall. Built 1839–40 for Don Ygnacio Palomares on the upper San José Rancho; restored 1939 and used thereafter as Pomona Valley Historical Society. 4 sheets (1934, including plan, elevations, section, details); 3 ext. photos (1934); 1 data page (1936). SHL

Portola Valley   □   San Mateo County

Buelna's Roadhouse (CA-2139). *3915 Alpine Rd.* Wood frame with channeled siding, one story, three-bay front, gable roof behind false front with bracketed cornice, one-story porch across front. Built 1852 for Felix Buelna as a roadhouse, use has continued to the present. 5 ext. photos (1975).

Our Lady of the Wayside Roman Catholic Church (CA-2140). *930 Portola Rd.* Reinforced concrete with stucco, three-bay front by six bays deep, one-and-a-half stories, gable roof with exposed rafter ends, Georgian doorway with scrolled pediment, round-arched windows, buttressed side walls. Built 1912, Timothy L. Pflueger, architect, fine example of Mission Revival with Georgian details. 7 ext. photos (1975), 5 int. photos (1975).

Portola Valley School (CA-1992). *775 Portola Rd.* Wood frame with channeled siding, 30' (three-bay front) × 50', one-and-a-half stories, hipped roof with three *espadaña*-type dormers, center dormer with Palladian-type window, flanking dormers with round louvers, recessed entrance with Doric columns. Built 1909, LeBaron R. Olive, architect; rare example of Mission Revival style in wood, one-room schoolhouse still in use as school. 4 sheets (1974, including plan, elevations, section); 4 ext. photos (1975); 3 data pages (1974).

Poverty Flat or Poverty Bar Stone Buildings Ruins (CA-1479). Stone ruins possibly from Poverty Bar, a well known camp in the 1850s on the Mokelumne River, now under Camanche Lake. 2 photocopies of photos (1932, n.d.).

Prado vicinity   □   Riverside County

Cota House (CA-332). Adobe, 68' × 35', two stories with rear one-story lean-to, shingled gable roof, one-story porch across front. Built ca. 1840 for Don Juan Bandini; in ruinous condition, 1936. 3 sheets (1936, including plans, elevations, details); 4 ext. photos (1936); 1 data page (1937).

Priests   □   Tuolumne County

Priest's Hotel (CA-1572). Wood frame with clapboards, two stories, double building, parapeted roof, porch across front with balustrade above. Built mid 19th c.; destroyed by fire, 1926. 1 photocopy of 1925 photo.

Quartz Mountain   □   Tuolumne County

Town of Quartz Mountain (CA-1196). One and two stories, commercial buildings with gable roofs and false fronts, porches across fronts. Town since disappeared. 1 photocopy of 1896 photo.

Red Dog   □   Nevada County

Wells Fargo Building (CA-1717). Ruinous brick walls. Built ca. 1850 in the once-prosperous town of Red Dog; this last remaining structure in the vanished town was finally demolished in 1943. 1 photocopy of ca. 1940 photo.

Redwood City ☐ San Mateo County

Bank of San Mateo County (CA-1991). 2000-02 Broadway. Brick with stone veneer, 56' × 52', two stories, flat roof with parapet, round corner bay has dome with pedimented gable dormers, corner bay open at first floor, supported by Ionic columns, bays divided by pilasters, topped by pediments; interior richly ornamented with coffered ceilings and marble counter. Built 1899–1900, Alfred I. Coffey, architect; in 1910, additional 26' frontage on Broadway added, Alfred I. Coffey, architect. 7 sheets (1974, including plans, elevations, sections); 8 ext. photos (1975), 3 int. photos (1975); 5 data pages (1974).

Diller-Chamberlain Store (Pioneer Store) (CA-2141). 726 Main St. Brick, three-bay front, one story, flat roof with parapet and denticulated cornice, pilasters across front delineate bays, original round-arched openings now mostly bricked in. Built 1859 as general store, oldest brick commercial building in town, served as social and civic center. 3 ext. photos (1975); 4 data pages (1974).

Fitzpatrick Building (CA-2142). 2010 Broadway. Brick, four-bay front, two stories, flat roof with parapet, bracketed and modillioned cornice, arcaded windows at second level, storefront entrance at first level, with side entrance to upper level; original interior cupboards and shelves, with mezzanine-level balcony. Built 1905, Alfred I. Coffey, architect. 5 ext. photos (1975), 3 int. photos (1975).

San Mateo County Courthouse (CA-2143). Middlefield, Hamilton, Broadway, and Marshall Sts. Brick with sandstone facing, cross-shaped, two stories, flat roof with balustraded parapet, glass dome with octagonal cupola, pedimented entrance bay has two-story pilasters, small doorway with pediment; rotunda lit by stained-glass dome, marble pilasters, mosaic tile floors. Built 1903–06, George A. Dodge and J. W. Dolliver, architects; rebuilt 1907–10, Glenn Allen, architect; front portion added 1933. W. H. Toepke, architect. 2 ext. photos (1975), 5 int. photos (1975); 6 data pages (1974). NR

Roaring Camp (Melones) ☐ Calaveras County

Frame Buildings (CA-1484). Wood-frame buildings.Community gone; name from Bret Harte's short story, "Luck of Roaring Camp;" not found on maps until 1948 when it was shown near Carson Hill; now under Melones Dam. 1 photocopy of ca. 1930 photo.

Rough and Ready ☐ Nevada County

Rough and Ready Hotel (CA-1540). Two buildings, both wood frame with clapboards, two stories, gable roofs extended over two-story porches with stick railings on both levels, buildings have different heights and not all of either one is shown in photo. Built 1850s in town of Rough and Ready, founded in 1849, named in honor of General Zachary Taylor, town was one of major settlements in early 1850s but a series of fires largely destroyed it. 1 photocopy of ext. photo (n.d.).

Round Top ☐ Amador County

Kirkwood Inn and Round Top Post Office (CA-1197). State Highway 88, 5.8 mi. E. of Carson Pass. Hand-hewn logs, three-bay front, one-and-a-half stories, gable roof, front porch, exterior brick chimney. Log portion built ca. 1858; frame addition 1863–64 when used by Zack Kirkwood, as a stage station, resort, and post office. 1 ext. photocopy (n.d.).

Sacramento ☐ Sacramento County

Adams & Co. Building (CA-1883). 1014 Second St. Plastered brick and granite, 37'-6" (five-bay front) × 75', three stories, flat roof with bracketed cornice and blind arcaded frieze, ground floor (now altered) had six granite piers, second floor has brick pilasters from which spring round arches, third floor has paired pilasters dividing windows, cast-iron balcony on third floor. Built 1853; the Adams & Co. Express and Banking House was the first to represent a large eastern firm on the Pacific coast and for almost three decades, 1853–83, was the center of pioneer communications and transportation; from 1858–82 the building housed Wells Fargo & Co. 6 sheets (1960, including plans, elevation, details); 2 ext. photos (1960), 1 photocopy of 1958 photo, 2 photocopies of drawings (1854, 1857); 6 data pages (1960). SHL

Apollo Building (CA-1716). 228-30 K St. Plastered brick, 40'-6" (five-bay front) × 100'-8" (eleven bays), two stories, flat roof, ground floor has round-arched openings, second floor has narrow round-arched openings separated by pilasters; upper floor interior has sky-lit rotunda at head of stairs and three marble mantels in adjacent rooms. Built 1852 as two 20' wide units for Priscilla Carswell; name from Apollo Seed &

Sacramento continued

Drug which occupied the corner space 1854–58; demolished 1965. 3 sheets (1964, including plans, elevations, section, detail); 2 ext. photos (1964); 4 data pages (1964).

Aschenauer Building (CA-1715). 1022 3rd St. Plastered brick, 20′ (three-bay front) × 81′-2″, two stories, flat roof, molded cornice, flat-arched windows. Built 1850 and owned by the Aschenauer family 1852–1962; one of the oldest buildings in the city; demolished 1965. 3 sheets (1964, including plans, elevation, section, detail); 2 ext. photos (1964); 4 data pages (1964).

Bank Exchange Building (CA-186). 1030 2nd St. Plastered brick, three-bay front, two stories, flat roof, first floor wood-framed storefront, second floor has two round-arched windows in one segmental-arched frame, flanked by round-arched windows. Built mid 19th c. 2 ext. photos (1965).

Bee Building (CA-1714). 1016-20 3rd St. Plastered brick, 60′-8″ (eight-bay front) × 80′-6″, two stories, flat roof with parapet, flat-arched windows. Built 1856 to house the "Daily and Weekly Bee," first published Feb. 3, 1857; southern third of building probably added later; newspaper moved in 1902; demolished 1965. 4 sheets (1964, including plans, elevations, section, details); 1 ext. photo (1964); 3 data pages (1964). SHL

Big Four Building (CA-1170). 220-226 K St. Brick, eight-bay front, two stories, stripped of detail. Originally three separate buildings erected after the fire of November, 1852: the Stanford Building, the Huntington & Hopkins Building, and the Miller Building; Stanford, Huntington, Hopkins, and Crocker formed the Central Pacific Railway with offices on the second floor; buildings combined behind new facade in 1878 for Huntington and Hopkins Hardware Store; demolished 1965; reconstructed to ca. 1867 appearance in 1970s, 7 sheets (1962, including plans, elevation, sections, details); 5 ext. photos (1962), 3 int. photos (1962), 1 photocopy of ca. 1935 photo, 2 photocopies of drawings (1861–77, 1880); 5 data pages (1962). NHL, SHL

Blake-Waters Assay Office (CA-1711). 222 J. St. Plastered brick, 20′ (three-bay front) × 63′, one story, flat roof, cornice missing, three round-arched openings on brick piers. Built 1852 and occupied by three firms of assayers and refiners, Blake & Co., Waters & Co., and J. Howell & Co., between 1852 and 1866; demolished 1965. 2 sheets (1964, including plan and elevations); 2 ext. photos (1964); 3 data pages (1964).

Booth Building (CA-182). 1019-21 Front St. Plastered brick, six-bay front, two stories, flat roof with parapet, second story has round-arched windows, first story bays divided by nine cast-iron pilasters with ornamental consoles. Built ca. 1879 as addition to northern portion built ca. 1866; headquarters of Booth & Co., wholesale grocers in Sacramento since 1850; Newton Booth, the founder, was state senator (1862–63), governor (1871–75), and U.S. senator (1875–81); northern portion of building destroyed by fire before 1940; building restored 1970s. 2 ext. photos (1965); 2 data pages (1969).

Brannan Building (CA-181). 106-110 J St. and Front St. Brick, seven-bay front, one story, flat roof with denticulated cornice on Front St., four round-arched openings and brick paneled piers, J St. front has seven round-arched openings with brick piers and cast-iron paneled pilasters. Built 1853 for Sam Brannan, Mormon merchant who was instrumental in the development of Sacramento; restored 1970s as part of the Old Sacramento State Historic Park. 3 ext. photos (1965); 1 data page (1980).

Cavert Building (CA-1254). 1207 Front St. Brick, five-bay front, one story, flat roof with parapet, bays divided by paired paneled cast-iron pilasters topped by consoles, fenestration altered. Built ca. 1856; restored 1970s in Old Sacramento State Historic Park. 2 ext. photos (1965).

Cienfuego Building (CA-1256). 1119 2nd St. Brick, two stories, three-bay front, flat roof with parapet, segmental-arched windows second floor, storefront altered. Built mid 19th c. 1 ext. photo (1965).

City Market (CA-199). 118 J St. Plastered brick, three-bay front, four stories, flat roof with parapet, upper floors have narrow doors flanked by wide windows, all segmentally arched, ground floor altered, two-leaf doors at corner entrance with decorative molded panels. Built ca. 1880 on the site of an 1849 market, one of the city's first meat markets; demolished 1965. 2 ext. photos (1965); 1 data page (1980).

Collicott Drug Store (CA-171). 127 J St. Brick, two-bay front, two stories, flat roof with parapet and brick denticulated cornice, segmental-arched windows on upper story, lower story altered. Built ca. 1856; the building housed W. G. Collicott, apothecary, and Sam Colville, publisher of the Sacramento Directory; now restored as the Haines Building. 1 ext. photo (1965); 1 data page (1980).

Cornwall, P. B., Building (CA-1257). 1011-13 2nd

St. Plastered brick, five-bay front with central bay projecting, two stories, flat roof, cornice missing, second floor has round-arched windows with hoodmolds, first floor has round-arched arcade with cast-iron pilasters, central bays and corner strip on second floor are scored to simulate masonry courses. First story built ca. 1853; second story added ca. 1865; building's name taken from owner of two previous buildings on this site who was a prominent local politician; restored as the Smith Building, 1970s. 2 ext. photos (1965); 3 data pages (1969).

Crocker Art Gallery (CA-1885). O and 3rd Sts. Art Museum. Originally two buildings now joined by connecting wing, restored 1970s. 4 sheets (1960, including site map and plans); 1 photocopy of 1880 drawing and site plan; 13 data pages (1960). See following entries for individual structures:

□ *Judge and Mrs. E. B. Crocker House.* Plastered brick, five-bay front, two stories with raised basement fenestrated with segmental arches, hipped roof with central balustrade, bracketed cornice with paneled frieze, quoins, one-story porches on north and east sides, projecting polygonal towered bay with straight-sided mansard roof on north side. Built 1853 for B. F. Hastings, Seth Babson, architect; porches and north tower added; altered nearly out of recognition, 1922 and after, to create the Annex to the Crocker Art Gallery. 1 photocopy of 1886 photo.

□ *Crocker Art Gallery.* Plastered brick, five-bay front with projecting central pavilion, two stories with raised basement, quoins on main and projecting sections, hipped roof, pavilions have triangular pediments with modillions, full Classical entablature with frieze panels punctuated with wreaths, dentil course, one-story balustraded front porch originally with branching stair; lavishly ornamented interior. Built 1872–73, Seth Babson, architect, to house the European art collection purchased by the Crockers in 1870; one of the best examples of the Mannerist Italianate villa style in the state and perhaps the state's first public art gallery; E. B. Crocker was closely associated with the fortunes of the Big Four and the

Crocker Art Gallery, Sacramento (CA-1885).

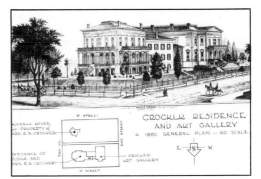

Crocker Art Gallery, Sacramento (CA-1885-1).

Crocker Art Gallery, Sacramento (CA-1885-3).

Crocker Art Gallery, Sacramento (CA-1885-17).

Mrs. E. B. Crocker House, Crocker Art Gallery, Sacramento (CA-1885-18).

Central Pacific Railroad and served as State Supreme Court Justice under Gov. Leland Stanford. 4 sheets (1960, including elevations, section, details); 1 ext. photo (1960), 9 int. photos (1960), 2 photocopies of ext. photos (1893, 1960), 3 photocopies of int. photos (1875, 1910). SHL

□ *Mrs. E. B. Crocker House.* Second-Empire design for Mrs. Crocker after Judge's death; designed late 1870s by Nathaniel Goodell, on lot south of older home; probably never built. 1 photocopy of 1880 drawing; 2 photocopies of architect's ca. 1879 elevations.

Democratic State Journal Building (CA-1251). SW corner 2nd and K Sts. Plastered brick, four bays by nine bays, flat roof with parapet and molded brick cornice, frieze with decorative swags, polygonal tower with pyramidal roof above corner entrance. Built 1852 by Boyd & Davis for office of Democratic State Journal which moved out 1855; several significant alterations; to be reconstructed. 2 ext. photos (1965); 1 data page (1980).

Diana Saloon (CA-1706). 205 J St. Plastered brick, 40' (five-bay front) × 114', one story, round-arched openings divided by paneled cast-

iron pilasters with Corinthian caps. Built in 1852 for D. A. Whipley; demolished 1965, to be reconstructed in Old Sacramento State Historic Park. 3 sheets (1964, including plans, elevation, section, detail); 4 ext. photos (1964); 4 data pages (1964).

Dingley Spice Mill (CA-167). 115 I St. Brick. 25'-4" (four-bay front) × 85', two stories, flat roof with parapet above denticulated brick cornice, upper-floor windows are slightly arched, fenestration altered, ground floor altered except for one corner brick pier. Built 1853 by Nathaniel Dingley, Maine-born '49er turned merchant, as headquarters for his coffee and spice business with residence above; building extended to the rear 25' ca. 1880. 3 ext. photos (1965); 9 data pages (1969).

Ebner's Hotel (CA-1252). 116 K St. Plastered brick, five-bay front, three stories, flat roof with stepped parapet, facade stripped of ornament, central bay accentuated by progression of one, two and three openings from ground to third floor. Built 1856 by Charles and Francis Xavier Ebner on the site of previous hotels and operated by them until 1863; continued as a hotel until the 1960s. 2 ext. photos (1965); 1 data page (1980). SHL

Eureka Swimming Baths (CA-177). 908-10 2nd St. Brick, six-bay front, two stories, flat roof with parapet, second-story windows have segmental arches with keystones, first story has round-arched arcade. Established 1854 by Wetzler & Bros. as the public baths with fourteen rooms including a barber shop; thereafter the building had a variety of uses; restored 1970s as the Schroth Building. 2 ext. photos (1965); 1 data page (1980).

Fashion Saloon (CA-1261). 209 J St. Brick and cast iron, 20′ (three-bay front) × 100′, two stories, flat roof with parapet, cast-iron front has wide paneled pilasters with Corinthian capitals supporting consoles under a belt cornice, second-floor windows have ornate flat heads on consoles and iron shutters folding back against the reveals. Built 1855 for owner John Keenan with fine cast-iron work from Eureka Iron and Brass Works, this was one of the most famous of the Sacramento saloons of the Gold Rush period, noted for its elaborate facade and interior decor; absorbed by the Forrest Theater next door in 1858; demolished 1965; to be reconstructed on another site in Old Sacramento State Historic Park. 6 data pages (1969).

Figg, E. P., Building (CA-1713). 224 J St. Plastered brick, 22′ (three-bay front) × 161′, two stories, flat roof with ornamented parapet, two fluted cast-iron pilasters with Ionic caps support a cast-iron lintel over altered shopfront, upper floor windows with squeezed pediment heads and ornamental plaster work, two ornate plaster medallions between windows. Built 1852 for E. P. Figg, merchant; demolished 1965, facade detail salvaged. 3 sheets (1964, including plans, elevation, section, details); 2 photocopies of 1964 ext. photos; 5 data pages (1964).

Fratt Building (CA-1255). 1103-09 2nd St. Brick, ten bays by nine bays, three stories, flat roof, bracketed cornice, brick quoins, segmental-arched windows with ornate hoodmolds, cast-iron balconies, ornate cast-iron pilasters with modified Corinthian capitals on ground floor. Built 1870 by Francis W. Fratt as a commercial and residential building and occupied on upper floor by Fratt until 1909; one of the largest and most lavish buildings in Old Sacramento; demolished 1969. 3 ext. photos (1965); 9 data pages (1969).

General View (CA-1669). 1 photocopy of 1852 drawing showing commercial area in flames during the town's first major fire.

General View (CA-1671). 2 photocopies of ca. 1880 photos looking northeast and northwest from roof of Capitol.

General View (CA-1705). 1 photocopy of 1850 lithograph showing the town inundated by flood waters.

Governor's Mansion (Gallatin House) (CA-1886). 1524 H. St. Wood frame with horizontal siding, three stories with raised basement, five-story square tower, mansard roofs with a variety of shingle patterns and round-arched dormers enriched with hoodmolds, polygonal bay on front of house, modillioned cornices with double frieze bands, round-arched windows with molded architraves, one-story front porch rounded at one end, surmounted by balustrade and supported by fluted Corinthian columns; interior has full panoply of decorative detail. Built 1877, Nathaniel D. Goodell, architect, for Albert Gallatin, manager-partner of Huntington, Hopkins & Co.; house sold in 1888 to Joseph Steffens, father of Muckraker Lincoln Steffens who grew up here; sold in 1903 to State of California and occupied by twelve successive governors, house is a lavish and exuberant example of late 19th c. eclecticism which draws simultaneously on the French Second Empire, the Italianate and the persistent Classic tradition. 3 ext. photos (1960), 15 int. photos (1960), 2 photocopies of drawings (1880, 1887); 5 data pages (1960). NR, SHL

□ *Governor's Mansion Stables.* Wood frame with horizontal siding, one-and-a-half stories, steeply pitched gable roof with cross gables, same style and ornament as the house. Built 1877, Nathaniel Goodell, architect; converted to garage. 1 ext. photo (1960).

Gregory-Barnes Store (CA-197). 126 J St. Brick, approx. 20′ (three-bay front) × 85′, two stories,

Fratt Building, Sacramento (CA-1255).

RESIDENCE OF ALBERT GALLATIN, COR. 16TH AND H STREETS,
SACRAMENTO, CAL.

Governor's Mansion (Gallatin House), Sacramento (CA-1886-1).

flat roof with simple cornice, upper story has tall narrow flat-arched windows, ground floor has three round-arched openings, brick piers at corners and cast-iron paneled pilasters on either side of center bay. Built ca. 1853; from 1860 the building served as produce market of Julius Gregory which expanded to 128 J St. in 1870. 1 ext. photo (1965); 1 data page (1980).

Hall, Luhrs & Co. (CA-176). *912-16 2nd St.* plastered brick, eight-bay front, two stories, flat roof with curvilinear parapet, second-floor windows segmentally arched, divided by pilasters with composite caps, ground floor altered. Built ca. 1880. 2 ext. photos (1965); 1 data page (1980).

Hastings, B. F., Bank Building (CA-1884). *128-32 J St.* Plastered brick, 40' (four-bay front) × 85', two stories, flat roof, flat-arched windows. Built 1852–53 as two 20' wide buildings; housed B. F. Hastings Bank, 1853–71, Wells Fargo & Co., 1853–57, State Supreme Court, 1854–57; restored as part of Old Sacramento State Historic Park, 1970s. 5 sheets (1960, including plans, elevations, details); 1 ext. photo (1960), 1 int. photo (1960), 1 photocopy of 1958 photo, 2 photocopies of drawings (1857, 1880); 5 data pages (1960). NR, SHL

Heywood Building (CA-1258). *1001-09 2nd St.* Plastered brick, six by fourteen bays, flat roof with parapet, upper floor flat-arched windows with hoodmolds, cast-iron balconies, ground floor much altered, only caps of pilasters remain. Built 1857 by Joseph Heywood, sold to J. McNulty in 1860 and to D. O. Mills & Co. Bank in 1865, remodeled thereafter; restored 1970s as part of Old Sacramento State Historic Park. 2 ext. photos (1965); 1 data page (1980).

Howard House (CA-184). *109-111 K St.* Plastered brick, approx. 40' (five-bay front) × 85', three stories, flat roof with stepped parapet, central projecting bay, third floor has round-arched windows with archivolt trim which forms a continuous molding across the building, second-floor window detail missing, first floor has round-arched arcade divided by cast-iron paneled pilasters with Corinthian caps. Built late 19th c.; restored 1970s as part of Old Sacramento State Historic Park. 2 ext. photos (1965); 1 data page (1980).

J Street Commercial Buildings (CA-1683). 1 photocopy of 1880s drawing of two-storied galleried commercial buildings.

Lady Adams Building (CA-190). 118-20 K St. Plastered brick, 28' (five-bay front) × 75', two stories, flat roof, second-floor windows have molded architraves with paneled spandrels, balcony removed, ground floor has rectangular openings stripped of ornament. Built in 1852, Lewis Fiedler, architect, of brick ballast from the Lady Adams brig; this was the only building to survive the fire of that year undamaged; restored 1970s in Old Sacramento State Historic Park. 6 sheets (1964, including plans, elevations, section, details); 2 ext. photos (1965) of unrestored state. SHL

Latham Building (CA-1710). 221-25 J St. Plastered brick, 40'-2" (five-bay front) × 157', four stories, flat roof with wide eaves supported by paired brackets and unusual strap-like braces at each end, upper-story windows with hoodmolds, ground-floor bays divided by cast-iron pilasters with Corinthian capitals. Built 1855 by Milton Slocum Latham, a lawyer who later became Governor of California and U.S. Senator; the building served as law offices with living quarters above for the Latham family until 1864; facade rebuilt in the 1880s and floor heights reduced to make four stories; demolished 1965. 4 sheets (1964, including plans, elevations, sections, details); 3 photocopies of 1964 ext. photos; 4 data pages (1964).

Leggett Ale House (CA-183). 1023 Front St. Plastered brick, three-bay front, three stories, flat roof with stepped parapet, cornice missing, tall narrow casement windows with flat molded heads on consoles with grotesque ornament, decorative cast-iron balcony between second and third floor, ground-floor bays divided by cast-iron pilasters. Built 1852 by Thomas W. Leggett, a Scot, who introduced ale as an exclusive article of trade in Sacramento; demolished 1965. 2 ext. photos (1965); 1 data page (1980).

Mechanics Exchange Hotel (CA-178). 116-22 I St. Brick, built in two sections: one has eight-bay front, three stories, flat roof with parapet and corbeled brick cornice, upper stories have flat-arched windows with segmental-arched brick hoodmolds, ground-floor arcade has brick arches defined by archivolts; two-story portion is four bays wide, flat roof with parapet and cornice, second-floor windows have flat heads on consoles, ground floor has similar arcade. Built 1860 by Henry Treichler; hotel served those connected with the iron works, mills, and railroad activities

north of I St.; buildings restored in Old Sacramento State Historic Park, 1970s. 4 ext. photos (1965); 2 data pages (1980).

Morse Building (CA-1259). 1025-31 2nd St. Plastered brick, 63' (six-bay front) × 20', two stories, flat roof with parapet, upper story has paired windows with segmental heads set in a shouldered architrave, seven of the original twenty round-arched ground-floor openings remain divided by ornate cast-iron pilasters with Corinthian caps. Originally a one-story building erected ca. 1853; upper story added after regrading of streets ca. 1864 following the 1861–62 floods; building named for Dr. John Frederick Morse, pioneer physician and one of the first directors of the Central Pacific Railroad who was a leader of Sacramento development from his arrival in 1849 to his departure for San Francisco in 1863; first restored structure in Old Sacramento State Historic Park, 1969. 4 ext. photos (1965); 6 data pages (1969).

Our House Saloon (CA-175). 926 2nd St. Plastered brick, three-bay front, flat roof with parapet and cornice with oversize dentils, second-story windows have flat molded hoods on consoles. Built early 1850s; restored 1970s. 1 ext. photo (1965); 1 data page (1980).

Pioneer Hall and Bakery (CA-198). 120-24 J St. Plastered brick, seven-bay front, two stories, flat parapeted roof with molded cornice and paired brackets, segmental hoodmolds and one remaining molded brick architrave on second floor, fenestration altered, ground-floor openings have elliptical arches with fluted cast-iron engaged columns with foliated caps, cast-iron balcony. Built 1854 and operated as bakery on ground floor and meeting hall on upper floor; demolished 1965. 2 ext. photos (1965); 1 data page (1980).

Pioneer Telegraph Building (CA-191). 1015 2nd

Mechanics Exchange Hotel, Sacramento (CA-178).

Sacramento continued

St. Plastered brick, 20'-1" (three-bay front) × 60'-4" with rear addition 20' long, two stories, flat roof with parapet, upper-floor windows have flat hoodmolds on consoles, ground floor has round-arched openings. Built after 1853, occupied from 1863–1915 by California State Telegraph Co. which was incorporated into Western Union Telegraph in 1868. 5 sheets (1964, including plans, elevations, section, details); 2 ext. photos (1965). SHL

Rialto Building (CA-192). *228-30 J St.* Plastered brick, originally two one-story structures, 20' × 70' and 20' × 80', combined into one two-story building, six-bay front, flat roof, first-floor round-arched openings divided by cast-iron pilasters, second-floor round-arched openings with hoodmolds divided by pilasters, denticulated cornice. Built 1853; remodeled by John J. Carroll & Co. in 1865; demolished 1965, to be reconstructed in Old Sacramento State Historic Park. 5 sheets (1965, including plans, elevations, section, details).

Sacramento Engine No. 3, Sacramento (CA-1249).

Rivett-Fuller Building (CA-1250). 128 K St. and 1108 2nd St. Brick, K St. portion 20' (three-bay front) × 65', two stories, flat roof with parapet, brick cornice with dentils, second-floor windows segmental-arched, paneled cast-iron pilasters on first level with modified Corinthian capitals, ornate paneled door; L-shaped plan, 2nd St. frontage similar. K St. portion built 1852 after the fire by John Rivett; 2nd St. portion built late in the 1850s; demolished 1965; reconstructed 1970s. 3 ext. photos (1965); 1 data page (1980).

Sacramento Engine No. 3 (CA-1249). 1112 2nd St. Plastered brick, 22'-6" (three-bay front) × 50', two stories, flat roof with false pedimented gable, corner pilasters supporting an entablature, "SACRAMENTO No. 3" in frieze, iron balcony is from Ebner's Hotel, ground-floor entrance with flat-arched openings. Built in 1853; oldest firehouse in California; remodeled 1959 as restaurant preserving much of the original appearance of facade; cupola not restored. 2 ext. photos (1965); 2 data pages (1969).

Sazerac Building (CA-172). 131 J St. Brick, three-bay front by seven bays, projecting polygonal bay above corner entrance, three stories, flat parapeted roof with modillioned cornice around the bay, third-story windows have segmental arches, second-story windows flat-arched with hoods on consoles, first story has three round-arched openings. Built ca. 1853 on site of the Gem Saloon, served as Sazerac Saloon, 1850s–60s, and a variety of uses thereafter; restored 1970s. 2 ext. photos (1965); 1 data page (1980).

Stanford Brothers Store (CA-1253). 1203 Front St. Brick, 42' (four-bay front) × 150' (fifteen bays), flat roof, four arched openings on front and five on side, both openings and fenestration altered, ornament stripped of detail. Built 1856, Seth Babson, probable architect; raised one story after 1861–62 flood; this was the second store owned by Leland Stanford, later Governor, U.S. Senator, and founder of Stanford University; the business of provisioning miners was purchased in 1861 by Booth & Co.; second story added ca. 1890, removed 1920s. 3 ext.photos (1965); 7 data pages (1969).

Stanford-Lathrop Memorial Home (CA-1709). 800 N St. Plastered brick, five-bay front with wings, two stories with raised basement and full attic, mansard roof with central section having a Palladian-type dormer window, round-arched dormers heavily ornamented, heavy cornice with frieze of recessed panels with inset cast-iron ornament, quoins and water table, entrance portico with full Classic entablature surmounted by a balustrade, flat-arched windows have squeezed segmental molded heads surmounted by a foliate motif, round-arched entrance; cross-shaped plan, center hall, fine interior detail. Built 1857, Seth Babson, architect for Shelton C. Fogus, as Georgian style in plan and format but incorporating Mannerist Italianate detail; 1862, altered after flood for new owner Leland Stanford; 1871–72, remodeled, Nathaniel Goodell and Seth Babson, probable architects; retained main block, but raised it a story to create space for a ground-floor ballroom built into a cross block which was connected to an existing rear south wing which was moved back to provide the space, retained much exterior detail, copied it for new portions, altered roof to mansard; 1874, Leland Stanfords moved to San Francisco; in 1893, Mrs. Stanford gave the house to Roman Catholic Diocese of Sacramento to use as orphanage; house a rare example of the high Victorian taste of California's "silver age" and comparable to the great houses on Nob Hill in San Francisco destroyed in the 1906 earthquake and fire. 6 photocopies of ext. photos (ca. 1860, ca. 1872, ca. 1886, 1902), 9 photocopies of int. photos (ca. 1872), 1 photocopy of photo of Stanfords, 1 photocopy of drawing (1862); 10 data pages (1960). NR, SHL

Stein Building (CA-1712). 218 J St. Plastered brick, 20' (three-bay front) × 74'-6", one story, flat roof with parapet and denticulated cornice, three elliptically arched openings divided by fluted cast-iron columns with modified Corinthian caps. Built 1854; demolished 1965, cast iron salvaged. 3 sheets (1964, including plan, elevations, details); 1 photocopy of ext. photo (1964); 3 data pages (1964).

Sutter's Fort (CA-1294). State Park. 2701 L St. Walls 18' high in vaguely rectangular plan form rear sides of one-story buildings on interior, consisting of stables, granary, store, kitchens and workshops; two bastions at opposite corners, main building in center. Built 1839 and after by John A. Sutter, a German-Swiss, to protect New Helvetia, his 76-square-mile Mexican land-grant, the fort became the political and social center of the only settled portion of the state's interior; abandoned by Sutter after the Gold Rush, the outer walls and buildings disappeared by the 1860s, but were reconstructed following state acquisition 1891–93. 2 ext. photos (1962), 2 aerial photos (n.d.), 1 photocopy of a drawing (n.d.), 2 photocopies of plans (1960, one a copy of 1848 plan). SHL. See following entries for individual structures:

□ *Ramparts (CA-1294 A).* 1 ext. photo (n.d.), 2 photocopies of undated photos.

U.S. Post Office, Sacramento (CA-1914-1).

U.S. Post Office, Sacramento (CA-1914-5).

Sacramento continued

□ *Southeast Bastion (CA-1294 B).* Square block-house at corner, pyramidal tile roof, segmental-arched opening. 3 photocopies of ext. photos (1925, n.d.).

□ *Main Building (CA-1294 C).* Adobe, one-and-a-half stories on raised basement, five-bay front, gable roof. 2 ext. photos (1962), 2 photocopies of ext. photos (1867, 1869), 1 photocopy of drawing (n.d.).

□ *Russian Cannon (CA-1294 D).* 5 photocopies of undated photos.

□ *Hay Press (CA-1294 E).* Heavy timber. 2 photo-copies of undated photos.

Union Hotel (CA-187). 1024-28 2nd St. Plastered brick, 60' (seven-bay) front, three stories, flat roof, small Greek fret at cornice, original cornice and hoodmolds removed. Built 1855 for J. P. Dyer, proprietor; ell on K St. recorded as Union Hotel Annex (CA-185); demolished 1965. 1 ext. photo (1965); 5 data pages (1969).

Union Hotel Annex (CA-185). 125 K St. Brick, one story, 20' (three-bay) front, flat roof, round-arched openings spring from pilasters. Built ca. 1855 as ell of Union Hotel (which see), fronting on 2nd St. 2 ext. photos (1965); 1 data page (1980).

U.S. Post Office (CA-1914). NE corner 7th and K Sts. Arizona red sandstone ashlar and structural steel, three stories with attic and six-story square tower, hip roofs in varied forms, large round-arched entrance, flat-arched triple windows on first floor, round-arched double windows on second floor, carved stone ornament; interior features marble floors. Built 1891–96, dedicated 1894; northern addition 1910–12 by Ambrose B. Stannard, contractor; important example of Richardsonian Romanesque style in Sacramento; demolished 1960s. 8 photocopies of ext. photos (1891, 1892, 1893, 1910, 1911, 1958), 1 photo-copy of int. photo (1921); 5 data pages (1961).

Vernon-Brannon House (CA-179). 112-14 J St. Brick, 43' (five-bay front) × 85', three stories, flat roof, molded brick cornice with enlarged consoles and dentils, third-floor windows have pedimental heads on consoles, second-floor windows have flat heads on consoles, first floor has round-arched openings, second-floor balcony across front. Built 1853 for H. E. Robinson, Sacramento's first postmaster, and operated as a hotel by various owners until 1918. 3 ext. photos (1965). 1 data page (1980).

Wormser, I. & S., Building (CA-196). 128 J St. Plastered brick, 20' (three-bay front) × 85', two stories, flat roof, tall narrow windows, ground floor has flat arches stripped of ornament supported by engaged fluted cast-iron columns with foliated caps, one set of paneled doors, other openings altered. Built 1853 by B. F. Hastings and rented to I. & S. Wormser, clothing merchants from Germany; in 1870, became part of the expanding produce market in the adjacent building owned by Julius Gregory; restored, 1970s, as part of Old Sacramento State Historic Park, Robert McCabe, architect. 2 ext. photos

Salinas vicinity □ Monterey County

El Colegio de San José (Hartnell College)—Academic Building (CA-1171). Rancho El Alisal. Adobe, two stories, five-bay front, gable roof. Built 1833 for W. E. P. Hartnell, first school of higher learning in California, opened January 1, 1834; this building served as residence, library, and classrooms; demolished 1961. 1 ext. photo (1933).

El Colegio de San José (Hartnell College)—Dormitory (CA-1172). Rancho El Alisal. No exterior description. Built 1833; this building served as dormitory, dining room, and kitchen; demolished 1961. 2 int. photos (1933) of details of brick fireplace.

Hartnell College. See El Colegio de San José (CA-1171, 1172).

Sherwood Ranch (CA-1121). Natividad Rd., approx. 3 mis. NE of Salinas. Adobe house in center of quandrangle formed by other adobe and frame buildings. Originally owned by Feliciano and Mariano Sobranes, acquired by Eugene Sherwood 1860; demolished except for part of center adobe 1960. 2 sheets (1938, 1959–60, including site plan, elevations); 1 ext. photo (1934), 1 photocopy of ext. photo (1934); 9 data pages (1960). See following entries for individual structures.

□ *Center Adobe (CA-1121 A).* One-and-a-half stories with porch and shed, tile roof, built 1824–30. 11 sheets (1938, 1959–60, including plans, elevations, sections, details); 1 ext. photo (1934), 3 photocopies of ext. photos (1934).

□ *Northeast Adobe (CA-1121 B).* Adobe and redwood siding, one story with arched gateway, shake roof, built in two sections 1830–45, 1853–60. 3 sheets (1938, 1959–60, including plan, elevations, section details); 5 ext. photos (1934).

□ *Main Frame Building (CA-1121 C)*. Horizontal siding, two stories with recessed porches, dining hall and servants' adobe attached, gable roofs, built 1853–60. 7 sheets (1938, 1959–60, including plans, elevations, section, details); 3 ext. photos (1934), 5 photocopies of ext. photos (1934).

□ *Barns (CA-1121 D)*. Adobe with horizontal sheathing, one story with shed roof, sawn shakes, probably built 1853–60. 2 sheets (1938, 1959–60, including plan, elevations, section).

San Andreas   □   Calaveras County

Adobe Store (CA-1481). Adobe, plastered, two-bay front, one story, shed roof, iron-shuttered openings. Built 1850s; demolished. 1 photocopy of undated photo.

Banque, J., Store (Agostini Building) (CA-1210). *Main St.* Brick central section has three-bay front, one-bay side lean-tos of adobe, one story, gable roof adjoining shed roofs on side wings, brick denticulated cornice across gable front, plastered brick side rooms. Built 1851 for Frenchman J. Banque, sold to Joseph Agostini 1870, adobe wings added later by Ciprian Agostini; demolished 1970. 1 ext. photo (n.d.), 1 photocopy of 1925 photo.

Friedberger Building (Calaveras Bar) (CA-1478). *SW corner Main and Court Sts.* Rubble stone, plastered and scored in courses, two stories, flat roof, corner of building is chamfered, iron shutters. Built 1855; demolished. 1 photocopy of undated photo.

Gravestones (CA-1487). *North Branch Cemetery.* Three carved headstones, stone, imported from the East for graves of miners who met violent deaths. Dated 1851 (carved by Cary of Boston), 1853, 1854 (carved by P. Mullaney). 2 photocopies of 1925 photos.

I.O.O.F. Building (CA-1496). *24 N. Main St.* Brick, five-bay front, two stories, flat roof, two-part cornice with enlarged brick dentils. Built 1856; restored 1979. 1 photocopy of undated photo.

Main Street Buildings (CA-1494). Brick, stone, and wood frame structures, one and two stories with canopies overhanging sidewalks, two-story Hall of Records building, 1893, with arched central entrance (restored 1979, now Historical Museum). Settled by Mexicans 1848, became county seat 1866; a rendezvous point for outlaw Joaquín Murieta, Black Bart tried and sent to prison here; gold from surrounding mines contributed greatly to Union's success in Civil War; general streetscape remains intact. 2 photocopies of undated photos.

Metropolitan Hotel (CA-1495). Brick, five-bay front by five bays deep, square, two stories on sloping site with raised basement in rear, parapeted roof with brick entablature and dentil course, engaged piers between openings, ornate cast-iron balcony around two sides at second-floor level. Built 1859; burned 1926. 3 photocopies of photos (1860, 1935, after 1941).

San Diego   □   San Diego County

Albatross Cottages (CA-2165). Four canyon cottages, wood frame with cement plaster finish, cube-shaped, plain exteriors with mission tiles, stained glass, ornamental iron; interiors without moldings; houses designed to set off and relate to landscaped canyon setting. Built as rental units for Alice Lee and Katherine Teats, designed by Irving J. Gill in 1912–13. 3 photocopies of architect's drawings (1912, including site plans, elevations); 7 data pages (1975).

□ *Lee Cottage (CA-2165 A)*. *3353 Albatross St.* Designed 1912, built after 1913. 2 photocopies of architect's drawings (1913, including plans, elevations); 10 data pages (1975).

□ *Lee Cottage (CA-2165 B)*. *3367 Albatross St.* Designed 1912, built 1912–13. 2 photocopies of architect's drawings (1912, including plans, elevations); 8 data pages (1975).

□ *Teats Cottage (CA-2165 C)*. *3407 Albatross St.* Designed 1912, built after 1918. 3 photocopies of architect's drawings (1912, including plans, elevations, details); 14 data pages (1975).

□ *Teats Cottage (CA-2165 D)*. *3415 Albatross St.* Designed and built 1912. 3 data pages (1975).

Backesto Block (CA-427). *5th Ave. and Market St.* Plastered brick, approx. 224' on 5th Ave. including 84' addition on north side, approx. 90' on Market St. with 20' addition on west, two stories, flat roof with parapet studded with square chimneys, pressed-metal bracketed cornice with dentil course, frieze panels, and architrave molding, broken-base pediment originally centered in each facade, paneled pilasters at corners and framing central bays, ground-floor openings altered, second floor has segmental windows with broken-base pediments on consoles; cross-hall plan with main hall through from 5th Ave., shop entrances on 5th, wood floors and stairway with

Backesto Block, San Diego (CA-427).

wainscoting. Built 1887, Burkett & Osgood, architects, as a commercial building by Dr. John P. Backesto of San Jose; upper floor originally had 39 sleeping rooms with fireplaces. 1 ext. photo (1960); 4 data pages (1963).

Bandini, Don Juan, House (CA-46). *2660 Calhoun St., Old Town State Historic Park.* Plastered adobe and wood frame, stone foundations, 117' (seven-bay front) × 82', L-shaped, two stories, hip roof extended over two-story porch on three sides with chamfered wood posts and wood stick railing on second-floor level. Built ca. 1830 by Juan Bandini for his home, originally one story, U-shaped adobe; headquarters of Commodore Stockton in 1846; purchased ca. 1865 by A. L. Seeley who added a wood-framed second story and converted structure to a hotel; restorations after 1929. 4 sheets (1936, including plans, elevations, section details); 4 ext. photos (1936, 1937); 1 data page (1937). SHL

Bank of Commerce Building (CA-1961). *835 5th Ave.* Brick faced with gray cut stone, 50' × 100', four stories, flat roof, sheet metal parapet with mansard form, projecting molded cornice on heavy scroll brackets that cap rusticated piers framing central bay and corners, two wood-framed stacked bays are polygonal on second and third story and square on fourth story, cornices of bays have molded squeezed pedimental heads, ground floor largely glazed and considerably altered; skylit lightwell lets light down to second-floor level, interior spaces much altered.

Built 1888, J. B. Stannard, architect, expressive of affluence of 1880s boom period that accompanied the arrival of the railroad in San Diego; two-story towers that surmounted projecting bays and pediment over center bay now missing. 1 sheet (1971, including elevation), 2 ext. photos (1971), 1 photocopy of 1889 drawing; 6 data pages (1971, 1979).

Botanical Building (CA-1970). *Balboa Park.* Wood lath, long barrel-vaulted building with dome at central crossing, stuccoed entrance, lily pond in front. Fabricated as railroad station by Santa Fe Railroad, assembled in 1915 for plant display at Panama-California Exposition, Carleton M. Winslow, architect. 3 ext. photos (1971), 2 int. photos (1971).

Cabrillo National Monument (Point Loma Lighthouse) (CA-41). *Point Loma.* Sandstone and brick, one story, 38' (five-bay front) × 20', chimneys at either end, round brick tower with light rises out of center of roof, balcony with metal railing, octagonal lantern originally with fixed white light of the wick type, French lens, now revolving red and white, domical metal roof. Built 1854–55, lighted November 15, 1855, Gibbon & Kelley, builders; first lighthouse in southern California and the loftiest in the continental U.S. at that time; use discontinued in 1891 when new light was built at lower elevation. 10 sheets (1934, including plans, elevations, sections, details); 6 ext. photos (1934), 5 int. photos (1934), 5 photocopies of ext. photos

San Diego continued

(1880s, ca. 1891, early 20th c., 1930s, 1934), 2 ext. photos of similar light of same manufacture at Point Pinos, Calif. (1934); 11 data pages (1936). NR, SHL

California Tower (Balboa Park, Entrance Building) (CA-1963). Balboa Park. Museum. Concrete and stone, one story with mezzanine, tiled roof, barrel vaulted, cruciform with dome over central crossing, four-stage tower, three upper stages form belfry, ribbed polychrome tiled dome with cross finial, encrusted with Chirrigueresque ornament, facade with curved gable end, recessed entrance framed by elaborate architectural composition of columns single and paired, statues in niches and curved cornice with coping, proliferation of decorative elements in the Chirrigueresque style and statuary, transept ends have large windows enframed with massive ornamented sculptural architraves, secondary tiled, domed one-story sections set in angles of transepts, half-domed apse end; rotunda with transepts in cruciform plan, entrance lobby precedes exhibition spaces. Built 1914 for the 1915 Panama-California Exposition, Bertram G. Goodhue, architect. Carleton M. Winslow, Sr., project architect, high relief sculptures on the tower entrance by Alfonso Ianelli, ornamental facade by the Piccirilli Brothers of New York City; pre-eminent example of Spanish Baroque Revival style, now Museum of Man; structural strengthening and repairs to the ornament anchorage have been carried out recently. 2 ext. photos (1971); 2 data pages (1971). NR

Casa de López (CA-47). 3890 Twiggs St., Old Town State Historic Park. Plastered adobe and wood frame, 100' (eight-bay front) × 45', one story, tiled hip roof extended over porches front and back with box columns, recessed openings with wood lintels; hall-less plan. Built ca. 1835 by Juan Francisco López; house, garden, and court restored. 2 sheets (1936, including plan, elevations, section, details); 3 ext. photos (1936); 1 data page (1937). SHL

Casa Machado (CA-411). 2745 San Diego Ave., Old Town State Historic Park. Plastered adobe and wood frame, six-bay front, one story, tiled gable roof; L-plan, hall-less. Built before 1843 by Don José Manuel Machado for María Machado and her husband José Silvas; also called Casa de la Bandera because Mexican flag was hidden there in 1846 when the Americans came; house restored to approx. 1869 appearance, serves as Community Church. 4 ext. photos (1937); 1 data page (1937). SHL

Cossitt, Mary, House (CA-2163). 3526 Seventh Ave. Wood frame thin-walled construction with cement plaster finish, two stories, 45'-7" × 77'-7", flat roof; interior has several levels, large studio with clerestory has sound-proofed walls. Built 1906, W. S. Hebbard and Irving J. Gill, architects. 4 photocopies of architect's drawings (1906, including plans, elevations, sections); 10 data pages (1975).

Davis, William Heath, House (CA-423). 227 11th St. Wood frame with drop siding, approx. 36' × 35' including rear shed addition, brick foundations, three-bay front, two stories, shingled gable roof, two brick chimneys, front entrance porch with square posts resting on wood railing, ornamental jigsawn brackets, porch across rear; central hall plan with open-string stairway, fairly elegant interior. Built 1851 for William Heath Davis, prominent early citizen and developer of the "New Town" of San Diego, who purchased this pre-framed house along with other cargo from Portland, Maine, in San Francisco and had it shipped to San Diego, probably first permanent house in New Town, first erected on State St. between Market and G Sts., moved to this site about 1873. 6 sheets (1975, including plans, elevations, section); 2 ext. photos (1960), 2 int. photos (1960); 4 data pages (1963). NR

Derby House (Pendleton House) (CA-430). 4017 Harney St., Old Town. Wood frame with drop siding, wood peg construction, 20' (two-bay front) × 74', two stories, low-pitched hip roof with 2' overhang on scroll-sawn brackets, molded boxed cornice, corner boards, one-story porch across front with box columns, one pair casement windows on ground-floor front, wood paneled doors in trabeated frames, other windows with double-hung sash, one-story rear addition of board-and-batten siding and adobe, approx. 26' long, shingled gable roof extended over porch along one side with square wood posts and wood floor. Built 1851 from pre-cut frame shipped from New England and assembled with pegs, only known remaining example of this type in southern California, by Juan Bandini for his daughter and her husband; in 1853 rented to Lt. George H. Derby who wrote under pseudonyms of John P. Squibob and John Phoenix; George Pendleton family owned and occupied house 1855–80; moved from 3877 Harney St. to present site in 1962 and restored by the County and the Historical Shrine Foundation. 3 ext. photos (1960), 2 int. photos (1960), 1 photocopy of undated photo; 5 data pages (1963). NHL

Estudillo House (Ramona's Marriage Place) (CA-

45). *400 Mason St., Old Town State Historic Park.* Plastered adobe and wood frame, 116' (seven-bay front) × 98', U-shape, one story, tiled shed roof with octagonal wood cupola, wood sash set in deep reveals with wood lintels, wooden doors; courtyard plan with central hall through from street, twelve rooms including a chapel and kitchen open on patio garden with well, wide corredor around patio, tile floors, ceilings of eucalyptus beams and matting tied with rawhide. Built ca. 1827 by Don José Antonio Estudillo and occupied by family until 1887; Helen Hunt Jackson made the chapel the fictitious place of marriage of her heroine, Ramona; house restored 1910 through generosity of John Spreckels; Hazel W. Waterman, architect; restored again 1968, Clyde Trudell, architect. 6 sheets (1936, including plan, garden plan, elevations, sections, details); 7 ext. photos (1936, 1937); 2 data pages (1937). NHL, SHL

Grand Hotel (Horton Hotel) (CA-1974). 311 Island Ave. Brick and frame, three stories, 60'-6" × 95'-0", flat roof, two two-story projecting bays, cast-iron balconies across front on second and third levels, bracketed and modillioned cornice; skylit stairwell in interior. Built 1887, Comstock and Trotsche, architects; first-floor storefront drastically altered, building dismantled, moved from original site and rebuilt as part of Horton Grand Saddlery Hotel, 1985. 5 photocopies of architectural drawings (ca. 1970, including plans, section), 1 photocopy of 1887 photo. NR

Independent Order of Odd Fellows Hall (CA-429). 526 Market St. Plastered brick and cast iron, 100' (seven-bay front) × 76', two stories, flat roof with balustraded parapet, blank segmental pediment over central bay, Classical entablature, rusticated piers on second floor mark bay divisions, paired fluted pilasters enframe center bay which has ornamental cast-iron balcony, ground-floor shop fronts enframed by cast-iron fluted pilasters, upper floor windows composed of round arches with keystones set under broken-base pediments; ground floor divided into seven rental spaces accessed from the street, second floor divided into two lodge halls. Built 1882, Levi I. Goodrich, architect, for the Masonic Lodge No. 35 and the Independent Order of Odd Fellows Lodge No. 153 which met in the building until 1974; at present occupied by the San Diego Ballet. 1 ext. photo (1960); 8 data pages (1963). NR

Derby (Pendleton) House, San Diego (CA-430).

Melville Klauber House, San Diego (CA-1962).

San Diego continued

Klauber, Melville, House (CA-1962). *3060 6th Ave.* Wood frame with brick veneer, stuccoed, approx. 73' (six-bay front) × 70', two-and-a-half stories, 10' × 21' covered porch with segmental-arched openings at one corner surmounted by open deck with brickwork railing, screened porch at opposite corner, shingled gable roof flared at eaves with broad overhang, redwood soffit, corbeled wood brackets, brick chimney at each end, balcony over entrance on oversized corbeled brackets with block-like ends; stairway with a distinctive, custom-designed railing of Port Orford cedar and cherry composed of stick sections alternating with solid panels, main rooms have Port Orford cedar dados with plaster walls above, flat board trim at corners, baseboards, and ceiling, built-in cabinetry. Built 1908–09, Irving J. Gill of Gill and Mead, architect, Kate Sessions, landscape architect, for Melville Klauber, founder of large wholesale grocery firm and community leader; design marks a transitional point in Gill's work from the earlier more traditional forms to his later, more stark

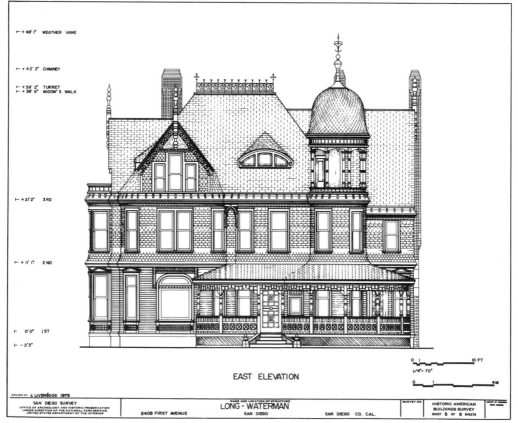

Long-Waterman House, east elevation, San Diego (CA-1964).

and cubistic work; demolished 1980. 2 sheets (1971, including isometric view); 6 ext. photos (1971), 6 int. photos (1971), 9 photocopies of architect's drawings (1907); 10 data pages (1971, 1979). NR

Lee, Alice, House (CA-2161). 3578 7th Ave. Wood frame thin-walled construction with cement plaster finish, two stories, L-shaped, hipped roof with tiles, garage in basement; community garden with house next door (Katherine Teats House, HABS No. CA-2162). Built 1905, W. S. Hebbard and Irving J. Gill, architect. 2 photocopies of architect's drawings (1911, including plans, elevations, section); 6 data pages (1975).

Long-Waterman House (CA-1964). 2408 1st Ave. Wood frame with a variety of cut shingles and board siding, approx. 49′ × 46′, irregular rectangle with a number of projecting bays and curved walls, two stories with unfinished attic, main roof is hipped with cross gables, eyebrow dormers, cresting, and finials atop ridge at gable ends, round tower with bell-shaped top and weathervane, upper stage of tower is open, front porch curves around corner tower, elaborate lattice-work railing, turned columns with fan brackets and spindle frieze, front doors richly carved with raised panel sections, leaded and stained glass in several windows, tripartite windows in gable ends; elaborate molded and carved redwood stairway and fireplace in hall, carved paneled wainscoting, molded chair rails, picture molding, molded window and door trim. Built 1889 for John S. Long, D. P. Benson, architect, most materials supplied by Long who owned a wood veneer firm; Robert W. Waterman, governor of California, 1887–1890, occupied the house just prior to his death in 1891; house is an outstanding example of the most elaborate phase of the Queen Anne style. 8 sheets (1975, including plans, elevations, section; plan, elevation of carriage house); 6 ext. photos (1971), 1 photocopy of undated photo; 12 data pages (1975). NR

Marston, Mrs. Arthur, House (CA-2164). 3575 7th Ave. Wood frame construction with brick veneer, two stories, approx. 63′ × 79′, gable roof. Built 1909, Irving J. Gill, architect. 1 photocopy

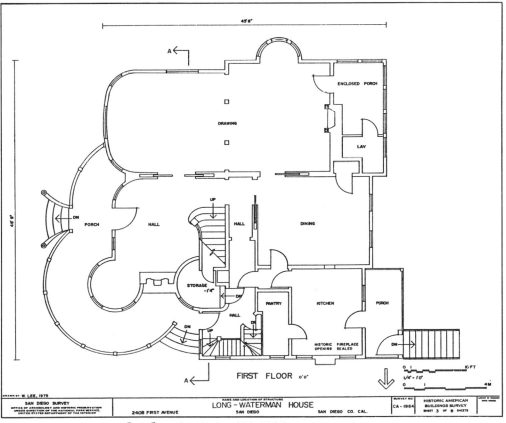

Long-Waterman House, first floor, San Diego (CA-1964).

McGurck Block, San Diego (CA-428).

of architect's drawing (1909, including site plan and sectional details); 7 data pages (1975).

Marston, George W., House (CA-1960). 3525 7th Ave. Wood frame with brick veneer on first level, wood frame with stucco on second level, irregular L-shape, approx. 66' × 64', two-and-a-half stories, shingled gable roof with flared eaves, exposed rafter ends, shed-roof dormers, paneled brick chimney, porte cochere in gable end has entrance, balcony above, second floor overhangs first with exposed joist ends; wood board wainscot on first floor with butterfly splices. Built 1904–05, Irving J. Gill, architect, for George W. Marston, San Diego pioneer, who helped in first bringing railroad to San Diego and secured recreational areas for city; an important transitional design in Gill's work with Craftsman character; setting on the edge of park is original. 5 sheets (1971, including site plan, isometric, elevation, section); 4 ext. photos (1971), 3 int. photos (1971), 1 photocopy of 1905 photo, 6 photocopies of architect's drawings (1904, including plans, elevations); 11 data pages (1970, 1971). NR

McGurck Block (CA-428). 605 5th Ave. Plastered brick with steel lintels and columns, approx. 101' (twelve-bay front) on Market St. and 90' (nine-bay front) on 5th Ave., three stories, low pitched roof with wood truss, square brick chimneys near eaves, parapet over central bay on each side, sheet metal Classical entablature with modillions and plain frieze, shallow paneled pilasters at corners and framing central bays, windows have pronounced segmental-headed architraves with label stops and keystones, ground floor with large glazed openings for shop fronts. Built 1887, Burkett & Osgood, architects, for Col. Ed Mc-Gurck as a commercial building with hotel rooms above. 1 ext. photo (1960); 3 data pages (1963).

Mission San Diego de Alcalá (CA-321). Mission Rd., State Highway 8 off Highway 5 in Mission Valley. Plastered adobe and stone, 70' × 150', one story, tiled gable roof, campanario with five round-arched openings with bells, heavy buttressing walls on either side of facade which end in espadaña, entrance composition very simplified, round-arched doorway with pilasters and pronounced archivolt below narrow segmental-arched opening above, wooden double doors; single nave with choir loft above entrance and baptistry to one side, altar and separate sacristy at other end, wood beamed ceiling, a few statues date from the mission period. Founded July 16, 1769, by Father Junípero Serra as the first of the Alta California Missions, moved from original site near the Presidio to present site in 1774, several structures preceded the present one begun 1808 and completed 1813, secularized 1834, the buildings fell into ruins; rebuilt 1930–31, I. E. Loveless, architect, of original structure only

San Diego continued

buttresses, front wall, and some side walls remained, foundations discovered by excavation, new walls built of reinforced concrete; further renovation in 1946. 24 sheets (1936, including plans, elevations, sections, details); 9 ext. photos (1936), 1 int. photo (1936); 1 data page (1937). NHL, SHL

Nesmith-Greely Building (CA-1971). 825 5th Ave. Brick with stone ornament, 50' × 100', asymmetrical three-bay facade, four stories, flat roof with brick parapet, entrance bay terminates in squeezed pediment with molded cornice, date 1888 and building name in raised letters over a squeezed round arch, entablature of two other bays has frieze of square brick bosses, bays divided by three-quarter round columns terminating in cone-shaped foliate finials above parapet, windows grouped in threes and set in stone architraves straight-headed on second and fourth floors and segmental-headed on third floor, three-story polygonal bay window inset in entrance bay, ground-floor commercial spaces altered; side hall entrance, central lightwell encircled by hall, elevator to all floors. Built 1888, N. A. Comstock and Carl Trotsche, architects; representative of the city's 19th-century commercial architecture during the boom period of the 1880s. 1 sheet (1971, including elevation); 1 ext. photo (1971); 5 data pages (1971, 1979).

Santa Fe Depot (CA-1965). 1050 Kettner Blvd. Stuccoed concrete over steel frame, two stories, tiled gable roof, central portion of facade has a monumental arch within which is set the recessed entrance arcade, upper part of which is largely glazed, two flanking towers have arched openings above which are murals, upper stage of towers recessed from a narrow balcony, arched openings in four sides, towers topped with polychromed tiled domes and lanterns; rectangular plan with main public space enriched with ceramic tile wainscoting and polychromed wood-beamed ceiling. Built 1915, Bakewell & Brown, architects, in Mission Revival style for Atchison, Topeka, and Santa Fe Railroad; arcaded entrance pavilion in front demolished 1954; now being rehabilitated as a transportation and commercial center. 4 ext. photos (1971), 2 int. photos (1971), 8 photocopies of architect's drawings (1914, including plans, elevations, sections), 6 photocopies of construction photos (1914), 1 photocopy of opening day ceremony (1915); 17 data pages (1975). NR

Sherman-Gilbert House (CA-1967). Heritage Park, headquarters for County Park and Recreation Dept. Wood frame with a variety of board siding,

fish-scale shingles, jigsawn work, one-and-a-half stories, hip and cross-gabled roof with gable braces, wide eaves with jigsawn brackets, two-story square tower with widow's walk above, one circular window in square frame, framing expressed decoratively on exterior with strip boards, X-ed panels and flat-sawn detail in stylized foliate forms; hand-carved fireplaces, carved stair rail. Built 1897, Comstock & Trotsche, architects, for John Sherman who occupied it a short time, various owners until 1897 when acquired by Mrs. Augusta E. Gilbert, musician and cultural leader in San Diego musical affairs including 1915 Exposition; house little altered except for 1920s addition of sun porch; acquired by Save Our Heritage Organization of San Diego and moved in 1971 from original site at 139 Fir St. 2 ext. photos (1971); 3 data pages (1969).

Spreckels Building and Theater (CA-1966). 123 Broadway. Steel frame with plastered concrete and brick, 17 bays by 19 bays, six stories, roof with parapet, full entablature enriched with dentils, modillions, and molded cornice, embossed spandrels, belt-cornice above mezzanine, piers studded with sculpted heads above, piers rusticated on mezzanine and ground floors, theater entrance with sculptural group over entrance bay; lobby has coffered ceiling, marble walls, rich variety of decorative motifs, Greek key, guilloche, bound laurel, bead and reel, rinceau and other motifs; theater with vaulted ceiling, monumental proscenium arch enriched with the same kind of Classical detail as the lobby, two tiers of balconies. Built 1911–12 for John D. Spreckels, Harrison Albright, architect, contained 1915 seats for the opening of the 1915 Exposition, allegorical paintings over the stage and ceilings by Emil T. Mazy, other art work by Arthur Hurlt in lobby and lounge. 1 ext. photo (1971), 6 int. photos (1971); 3 data pages (1972). NR

Teats, Katherine, House (CA-2162). 3560 7th Ave. Wood-frame thin-walled construction with cement plaster finish, two stories, approx. 40' × 45', hipped roof; community garden with house next door (Alice Lee House, HABS No. CA-2161). Built 1905, W. S. Hebbard and Irving J. Gill, architects. 3 photocopies of architects' drawings (1905, including plans, elevations, details); 7 data pages (1975).

Temple Beth Israel (Fraternal Spiritualist Church) (CA-1999). Heritage Park. Wood frame with horizontal siding, T-shaped, 55' (three-bay front) × 41', one story, gable roof, false-front cornice, pilasters extend above cornice and terminate in round arches, round windows at gallery level with six-pointed stars of colored glass,

Temple Beth Israel, San Diego (CA-1999).

barrel-vaulted porch on front; vestibule and sanctuary. Built 1889; porch added early; one of earliest surviving synagogues in California; Fraternal Spiritualist Church which occupied beginning 1932 sealed off balcony and added wing to rear ca. 1938. Moved from 1502 2nd Ave. 5 sheets (1975, including plan, elevations, section); 2 photocopies of ext. photos (n.d.); 8 data pages (1975). NR

Villa Montezuma (Jesse Shepard House) (CA-432). *1925 K St.* Museum. Wood frame with variety of cut shingles, approx. 70' × 45', cross

gable roof with gable dormer and metal cresting, polygonal two-story tower with round top and conical roof, three-story square tower with onion dome, other small turrets, flat- and round-arched windows in bays, wall surface textured overall, great variety of decorative detail around openings, gable ends, and on towers, extensive use of stained glass; irregular plan, main rooms have wainscot of walnut and redwood paneling, lincrusta walton wall covering, five individually designed fireplaces with decorative tiles and elaborate mantles, pictorial colored glass designed by owner and made by San Francisco firm of John Mallon; wood coffered ceilings with lincrusta walton in coffers, period furniture. Built 1887 for Jesse Shepard, musician, writer, poet, and world traveler, Comstock and Trotsche, architects; house was largely the creation of Shepard who was financially sponsored by wealthy townspeople; Shepard occupied the house until December 1889 when he changed his name to Francis Grierson, became an author and left San Diego, selling his house; in 1970 the San Diego Historical Society and the Save Our Heritage Organization purchased the house for the City which restored it with HUD and Model Cities funds as a museum and cultural center; house is

Villa Montezuma (Jesse Shepard House), San Diego (CA-432).

Whaley House, San Diego (CA-422).

notable for the integrity and quality of its decorative detail. 8 sheets (1971, including plans, elevations, section); 2 ext. photos (1964), 9 int. photos (1964, 1971); 7 data pages (1964). NR

Whaley House (CA-422). 2482 San Diego Ave., Old Town. Brick, 63′ front, one- and two-story sections each with three-bay fronts, one-story section with gable roof extended over porches front and back, windows with double-hung sash, two-story portion with flat parapeted roof, one-story porch with balustrade on top, all railings have turned spindles, casement windows with straight wood lintels. Built 1856 for Thomas Whaley, a prominent early citizen, the first brick house in San Diego; brick made in owner's brickyard nearby, one-story part originally a granary; Whaley leased house after 1868, served as county courthouse 1869–70; house ruinous by 1956, restoration followed county acquisition. 3 ext. photos (1960), 5 int. photos (1960), 1 photocopy of ca. 1868 plan; 11 data pages (1963). SHL

San Diego vicinity □ San Diego County

Johnson-Taylor Ranch House (CA-2072). Black Mountain Rd., Rancho Penasquitos. Adobe and wood frame, U-shaped around court, 116′-4″ × 90′-3″, one story, gable roof. Built 1862 for George Alonzo Johnson, two wings added by 1868, wood-frame additions by 1883, wood-frame portions rebuilt 1913 after fire; now part of Rancho Penasquitos Regional Park. 3 sheets (1975, including site plan, plan, elevation, section); 1 photocopy of 1883 lithograph; 13 data pages (1975). NR

San Dimas vicinity □ Los Angeles County

Casa de Saturnino Carrión (CA-315). Mountain Meadows Rd. Adobe and wood, stone foundations, irregular L-shape, one story, shingled gable roof pitches out over porch, wood plank doors, windows without sash screened with vertical wood bars and shuttered; six-room, hall-less plan. Built 1868 by Saturnino Carrión on a portion of the Rancho San José de Arriba given him by his uncle, Ygnacio Palomares; demolished. 4 sheets (1934, including plan, elevations, details); 2 ext. photos (1934); 1 data page (1937).

San Fernando □ Los Angeles County

Casa de Gerónimo López (CA-341). 1102 Pico St. Plastered adobe and wood, main section 25′ × 50′, two stories, southeast one-story wing originally detached, original gabled roof was shingled, now tile, gables originally board-and-batten siding, now plastered, two-story porch on three sides, chamfered columns with scroll-sawn brackets, jigsawn balustrade; originally two-room rectangular plan with detached kitchen, second-floor bedrooms reached by exterior stair. Built 1878, one of the first houses in what is now the City of San Fernando; remodeling ca. 1926 connected kitchen to main house, tiled the roof, altered the porch, and converted house to apartments. 2 ext. photos (1960), 2 photocopies of ext. photos (ca. 1900, ca. 1912); 7 data pages (1963). NR

Mission San Fernando Rey de España (CA-325). 15151 San Fernando Rd. Museum. Founded 1797 as seventeenth in chain of twenty-one missions. 2 ext. photos of fountain and statue (1936); 1 data page (1936). SHL

□ *Church (CA-325).* Adobe, stone foundations, 72′ × 163′, tiled gable roof, buttressed side walls; single-nave plan, chapel. Church built 1806; rebuilt after 1812 earthquake, restored in 1896 and 1935; 1971 earthquake required demolition, structure rebuilt 1974 in reinforced concrete. 8 sheets (1935, including plot plan, plans, elevations, sections, details); 6 ext. photos (1934, 1935, 1936), 1 int. photo (1936); 1 data page (1937).

□ *Monastery (CA-37-5).* Plastered adobe, 234′ (nineteen-bay front) × 65′, two stories, tiled gable roof extends to cover arcade across front; interconnecting rooms, outside entrances. Built ca. 1810–22 as living quarters for the padres, guest rooms, winery and offices, Padre Antonio Anzado, architect; restored ca. 1897–1916 by the Landmarks Club. 7 sheets (1934, including plans, elevations, section, details); 7 ext. photos (1934); 1 data page (1936).

Pico, Andrés, House (CA-324). 10940 Sepulveda

San Fernando continued

Blvd. Plastered adobe, stone foundations, irregular U shape, 75' (five-bay front) × 52', two stories with one-story lean-to kitchen and rear wing, gable roof with shakes, shed-roofed porch or corredor in front and rear with tile floors; shallow courtyard plan, five main rooms. Built ca. 1834 by Andrés Pico, brother of Governor Pío Pico; purchased and enlarged 1846 by Eulogio de Celis; restored from ruinous condition in 1930 by M. R. Harrington. 8 sheets (1935, including plans, elevations, details); 4 ext. photos (1936); 1 data page (1937).

San Francisco   □   San Francisco County

Note: A number of HABS records of San Francisco are historic views that have been photocopied for the collection. These are arranged at the end of the regular San Francisco listings under the heading HISTORIC VIEWS OF SAN FRANCISCO. In addition, a number of the buildings that were recorded by HABS also have historic views as part of their documentation. In these cases, the historic views are listed as part of this first section, where they are filed with the building name.

Bank Building (CA-1728). NW corner California and Leidesdorff Sts. Cast-iron facade painted to simulate stone, three-and-a-half stories, entrance in chamfered corner bay, three-bay front on California St., eight-bay front on Leidesdorff St., windows separated by three-quarter columns, paired on California St., single on Leidesdorff St., in Doric order first level, Ionic order second level, Corinthian order third level, modillioned and denticulated cornice, balustrade above. Built 1873 for Bank of London and San Francisco, David Farquharson, architect; fourth story added, some ornament altered; gutted in 1906 fire, renovated by Daniel Burnham of Chicago and Willis Polk of San Francisco; demolished 1959; some elements preserved. 7 ext. photos (1959), 1 int. photo (1959), 2 photocopies of late 19th c. photos; 4 data pages (1960).

Blackstone House (CA-1224). Blackstone Court. Wood frame with clapboards and channeled siding, two stories, salt-box form, three-bay front by two bays, second-floor porch across front with split columns and simplified Tudor arches, three-light casement windows on upper floor, second-story bathroom attached to rear lean-to. Built 1850. Captain Blackstone was well-known early San Franciscan and owner of a flour mill. 2 ext. photos (1939).

Bolton and Barron Building (CA-1232). NW cor-

ner Montgomery and Merchant Sts. Stuccoed brick, stone trim, cast-iron storefront, three stories, four bays by six bays, parapeted roof with projecting molded cornice, storefront arcaded with paneled cast-iron pilasters and consoles supporting cornice, flat-arched double-hunt windows in deep reveals, stone sills. Built before 1854; demolished 1950s. 1 ext. photo (1940).

Booth, Edwin, House (so-called) (CA-1242). 35 Calhoun St. Wood frame with channeled siding, two stories, three-bay front, hip roof, paired windows with plain frames. Built 1850s, remodeled after 1940 and extended to south; said to have been a residence of actor Edwin Booth whose name is also linked to another house to the north on Calhoun. 1 ext. photo (1940).

Bourn, William, House (CA-2219). 2550 Webster St. Brick walls with sandstone detail. Three-and-a-half stories, gable roof with balustrade, denticulated molded cornice, double brick chimneys on each end, three dormers with broken segmental window heads, three-bay facade, brick quoins, ground floor brick rusticated, molded belt cornice, central recessed entry with brick bands on either side, surmounted by central aedicule with balustraded balcony on consoles, architrave with ornamented pilasters and molded segmental pediment, French doors with glazed transom, three double-hung third floor windows with sandstone sills and keystones; L-plan with rear wing, central hall with reception rooms on either side, stair at rear, second floor living room across front with polygonal bay at one end, redwood paneling, stair hall walls with landscape paintings by Bruce Porter. Built 1895–96, Willis Polk, architect. A personal version of the Georgian Revival style townhouse built for mining magnate William Bourn, Jr. 1 ext. photo (1981).

Brickell, John, House. See Historic View (CA-1737).

Brooklyn Hotel. See Historic View (CA-1163).

California Historical Society's Mansion. See Whittier Mansion (CA-1907).

Call Building. See Historic Views (CA-1778, CA-1780).

City Hall (CA-1881). Civic Center, Van Ness Ave. Granite over steel frame, 390' × 273', first floor rusticated, second- and third-floor windows divided by two-story colonnade supporting a cornice, fourth floor set back behind balustrade, center pavilion has three-story Doric columns supporting pediment with bas-relief sculpture in tympanum, central dome rising 308' above ground, 112' interior height, first stage is windows separated by Doric colonnade, copper and lead dome with ornamental occuli, surmounted by elaborate lantern; central-hall plan with flanking halls, central rotunda is open stair hall, monumental marble stair leads from main to second floor, interior finished in marble, Indiana limestone, and Eastern oak. Built 1915, Arthur Brown, Jr., and John Bakewell, Jr., architects, winners of 1912 competition to replace previous City Hall that collapsed in 1906 earthquake; finished for opening of Pan-Pacific Exposition, San Francisco's celebration of recovery; major element of the Civic Center, exemplary City Beautiful complex in the best of the American academic Beaux Arts tradition. 6 ext. photos (1956, 1981), 2 int. photos (1956); 12 data pages (1964).

City of Paris Dry Goods Company (Spring Valley Water Company Building) (CA-2019). *SE corner Geary and Stockton Sts.* Brick, granite, plaster, terra cotta and metal, 135′-6″ (seven-bay front) × 135′-6″, six stories, flat roof, pilasters on first through second floors, Ionic half-column on third through fourth floors, Corinthian half-columns on fifth through sixth floors, ornate terracotta frieze and cornice at roof line, elaborate spandrel panels between floors, entrances flanked by engaged columns and pilasters; retail spaces arranged around light well that extends through fourth floor, office spaces on sixth floor, notable glass dome. Built 1896, Clinton Day, architect; burned and interior gutted, 1906; interior and structural system reconstructed 1908,

James R. Miller, architect, with Bakewell and Brown, architects, responsible for interior and dome; demolished 1982, rotunda and glass dome incorporated in new structure, 1982, Johnson/Burgee, architects. 45 sheets (1979, including title sheet, site plan, plans, elevations, sections, details of building, rotunda, glass dome); 25 ext. photos (1979), 44 int. photos (1979), 10 photocopies of 1898, 1906, ca. 1914, ca. 1922, 1930s photos; 30 data pages (1979); field records. NR

Clay Street Bank. See Historic View (CA-1744).

Cliff House. See Historic View (CA-1736).

Daily Morning Call Building. See Historic View (CA-1743).

Dakin, Captain, House (CA-1240). *SE corner Taylor and Vallejo Sts.* Wood frame, shingled, two stories on sloped site, square with rear one-story addition, hip roof, one-story rectangular entrance bay. Built 1850s, roof altered, minor additions. 1 ext. photo (1940), 1 photocopy of 1850s photo.

DeYoung Building. See Historic View (CA-1778).

Eagle Cafe (McCormick Steamship Office) (CA-2046). *2566 Powell St.* Wooden frame with shingles, one story, four-bay front, hip roof, front porch; dining area with kitchen bar. Built 1911 as McCormick Steamship Office, on edge of wharf between Powell and Mason; moved 1914 to present site; rear addition of decorative siding, n.d.; moved to Pier 39 on North Point Pier, 1977.

City of Paris Dry Goods Company, north elevation, San Francisco (CA-2019).

City of Paris Dry Goods Company, interior detail, San Francisco (CA-2019).

First steamship passenger waiting room in San Francisco. 4 ext. photos (1977), 3 int. photos (1977); 3 data pages (1977).

Engine 15 Firehouse (CA-1882). *2150 California St.* Brick with stone trim, 30′ (three-bay front) × 107′, two stories, parapet has crenellated stone coping and pedestals with finials of firemen's gear, center one in form of fire hydrant capped with fireman's helmet, corner finials have corbel stops in form of fire chiefs' heads, ground floor fire engine entrance in center, pointed arch with stone drip mold and keystone with "15," double wooden doors with tracery in transom, second floor has Tudor-arched windows with stone drip molds, ornamental label stops, hose tower with hip roof rises in two stages above roof; engine room and waiting room below and living quarters above. Built 1885, P. J. O'Connor, architect; tower altered; one of the most fanciful

San Francisco continued

Gothic Revival structures in the city, its capricious qualities were the product of an era when fire-fighting units competed among themselves; demolished 1959. 10 sheets (1959, including site plan, plans, elevation, section, details); 4 ext. photos (1957, 1959), 2 int. photos (1959), 3 photocopies of ext. photos (late 1880s, 1894); 4 data pages (1959).

Express Building. See Historic View (CA-1769).

Fairmont Hotel. See Historic View (CA-1817).

Ferry Building (CA-1910). Embarcadero at Market St. Colusa sandstone over steel and brick, approx. 660′ × 150′, three stories with multi-stage tower approx. 240′ high, projecting central section with three arches rising to top of second story, divided by giant Corinthian columns and framed with two more columns to either side, flanking sections have open arcade at ground level and round-arched openings extending through second and third floors, tower has clock faces 22′ in diameter on each face at top of first stage, open loggia above, topped by three more set-back levels; ground-floor arcade led to waiting rooms of ferry lines and service areas, second floor features a grand nave 42′ wide running the full length of building. Commissioned in 1894, opened in 1898, (Historic View CA-1730), but not completed until 1903, A. Page Brown, architect, finished under Edward S. Swain and Willis Polk; structure replaced wooden terminal of 1877 (Historic View CA-

Engine 15 Firehouse, ca. 1890 photo, San Francisco (CA-1882).

Engine 15 Firehouse, 1894 photo, San Francisco (CA-1882-1).

Engine 15 Firehouse, 1957 photo, San Francisco (CA-1882-9).

San Francisco continued

1749), undamaged by 1906 earthquake, service ceased during World War II, interior remodeled 1956 by William Merchant Association as World Trade Center and offices. 2 ext. photos (1960), 1 photocopy of ca. 1900 int. photo; 10 data pages (1964). NR. See also Historic View (CA-1780).

Feusier Octagon House. See Historic View (CA-1737).

Filbert Street Houses. See Telegraph Hill, Filbert Street Houses (CA-1246).

Fireman's Fund Insurance Building. See Historic View (CA-1167).

Fleishhacker Pool and Bath House (CA-2075). Corner Sloat Blvd. and Great Highway. Pool of reinforced concrete, 1000' × 150', largest swimming pool in world at time it was built; bath house two stories, stucco, green-tiled hip roof. Built 1924–25, Earl Clements, engineer for pool; Ward & Blohme, architects of bath house; demolished 1970s. 14 ext. photos (1979), 3 int. photos (1979), 3 photocopies of undated photos, 6 photocopies of 1922, 1924 architectural drawings; 20 data pages (1977); field records.

Flood Building. See Historic View (CA-1819).

Flood, James, Mansion (now Pacific Union Club) (CA-1230). 1000 California St. at Mason St. Connecticut sandstone, two-and-a-half stories on raised basement, seven-bay front, rectangular block with flanking one-story wings rounded at ends, low-pitched roof with balustraded parapet having low paneled posts above bay divisions, main facade has projecting central element over three-bay entrance portico with paired box columns and full Classical entablature surmounted by balustrade, second floor of entrance pavilion has three round-arched windows, quoins on all corners, wall elevations terminate in architrave molding with two fascias, plain frieze, modillions and wide cornice molding, parklike setting with masonry retaining wall and bronze fence with enriched rinceau; center-hall plan with wood paneling, richly appointed interiors, dining room in wing. Built 1885–86 for James Clair Flood; Augustus Laver, architect. Flood, who began as a bartender, became one of the city's wealthiest men through mining speculation in the Comstock Lode and established the Nevada Bank, 1875, that merged with the Wells Fargo Bank after his death in 1889; only Nob Hill mansion to survive 1906 earthquake, then acquired by Pacific (and) Union Club, remodeled for club use by Willis Polk, architect, in 1910–11, wings

added, front central tower removed, third floor set into attic. 3 ext. photos (1940).

Fortman House (CA-1161). NW corner Gough and Eddy Sts. Wood frame with channel siding, two-and-a-half stories on raised basement, square with square bay windows on side and polygonal bay on front, low pitched roof with parapet, bracketed molded cornice, entablature, and frieze panels, bays have triple windows with colonettes and ornamental detail, other windows have ornamented hoods on consoles, classical entrance portico approached by broken flight of steps; center-hall plan. Built 1882; occupied by Fortman, President of Alaska Commercial Lines in the 1930s; demolished 1959. 1 ext. photo (1956).

Fort Mason (CA-1119). Van Ness, Bay, and Laguna Sts. Declared military area 1851, U.S. Army under Colonel Mason dispossessing Fremont and others who had claimed land, troops quartered here after 1863, named Fort Mason 1882. 3 ext. photos (1939), 3 photocopies of ext. photos (before 1855, ca. 1887, 1920). See also Historic Views (CA-1733, CA-1781).

□ *Quarters #1 (Commanding Officer's House, Officer's Club) (CA-1877).* Clapboard over frame, two stories, seven-bay front, hip roof. Built 1855 as Brooks House, only kitchen wing retains original fabric; rebuilt 1863, improved 1887, commanding officer's house 1866–1943, officers' club since. 1 ext. photo (1939), 1 photocopy of ca. 1885 photo.

□ *Quarters #2 (CA-1878).* Channeled siding over frame, one-and-a-half stories, gable roof, with hip-roof two-story addition, gable and shed dormers, modillioned cornice, one-story porch on two sides. Built after 1863, perhaps with pieces of Brooks House. 2 ext. photos (1940), 1 photocopy of undated ext. photo.

□ *Quarters #3 (CA-1879).* Clapboard over frame, two stories, hip roof, one-story bays. Rubble walls of basement and first floor thought to date from Moody House (1855); built largely after 1863. 1 ext. photo (1939).

□ *Quarters #4 (CA-1880).* Clapboard over frame, two stories, four-bay front, oriels on first story, modillioned cornice between first and second floors. Built 1855 by Haskell and Co., sold to Joseph Palmer; seized by U.S. Government 1863 and reworked by Army, now a duplex. 1 ext. photo (ca. 1939), 1 photocopy of ca. 1857 ext. photo.

Fort Point (Fort Winfield Scott) (CA-1239). Below

Golden Gate Bridge. Brick and granite, trapezoidal form with interior courtyard, three main stories, walls average 5′ to 12′ in thickness, parapets and 36 gun positions on top floor barbette, casemate rooms with parabolic brick vaulting on north side, brick arches, 30 gun rooms to a floor, open gun ports on outer wall, three granite spiral staircases open on the courtyard, 1864 lighthouse atop one stairwell, cisterns located under southeastern rooms; courtyard plan, main power magazine, jail, storerooms on main floor south, second floor contains officers' quarters, small hospital, kitchen; third floor has enlisted men's quarters. Original adobe brick fort of 1794 built by Spanish and called Castillo de San Joaquín, leveled 1853 for construction of Fort Winfield Scott, constructed with much difficulty and delay 1853–1861, designed to mount 126 cannons and house 600 soldiers to protect entrance to the Bay, called Fort Point after 1861, abandoned 1886 when powerful rifled cannon made brick forts obsolete, 1933–37 served as base of construction operation for Golden Gate Bridge, 100 soldiers garrisoned here during World War II as submarine watch, dedicated Fort Point National Historic Site in 1970, restored. A classic example of brick seacoast forts. 35 ext. photos (1934, 1968, 1975, 1981), 12 int. photos (1934, 1968, 1975), 3 photocopies of aerial photos (1920s, 1950s, ca. 1968). NR, SHL

Fort Winfield Scott. See Fort Point (CA-1239).

Fremont Hotel. See Historic View (CA-1726).

Fremont House. See Historic View (CA-1175).

Golden Gate Park Conservatory (CA-2227). John F. Kennedy Drive. Cast-iron and glass frame, one-story, central polygonal block surmounted by a two-tiered central dome capped with a finial, polygonal base with four gable-roofed dormers, flanking wings turn at right angles toward front and have large finials, entrance wing with cantilevered gabled dormer, rich cast-iron ornamental detail in banded windows and at edges of dormers and dome; E-plan, interior replicates exterior. Erected in Golden Gate Park in 1878, made some time earlier by Hammersmith Works in Dublin, Ireland, for James Lick and sold by his estate to Leland Stanford, Charles Crocker and others who gave it to Golden Gate Park. 6 ext., 3 int. photos (1981).

Grace Church. See Historic View (CA-1817).

Haas-Lilienthal House (CA-1160). 2007 Franklin St. House/Museum. Wood frame with channeled siding, clapboards, fish-scale shingles, two-and-a-

half stories on raised basement, cross-gabled roof with flat central section, wooden cresting and finials at end of ridges, boxed, molded cornice with modillions, round corner bay terminates in a shingled tower with domical roof and finial, double-hung tower windows have gable roofs and consoled aprons, foliated frieze in high relief around tower, gable ends have stepped out section at top with foliated ornament, entrance portico with turned and square posts, gable roof and finial, first-floor polygonal bay at corner has elaborate foliated frieze below window sills, two windows have swan-necked hoods on consoles that break into belt course marking second floor, second-floor windows have transom lights with patterned glass, frieze above tripartite window section has swags, third floor has balcony across portion of gabled roof form, projecting wing on west side; parlors and dining room on west side, hall, two stairways, and kitchen on east side; second floor bedrooms, third floor ballroom/playroom and servants' rooms, richly ornamented interior retaining original furnishings from several periods. Built 1886 for William Haas, Bavarian-born wholesale grocer and later prominent member of San Francisco Jewish community; Peter R. Schmidt, architect, McCann & Biddell, contractors; slight alterations include addition of brick chimney and bath to west wall and sleeping porch in rear, 1927 rear wing on west side designed by Gardner Dailey. One of the Bay Area's most outstanding late 19th c. townhouses in the Queen Anne mode, largely intact through continuous ownership by the original family, donated in 1973 to the Foundation for San Francisco's Architectural Heritage. 7 ext. photos (1956, 1960, 1975), 1 photocopy of 1885 ext. photo; 8 data pages (1964).

Hallidie Building (CA-2221). 130-150 Stutter St. Steel and concrete frame, ten stories, five bays wide, flat parapeted roof with elaborate Gothicized cast iron ornament, similar belt cornice below top story with balcony, filigreed belt cornices on second and third stories, metal fire escapes on each end of facade, a glazed curtain wall with a metal grid is hung before the building frame above the first three stories, arched entrance on one end; rectangular plan, conventional office floors. Built 1917–1918, Willis Polk, architect; this is reputed to be the first use of "curtain wall" construction in a multi-story office building. It was named for Andrew S. Hallidie, inventor of the cable car. 1 ext. photo (1981).

Mills Building (CA-2223). 220 Montgomery St.

Haas-Lilienthal House, San Francisco (CA-1160-20).

Steel frame with brick, terra cotta and white marble facing. 13 bays wide, ten stories, flat roof with parapet, projecting molded cornice with entablature and modillions, molded belt cornice with modillions below attic story, other molded belt cornices above ground floor and mezzanine floor, three-part block with differentiated end bays, mid-zone of office floors terminates in round arches, ornamentation is Romanesque with foliate forms and other ornamental detail in terra cotta, ground floor and massive rounded entrance arch clad in white Inyo marble, finely carved Romanesque capitals with heads and foliate detail; square plan with large central light court, continuous corridors on each floor, marble-clad entrance lobby with graceful wrought-iron stair railings. Built 1891; Burnham & Root, architects; additions 1908, 1914, 1918 by Willis Polk; Mills Tower addition, 1931 by Lewis Hobart. The first steel-framed skyscraper in San

San Francisco continued

Francisco and the only remaining building in the city by this famous Chicago firm. 4 ext., 3 int. photos (1981).

Hibernia Bank (CA-2224). *NW corner McAllister St. at Market St.* Steel frame with granite cladding. 8 bays square with rounded corner bay, flat roof with balustraded parapet, copper dome with ornamental oculus on a masonry drum with three windows with triangular pediments, differentiated end bays of each elevation have triangular pediments, continuous molded and denticulated cornice with blank frieze, giant Composite order engaged columns with fluted shafts rest on water table above low base story, end bays have windows with architraves of Ionic pilasters and segmental heads, entranceway is a rotunda under domed element; square plan with elaborate banking hall with Classical detail dominated by a stained glass dome. Built 1892, enlarged in 1905, rebuilt in 1907, Albert Pissis, architect; the oldest and among the finest of San Francisco's modified temple-form banks with Baroque elements. 1 ext., 4 int. photos (1981).

Hibernia Savings and Loan Society Building. See Historic Views (CA-1729, CA-1735, CA-1739, CA-1797).

Hindu Temple (Vedanta Society) (CA-1286). *2936 Webster St.* Wood frame with horizontal siding and shingles, three stories, two-bay front by six bays, flat roof with hipped parapet clad in fish-scale shingles, four cupolas, one surmounting round corner bay with two-stage onion dome in pressed metal with swags, one with two-stage lobed dome with metal roofs and weather vane, one with tear-drop domes in two tiers around base of large pointed dome also of metal, continuous open veranda around third floor with cusped arches on ornate caps and round columns, bowed metal railing with bosses, wide cornice molding at top of second floor caps an ornate plaster frieze, second floor has four oriels. Built 1905, Joseph A. Leonard, architect; Swami Triguenatitamanda advised designer on doctrinal matters; Vedanta is the common doctrinal basis of all Hinduism; Society established in San Francisco as result of popularity of Swami Vivhananda's teachings at Columbian Exposition in Chicago in 1893. 3 ext. photos (ca. 1960).

Holy Cross Parish Hall (St. Patrick's Church) (CA-1908). *Eddy St. between Scott and Divisadero Sts.* Wood frame with lapped siding, three-bay front by six bays, one story, gable roof with cornice returning one-third width of end, facade divided by four pilasters, double window above entrance; single nave with raised sanctuary. Building said to have been shipped in pre-fabricated sections around the Horn ca. 1851 and erected on Market Street between Second and Third Sts. as St. Patrick's Church; moved in 1873 for building of Palace Hotel to site on Eddy St., moved again in 1891 to present site; a modest Greek Revival design and a rare survivor of this early period of building in the city; alterations of 1899 for Parish Hall include addition of paired windows, interior also remodeled for use as Parish Hall for Holy Cross Church. 1 ext. photo (1960), 2 photocopies of ca. 1865, ca. 1937 ext. photos; 8 data pages (1964). See also Historic View (CA-1233A).

Hotaling Building (CA-1475). *451-461 Jackson St.* Brick with cast-iron facade, 48' (six-bay front) × 88', three stories, flat roof with raised parapet bearing elaborate modillioned cornice, quoins, ground floor has cast-iron pilasters, windows have cast-iron hoodmolds, iron shutters in reveals. Built 1866 for Anson Parson Hotaling, wholesale dealer in spirits and tobacco, restored 1952 by Mr. and Mrs. Henry Lawenda as center for interior design and import firms with minor alterations, still the most ornate of the cast-iron front commercial buildings to survive the 1906 earthquake and fire, part of the Jackson Square Historic District. 3 ext. photos (1960); 8 data pages (1964).

Humphrey House (CA-155). *Chestnut and Hyde Sts.* Wood frame with tongue-and-groove siding, five-bay front by two bays, two stories with basement under east end, low pitched roof with crenellated parapet, Classical entablature, and off-center octagonal fenestrate cupola, one-story porch wraps around east side and has a crenellated parapet above an entablature with molded cornice, four-paneled door with side lights and transom, six-over-six-light double-hung windows with label stops, south rear elevation has six-bay porch with same treatment as front porch, polygonal corner tower with crenellated parapet on west elevation; center-hall plan. Built 1851–52 by William Squire Clark, owner of Clark's Point (1847), first redwood pile wharf on Pacific coast; doors and moldings probably shipped from Maine; acquired by William Penn Humphrey in 1868, moved 70' west in 1898 and somewhat altered, east side extended, Tudor arches removed; demolished ca. 1949. 4 ext. photos (1936), 1 photocopy of ca. 1860 ext. photo.

Jackson Square—Commercial Buildings, *463-73*

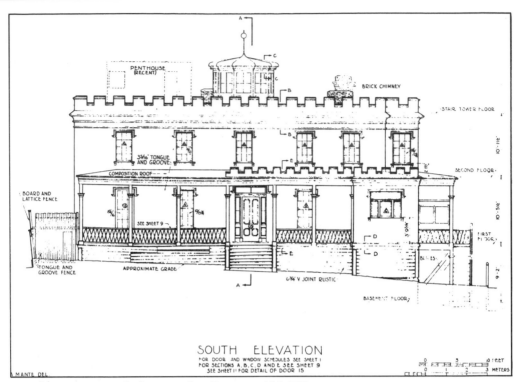

Humphrey House, south elevation, San Francisco (CA-155).

Jackson St., (**CA-1900**), *445 Jackson St.* (**CA-1901**), *441 Jackson St.* (**CA-1902**), *415-31 Jackson St.* (**CA-1903**). Brick, two and three stories, cast-iron storefronts, elaborate hoodmolds and cornices. This two-block stretch of Jackson St. was one of few areas to survive 1906 earthquake and fire, virtually only downtown remnant of mid-19th c. city. 6 ext. photos (1960).

*Jackson Street—Commercial Buildings (**CA-1473**). Between Montgomery and Sansome Sts.* Row of two- and three-story commercial buildings, stone and stucco, cast-iron storefronts, hoodmolds, cornices. Built mid to late 19th c. 2 ext. photos (1934). Originally recorded as Building.

Leese, Jacob, House. See Historic Views (CA-1866, CA-1869).

Lick House. See Historic View (CA-1727).

Lilienthal House. See Haas-Lilienthal House (CA-1160).

Lincoln School. See Historic View (CA-1868).

Maguire's Music Hall. See Historic View (CA-1724).

Masonic Temple. See Historic Views (CA-1739, CA-1747, CA-1797).

McCormick Steamship Office. See Eagle Cafe (CA-2046).

McCoy Label Company Building. See U.S. Sub-Treasury and Mint (CA-1218).

McElroy Octagon House. See Octagon House (CA-1223).

McGaw Octagon House. See Historic View (CA-1737).

Mechanics' Institute. See Historic View (CA-1823).

*Medical Dental Building (**CA-2226**). 450 Sutter St.* Steel frame with terra cotta cladding. Nine bays wide at base, thirty stories high, flat parapeted roof with elevator tower, both with ornamental pier caps, prismatic form of splayed piers and bay windows, set-backs at 18th and 24th floors, recessed three-story entrance with canopy bearing Mayan motif, glazed ornamented transom above entrance doors, window spandrels enriched with Mayanesque cast terra cotta ornament; T-plan, elevator lobby has marble revetment and floors, pseudo-corbel-arched ceiling with elaborate Mayanesque ornament in gilded terra cotta relief. Built 1929–30. Miller & Pflueger, architects; an outstanding early Modern skyscraper designed by a firm noted for innova-

San Francisco continued

tion in skyscraper and theater design. 6 ext., 3 int. photos (1981).

Mercantile Library Building. See Historic View (CA-1163).

Merchants' Exchange. See Historic View (CA-1723).

Metropolitan Theater. See Historic View (CA-1745).

Mexican Custom House. See Historic Views (CA-1293, CA-1732).

Miner's Exchange Bank. See Historic View (CA-1731).

Mission Dolores. See Mission San Francisco de Asís (CA-113).

Mission San Francisco de Asís (Mission Dolores) (CA-113). *Dolores Street near 16th Street.* Church/museum. Plastered adobe and wood, approximately 32′ × 152′, one story, tiled gable

Jackson Square, 463-73 Jackson Street, San Francisco (CA-1900).

Jackson Square, 445 Jackson Street, San Francisco (CA-1901).

roof, east facade divided horizontally by wooden balcony with railing, structure raised above street on masonry plinth, round-arched central entrance with plain pilasters, molded caps, and pronounced archivolt molding, wood paneled doors with brass rosettes, flanked by paired engaged columns on stepped bases, belt cornice with central pendant over entrance, upper division in *espadaña* form with three openings for bells and six half-columns topped with stepped pyramidal capitals, pair of four-light wood-framed windows above balcony floor, 4′ thick adobe side walls buttressed on south side, recessed round- and square-headed openings, flat apse; single nave with sanctuary at east end set off by two steps and wrought-iron railing, choir loft at west end, baptistry niched against south wall in mid-nave, polychromed altars on either side of nave at sanctuary steps, polychromed, wooden beamed ceiling, elaborate gilded and polychromed wooden reredos covers east end wall, five of six niches hold statues of saints. Founded

Mission San Francisco de Asís, San Francisco (CA-113-7).

by Father Francisco Palou October 9, 1776, called "Dolores" from name of nearby pond or creek, first church 1782–1791; present church built 1972–ca. 1810; only the church and cemetery, which has the 1830 grave of Don Luís Antonio Arguello, first governor, remain from mission complex; church restored 1916, Willis Polk, architect, steel frame inserted in walls and roof to reinforce original structure, east facade restored as well as portions of the ceiling and other details, street downgraded and church set on brick foundations with steps about 1901, cemetery walls set back from sidewalk. This is the sixth in the chain of California missions and one of the most intact in respect to original building fabric and interior furnishings. 39

San Francisco continued

sheets (1934–37), including plot plan, plans, elevations, section, details); 11 ext. photos (1936), 8 int. photos (1936), 1 photocopy of 1854 site plan, 5 photocopies of drawings (ca. 1816, 1849, ca. 1860s, 1883), 10 photocopies of ext. photos (ca. 1860, ca. 1865, 1870, ca. 1880, before 1906, and undated); 9 data pages (1937). SHL

Montgomery Block (CA-1228). 628 Montgomery at Washington Street. Plastered brick, redwood pile foundation, stone trim, four stories, 122′ (nineteen-bay front) on Montgomery by 138′, flat roof, ground-floor arcade with box columns, segmental rusticated arches, heads of famous Americans in relief on keystones, wide molded belt course at second floor, full entablature with architrave course, Vitruvian scroll frieze, ovolo course, modillions, projecting cornice molding; U-plan with interior open court closed at street by fire wall, basement and first floor housed 28 commercial spaces, about 150 office spaces on other floors, artesian well in court furnished water; iron shutters, mahogany doors. Built 1853 for Henry W. Halleck and his law partners Archi-

Mission San Francisco de Asís, 1854 plot, San Francisco (CA-113-25).

bald Peachy and Frederick Billings, Gordon P. Cummings, architect; structure was only building in this downtown area to survive the 1906

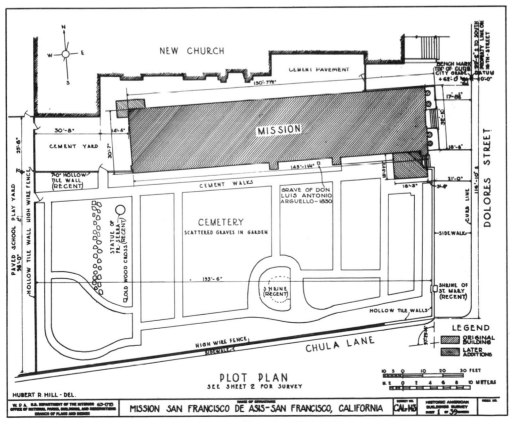

Mission San Francisco de Asís, plot plan, San Francisco (CA-113).

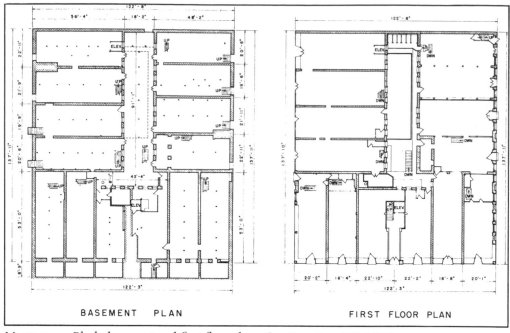

Montgomery Block, basement and first floor plans, San Francisco (CA-1228).

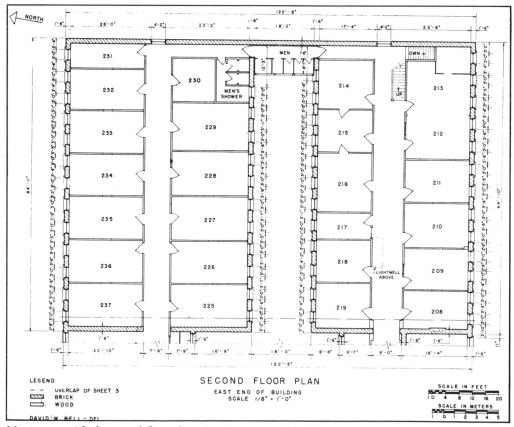

Montgomery Block, second floor plan, San Francisco (CA-1228).

San Francisco continued

earthquake, though losing some decorative trim; then the largest and best equipped commercial building in San Francisco, first occupied by mining engineers and lawyers, later by writers and artists including Bret Harte, Mark Twain, Frank and Kathleen Norris, and Jack London. Demolished 1959. 13 sheets (1958, including plans, elevations, sections, details); 6 ext. photos (1940, 1956, 1958), 3 int. photos (1958), 3 photocopies of ext. photos (ca. 1856, ca. 1860); 7 data pages (1958). SHL

Montgomery Street—Commercial Buildings (CA-1474). E. side Montgomery Street between Washington and Jackson Streets. Row of two- and three-story brick buildings, four-story Montgomery Block at end. Built 1850s–70s, typical late 19th c. commercial streetscape virtually unaltered in 1934. 1 ext. photo (1934). Originally recorded as Buildings.

Montgomery Street—Commercial Building (CA-1472). 802 Montgomery Street. Plastered brick, two stories, seven-bay front by seven bays deep, flat roof with parapet, ground floor rusticated,

segmental-arched openings with pronounced voussoirs. Built 1850s. 1 ext. photo (1934). Originally recorded as Building.

Montgomery Street House. 1301 Montgomery Street. See Telegraph Hill—Brick House (CA-1241).

Montgomery Street Houses (CA-1245). Wood frame houses lining the street north of Union Street looking toward the Bay, some modern apartment houses. Built ca. 1850–ca. 1940, the street preserves the 19th-century scale of Telegraph Hill. 1 ext. photo (1940).

Morris Store (V. C.) (CA-2216). 140 Maiden Lane. Art Gallery. Concrete frame with brick veneer, one story with mezzanine, rectangular shape, low pitched skylit roof with parapet, windowless facade with round-arched glazed entrance with triple arches on one side, expressed vertical row of bricks to left of entrance conceals lights; ground floor open to sky-lit ceiling, spiral ramp curving up from ground floor to mezzanine with circular display windows at intervals, translucent hung ceiling of inverted bowl-like forms. De-

Montgomery Street, between Washington and Jackson Streets, San Francisco (CA-1474).

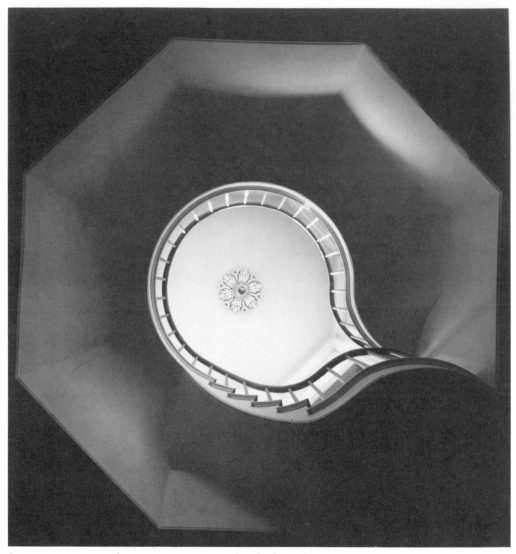

Octagon House (McElroy Octagon House), detail of circular stairway and ceiling medallion, San Francisco (CA-1223).

signed 1948–49 as a remodeling of a 1911 ware-house by Frank Lloyd Wright for V. C. Morris for the sale of fine crystal and china, interior very similar to Wright's Guggenheim Museum in New York. 1 ext. photo, 8 int. photos (1981).

Napier Lane Houses. See Telegraph Hill, Napier Lane Houses (CA-1244).

Nevada National Bank. See Historic View (CA-1164).

Niantic Hotel. See Historic View (CA-1719).

North Point Pier Bulkhead Buildings #1, 3, 5, 9, 15, 19, 23, 29, 31, 33, 35, 39, 41 (CA-2047). N. of Ferry Building along Embarcadero between

Kearny and Powell Streets. Steel, wood and plas-ter, one-and-a-half or two stories, five major front bays, flat roofs with parapets, large arched en-trances with keystones and voussoirs, flanked by battered piers and capped by pediments with denticulated cornices; piers, sheds and docks be-hind bulkhead buildings. Built 1910–20; piers #39 and 41 demolished, 1978. 27 ext. photos (1977); 3 data pages (1977, 1979).

O'Brien House (CA-1236). 1045 Green Street. Wood frame, shingled, two stories on raised basement, three-bay front with central rectangu-lar oriel at second floor, gable roof, boxed cor-nice, cupola with conical roof, variety of

San Francisco continued

windows, rectangular bay window on side, steps to one side; side-hall plan. Built ca. 1890, one of a group of houses that survived the 1906 fire; somewhat altered, good example of an eccentric 19th-century rustic cottage with a mixture of stylistic elements. 1 ext. photo (1940).

Occidental Hotel. See Historic View (CA-1162).

Octagon House (McElroy Octagon House) (CA-1223). 2645 Gough Street. House/museum. Concrete with redwood clapboards and wooden quoining, two stories, octagonal shape, 16' sides, pyramidal roof with central cupola, paired windows on each face, entrance portico with hipped roof, two box columns and two pilasters, plain frieze, dentil course and molded cornice; large first-floor room with spiral stair to one side. Built ca. 1860–61 for William C. McElroy on site across street, severely damaged in 1906 earthquake but escaped fire, acquired by Colonial Dames and moved to present site; Warren Perry remodeled the house, changing the interior significantly on the first floor and reconstructing the stair, 1953; house well-furnished with largely 19th-century American pieces. 4 ext. photos (1939, 1956, 1960, 1981), 4 int. photos (1960), 2 photocopies of ext. photos (undated, 1906); 8 data pages (1965).

Old Mint. See U.S. Branch Mint (CA-160).

Orphan Asylum. See Historic View (CA-1233 A).

Osbourne, Lloyd, House. See Stevenson, Mrs. Robert Louis—Lloyd Osbourne House (CA-1229).

Pacific Union Club. See Flood, James, Mansion (CA-1230).

Palace of Fine Arts (CA-1909). Baker between Jefferson and Bay Streets. Complex consisting of a semi-circular exposition building 1100' on outer circumference, 135' wide, 48' high, and rotunda backed by peristyle following curve of exposition building consisting of Corinthian colonnade terminating in open pavilions, rotunda supported on eight large triangular piers buttressed on the exterior by paired Corinthian columns, drum with pseudo-Classical relief sculptures in variety of themes on Greek culture; interior of rotunda has polychromed coffering with enriched divisions, murals in coffers, plaster tinted to simulate Numidian marble for columns, and travertine for other elements, interior of exposition building continuous space divided into 114 galleries supported by hinged steel truss. Built 1915, Bernard Maybeck, architect, for the Pan-Pacific International Exposition, focal element at end of fair

grounds; only building left standing from the fair, deteriorated because of the ephemeral nature of its materials, rebuilt in concrete from casts of original, 1959–62, as result of generous contribution and zeal of Walter Johnson, San Francisco financier. 13 photos (1956, 1981), 13 data pages (1964).

Palmer, Silas, House (CA-1289). NW corner Van Ness Avenue and Washington Street. Wood frame, variety of sidings, two-and-a-half stories, gable roof, central tower, canted bay on corner, square bays, variety of decorative detail typical of 1880s. Built ca. 1886; demolished ca. 1940. 1 ext. photo (1940).

Parrott's Granite Block. See Historic Views (CA-1770, CA-1778, CA-1819).

Phelan Building. See Historic View (CA-1778).

Phelps House (CA-1904). 329 Divisadero Street. Wood frame with clapboards and channeled siding, two-and-a-half stories, five-bay front, gabled roof with four gabled wall dormers, central cross-gable and gable ends have scalloped bargeboards, two-story porch runs across front, turned wood balustrade both levels, French doors both levels; central-hall plan, wainscoting with wide and narrow vertical boards. Built ca. 1850 at foot of Buena Vista Hill, purchased by Abner Phelps, alleged to have been built with pre-fabricated sections shipped around the Horn from either Maine or New Orleans, but restoration research indicates house built of local redwood; one of city's oldest houses, transitional style combining both Greek and Gothic Revival elements; Phelps family occupied the house until

Silas Palmer House, San Francisco (CA-1289).

San Francisco continued

1939, moving it several times; moved once more and restored 1970s. 4 ext. photos (1960), 3 int. photos (1960); 7 data pages (1960).

Polk-Williams House (CA-2217). 1013-1019 Vallejo St. Wood frame with shingles. A double house, two stories in front, four and five stories in back, irregular shape, gable roof with two cross gables, facade has two projecting bays, one polygonal, the other with a flat front, two entrances, one in a small entrance porch at the west end, the other recessed in center of east side, variety of windows; irregular plan, east unit has living room open through second floor to the roof with massive hearth and redwood mantle continuing from first to second floor. Designed 1892, Willis Polk, architect, for the Polk family and Mrs. Virgil Williams, one of Polk's most distinctive designs and a hallmark of the turn-of-the-century San Francisco Bay region style. 1 ext. photo 1981.

Presidio (CA-1114). Site of a military post since 1776, first Spanish, Mexican after 1822, U.S. post since 1846; most buildings date from U.S. period; now 1540 acres; oldest active military post in U.S. 5 photocopies of drawings (ca. 1816, ca. 1830, ca. 1847, ca. 1854, ca. 1856), 3 photocopies of photos (ca. 1850s, ca. 1856, n.d.). NHL

☐ *Barracks (CA-1173).* Row of houses, brick, two-and-a-half stories, four- and five-bay fronts, hip roofs with hip-roofed dormers, one-story frame porches in front. Built turn of 20th century. 4 ext. photos (1975).

☐ *Chapel of Our Lady (CA-1217). Moraga Avenue.* Wood frame, vertical boards and rounded battens, one story, gable roof, square louvered belfry with sharply peaked roof, single-bay front by four bays, boxed cornice with ornamental brackets with pendants, double-hung pointed-arched windows with hood molds, rose window in gable, entrance vestibule; single nave, exposed wood truss, apse. Built 1860s, slightly remodeled in the Spanish Mediterranean revival mode in the 1950s. 2 ext. photos (1940, 1975), 1 int. photo (1940), 3 photocopies of ext. photos (1873, 1926).

☐ *Comandancia (Officers' Club), (CA-1100). Moraga Avenue.* Adobe and wood, seven bays by one bay, rectangular, one story, tiled gable roof extends over porch with square wood posts, square bay window on one end, other end attached to larger buildings, one-room interior with wood beamed ceiling and plastered fireplace (not original). Built 1776 as headquarters of the Presidio; taken over by U.S. Army 1846 as Officers' Club; remodeled ca. 1880; restored 1933 to a pseudo-

Barracks, Presidio, San Francisco (CA-1173).

Spanish Colonial appearance with totally new interior and exterior; only portion of adobe wall remains from the original structure. 3 ext. photos (ca. 1940), 1 int. photo (1934), 3 photocopies of ext. photos (ca. 1925, ca. 1930).

□ *Gun Emplacements (CA-1212).* Concrete emplacements for at least two guns, two stories, platform above, rooms below. Built 20th century. 6 ext. photos (1975).

□ *Officers' Club.* See Comandancia (CA-1100).

□ *Officers' Quarters (CA-1214). Funston Avenue.* Wood frame with clapboards, one-and-a-half stories on raised foundation, five-bay front, gable roof, gabled dormers, boxed cornice with returns at gable ends, front porch with split columns, polygonal bays on front and side elevations of living room, double-hung windows with straight cornice heads; irregular L-plan. Row of twelve residences built ca. 1865 as officers' quarters. 3 ext. photos (1940, 1975).

□ *Old Station Hospital (Post Hospital) (CA-1216). Funston Avenue near Lincoln Blvd.* Wood frame with clapboards, two stories on raised, fenestrated, brick basement, eight-bay front, low-pitched hip roof, Classical entablature with wide overhanging cornice, three-story porch across front has box columns and balustrade with

turned balusters; rectangular plan with wards off through halls. Built 1857, upper level of porch glazed later; the oldest U.S. Army building in the Presidio. 3 ext. photos (1975), 1 photocopy of undated ext. photo.

□ *Pershing House (CA-1215).* Wood frame with clapboards, three-bay front, gable roof with clipped-gable end, brick chimneys, bracketed cornice, porch across front with scalloped frieze and chamfered posts, square bay window on side; L-plan. Built ca. 1885, occupied by Gen. Pershing and family after 1914, wife and three daughters killed in fire which destroyed house, 1915. 2 photocopies of ext. photos (late 19th century, 1915).

□ *Post Hospital.* See Old Station Hospital (CA-1216).

□ *Powder Magazine (CA-1213). Graham Street.* Stone, random ashlar, 23' × 28', one story, tiled hip roof, heavy wood entablature with overhanging cornice, quoins, single round-arched entrance door, slit openings on either side; single room interior, stone vaulted ceiling. Built 1845 by Mexicans. Presidio taken over by U.S. Army in 1846. 2 photocopies of ext. photos (ca. 1930s, 1940).

□ *Stables (CA-1174).* Two stables, brick, one

Post Hospital, Presidio, San Francisco (CA-1216-1).

San Francisco continued

story with clerestory, five-bay front by eighteen bays, gable roof, segmental-arched openings. Built late 19th century. 1 ext. photo (1975).

Railroad House. See Historic View (CA-1720).

Reservoir Keeper's House (CA-1234). SW corner Bay and Hyde Streets. Clapboard over frame, one story, gable roof, one-story porch with Moorish arches across front. Probably built ca. 1860–65; demolished ca. 1950. 1 ext. photo (1940).

Roos Brothers Store. See Historic View (CA-1721).

Russ Building. See Historic View (CA-1754).

Sacramento Block. See Historic View (CA-1746).

Sacramento Stree House (CA-2044). 3397-99 Sacramento St. at corner of Sacramento and Walnut Sts. Wood frame with clapboards, three stories, 37' (three-bay front) × 100', flat roof, cornice frieze with rinceau ornamentation, original storefront first story, two-story octagonal oriel on corner, two-story rectangular oriels at both ends. Built ca. 1895, first floor originally a grocery store; demolishéd 1979. 8 ext. photos (1978).

Sailors' Home. See Historic View (CA-1741).

St. Francis Church. See Historic View (CA-1219).

St. Francis Hotel. See Historic View (CA-1818).

St. Mary's Church (CA-1237). 660 California, NE corner of Grant Avenue. Brick, one-story nave and side aisles, 75' × 130', four-stage tower with clock face on three sides, fourth-stage belfry with paired louvered openings, angled stepped buttresses, crenellated parapet with raised center pieces, stone coping, gable roof with parapet, primary windows have lancet form with central stone mullion and tracery, entrance in tower base; central nave plan, 45' high. Built 1853–54, William Craine and Thomas England, architects, under Bishop Alemany; church gutted by fire 1906, rebuilt by T. Welsh after 1907; served as Cathedral until 1891; taken over by Paulist Fathers ca. 1894. Good example of the academic Gothic Revival style as it was used in largely urban parish churches of 19th-century California. 12 photocopies of ext. photos (ca. 1854, 1850s, 1863, 1868, ca. 1880, 1890, ca. 1900, after 1906). See also Historic Views (CA-1718, CA-1814, CA-1817). SHL

St. Patrick's Church (First). See Holy Cross Parish Hall (CA-1908) and Historic View (CA-1233 A).

St. Patrick's Church (Third) (CA-1233 B). 756 Mission Street. Brick, three stories, four-story central tower, Gothic-arched openings, buttresses, pinnacles. Built 1870; burned 1906; rebuilt. 1 ext. photo (1940), 1 photocopy of 1906 ext. photo, 1 photocopy of undated int. photo.

St. Rose's Church (CA-1311). Brannan near 5th

San Francisco Maritime Museum, San Francisco (CA-2225).

Street. Brick with stone trim, two three-stage towers with different tops, louvered belfries, pointed-arch windows with hoodmolds, tripartite entrance, buttresses; cast-iron supports on interior. Built ca. 1880; demolished after fire, 1940. 1 ext. photo (1940), 2 int. photos (1940).

San Francisco and San Jose Railroad Building. See Historic Views (CA-1729, CA-1735, CA-1739, CA-1797).

San Francisco Maritime Museum (CA-2225). *Foot of Polk St.* Concrete and steel frame, 125′ long, three stories, flat roof with metal masts and flagpole, three-tiered form, second story set back on deck-like terrace with metal railings, rounded ends largely glazed with metal sash, central projecting balcony, recessed entrance centered in ground floor faced with marble, rectangular cantilevered entrance canopy flanked by three vertical windows, porthole windows grouped in threes at each end on front elevation, rear has large square glazed openings; elliptical plan, ground floor exhibition area enriched with nautical detail, murals by Hilaire Hiler and Sargent Johnson, houses historical material on West Coast shipping, many fine ship models. 1939, William Mooser Sr. and Jr., architects. A fine example of the "streamlined" Moderne style with a nautical form suited to its purpose. 4 ext., 3 int. photos (1981).

Seawall Warehouse (CA-1263). *1501 Sansome Street.* Brick with heavy timber framing on interior, sixteen-bay front, two stories, flat roof with parapet, elliptical-arched openings. Built mid 19th c.; demolished. 3 ext. photos (1968), 3 int. photos (1968).

Second U.S. Branch Mint. See U.S. Branch Mint (CA-160).

Spreckels Building. See Historic View (CA-1778).

Spreckels Mansion (CA-1906). *2080 Washington Street.* Reinforced concrete with Utah limestone, 80′ (five-bay front) × 50′, two stories on sloped site, flat roof with paneled and balustraded parapet, Corinthian cornice, giant order of fluted composite three-quarter columns paired on front except at corners, round-arched ground-floor openings with French doors, second-floor flat-arched French doors with curved metal balconies; central hall with stair curving upward to the west, at north, facing view, circular "Pompeian" room with fountain, Adamesque fireplaces and detail, indoor pool in basement. Built 1913 for Adolph B. Spreckels, George Applegarth, architect; conversion to apartments caused suppression of monumental entrance stair on south side and some interior alterations. 2 ext. photos (1960); 10 data pages (1966).

Spring Valley Water Company Building. See City of Paris Dry Goods Company Building (CA-2019).

Stevenson, Mrs. Robert Louis—Lloyd Osbourne House (CA-1229). *Hyde and Lombard Streets.* Wood frame, stuccoed, rectangular, three and four stories, sloped site, tiled hip and gable roof. Hyde Street elevation a hodge-podge of windows and doors, some with Classical detail, most are casements in groups of three, glazed porch on third floor with twisted columns, corner pavilions on fourth floor, tiled vent sections, tiled hood on consoles over Lombard Street entrance. Built 1900 for Fanny Osbourne, who married Robert Louis Stevenson in 1881, Willis Polk, architect; remodeled by Lloyd Osbourne 1930s, extensively enlarged March 1940. 2 ext. photos (before and after 1940 addition), 2 photocopies of ca. 1900 ext. photos.

Sutro, Adolph, House (CA-1238). *Sutro Heights, Point Lobos and 48th Ave.* Wood frame, horizontal siding, two stories with wings and a high observation tower with sloping walls and deck near top, gable and hip roofs, pointed- and round-arched windows, variety of decorative detail, open decks and glazed porches; irregular plan, lavishly appointed and furnished; granite promenade with wooden walk below, elaborate landscaped grounds with statuary. Built ca. 1870s, acquired by Adolph Sutro, mayor of San Francisco and Nevada capitalist, from S. Tetlow in early 1880s, continuously remodeled with particular attention lavished on the twenty-acre garden and the statuary purchased in Europe, major social center during Sutro's lifetime, inherited by his daughter, Dr. Emma Sutro Merritt in 1898, who left it to the city in 1938; house condemned and razed in 1939, foundations, stairs, and traces of garden remain. 2 photocopies of ext. photos (ca. 1885, undated), 1 photocopy of 1928 aerial view, 5 photocopies of ext. drawings, 2 photocopies of int. drawings.

Telegraph Hill:

□ **Alta Street Houses (CA-1243).** Row of wood frame houses with horizontal siding, two and three stories on sloped sites, gabled roofs, some with parapets and bracketed cornices. No. 31 has two-level gallery with box columns and turned brackets. Row built 1850s and 1860s. 1 ext. photo (1940).

San Francisco continued

□ **Brick House (CA-1241)**. *1301 Montgomery Street, NW corner Union Street.* Stuccoed brick, two stories, three-bay front, stone sills, very severe. Built ca. 1858–60; altered 20th century. 1 ext. photo (1940).

□ **Filbert Street Houses (CA-1246)**. *S. side of street west of Montgomery.* Row of wood-framed houses, horizontal siding, two stories, gabled roofs. Built 1850s, altered. 1 ext. photo (1940).

□ **Montgomery Street Houses**. See Montgomery Street Houses (CA-1245).

□ **Napier Lane Houses (CA-1244)**. Wood frame with horizontal siding, one, two, and three stories, gabled roofs, some with parapets bearing bracketed cornices, some porches. Built in 1850s and 1860s along a narrow north-south lane on the steep eastern side of the hill, the whole setting a rare, fairly intact survivor of the mid 19th-century environment of Telegraph Hill. 1 ext. photo (1940).

□ **Union Street Houses (CA-1226)**. *Union Street, both sides, east of Montgomery Street.* Rows of wood-framed one- and two-story houses, some gable-roofed with carved bargeboards, some with parapeted fronts and Classical cornices, wooden sidewalks. Some houses remain. 2 ext. photos (1940).

Trinity Church. See Historic View (CA-1739).

Trocadero Inn (CA-119). *19th St. and Sloat Blvd.*

Wood frame with horizontal siding, vertical siding, and variety of decorative shingles, irregular rectangle, one-and-a-half stories, cross-gable roof with gabled dormers, decorative iron cresting, square cross-gabled cupola at roof crossing, front porch with pedimented entrance bay, turned posts, tripartite window in front gable, other windows single and paired with ornamented architraves and label stops below sills, both clear and colored glass; tongue-and-groove wainscoting, picture and cornice moldings, later river boulder fireplace. Built ca. 1890 by George M. Greene as an inn. Hideout of political boss Abe Ruef in 1907, acquired by Mrs. Sigmund Stern in 1931 as a memorial to her husband and given to the city for recreational and cultural purposes, part of Stern Grove, now in a deteriorated condition. 12 sheets (1934–37, including plans, elevations, section, details); 4 ext. photos (1936), 5 int. photos (1936), 2 data pages (1937).

Union Depot and Ferry House. See Historic View (CA-1749).

Union Street Houses. See Telegraph Hill, Union Street Houses (CA-1226).

U.S. Branch Mint (Second U.S. Branch Mint, Old Mint) (CA-160). *5th and Mission Streets.* Stone, cast-iron columns and wrought-iron girders, brick arches, 165' × 220', narrow interior court, two stories on raised, fenestrated basement, metal roof with parapets slightly raking over corner pavilions, square brick chimneys 130' high, main facade has Doric hexastyle portico, pedi-

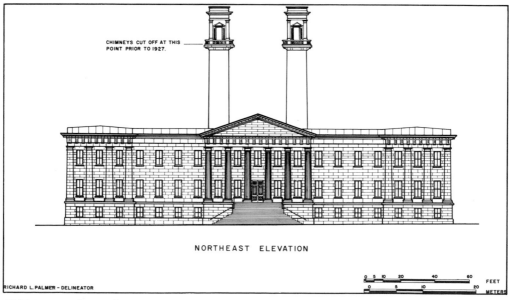

NORTHEAST ELEVATION

CHIMNEYS CUT OFF AT THIS POINT PRIOR TO 1927.

RICHARD L. PALMER – DELINEATOR

Old Mint, northeast elevation, San Francisco (CA-160).

ment with full entablature, corner pavilions have Doric pilasters, frieze and cornice, windows have stone sills; court plan, main front lobby, large main hall with rich decor in stamped metal, coved ceiling, Classical piers, basement storage areas have brick groin vaults, golden mahogany woodwork throughout, folding iron shutters inside openings. Built 1869–74 under auspices of the Treasury Department, A. B. Mullet, architect. The most active 19th-century mint in the country, this building supplanted the First Branch Mint (1854) on Commercial Street and was itself supplanted by the 1937 Mint; a late, but major Pacific coast federal building design of this period in the Classical Revival mode, restored 1972–76 by Mint Director Mary Brooks, Walter Sontheimer, architect. 22 sheets (1962, including site plan, plans, elevations, sections, details); 7 ext. photos (1936, 1958), 4 int. photos (1958), 6 photocopies of ext. photos (ca. 1870, ca. 1871, ca. 1882, 1906), 15 photocopies of int. photos (ca. 1882–85) 1 photocopy of architect's perspective (ca. 1870); 3 data pages (1958). NR, SHL

U.S. Custom House. See Appraiser's Building (CA-1231) and Historic View (CA-1556).

U.S. Marine Hospital. See Historic View (CA-1741).

U.S. Naval Buildings. See Historic View (CA-1793).

U.S. Post Offices. See Historic Views (CA-1225, CA-1751, CA-1791).

U.S. Sub-Treasury and Mint (McCoy Label Co.) (CA-1218). *608 Commercial Street.* Brick on granite foundation, originally four stories, now one, flat roof with parapet above molded cornice, brick and stone pilasters, two pairs of doors with glazing, large eight-light shop windows, transom windows over all openings. Built 1875–77, partially destroyed and dynamited in 1906, rebuilt as one-story building, restored 1984. 1 ext. photo (1940).

Van Ness Frame Houses (CA-1235). *2213–17 Van Ness Avenue.* Wood frame with channeled siding, fish-scale shingles, two stories on raised basements, parapeted roof with false gable ends, bracketed cornices with frieze panels, two-story rectangular bay windows have pent roofs over paired windows on each story, turned-column porticoes at entrances have variety of woodwork and broken-base pediments, #2215 has Classical balustrade on portico; side-hall plan. Row of three speculative houses built in the 1880s with characteristic form and decorative detail; demolished. 1 ext. photo (1940). Originally recorded as Row of Frame Houses.

Vedanta Society. See Hindu Temple (CA-1286).

Warner's Cobweb Palace. See Historic View (CA-1740).

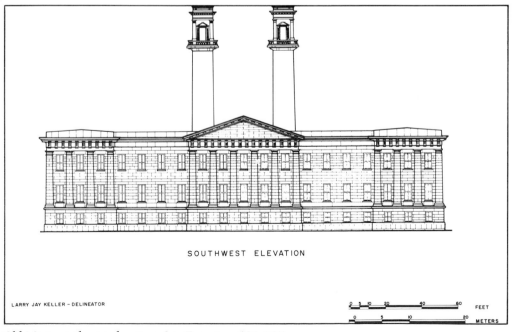

SOUTHWEST ELEVATION

LARRY JAY KELLER – DELINEATOR

Old Mint, southwest elevation, San Francisco (CA-160).

San Francisco continued

Wells, Fargo & Company Buildings. See Historic Views (CA-1768, CA-1769, CA-1770, CA-1771).

Whittier Mansion (California Historical Society's Mansion) (CA-1907). *2090 Jackson Street.* Wood frame and brick sheathed in Arizona sandstone, 55′ × 75′ plus east wing, three stories, tiled hip roof with dormers and cross gables, round corner bays capped with conical tiled roofs, central one-story portico, second floor has five-bay temple front with Ionic pilasters; interior decor in Louis XVI style, Ionic columns support arched room entrances, halls paneled in quarter-sawn white oak with golden oak finish, central focus of main living room is a profusely carved mahogany mantelpiece with grotesques, foliage and other motifs, Turkish smoking room or lounge with elaborate carved and polychromed plaster ceiling, dining room with coved plaster ceiling and central bay. Built 1894–96 for William Franklin Whittier, pioneer merchant who came to San Francisco in 1854 and established a paints, oils, mirrors, and glass firm, Edward R. Swain, architect; combination of Richardsonian Romanesque and Queen Anne styles with Classical Revival elements on exterior and interior, one of the few turn-of-the-century mansions to survive largely intact; acquired by California Historical Society in 1956, ext. restoration in progress, 3 ext. photos (1960), 6 int. photos (1960), 1 photocopy of ext. photo (ca. 1910), 6 photocopies of int. photos (ca. 1900); 19 data pages (1964). NR

Wrights' Exchange Bank. See Historic View (CA-1731).

Yerba Buena Island—Lighthouse Buildings (CA-1554). Three wood-framed buildings including lighthouse tower and keeper's residence at top of hill, ca. 1860. 1 photocopy of 1910 photo.

Yerba Buena Island—Naval Buildings (CA-1793). Brick and stone, two stories, U-shaped, central pavilion with hyphens and projecting wings, parapet roof, low dome over central building, hexastyle Doric portico on central building, pilasters on hyphens, in antis porticoes on wings. U.S. Naval Training Station 1898–1923. 3 photocopies of 1928, 1931, 1936 aerial photos; 1 photocopy of undated photo.

Historic Views of San Francisco

The following entries refer to historic views of San Francisco, arranged in order of HABS survey numbers. These views, from a variety of sources, depict scenes and buildings from 1836 to 1906. Only historic views are noted in this section. Photographs taken by HABS photographers are included in the preceding section, filed by building name. When the documentation consists of both historic views and views taken by HABS photographers, it will be filed by building name. Historic views noted in previous HABS catalogs have been cross-referenced in the alphabetical listing.

(CA-1159). 1 photocopy of 1850 watercolor by Francis Marryatt of SE corner of Montgomery and California Streets showing celebration of Admission Day on October 29, 1850. Originally recorded as Admission Day Celebration.

(CA-1162). 1 photocopy of 1861 photo of Occidental Hotel, SE corner Montgomery and Bush Streets. Four-and-a-half-story building with twenty-one-bay front and low hipped roof built 1861 for J. Donohue, Johnson and Mooser, architects; 1865 addition; with 412 rooms, considered city's finest hotel at the time; demolished. Originally recorded as Occidental Hotel.

(CA-1163). 1 photocopy of 1875 photo of Mercantile Library Building, north side Bush Street west of Sansome. Three-and-a-half-story structure with mansard roof with brick chimneys, arcaded central section with enriched round-arched hoods on colonettes, built ca. 1872; demolished. Brooklyn Hotel also shown. Originally recorded as Mercantile Library Building.

(CA-1164). 1 photocopy of late 19th century photo of intersection of Montgomery and Pine Streets showing Nevada National Bank, four-story structure with round corner entrance bay, built 1875, later part of Wells Fargo Nevada Bank. Originally recorded as Nevada National Bank.

(CA-1165). 1 photocopy of 1851 drawing of Montgomery Street from Sacramento Wharf during fire of June 27, 1851. Originally recorded as View of Montgomery Street from Sacramento Wharf.

(CA-1166). 1 photocopy of photo (before 1906) of Sacramento Street showing Broderick Engine #1 and Italianate buildings lining street. Originally recorded as "Broderick Engine #1."

(CA-1167). 1 photocopy of 1872 photo of SW corner California and Sansome Streets, showing Fireman's Fund Insurance Building at corner, other Renaissance Revival buildings, all de-

Historic View (CA-1167), California and Sansome Streets, San Francisco.

stroyed by 1906 fire. Originally recorded as California and Sansome Streets (1872).

(CA-1175). 1 photocopy of ca. 1860 ext. photo of Fremont House in Fort Mason area. One-story, hip-roofed, frame cottage built 1854 for George Eggleston, acquired 1857 by John C. Frémont, demolished 1863. Originally recorded as Fremont House.

(CA-1219). 2 photocopies of ca. 1880 ext. photos, 1 photocopy of a general view just after 1906 fire, of St. Francis Church, a three-story brick church with two four-story square towers, Gothic-arched openings; built 1859–60, Thomas England, architect; gutted by 1906 fire; rebuilt. Originally recorded as St. Francis Church.

(CA-1220). 2 photocopies of 1859 plat of San Francisco. Originally recorded as 1859 plat (map) of San Francisco City.

(CA-1221). 2 photocopies of 1853 plat of San Francisco. Originally recorded as 1853 plat (map) of San Francisco City.

(CA-1222). 1 photocopy of 1852 plat of San Francisco. Originally recorded as 1852 plat (map) of San Francisco City.

(CA-1225). 1 photocopy of ca. 1853 lithograph of Second U.S. Post Office, SW corner Clay and Pike Streets. One-and-a-half-story gable-roofed structure with porches, built ca. 1849, moved twice, demolished. Originally recorded as Second Post Office (ca. 1849).

(CA-1227). 1 photocopy of 1850 watercolor of Sansome Street by Francis Marryatt, showing several buildings, including one two-story structure with two-level gallery, hipped roof. Origially recorded as Sansome Street (1850).

(CA-1233 A). 1 photocopy of ext. photo (before 1873) of St. Patrick's Church, one-story, gable-front frame structure built ca. 1851, moved 1873 and 1891, see Holy Cross Parish Hall (CA-1908); and Orphan Asylum, two-story brick structure with center pavilion, quoining, flat roof. Originally recorded as St. Patrick's Church (first).

(CA-1247). 3 photocopies of 1860s, 1880s, 1890 photos of Telegraph Hill. Originally recorded as Telegraph Hill—General View.

(CA-1248). 1 photocopy of ca. 1885 photo of Greenwich Street from Powell Street east to top of Telegraph Hill, showing frame buildings lining street, cable cars, and four-story wooden castle built as a resort by Gustav Walter ca. 1885. Originally recorded as Telegraph Hill (w. side).

(CA-1293). 3 photocopies of 1916, 1931, undated, drawings of Mexican Custom House, Portsmouth Square. Adobe and wood one-story structure with tiled gable roof extending over sides and ends to form galleries, built 1844–45, center of San Francisco's civic life; destroyed by fire, 1851. Originally recorded as Mexican Custom House.

(CA-1555). 3 photocopies of ca. 1849, ca. 1851, early 1850s drawings; 2 photocopies of photos (ca. 1860, n.d.) of Portsmouth Plaza, the square where Commodore J. B. Montgomery of USS Portsmouth raised American flag, July 9, 1846. Originally recorded as Portsmouth Plaza.

(CA-1556). 1 photocopy of undated photo of U.S. Custom House, SW corner Battery and Washington Streets, stuccoed brick structure with granite base, eleven-bay front with projecting central section and two-story pedimented portico, built 1855, Gridley J. Bryant, architect; demolished. Originally recorded as Old U.S. Custom House.

(CA-1557). 1 photocopy of 1849–50 photo of Yerba Buena Cove showing harbor jammed with sailing ships abandoned by crews who went to the Gold Rush in 1849–50. Originally recorded as Abandoned Ships.

(CA-1718). 1 photocopy of 1856 photo of Second Street at Folsom, showing wood-frame houses and commercial buildings on rolling terrain, St. Mary's Church visible in distant center. Originally recorded as General View from Second and Folsom Streets to North.

(CA-1719). 1 photocopy of drawing taken from Francis Marryatt's sketch "High and Dry" from *Mountains and Molehills* (1855) of Clay and Sansome Streets showing wooden whaling ship, the

San Francisco continued

Niantic, beached and converted to hotel in spring of 1849. Originally recorded as Niantic Hotel.

(CA-1720). 1 photocopy of ca. 1855 lithograph of Railroad House, 48 Commercial Street, four-story, four-bay front, parapeted roof with modillioned pediment, cupola, built 1854 as a hotel for Haley & Thompson, Thomas Boyd, architect; demolished. Originally recorded as Railroad House.

(CA-1721). 1 photocopy of late 19th century photo of Roos Brothers Store, SW corner Post and Kearny Streets, three-story, seven-bay brick structure, built after 1865 for Adolphe and Achilles Roos, became leading San Francisco department store; destroyed by fire, 1906. Originally recorded as Roos Brothers Old Store.

(CA-1722). 1 photocopy of ca. 1874 photo from roof of Palace Hotel looking east on Market Street. Originally recorded as San Francisco View (ca. 1874).

(CA-1723). 1 photocopy of 1856 photo, Battery Street north from California Street, showing two- and three-story brick and stucco buildings, Merchants' Exchange in distance, street paved with planking. Originally recorded as General View.

(CA-1724). 1 photocopy of ca. 1868 photo of Pine Street between Montgomery and Sansome Streets showing 1860s buildings including Maguire's Music Hall, since demolished. Originally recorded as Maguire's Music Hall.

(CA-1725). 1 photocopy of ca. 1851 lithograph, apparently a letterhead published by Marvin and Hitchcock, Pioneer Bookstore, showing San Francisco looking east from Portsmouth Square. Originally recorded as General View (1851).

(CA-1726). 1 photocopy of 1850 lithograph from the *Illustrated London News* showing Battery Street Bluff and the Fremont Hotel, a five-bay, two-and-a-half-story structure with gable roof. Originally recorded as Fremont Hotel.

(CA-1727). 1 photocopy of 1879 photo of Lick House, W. side Montgomery Street between Post and Sutter Streets, three-story, 23-bay front, brick, stucco, and stone Italianate building with cast-iron storefront; built 1862, Kenitzer and D. Farquaharson, architects, for James Lick. Originally recorded as James Lick House.

(CA-1729). 1 photocopy of 1865 photo of San Francisco and San Jose Railroad Building, north side Post Street at Montgomery and Market, a three-story building with Florentine Palazzo styl-ing and Gothic Revival details. Built ca. 1864–65; remodeled as Hibernia Savings and Loan Society Building, 1870s; destroyed by fire, 1906. Originally recorded as San Francisco and San Jose Railroad Building.

(CA-1730). 1 photocopy of ca. 1851 drawing of Kearny Street looking towards Telegraph Hill, showing aftermath of May 4, 1851, fire. Originally recorded as San Francisco after fire of May 4, 1851.

(CA-1731). 1 photocopy of 1856 photo of Montgomery Street at corner of Jackson Street showing frame buildings on Telegraph Hill and Wright's or Miner's Exchange Bank, a four-story, galleried structure with large cupola. Built 1854, Peter Portois, architect; cupola removed by 1868; demolished. Originally recorded as Wright's or Miner's Exchange Bank (1856).

(CA-1732). 1 photocopy of 1886 lithograph after 1845 drawing by Captain William Swasey, showing San Francisco with street names indicated, Mexican Custom House flying U.S. flag, U.S. Naval ships in harbor. Originally recorded as Early San Francisco (1846) (sic).

(CA-1733). 1 photocopy of 1865 photo of North Beach showing buildings of Fort Mason under construction and Telegraph Hill in distance. Originally recorded as San Francisco (1865).

(CA-1734). 1 photocopy of 1868 drawing of San Francisco, and Telegraph Hill in lower right and Market Street receding. Originally recorded as San Francisco—Panorama (1868).

(CA-1735). 2 photocopies of 1880, 1884 photos of NE corner of Post and Montgomery at Market Streets showing Hibernia Savings and Loan Society Building, built as San Francisco and San Jose Railroad Building ca. 1864–65; remodeled 1870s; destroyed by fire 1906. Originally recorded as Hibernia Savings and Loan Society Buildings.

(CA-1736). 1 photocopy of 1907 photo showing Cliff House at Point Lobos and Western Beach on fire; built for Adolph Sutro 1896, Cotley and Lemme, architects; burned September 1907. Originally recorded as Cliff House.

(CA-1737). 2 photocopies of ca. 1865 and late 19th century photos showing Russian Hill, one of which shows Green Street west from Jones, including Feusier Octagon House, McGaw Octagon House, and John Brickell House. Originally recorded as Russian Hill Houses (ca. 1865).

(CA-1739). 1 photocopy of 1868 photo of NW corner of Post and Montgomery Streets showing

Masonic Temple Center (1860), San Francisco and San Jose Railroad Building (ca. 1864–65), and Trinity Church. Originally recorded as Masonic Temple Center.

(CA-1740) 2 photocopies of late 19th century interior photos of Warner's Cobweb Palace, at Lumber Street and Francisco, bar renowned for its 6' to 8' long festoons of cobwebs. Originally recorded as Warner's Cobweb Palace.

(CA-1741). 1 photocopy of undated photo of U.S. Marine Hospital (Sailors' Home) at NE corner Spear and Harrison Streets. The four-story brick and stone structure with wide eaves was built before 1868; demolished 1920s. Originally recorded as U.S. Marine Hospital.

(CA-1743). 1 photocopy of 1856 lithograph showing Cunningham's Wharf at foot of Commercial Street. Originally recorded as Cunningham's Warf (sic).

(CA-1744). 1 photocopy of 1865 photo of Clay Street Bank at 35 Clay Street, a three-story cast-iron front structure built ca. 1860, and adjacent buildings in Italianate style. Originally recorded as Clay Street Bank.

(CA-1745). 1 photocopy of 1868 photo of Metropolitan Theater on west side Montgomery Street south of Jackson Street, a three-story, stuccoed-brick structure built 1861 for Tom Maguire; demolished 1873. Originally recorded as Metropolitan Theater.

(CA-1746). 2 photocopies of 1856 and undated drawings; 1 photocopy of 1856 photo. Sacramento Block ("Fort Gunnybags"), Sacramento Street near Battery, two-story, fifteen-bay structure built early 1850s, used as headquarters of Vigilance Committee in 1856. Originally recorded as Sacramento Block.

(CA-1747). 1 photocopy of 1853 watercolor of

Historic View (CA-1735-2), Hibernia Savings and Loan Society Building, San Francisco.

San Francisco continued

Masonic Hall on Montgomery between California and Sacramento Streets, a four-story, stuccoed brick and stone structure built 1853; demolished. Originally recorded as "Old" Masonic Hall.

(CA-1749). 1 photocopy of 1887 photo of Union Depot and Ferry House, foot of Market Street. Two-story shed-like structure built 1877, served as terminus for steam, cable, and horse car lines until replaced by new Ferry Building in 1898. Originally recorded as Union Depot and Ferry House.

(CA-1751). 1 photocopy of 1856 photo of U.S. Post Office at NE corner of Kearny and Clay Streets. Two-story brick structure built before 1854. Originally recorded as "Old" Post Office.

(CA-1753). 1 photocopy of 1859 photo of Daily Morning Call Building, SE corner Clay and Montgomery Streets. This two-and-a-half-story wood-frame building with gable roof with returns, five-bay front, was built early 1850s, gutted by fire 1859 as this photo shows. Originally recorded as San Francisco Morning Call (1859).

(CA-1754). 1 photocopy of 1860 photo of Russ Building, SW corner Montgomery and Pine Streets. This one-and-a-half-story, wood-frame structure with gable roof was built 1850s for J. C. Christian Russ, New York jeweler who ran jewelry shop and assay office and invested in downtown real estate; replaced 1862 with the 300-room Russ House, which was replaced 1927 with Russ Building. Originally recorded as First Russ Building.

(CA-1756). 1 photocopy of 1851 photo of San Francisco from near Portsmouth Square showing the estimated 800 ships abandoned in harbor when their crews joined the Gold Rush. Originally recorded as Early San Francisco (1851).

(CA-1758). 1 photocopy of 1849 lithograph showing San Francisco, accentuating early shanty-town appearance. Originally recorded as Early San Francisco (1849).

(CA-1759). 1 photocopy of 1849 drawing of San Francisco, showing isolated buildings, topography inaccurate. Originally recorded as Early San Francisco (1849).

(CA-1760). 1 photocopy of 1848 drawing by J. W. Orr showing one-story buildings and Portsmouth Square. Originally recorded as Early San Francisco (1848).

(CA-1761). 1 photocopy of 1853 photo from a panorama by Shew of San Francisco looking northwest from Rincon Hill. Originally recorded as Early San Francisco (1853).

(CA-1762). 1 photocopy of ca. 1856 drawing of San Francisco from Rincon Hill; 1 photocopy of ca. 1856 photo looking northeast from First and Harrison Streets. Originally recorded as General View—Early San Francisco (1856).

(CA-1764). 6 photocopies of 1906 panoramic photo of Pine Street near corner of Jones showing city in ruins. Originally recorded as General View Panorama After Fire 1906.

(CA-1767). 1 photocopy of ca. 1875 drawing of San Francisco looking west from 16th Street and Potrero Avenue. Originally recorded as San Francisco (ca. 1875).

(CA-1768). 1 photocopy of ca. 1852 photo of Wells, Fargo & Co. Building at 114 Montgomery between Sacramento and California Streets. Two-story brick building opened in July 1852, housed bankers and express agents until 1854. Originally recorded as Wells, Fargo & Co. Building.

(CA-1769). 1 photocopy of an 1856 engraving from an 1856 daguerreotype; 3 photocopies of 1856, 1865, and ca. 1880 photos; all of Express Building, NE corner California and Montgomery Streets, location of Wells, Fargo & Co. 1854–56; destroyed by fire, 1906. Originally recorded as Express Building.

(CA-1770). 2 photocopies of ca. 1860–70 and 1880s photos of Parrott's Granite Block, NW corner of California and Montgomery Streets, home of Wells, Fargo & Co. from 1856–76; destroyed by fire, 1906. Originally recorded as Parrott's Granite Block.

(CA-1771). 1 photocopy of ca. 1880 photo of Wells Fargo Bank at NE corner of California and Sansome Streets. Three-story cast-iron-fronted structure built 1876; destroyed by fire, 1906. Originally recorded as Wells Fargo Bank.

(CA-1776). 1 photocopy of April 1850 drawing showing long wharf at foot of Commercial Street and harbor crowded with ships abandoned by their crews for the Gold Rush. Originally recorded as Early San Francisco (1850).

(CA-1778). 1 photocopy of 1906 photo of Market Street showing smoke around DeYoung Building, Call (Spreckels) Building a shell, Parrott Building, and Phelan Building apparently being dynamited. Originally recorded as San Francisco (1906 Fire).

(CA-1780). 1 photocopy of ca. 1900 photo showing Ferry Building tower (finished 1903) and

Call Building on Market Street. Originally recorded as San Francisco (ca. 1900).

(CA-1781). 1 photocopy of ca. 1880 photo from Telegraph Hill toward Golden Gate with Fort Mason in upper center and Lombard Street on right. Originally recorded as San Francisco (ca. 1880).

(CA-1782). 1 photocopy of 1849 drawing of San Francisco looking toward Telegraph Hill showing busy, small-scale town. Originally recorded as Early San Francisco (1849).

(CA-1790). 1 photocopy of 1866 illustration of Powell Street from Market.

(CA-1791). 1 photocopy of 1848 painting of first Post Office, Stockton and Washington Streets. One room, wood frame with board-and-batten siding, housed post office 1848–49. Originally recorded as First Post Office.

(CA-1796). 1 photocopy of ca. 1864 photo of south side of Market Street looking west. Originally recorded as Market Street.

(CA-1797). 3 photocopies of 1864, 1865, and 1906 photos of Montgomery Street looking north from Post, showing Masonic Temple and San Francisco and San Jose Railroad Building. Originally recorded as Montgomery Street.

(CA-1798). 2 photocopies of April 18, 1906, photos looking south to Market Street during fire. Originally recorded as San Francisco After Fire of 1906.

(CA-1814). 1 photocopy of ca. 1856 photo of Sacramento Street looking east from Stockton Street, also showing St. Mary's Church on California Street. Originally recorded as Early San Francisco (ca. 1856).

(CA-1815). 1 photocopy of ca. 1870 photo of Stockton Street looking north towards Angel Island. Originally recorded as Stockton Street Houses.

(CA-1817). 1 photocopy of 1906 photo of California Street looking to Mason Street showing ruins of Old St. Mary's Grace Church tower, and incomplete Fairmont Hotel. Originally recorded as San Francisco (1906 Fire).

(CA-1818). 1 photocopy of 1906 photo of Powell Street showing ruined area, including gutted shell and unfinished wing of St. Francis Hotel. Originally recorded as San Francisco (1906 Fire).

(CA-1819). 1 photocopy of 1906 photo looking north toward shell of Parrott Building and Floor

Building at Powell and Market Streets. Originally recorded as San Francisco (After 1906 Fire).

(CA-1820). 1 photocopy of 1906 photo of California Street looking east to Sansome Street showing firefighting equipment in middle of fire. Originally recorded as San Francisco (1906 Fire).

(CA-1823). 1 photocopy of ca. 1859 lithograph of Market Street from Montgomery Street, showing Mechanics' Institute (1857). Originally recorded as Early San Francisco (ca. 1859).

(CA-1866). 1 photocopy of 1837 watercolor showing San Francisco, Jacob Leese House in center. Originally recorded as Early San Francisco (1837).

(CA-1868). 1 photocopy of 1866 photo of Lincoln School, east side 5th Street south of Jessie Street. Stuccoed brick and stone, three stories plus mansard roof, built 1865, William Craine, architect; destroyed by fire, 1906. Originally recorded as Lincoln School.

(CA-1869). 1 photocopy of 1836 drawing of Jacob Leese House on Grant Avenue south of Clay. One of first two houses in Yerba Buena town, one-story gable-roofed wood-frame structure. Originally recorded as Jacob Leese House.

San Gabriel □ Los Angeles County

Casa Vieja de López (CA-316). 330 N. Santa Anita Ave. Plastered adobe and wood frame, approx. 67' (seven-bay front) × 26', one story, wood-frame rooms across rear; no hall. Built between 1796 and 1804, interior and exterior substantially altered in 1925. 4 sheets (1934, including plan, elevations, section, details); 1 ext. photo (1937); 1 data page (1937).

Mission San Gabriel Arcángel (CA-37-8). W. Mission Dr. and Junipero Serra St. Church is stone and fired brick, 172' × 45', one story, shingled hip roof, south side has heavy stepped buttresses capped with pyramidal forms, campanario at one end has six arched openings for bells, adjoining campanario is padres' residence, plastered adobe, 70' (five-bay front) × 26', one story, shingled gable roof, porch across front. Founded in 1771 as fourth in chain of twenty-one missions, moved to this site in 1775 by Father Lasuén, present church with stone vaulted roof begun 1791, roof replaced with flat roof in 1805, severe earthquake damage in 1812, campanario and shops destroyed, repaired by 1828, original architect Padre Antonio Cruzado, succeeded by

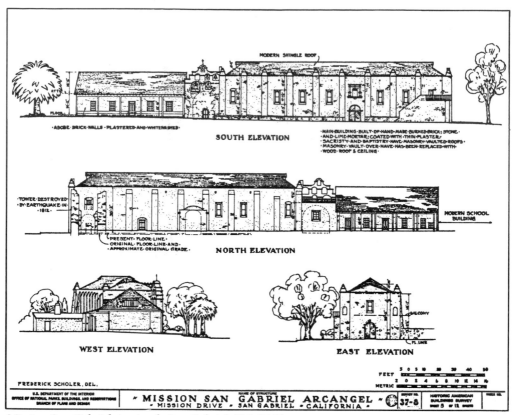

Mission San Gabriel Arcángel, San Gabriel (CA-37-8).

José María de Zalvidea. 12 sheets (1934, including plans, elevations, sections, details); 12 ext. photos (1934, 1937); 3 data pages (1936, 1937). SHL

□ *Industrial Shops Ruins (CA-37-8A).* 7 sheets (1937, including plot plan; elevations, section of soap factory ruins; plan, sections of tannery ruins; plan, elevation, details of reredos; details of old door confessional booth); 9 ext. photos of ruins (1934, 1937).

Padillo Adobe (CA-328). Mission Dr. Plastered adobe and wood frame, stone foundations, approx. 44' (four-bay front) × 36', one-and-a-half stories, gable roof with shakes, lean-to additions across front and rear, one chimney, first floor adobe brick, upper floor sheathed in board-and-batten siding, variety of wood-framed openings with triangular lintels, upper-floor balcony with wood railing. Built ca. 1840 as three-room house with flat tarred roof; enlarged ca. 1854; demolished. 3 sheets (1935, including plans, elevations, section, details); 2 ext. photos (1936); 1 data page (1937).

Purcell House (Las Tunas Ranch) (CA-35). 308

Mission Blvd. Adobe and wood, irregular plan, 85' × 89', two stories with one-story wings, hip roof extended over porches on several sides. Built ca. 1791 as one-story adobe structure with flat brea (tar) roof, possibly as residence for the padres; known also as Las Tunas Ranch because of "tuna" or cactus hedge; second floor, shingled roof, porches and wings added after 1858. 3 sheets (1934, including plans, elevations, details); 3 ext. photos (1934); 1 data page (1937).

San Gregorio □ San Mateo County

San Gregorio House (CA-1993). San Gregorio Rd. Wood frame with clapboards, 89' (ten-bay front) × 20', two stories, gable roof, porch across front with turned-wood balustrade above; extensive set of outbuildings, including water and tower and barn. Built ca. 1865 for George Washington Tully Carter as building with three-bay front; in 1875 northern seven bays added for John W. Evans; hotel closed 1930. 2 sheets (1974, including site plan, elevations); 7 ext. photos (1975), 2 int. photos (1975), 5 photos of outbuildings (1975); 5 data pages (1974). NR

San Jose □ Santa Clara County

Allen, Horace, Gasoline Station (CA-2105). 505 E. San Carlos St. Brick, 21' (three-bay front) × 18', T-shaped one story, gable roof with vertical boards in two gables, stuccoing in other two, porte cochere arrangement over gas pumps, exterior chimney on one gable end. Built 1931 or 1932, possibly designed by Horace Allen. 3 sheets (1980, including site plan, plans, elevations); 6 ext. photos (1980); 9 data pages (1980).

Blanchard House (CA-1787). Wood frame with clapboards, five-bay front, two-and-a-half stories, gable roof with central cross gable, boxed cornice with molding and returns, one-story porch across front. Built ca. 1865; not located. 1 photocopy of undated photo.

Col, Peter E., House (CA-2008). 1163 Martin Ave. Stuccoed wood frame, 52' × 50', one-and-a-half-story center section flanked by one-story sections, flat roofs with deep eaves, large concrete terrace across front, art glass windows with geometric detailing. Built 1913, Wolfe and Wolfe, architects. 5 sheets (1978, including site plan, plan, elevations, sections); 5 ext. photos (1980), 2 int. photos (1980); 7 data pages (1978, 1979).

College Park Association of Friends' Meeting House (Friends' Meeting House) (CA-2061). 1041 Morse St. Wood frame with channeled siding, 19' (three-bay front) × 52', T-shaped, one story, gable roof, enclosed entrance porch with gable roof. Built 1885, oldest extant Quaker meeting house in California. 2 sheets (1979, including plan, elevations); 3 ext. photos (1980); 9 data pages (1979).

Cottage (CA-2109). 1147 Chapman St. Wood frame with channeled siding, three-bay front, one-and-a-half stories, hip roof with gable-roofed projections, one-story porch on front, jigsawn ornamentation. Built last quarter of 19th c. 4 ext. photos (1980).

Gates, Howard B., House (CA-2077). 62 S. 13th St. Stuccoed wood frame, 44' (two-bay front) × 33', three stories, gable roof with shed dormer, large balconied window on front; open plan on interior, dramatic winding staircase and oversized fireplace. Built 1904, Bernard Maybeck, architect. 10 sheets (1980, including site plan, plans, elevations, sections, details); 6 ext. photos (1980), 6 int. photos (1980), 1 photocopy of ca. 1910 photo; 18 data pages (1980).

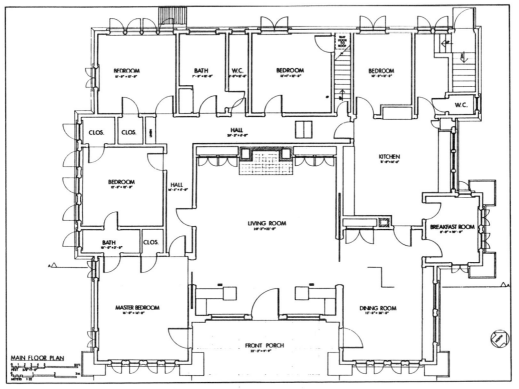

Peter E. Col House, main floor plan, San Jose (CA-2008).

San Jose continued

Greenawalt, David, Farm (CA-2009). *14611 Almaden Expwy.* House: Wood frame with horizontal siding, two stories, bracketed and denticulated cornice. Built 1877. 1 sheet (1978, site plan); 4 ext. photos (1980); 6 data pages (1978, 1979).

□ *Tank House.* Heavy timber framing with horizontal siding, 18'-2" square, two stories, hip roof. Built ca. 1877. 3 sheets (1978, including plans, elevation, section, isometric cut-away); 1 ext. photo (1980).

Hanchett Residence Park (CA-2010). *1225, 1233, 1241, 1249, 1257 Martin Ave.* Five California bungalows, all with rectangular outlines, one or one-and-a-half stories, covered with stucco, cobblestone and wooden shiplap siding, wide projecting gable roofs supported by exposed rafter and purlin ends. Real estate development designed in 1907 by John McLaren, landscape architect; 1225 and 1249 built in 1911 by Wolfe and McKenzie, architects; deed restrictions have preserved layout and character of park. 4 sheets (1978, including map, site plan, elevations, sec-

tion); 6 ext. photos (1980); 14 data pages (1979).

Horn, Emily, House (CA-2108). *2341 N. 1st St.* Wood frame with horizontal board siding, one-and-a-half stories, 33' (three-bay front) × 72', hipped roof with hipped dormer, porch across front rounded at both ends, rounded bay on one corner of house. Built 1906. 6 ext. photos (1980); 6 data pages (1980).

Kennedy House (CA-1789). Wood frame with horizontal siding, six-bay front, two-and-a-half stories, gable roof with cross gable and square cupola with pinnacle and balustrade, one-story wrap-around veranda with balustrade on both levels, polygonal outbuilding with pointed roof extended from one side of house. Built ca. 1865; called the Stockton Ranch House of James F. Kennedy, agent of Commodore Stockton; not located. 1 photocopy of undated photo.

Kirk-Farrington House (CA-2090). *1615 Dry Creek Rd.* Wood frame with horizontal siding, approx. 46' × 75', two stories, irregular plan, hipped roof with paired brackets and dentils, two-story polygonal bay on front, front porch re-

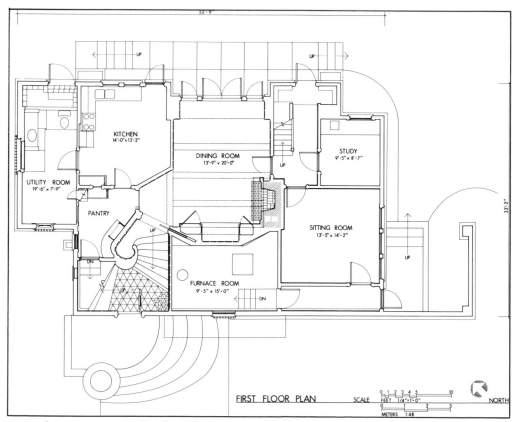

Howard B. Gates House, first floor plan, San Jose (CA-2077).

cessed under upper story, quoining. Built ca. 1878 for Theophilus Kirk, early settler. 7 sheets (n.d., including plans, elevations, section).

Lick Observatory (CA-2110). West peak of Mt. Hamilton. Stuccoed brick, one story, 295' long, domed tower 40' in diameter, another smaller domed tower. Built 1888, Wright and Sanders, architects, directed by Richard S. Floys and Thomas E. Fraser of observatory. 5 ext. photos (1980); 1 data page (1981).

Masonic Temple (CA-2045). 262–272 S. 1st St. Stuccoed brick, three stories, six-bay front, flat roof with balustrade on facade, cornice below balustrade with frieze containing name and date of structure, fluted Ionic pilasters flank end bays on second and third stories, windows surrounded by decorative molding, second story pedimented window heads on each end bay, frieze with fret motif, recessed main entrance crowned by Masonic emblem, framed by rusticated stone quoins. Built 1908; first floor commercial units modernized, n.d.; demolished 1979. Structure served as a local meeting place for several Masonic lodges until early 1970s. 4 ext. photos (1978).

O'Brien Court (CA-2106). 1076–78, 1084, 1086, 1088, 1090, 1092 O'Brien Court. Six bungalows, all wood frame with stucco, all one story, flat roofs with parapets or tiled gable roofs, round-arched openings, *espadaña*-like projections. Built 1920s as middle-class residential development. 3 sheets (1980, including site plan, plan, elevations); 8 ext. photos (1980); 14 data pages (1980).

Pina House (CA-1846). 3260 The Alameda. Alameda Women's Club. Adobe, four-bay front, one story, tiled gable roof extended over front porch. Built ca. 1800 as one of a row of adobes built to house the Indians of the Mission Santa Clara; acquired, refurbished and modernized by the Santa Clara Women's Club as headquarters in 1914. 1 ext. photo (1940). SHL

Winchester House (Winchester Mystery House) (CA-2107). 525 S. Winchester Blvd. Museum. Wood frame with variety of coverings, large rambling house with numerous finial-crowned gables, two chateauesque towers, porches, stained-glass windows, pargeting, cut shingle-work, many skylighted rectangular cupolas; 160 rooms, maple-paneled ballroom with pipe organ,

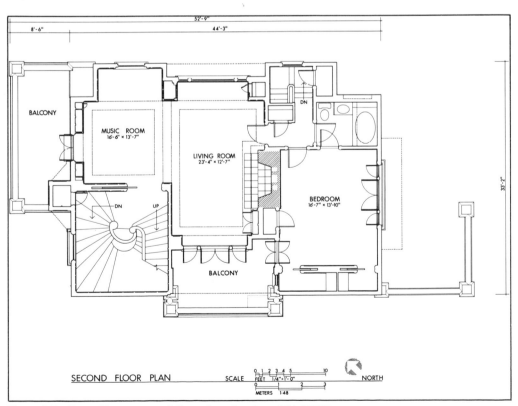

Howard B. Gates House, second floor plan, San Jose (CA-2077).

San Jose continued

some of the 40 stairways and 2,000 doors lead nowhere. Built between 1884 and 1922 because owner Sarah L. Winchester, heiress of Winchester Rifle fortune, believed she would live as long as construction continued. 7 ext. photos (1980), 3 int. photos (1980); 1 data page (1981). NR, SHL

San Juan Bautista □ San Benito County

Castro, José, Adobe (CA-1120). SW corner of Plaza. Plastered adobe, six-bay front, two stories, tiled gable roof extends to cover balcony across front, two-story wood veranda across rear. Built 1840–41 for José Castro, Commandant General of California, as a residence and military quarters; sold 1854 to Patrick Breen; restored as a museum 1960s. An outstanding example of the two-story adobe house in the so-called Monterey style. 5 ext. photos (1934). NR, SHL

House of the Mexican Period (Juan de Anza House) (CA-15). 101 3rd St. Plastered adobe front

section, wood frame with horizontal siding rear section, 50' (four-bay front) × 32', one story, gable roof, canopy over sidewalk. Built 1820–40. 3 sheets (1934, including plan, elevations, sections, perspective, details); 2 ext. photos (1934).

Mission San Juan Bautista (CA-14). NW side of Plaza. Church: Plastered adobe, brick and wood, three-aisled basilica, 72' × 199', one story with loft, tiled gable roof, deep recessed windows and doors of various kinds, simple belt course molding across front, square opening above, piers with simple molded caps frame round-arched entrances; central nave with side chapels and cruciform plan with large chapels in transept arms, transverse arch at sanctuary and sanctuary ceiling polychromed, nave arcade with round arches and square piers with simple molding at the springing of the arches, string course near top of nave wall, flat wood ceiling, elaborate painted wood reredos made by Thomas Doak, an early settler. Monastery at right angle to church, adobe, one story, eighteen-bay arcade across front, round arches of brick, tiled gable roof; several interior rooms furnished as a museum, re-

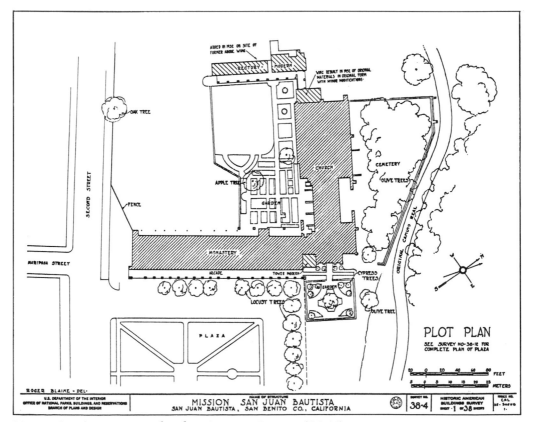

Mission San Juan Bautista, plot plan, San Juan Bautista (CA-14).

stored. Courtyard garden with buildings on three sides. Mission founded 1797 as fifteenth in chain of 21 missions; church cornerstone laid 1803, completed 1812; damaged by earthquake 1906; wooden tower with steeple added 1865, steeple removed 1915, tower plastered and remodeled 1929, tower removed 1949; church restored 1949–50; now a parish church. 38 sheets (1934, including plans, elevations, perspective, sections, details); 17 ext. photos (1934), 4 int. photos (1934); 1 data page (1936). NHL, SHL

Plaza Hotel (Mexican Barracks) (CA-1954). NW corner of Plaza. Adobe and wood frame, 92′ (seven-bay front) × 94′, U-shaped, two stories, hip roof, casement windows, second-floor balcony. Built 1815 as one-story adobe barracks for Spanish soldiers and two-story guard house; combined into one structure and wood-frame second story added by Angelo Zanetta, 1855; operated as a hotel on stage line between San Francisco and Los Angeles; restored 1960s. 11 sheets (1966, including plans, elevations, sections, details); 1 photocopy of 1925 photo. SHL

Zanetta House (CA-1501). E. side of Plaza. Adobe and wood with horizontal wood siding, four-bay front by two bays deep, two-story main section, roof with high parapet and bracketed cornice, one-story porch across front with balcony above, turned balustrade. Built 1815 as two-story adobe house for unmarried Indian women; General Castro also used it as military quarters; acquired by Zanetta in 1868 and remodeled as residence on first floor and large room, Plaza Hall, on second floor. 1 ext. photo (1930s).

San Juan Capistrano □ Orange County

Mission San Juan Capistrano (CA-331). Olive St. and Hwy. 101. Mission founded 1776 as seventh in chain of 21 missions. 1 sheet (1936, including plot plan, perspective); 2 ext. photos (1936); 2 data pages (1937). SHL

□ *Stone Church (CA-331 A).* Sandstone, 84′ × 136′, ruinous condition, only sacristy, sanctuary, transept, and part of nave walls remain, dome over sanctuary, evidence of fine moldings, arches, pilasters. Built 1796–1806; partially destroyed by earthquake, 1812, not used since. 9 sheets (1936, including plan, elevations, sections, details); 24 photos (1936).

□ *Serra's Church (CA-331 B).* Adobe, 27′ × 152′, one story with two-story portion, tiled gable roof, heavy buttresses on one side, round-arched cloister along other side; elaborate gilt reredos

installed 1922–24. Built ca. 1777. 9 sheets (1936, including plans, elevations, sections, details); 5 ext. photos (1936), 4 int. photos (1936).

□ *Fountain (CA-331 C).* Built 1920s. 1 photo (1936).

□ *Padres' House and Campanario (CA-331 D).* Adobe and brick, 24′ front has *espadaña*-like parapet, wall extends to one side with four round-arched openings for bells, tiled gable roof. 8 sheets (1936, including plan, elevations, sections, details); 8 ext. photos (1936), 1 int. photo (1936).

□ *Living Quarters (CA-331 E).* Adobe and brick, one story with two-story section, segmental-arched eleven-bay cloister along both sides, tiled gable roof. 7 sheets (1936, including plans, elevations, details); 5 ext. photos (1936).

□ *Guest House (Barracks) (CA-331 F).* Adobe and brick, 24′ × 108′, one story, gable roof extends to cover cloister along one side. 4 sheets (1936, including plan, elevations, details); 4 ext. photos (1936).

□ *Industrial Shops (CA-331 G).* Adobe ruins. 2 sheets (1936, including plan, elevation, section); 7 photos (1936).

San Leandro □ Alameda County

Estudillo House (CA-1662). 1291 Carpenter St. Wood frame with channeled siding, rectangular, one story over raised basement, veranda surrounds house. Built 1868 by José Joaquín Estudillo, grantee of the Rancho San Leandro and founder of the town. Demolished. 2 ext. photos (1940).

Peralta, Ignacio, House (CA-1896). 561 Lafayette Ave. Brick, plastered, three bays by three bays, one story on raised foundation, hip roof, bracketed cornice, rear extension; central-hall plan. Built 1860 by Ignacio Peralta on southern portion of Rancho San Antonio, remodeled into private club. 4 ext. photos (c. 1860, 1960), 6 int. photos (1960); 8 data pages (1966). SHL

San Luis Obispo □ San Luis Obispo County

Mission San Luís Obispo de Tolosa (CA-210). 782 Monterey St. Founded 1772 as fifth in chain of 21 missions; church completed 1793 with first roof tiles used at a mission; front portion added 1820; front torn down and wooden siding added to fa-

San Luis Obispo continued

cade ca. 1880; restored 1934. 1 sheet (1936, plot plan); 2 data pages (1937). SHL

□ *Church (CA-210)*. Adobe, 34' (three-bay front) × 195', one story with loft, tiled gable roof, round-arched openings to narthex, round-arched openings to belfry above, chapel at right angle to nave. 10 sheets (1936, including plans, elevations, sections, details); 8 ext. photos (1936); 2 int. photos (1936).

□ *Monastery (CA-210 A)*. Adobe, wood frame with horizontal siding and plaster stone, 229' (nineteen-bay front) × 27', one story, hipped roof, corredor faces on courtyard. Corredor across front removed early 20th c., rebuilt 1937, has square openings and round pillars. 4 sheets (1936, 1937, including plans, elevations, section, details); 4 ext. photos (1936).

San Marino □ Los Angeles County

Casa de Miguel Blanco (CA-322). Huntington Dr. One-story adobe, 32' × 40', joined at corner to two-story wood frame with shiplap siding, 26' × 22', shingled gable roofs, L-shaped porch on one-story and part of two-story sections, box columns. Original one-story section built 1830–40; two-story addition built 1865–80 for Michael

White, who came to California in 1829 and married daughter of Doña Eulalia Pérez de Guillén, keeper of the keys at San Gabriel Mission; demolished. 6 sheets (1935, including plans, elevations, details); 4 ext. photos (1935, 1936); 1 data page (1937).

San Martin □ Santa Clara County

Krohn, John, Tank House (CA-2111). 13000 Foothill Ave. Wood frame with drop siding, approx. 15' square, three stories, hipped roof, exposed rafter ends, third floor cantilevered over second, wind-pump attached to one side. 3 sheets (1980, including site plan, plan, elevations); 6 ext. photos (1980); 7 data pages (1980).

San Mateo □ San Mateo County

St. Matthew's Episcopal Church (CA-2144). El Camino Real and Baldwin St. Steel frame with reinforced concrete faced with sandstone, one story, gable roof, gable front filled with pointed-arch opening with series of slender ogee and lancet arches topped by a trefoil all in stained glass, buttressed side walls. Built 1906–10, Willis J. Polk, architect, to replace former church built in 1865 and destroyed in earthquake, in same vil-

Mission San Miguel Arcángel, San Miguel vicinity (CA-138).

lage Gothic style; in 1956, Milton T. Pflueger, architect, made addition by moving one end forward and adding to the middle. 7 ext. photos (1975), 6 int. photos (1975).

San Miguel vicinity ◻ San Luis Obispo County

Caledonia Inn (CA-1300). E. side Hwy. 101. Adobe, two-and-a-half stories, three-bay front, gable roof extends to cover two-level porch across front. Built ca. 1846 by Petronillo Ríos, one of the buyers of Mission San Miguel after secularization, with local Indian labor, named Caledonia in 1860s when used as a hotel on stage route between Los Angeles and San Francisco; restored 1968 by the Friends of the Adobes as a museum. 2 ext. photos (1930s). SHL

Mission San Miguel Arcángel (CA-138). Hwy. 101. Church: plastered adobe and stone, 38' (one-bay front) × 157', one story with loft, tiled gable roof, single entrance opening with relieving arch, window above with relieving arch; brightly decorated interior. Monastery: plastered adobe and stone, 178' × 39', one story, tiled gable roof, round-arched cloister along most of front. Mission founded 1797 as sixteenth in chain of 21 missions; church built 1816–18; restored 1901 and 1928. 36 sheets (1934, including plans, elevations, sections, details); 4 ext. photos (1934), 4 int. photos (1934), 1 photo of ruined walls at rear (1934), 1 photocopy of 1854 plat, 3 photocopies of drawings (ca. 1861–85, before

1850, 1850), 20 photocopies of ext. photos (ca. 1880, ca. 1890, ca. 1900, 1930s, 1936), 3 photocopies of int. photos (n.d.); 1 data page (1936). NR, SHL

San Pablo ◻ Contra Costa County

Castro-Alvarado Adobe (Rancho San Pablo) (CA-1654). 2748 San Pablo Ave. and Church St. Museum. Adobe, plastered, two-bay front, rectangular plan, two stories, gable roof, second floor balcony. Built 1842 by Jesús María Castro for his mother, widow of Francisco María Castro, grantee in 1823 of the Rancho San Pablo. Restored 1977–78 as museum in San Pablo Civic Center complex. 1 photocopy of ext. photo (n.d.) shows only gable roof and second floor balcony. SHL

San Pedro Valley ◻ San Mateo County

Sánchez, Francisco, Adobe (CA-156). Linda Mar Blvd. and Adobe Dr. House/museum. Adobe, 96' × 34', two stories, hip roof, two-story porch on three sides, wood-frame, one-story addition on one end. Built 1842; reconstructed 1953, wood-frame portions removed, double gallery added, building now 64' × 22' plus porches. 8 sheets (1938–40, 1958, including plans, elevations, sections, details); 6 ext. photos (1936, 1958), 2 int. photos (1936), 1 photocopy of ca. 1891 photo, 1 photocopy of 1865 or 1885 painting; 5 data pages (1958). SHL

Francisco Sanchez Adobe, San Pedro Valley (CA-156-10).

Covarrubias Adobe, Santa Barbara (CA-26).

Santa Barbara □ Santa Barbara County

Birabent Adobe (CA-247). 820 Santa Barbara St. Adobe with clapboards, one story, porch across front; rest of structure not ascertainable. 1 ext. photo (1960).

Buena Ventura Pico Adobe (CA-243). 920 Anacapa St. Adobe, 26′ (two-bay front) × 20′, one story, gable roof pitches out to cover porch across front, wood frame addition in rear. Built before 1852. 1 ext. photo (1960), 1 photocopy of 1965 sketch plan; 6 data pages (1965).

Caneda Adobe (Presidio Adobe) (CA-242). 121 E. Canon Perdido. Adobe, 35′ (three-bay front) × 16′, one story, tiled gable roof extends to cover porch across front. Built 1782 inside northwest wall of Presidio; incorporated in adobe house built in 1946 for Mr. and Mrs. Elmer H. Whittaker; this adobe and El Cuartel (CA-37-36) are only two fragments remaining from Presidio. 1 ext. photo (1960), 2 int. photos (1960), 1 photocopy of 1965 sketch plan; 5 data pages (1965). NR

Commercial Building (CA-245). E. de la Guerra Street. Plastered exterior, three-bay front, one story, flat roof with parapet, round-arched openings. 1 ext. photo (1960).

Covarrubias Adobe (CA-26). 715 Santa Barbara St. Adobe, 60′ (three-bay front) × 71′, L-shaped, one story, tiled gable roof, walls have heavy buttresses on one side and ends, massive end wall chimney. Built 1817 with Indian labor for Don Domingo Carrillo whose daughter married Don José María Covarrubias in 1838, descendants lived in house for over a century; moved and restored by John Southworth in 1924, acquired by Los Adobes de los Rancheros in 1938, open to the public. 3 sheets (1936, including plan, elevations, details); 4 ext. photos (1934, 1960), 3 int. photos (1934, 1960); 1 data page (1937). SHL

El Cuartel (CA-37-36). 122 E. Canon Perdido St. Adobe, 18′ × 40′, one story, tiled gable roof, structure built into wall with arched openings on street; wood frame additions. Built 1782 as part of Presidio; one of two important fragments remaining from the Presidio. 3 sheets (1934, including plan, elevations, details); 2 ext. photos (1934, 1960), 1 int. photo (1960), 3 photocopies of ca. 1890 and undated photos; 1 data page (1934). NR, SHL

Fernald, Charles, House (CA-240). 412 W. Montecito St. Brick and wood frame, 51′ × 37′, two stories, gable roof with cross gables and finials, second-story projecting bays cantilevered over first-story bay windows, one-story porch with jigsawn ornament, other stick-style features. Built 1862 as 31′ square brick building, Roswell Forbush, probable architect; remodeled and enlarged 1877, Thomas Nixon, probable architect; moved from original site at 422 Santa Barbara St.

in 1959. 3 ext. photos (1960), 7 int. photos (1960), 2 photocopies of architectural drawings (1965, including plat and plan); 9 data pages (1965).

Historic Adobe (CA-249). 715 Santa Barbara St., in rear of Covarrubias Adobe. Adobe, one story, tiled roof extends to cover porch across front. Built 1836, moved to present site 1922. 1 ext. photo (1960).

Hunt-Stambach House (CA-241). 404 W. Montecito St. Wood frame with horizontal siding, 36' (three-bay front) × 30', two stories, hipped roof with cupola, wide eaves with brackets and modillions, consoles support hoodmolds over windows, one-story, one-bay portico at entrance. Built 1879–80, Peter J. Barber, architect; originally located on east side State St. between E. Anapamu and E. Victoria Sts.; in 1891 moved to south side Victoria St. and Mora Villa Ave.; moved to present location 1955. 2 ext. photos (1960), 4 int. photos (1960), 2 photocopies of architectural drawings (1965, plans); 7 data pages (1965).

Knox Brick House (CA-244). 914 Anacapa St. Brick, 35' (five-bay front) × 43', one story, flat roof with parapet. Built 1871 for José Lobero for his mother-in-law; rear wood frame additions. 1 ext. photo (1960), 1 int. photo (1960), 1 photocopy of ca. 1880 ext. photo, 1 photocopy of 1965 sketch plan; 7 data pages (1965).

La Casa de la Guerra (CA-313). 11-19 E. de la Guerra St. Adobe, U-shaped, approx. 111' × 75', one story with two-story addition in rear, tiled gable roof, *corredor* around courtyard. Built ca. 1819–26 for José Antonio Julián de la Guerra y Noriega; renovated 1919–22, James Osborne Craig and Carleton M. Winslow, architects. 6 sheets (1934, including plans, elevations, section, details); 5 ext. photos (1935, 1936), 2 photocopies of ca. 1901 ext. photos; 12 data pages (1937, 1965). NR, SHL

La Casa de Joaquín Carrillo (CA-25). 11 E. Carrillo St. Adobe, 71' (six-bay front) × 31', one story, tiled gable roof extended over front porch. Built 1828 by Daniel Hill of Massachusetts for his bride, Rafaela Ortega y Olivera, granddaughter of the founder and first *comandante* of the Royal Presidio in Santa Barbara; restored and open to the public. 4 sheets (1936, including plan, elevations, section, details); 3 ext. photos (1936, 1960), 1 int. photo (1960), 5 photocopies of 1880 and undated photos; 1 data page (1937).

Miranda House (CA-37-35). 806 Anacapa St. Adobe, 80' × 68', L-shaped, one story, gable roof

Charles Fernald House, detail of entrance, Santa Barbara (CA-240).

extends to cover porches. Built ca. 1820 for Pacifico Ortega. 4 sheets (1934, including plan, elevations, sections, details); 1 ext. photo (1934); 1 data page (1934).

Mission Santa Barbara (CA-21). Laguna St. and Mission Canyon Rd. Church and monastery in L-plan with other modern buildings completing the quadrangle. Church: stone with some reinforced concrete, 97' × 211', one story, tiled gable roof, square towers at front corners have two stages of belfry with round-arched openings, domes with cupolas, round-arched entrance flanked by three Ionic engaged columns supporting denticulated pediment. Monastery: adobe and brick with some reinforced concrete, 90' (twelve-bay front) × 42', two stories, tiled gable roof, cloister along front has round-arched openings. Mission founded 1786 as tenth in chain of 21 missions; church built 1815–20; reconstructed 1925–26 after earthquake. Ross Montgomery, architect; facade rebuilt 1950. 30 sheets (1936, including plot plan, perspective view, plans, elevations, sections, details); 10 ext. photos (1936), 1 int. photo (1936); 2 data pages (1937). NHL, SHL

Santa Barbara continued

Orena, Gaspar, House (CA-246). *E. de la Guerra St.* Adobe, four-bay front, one-and-a-half stories, tiled gable roof extends to cover porch across front, gable dormer. Built mid 19th c., 2 photocopies of undated photos.

Trussell House (CA-248). *327 Castillo St.* Wood frame with clapboards, two-and-a-half stories, three-bay front in gable end, gable roof, one-story porch across front. Built mid-19th c. 1 ext. photo (1960).

Trussell-Winchester Adobe (CA-239). *412 W. Montecito St.* Adobe, 36′ (five-bay front) × 27′ with wood frame additions on sides, one story, gable roof pitches out to cover porch across front. Built 1854 by Capt. Horatio Gates Trussell, probable designer. 3 ext. photos (1960), 1 int. photo (1960), 1 photocopy of 1965 sketch plan; 7 data pages (1965). SHL

Vhay, Mrs. A. L. M., House (CA-37-37). *835 Laguna St.* Adobe, 90′ (eight-bay front) × 35′, one story, tiled gable roof, shingled roof covers porches across front and rear with enclosures at either end. Built 1825. 4 sheets (1934, including plan, elevations, details); 10 ext. photos (1934); 1 data page (1934).

Yorba-Abadie House (CA-37-33). *De la Guerra Plaza.* Adobe, 72′ (five-bay front) × 66′, L-shaped, one story, gable roof, partially tiled, pitches out to cover porch across front. Built 1826 for José Joaquín Maitorena; walls of west wing raised in 1850, tiled roof on west wing replaced with shingles. 4 sheets (1934, including plan, elevations, sections, details); 2 ext. photos (1934); 1 data page (1936).

Santa Clara □ Santa Clara County

Harrison Street Block (CA-2063). *1009, 1025, 1037, 1051, 1065, 1077, 1091 Harrison St.* Seven houses, all wood frame with horizontal siding, one-and-a-half to two-and-a-half stories, gable and hip roofs with cross gables, variegated shingles, decorative bargeboards, scrolled brackets, incised ornamentation. Built ca. 1890–1900, forming harmonious and picturesque streetscape. 4 sheets (1979, including elevations); 8 ext. photos (1980); 19 data pages (1979).

Landrum, Andrew, House (CA-2064). *1217 Santa Clara St.* Wood frame with channeled siding, 32′ (three-bay front) × 18′ with rear wing 25′ × 17′ forming T-shape, one-and-a-half stories, gable roof with cross gable, pointed-arch windows, quoining, one-story porch on front. Built 1875,

Andrew Landrum, builder. 3 sheets (1979, including site plan, plans, elevations); 5 ext. photos (1980); 7 data pages (1979).

Larder House (CA-2112). *1065 Alviso St.* Wood frame with horizontal siding, three-bay front, flat roof with wide eaves and paired brackets, broken pediment over second-floor window, one-story porch across front, quoining. Built ca. 1875. 2 ext. photos (1980).

Mission Santa Clara de Asís (CA-1133). *University of Santa Clara campus, the Alameda.* Stuccoed concrete, one-and-a-half stories, one-bay front in gable end, tiled gable roof, one-story shed-roofed portions along each side, square campanile on one corner with two round-arched openings on each side of belfry with polygonal roof with lantern, gable front has pilasters flanking niches, elaborate architrave and other embellishments all in bold relief. Built 1927–29, mission founded 1777 as eighth in chain of 21 missions; early log structures replaced in 1823–25 by adobe church; campanile replaced by frame one, 1839; roof extended on sides, 1861; in 1885, adobe walls taken down, wood frame ones built on extended line, two towers, pedimented front, much quoining and classical detailing; structure destroyed by fire, 1926; present structure designed to resemble 1825 appearance. Present structure: 1 aerial photo (1940), 1 photocopy of 1927 construction photo, 2 photocopies of ca. 1930 ext. photo, 1 int. photo (1940), 1 photocopy of 1928 int. photo; present adobe wall in quadrangle: 4 ext. photos (1940); 1825 structure: 1 photocopy of 1854 plat, 7 photocopies of drawings (1843, 1849, 1850, ca. 1861–85, ca. 1870, ca. 1880, 1901), 2 photocopies of photos (1950s, 1856); 1885 renovation: 2 photocopies of undated ext. photos, 4 photocopies of undated int. photos, 9 photocopies of 1926 photos of fire and ruins. SHL

Lick, James, Mill (CA-2011). *Guadalupe River, off of Montague Rd.* Flour mill built ca. 1855, brick with mahogany interior, converted to paper mill, destroyed by fire 1882. 3 sheets (1978, including site plan, site section); 12 data pages (1979).

□ *Granary.* Brick, round, 62′ diameter, two stories, conical roof, denticulated cornice. Built ca. 1855, wood frame interior destroyed by fire, 1882; rebuilt. 3 sheets (1978, including plans, elevation, section); 2 ext. photos (1980).

□ *House.* Heavy timber with shiplap siding, three-bay front, two stories, gable roof with cross gable, brackets, one-story porch across front wraps around. Built ca. 1860. 4 ext. photos (1980), 6 int. photos (1980).

□ *Office.* Wood frame with shiplap siding, three-bay front in gable end, gable roof with cross-tie brace on gable end. Built ca. 1880–87. 2 ext. photos (1980).

Santa Clara Verein (CA-2068). 1082 Alviso St. Wood frame with channeled siding, approx. 60′ (six-bay front) × 62′, one story, gable and flat roofs with parapet; interior has stenciled ceiling and proscenium arch. Built ca. 1880 by German community as social hall. 2 sheets (1979, including plan, elevation, section); 1 ext. photo (1980), 2 int. photos (1980); 9 data pages (1979).

Santa Cruz □ Santa Cruz County

Covered Bridge (CA-1549). San Lorenzo River. Wood frame with vertical plank siding, gable roof, opening between siding and roof exposes trusswork, great length. Built 1850s, since demolished. 1 photocopy of 1870s photo also shows wood frame houses in foreground.

Hall of Records (CA-1548). Front and Cooper Sts. Museum. Brick, octagonal, one story, hipped roof, pilasters at corners, pedimented doorway. Built 1882; restored. 1 photocopy of ca. 1900 photo, also showing two-story County Courthouse, built 1894, and other commercial buildings in town center.

Mission Santa Cruz (CA-1552). Emmet and School Sts. Misión La Exaltación de la Santa Cruz founded 1791 as twelfth in chain of 21 missions; built 1793–94 as one-story adobe church with two-stage buttresses on front gable end, tiled gable roof, square tower to side with open belfry and domical roof; bell tower collapsed 1840; remainder collapsed after 1857 earthquake; wood frame church with two square towers and taller central tower with bell-shaped roof built 1858, demolished 1889; brick church with tall central tower with spire built 1889; replica of original mission church at one-third size built 1931. 3 photocopies of maps (1834, 1853, 1854); 4 pho-

tocopies of drawings of original mission church before its destruction (n.d., after 1861, 1886, ca. 1925), 2 photocopies of drawings of church after partial destruction, showing interior (1857); 1 photocopy of photo of frame church (n.d.); 2 ext. photos of brick church (1930s), 1 photocopy of photo of brick church (n.d.); 2 ext. photos of church replica (ca. 1940), 2 int. photos of church replica (1940); 2 ext. photos of adobe soldiers' quarters (1936, 1937); 4 ext. photos of stone walls and cemetery (ca. 1940). SHL

Town of Santa Cruz (CA-1550). Thriving town of one- and two-story houses with some three- and four-story commercial buildings, also frame Mission church. 1 photocopy of 1870s photo.

Santa Margarita □ San Luis Obispo County

Santa Margarita Asistencia (Mission Chapel of Santa Margarita) (CA-1182). Rubble stone and adobe, gable roof, walls with stone relieving arches over openings. Built early 19th c. as an outpost chapel and storehouse for the extensive grain farming of the monks and Indians from Mission San Luis Obispo; demolished. 1 photocopy of 1834 drawing, 21 photocopies of photos of ruins (ca. 1925, 1930s).

Santa Monica □ Los Angeles County

Horatio West Apartments (CA-1984). Four units on a 75′ wide lot oriented to a central court with service area in rear, concrete and wood frame, irregular rectangles, two stories, flat roofs, small entry porches with two arched openings, wood and glass doors, variety of wood-framed windows, banded casement windows at corners with transoms, continuous band of paired, two-light casement windows on three sides of top floor under cornice line; living rooms on second

James Lick Mill, Santa Clara (CA-2011).

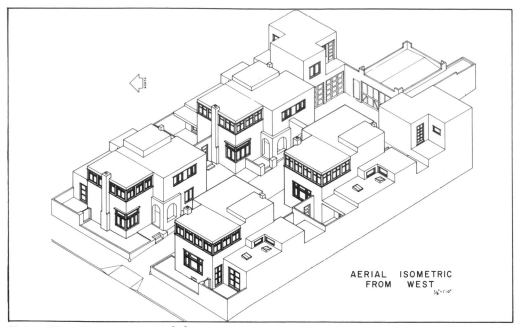

AERIAL ISOMETRIC
FROM WEST

Horatio West Apartments, aerial elevation, Santa Monica (CA-1984).

floors. Built 1919, Irving J. Gill, architect; a good example of his innovative work in low-cost housing. 11 sheets (1968, including aerial isometric, plans, elevations of complex; plans, sections of one unit); 6 ext. photos (1968); 6 data pages (1968). NR

Santa Rosa   □   Sonoma County

Carrillo Adobe (CA-1442). *Montgomery Dr. and Franquette Ave.* Adobe, approx. 83′ × 21′, one story, hip roof covers 10′ wide porch on all sides. Built ca. 1829 as the Asistencia de Santa Rosa de Lima on the south bank of Santa Rosa Creek; abandoned, 1835, after secularization; subsequently occupied by General Mariano Vallejo's mother-in-law, Señora María Ignacia López de Carrillo; originally L-shaped, one wing of L destroyed by 1961; partially restored. 3 sheets (1961, including plan, elevations, section, details); 4 ext. photos (1936), 3 int. photos (1936); 4 data pages (1962).

Santa Rosa Post Office and Federal Building (CA-2051). *401 5th St.* Stuccoed brick with limestone trim, 82′ (seven-bay front) × 52′, two stories, hip roof, bracketed eaves, main entrance through five-bay portico with limestone columns with composite capitals, double doors with transoms, keystones on first-floor windows, original exterior cast-iron lighting fixtures; main workroom

and lobby flanked by offices, notable plaster work in lobby. Built 1909, James Knox Taylor, architect; addition to the rear, open stair well enclosed for office space, 1926; work room altered, 1967; moved to 7th St., 1979. First structure constructed by federal government in Santa Rosa; noted for its small scale and attempt to be compatible with the neighborhood. 3 ext. photos (1977), 6 int. photos (1977), 14 photocopies of 1908 architect's drawings (including elevations, plans, details); 9 data pages (1977).

Santa Rosa vicinity   □   Sonoma County

Fountain Grove (CA-1917). *Highway 101.* Wood frame with channeled siding, three-bay front, two stories, bracketed hip roof, central section of facade projected, quoining on all corners, polygonal one-story bay on front, one-story porches on three sides; central-hall plan, enriched mantels and interior detail. Built 1875 as a utopian community; demolished 1960s. 2 ext. photos (1960), 5 int. photos (1960).

□ ***Barn (CA-1915).*** Wood frame with board-and-batten siding, sixteen-sided, 71′ diameter, 55′ high above main floor, built into hill with battered base on lower side, conical roof with open lantern at peak, one large round-arched entrance; polygonal plan with radiating stalls, heavy timber framing on main floor and raised center platform. Built 1875. 5 sheets (1960, including site plan, plans, elevation, section); 5 ext. photos (1960), 3 int. photos (1960).

□ *Winery Buildings (CA-1916).* Brick champagne storage building with wood frame second story, stone wine shop, large vats. Built 1870s, demolished 1960s. 3 ext. photos, 1 of general view, 1 of champagne storage building, 1 of vats (1960); 1 int. photo of vat building (1960).

□ *Hop Kilns (CA-1651).* Stone, rectangular with square portion in rear, two steep-pitched pyramidal roofs with vented peaks. Built 1870s; demolished 1960s. 3 ext. photos (1960).

Saratoga □ Santa Clara County

Saratoga Foothill Club (CA-2014). 20399 Park Pl. Wood frame with redwood shakes, 74′ × 67′, one-and-a-half stories, cross gable roof, projecting bracketed bays, paired brackets between windows; circular multi-pane rose window in gable; redwood paneling on interior. Built 1914–15, Julia Morgan, architect, for women's study group. 10 sheets (1978, including site plan, plans, elevations, sections, details); 7 ext. photos (1980); 10 data pages (1978, 1979).

Villa Montalvo (James Duval Phelan House) (CA-2048). Montalvo Rd. Wood frame and concrete covered with stucco, 104′ (five-bay front) × 40′ with wings forming a U-shape, two stories, tiled hip roof, round-arched openings at first level, loggia in center three bays. Built 1912–14, William Curlett and Sons, architects, John McLaren, landscape architect. 5 ext. photos (1980), 4 int. photos (1980); 10 data page (1977, 1979).

Welch-Hurst (CA-2006). 15800 Sanborn Rd., Sanborn Skyline County Park. Halved redwood logs, horizontal on first floor, set in vertical columns on second floor, approx. 82′ × 128′, irregular plan, two stories, hip and gable roofs. Built ca. 1913 for Judge and Mrs. James R. Welch, designers, as family retreat. 5 sheets (1977, including site plan, plans, elevations, section); 6 ext. photos (1980); 8 data pages (1977, 1979). NR

Saratoga vicinity □ Santa Clara County

Dyer, H. P., House (CA-2050). 16055 Sanborn Rd., Sanborn Skyline County Park. Stone first story, lap-jointed squared timbers upper story, two stories, hipped roof, one-story stone porch, exterior stone chimney on front; dramatic two-story living hall, rooms paneled with redwood. Built 1915. 6 ext. photos (1980), 2 int. photos (1980); 4 data pages (1977).

Sawyers Bar □ Siskiyou County

Catholic Church (CA-1190). Wood frame with clapboards, one-bay front in gable end, one story, gable roof with cross at ridge. Built 1855 during first mining boom on Salmon River; demolished.

Fountain Grove, Barn, Santa Rosa vicinity (CA-1915).

Sawyer's Bar continued

1 photo also shows river bank with tailings from hydraulic mining (1937).

Shasta   □   Shasta County

Bystle House (CA-1445). Trinity and High Sts. Wood frame with horizontal siding, three-bay front in gable end, two-and-a-half stories, gable roof extended over two-story front porch with simple columns, triangular window in gable. Built ca. 1850, later side addition, openings altered. 1 ext. photo (1934).

Commercial Buildings (CA-1305). Main St. Rows of one- and two-story brick buildings, iron-shuttered openings at ground level, some with round arches, variety of parapets. Built 1850s; stabilized ruins; the remains of a once-booming town of 2,500 of the northern gold-mining country; county seat 1851–88. 2 ext. photos (1934), 5 photocopies of 1930s photos; 1 photocopy of 1850 plat.

Foster House (CA-1443). Wood frame with horizontal siding, four-bay front in gable end, two-and-a-half stories, gable roof, attic story built out over two-story front porch, casement windows and French doors on ground floor, round-arched window in gable. Built ca. 1860, reconstructed on original foundations. 1 ext. photo (1934).

Masonic Hall and Store Building (CA-1303). Museum. Masonic Hall: brick, three-bay front, two stories, flat roof, brick parapet with inset panel, entablature with molded cornice, dentil course and blank frieze, brick pilasters with simple caps, two paneled iron shuttered openings on each level. Store: brick, two stories, five-bay front, flat roof with parapet, round arches on second level, iron-shuttered openings. Masonic Hall built 1854, store built shortly after; Hall restored. 3 ext. photos (1934, 1930s).

Shasta County Courthouse (CA-1297). Museum. Brick, nine-bay front, one story, flat roof, high brick parapet with bracketed cornice and three inset panels, round-arched doors with relieving arches and keystones, paneled iron shutters. Built 1855; restored. 5 ext. photos (1934, 1930s), 1 int. photo (1934), 1 photocopy of 1938 ext. photo, 1 photocopy of 1930s int. photo, all before restoration.

Shurtleff, Dr., House (CA-1944). Wood frame with horizontal siding, three-bay front in gable end, two-and-a-half stories with one-story wings, gable roof extended at gable end over two-story porch, side porches. Built ca. 1850; destroyed by fire, 1960s; an outstanding example of a frontier Classic Revival house. 2 ext. photos (1934).

Shaw's Flat   □   Tuolumne County

Mississippi House and Post Office (CA-1579). Shaw's Flat and Mt. Brow Rds. Wood frame with clapboards, six-bay front, one story with loft, gable roof extended over porch across front with plain box columns. Built 1850 as general store, saloon, post office and courtroom. Demolished. 2 photocopies of 1925 photo.

Shingle Springs   □   El Dorado County

Phelps Store (CA-1357). U.S. Hwy. 50. Fieldstone, three-bay front in gable end, three bays deep, two-and-a-half stories, gable roof with vertical board siding in gable, segmental-, round- and flat-arched openings. Built ca. 1855; ruinous condition, shell remains. 1 ext. photo (1934), also shows a one-story, shed-roofed, board-and-batten siding shed built on side of the store.

Sierra City   □   Sierra County

Buildings (CA-1477). Main St. Row of wood frame buildings with sidewalk canopies and gable roofs, Wells Fargo Building (CA-1426) in distance. 1 ext. photo (1934).

Commercial Buildings (CA-1422). Main St. Two gable-roofed, two-story structures, one of rubble stone with brick front, other wood frame with horizontal siding, both have fronts in gable ends and sidewalk canopies. Built 1860s. 1 ext. photo (1934).

Frame House (CA-1423). Main St. Wood frame with horizontal siding, four-bay front, one-and-a-half stories, gable roof extended on both sides to form front porch and rear lean-to. Built 1860s, a good example of a vernacular cottage typical of the mining country. 1 ext. photo (1934).

Houses (CA-1425). Main St. Two very similar houses, wood frame with horizontal siding, three-bay fronts in gable ends, two-story house has gable roof with raking cornice and returns, round louvered window in gable, gabled hood over door on braces, side lean-to; two-and-a-half story house has two-story porch on gable end. Built 1860s; two-story house altered and converted to apartments. 2 ext. photos (1934).

Old Mine (CA-1421). Wood frame buildings with gable roofs of utilitarian character sited around an open meadow or field. 2 ext. photos of general views (1934).

Town of Sierraville (CA-1676). Collection of wood frame buildings that formed the supply center for the area's mines and camps. Built 1850s; largely demolished. 1 photocopy of 1852 photo.

Wells Fargo & Co. Building (August C. Bush Building) (CA-1426). Main St. Brick and wood, six-bay front, three-and-a-half stories with upper story-and-a-half sided with wood and first two stories of brick, built into hill, gable roof extended to ground level in rear, two-story front porch, four paneled iron shuttered doors at ground level. Built 1871 of local brick as the August C. Bush Building; housed the Wells Fargo Company; veranda and rear saltbox extension removed; roof lowered to second story. 1 ext. photo (1934).

Smartville   □   Yuba County

O'Brian, James, House (CA-1809). O'Brian Rd. Wood frame with clapboards, four-bay front by two bays, two stories, gable roof, boxed cornice, one-story porch on two sides supported by split wood columns with spacer blocks, rear one-story addition with porch. Built 1856 for James O'Brian, this fine Greek Revival house retains much of its early landscaping planted by Chinese who worked for the family. 1 photocopy of 1905 lithograph.

Soledad vicinity   □   Monterey County

Mission Nuestra Señora de la Soledad (CA-1130). Off Hwy. 101, Salinas Valley. Adobe, 24'-6" × 67'6", tile gable roofs of hewn beams on peeled limb rafters. Founded 1791 by Father Lasuén; this building begun 1808; abandoned 1835; restored and dedicated 1955 under the auspices of the Native Daughters of the Golden West. 5 ext. photos (1939, n.d.) 1 int. photo (1939), 38 photocopies of ext. photos (1850s, ca. 1870, 1870s, 1880, 1881, ca. 1882, ca. 1884, 1884, 1888, ca. 1890, ca. 1895, 1898, 1900, 1902, ca. 1902, ca. 1905, 1918, 1932, 1938, 1939, n.d.), 14 photocopies of int. photos (1890s, 1898, 1902, ca. 1904, ca. 1920, 1938, 1939, n.d.), 5 photocopies of drawings (1850, 1861–85, early 1870s, 1873), 1 photocopy of plat (ca. 1854). Most photographs show mission in ruins. SHL

Solvang   □   Santa Barbara County

Mission Santa Ynéz (CA-24). State Hwy. 150. Church and monastery in L-plan all that remains of quadrangle. Mission founded 1804 as 19th in chain of 21 missions; church built 1813–17; campanario rebuilt 1911; church and monastery restored 1946; campanario again rebuilt 1948. 5 ext. photos of mission (1936); 2 data pages (1937). SHL

□ *Church (CA-24 A).* Adobe and brick, 38' (one-bay front) × 168', tiled gable roof, round-arched entrance, round-arched entrance, round-arched opening above, pilasters at front corners, buttresses on side walls, campanario to one side has three round-arched openings with one round-arched opening above. Campanario altered since recording. 5 sheets (1936, including plan, elevations, sections, details); 5 ext. photos (1936), 3 int. photos (1936).

□ *Monastery (CA-24 B).* Adobe with brick piers, 144' (nine-bay front) × 70', one story, tiled gable roof extends to cover cloisters on both front and back, wood-frame corner has horizontal siding. Altered since recording. 4 sheets (1936, including plan, elevations, section, details); 4 ext. photos (1936), 1 int. photo (1936).

□ *Tannery (CA-24 C).* Stone, foundation only remains, plan and design of superstructure unknown. 2 sheets (1936, including plans, elevations, sections); 2 photos of ruins (1936).

Sonoma   □   Sonoma County

Blue Wing Inn (Sonoma House) (CA-1438). 133 Spain St. E. Adobe, two stories, ten-bay front, hip roof extends to cover two-story porch across front, porch enclosed with clapboarding on sides of house. Built ca. 1835. 2 ext. photos (1934). SHL

Mission San Francisco Solano de Sonoma (CA-1138). Spain St. E. and 1st St. E. Museum. Plastered adobe chapel and convento: chapel one-and-a-half stories, one-bay front with two flat-arched openings, three bays deep, tiled gable roof; convento one story, nine-bay front, tiled gable roof extends to cover corredor across front, building set at right angle to chapel. Mission founded 1823 by Padre José Altimira as last in chain of 21 missions; present chapel built as parish church for Sonoma in 1841; restored 1911–13, when all round-arched openings replaced by flat-arched ones, belfry removed. 7 ext. photos (1930s), 20 photocopies of photos (n.d., 1850s, ca. 1880, ca. 1890, ca. 1895, ca. 1902, ca. 1903, 1909, ca. 1912, ca. 1923, ca. 1925), 1 photocopy

Temelec Hall, Sonoma (CA-1563).

Temelec Hall, Sonoma (CA-1563).

Sonoma continued

of site plan (1854), 6 photocopies of drawings, including 2 of chapel as a separate structure, 1 of original church, 3 general views of plaza with other buildings (n.d., before 1846, ca. 1870, 1879, 1883). NHL, SHL

Ray House (Adler Adobe) (CA-1439). 205 Spain St. E. Wood frame with channeled siding and adobe plastered and scored to resemble stone, two stories, nine-bay front, hip roof extends to cover porch. Frame portion built 1846, adobe portion 1850. 1 ext. photo (1934).

Sonoma Barracks (Mexican Army Barracks) (CA-1560). Spain and 1st St. E. Adobe plastered and scored to imitate stone masonry, three-bay front, two stories, gable roof, central polygonal oriel with domed roof, ornate heads on windows, balcony with latticed railing across front. Built 1836 for General Mariano Vallejo as part of fortification of Sonoma Pueblo; altered later in the Italianate style; restored, 1970s, to original adobe structure. 1 ext. photo (1933). SHL

Sonoma Plaza (CA-1436). N. side of Plaza. Two story adobe buildings, including Sonoma Barracks (CA-1560) and Don Salvador Vallejo's house; Mission Chapel (CA-1138); one-story shops, and Bear Flag flagstaff. 1 photocopy of 1851 drawing. NHL

Temelec Hall (CA-1563). 20750 Arnold Ave. Stone, dressed and rough dressed ashlar, eight-bay front, two stories, low-pitched hip roof with square cupola and widow's walk surrounded by balustrade, two-story veranda on north, east, and west sides, square rusticated columns on ground level, Ionic columns on upper level, entablature with modillions and carved frieze in relief of stylized running vine, windows have triangulated pediments, two-story wing on one side of rough-dressed fieldstone, same entablature, quoins on corners; central-hall plan; grounds have fieldstone gazebos with dressed ashlar quoins, cross-gable roofs with cornice molding, scroll bargeboards, finial, round-arched openings; rough-coursed ashlar stable, three-bay front, square, two stories, hip roof with square dovecote. Built 1858 for "Captain" Granville P. Swift who came West in 1843 with Kelsey Party, prospered in gold mining and was a member of the Bear Flag Party centered in Sonoma; Temelec Hall, possibly built to surpass the Casa Grande of General Mariano Vallejo, is an outstanding example of a modified Classical Revival design with Italianate Villa overtones; interior has been modernized;

house now community center. 16 ext. photos (1960), 4 int. photos (1960), 1 photocopy of 1968 photo. SHL.

Vallejo, General Mariano, House (Lachryma Montis) (CA-1440). N. end of 3rd St. W. House/museum. Wood frame with adobe nogging, horizontal siding, T-shaped, 41' × 58', one-and-a-half stories, gable roof with gable dormers, elaborately carved bargeboards with finial and pendant at gable peak, carved bargeboards also on dormers, one gable end has pointed-arch window with drip mold and corbel stops at second level, polygonal bay window on first level, other windows have rectangular drip molds with label stops, one-story porches with chamfered wood posts and carved trim, rear kitchen building; central-hall plan featuring cast-iron ceiling rosettes, several marble mantels on both floors, period furnishings and some family pieces. Built 1851–53, from a prefabricated frame shipped around the Horn and purchased by Vallejo with two others in San Francisco (the other remaining frame is the Frisbie-Walsh House in Benicia, CA-2087); General Vallejo was a principal figure in early California history, a general in the Mexican Army, founder of the town of Sonoma, and member of the first State Constitutional Convention at Monterey, 1849; Vallejo's ten surviving children grew up in the house and when the General died in 1890 the house continued in the family until presented to the state in 1932; Vallejo's fifteenth daughter remained as custodian of the house until her death in 1943; restored by the National Park Service. 6 sheets (1960s, including plans, elevations, section, details); 4 ext. photos (1934); 7 data pages (1964). NHL, SHL

Vallejo Swiss Chalet (CA-1441). State Historic Park. Half-timber construction with brick nogging, one-bay front by five bays deep, two stories, upper-story walls extended on joists, gable roof, variety of openings, wooden loft doors at ends. Built ca. 1852 from pre-cut and numbered timbers shipped around the Horn and purchased by Vallejo in San Francisco; restored by National Park Service. 1 ext. photo (1934).

Sonora □ Tuolumne County

Cady House (CA-116). NW corner, Dodge and Norlin Sts. Wood frame, 45' (three-bay front) × 71', one story, gable roof, front porch with pedimented portico with box columns and raking cornice, entrance door with sidelights and tran-

Sonora continued

som framed by pilasters. Built 1856 for Charles Haley, sold to J. S. Cady, Sonora miner and merchant. 6 sheets (1934, including plans, elevations, details); 3 ext. photos (1934), 1 photocopy of ext. photo (late 19th c.), 1 photocopy of int. photo (late 19th c.); 1 data page (1937).

City Hotel (CA-1566). Stone and adobe, two stories, gable roof, two-story porch across front with elaborate balustrade and spindlework frieze at second level. 1 photocopy of 1925 photo.

Commercial Building (CA-1699). Brick building adjoining Stockton Record Building, iron doors. 2 photocopies of 1937 photos of details of iron doors.

Dorsey House (CA-1134). Brick, three-bay front, square, two stories, hipped roof (not original), fanlight over entrance door, small one-story extension with shed roof. Built 1854 for Caleb Dorsey, who came to area via Panama in 1850; Dorsey later served as county District Attorney and was a major figure in county development; demolished 1950s. 2 ext. photos (1934).

First (Frame) Post Office (CA-1575). Wood frame with clapboards, two-and-a-half stories, gable roof overhanging two-story porch. Built ca. 1860; George W. Patrick, one of Sonora's early postmasters, had his post office here; demolished. 1 photocopy of undated photo.

Gem Café. See Store Building (CA-1688).

Gunn, Dr. Lewis, Adobe. See Italia Hotel (CA-1135).

House (CA-1139). Dodge and Stuart Sts. Stone and brick, four-bay front, one story with fully exposed basement on low side of hill site, flat roof, upper-floor balcony on two sides with ornate flat-sawn balustrade and frieze, turned columns with brackets on main floor. Built 1860s and '70s; altered, decorative woodwork removed, brick plastered. 1 ext. photo (1934).

House (CA-1136). Washington St. Wood frame

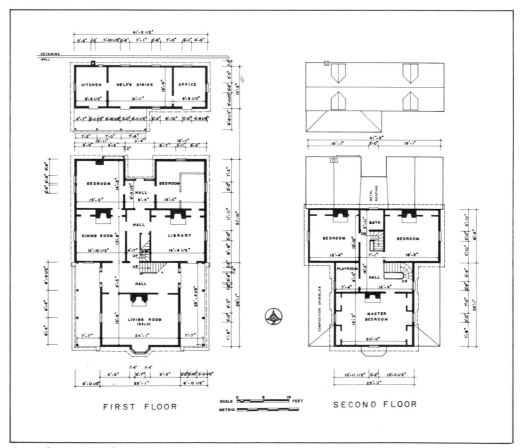

General Mariano Vallejo House (Lachryma Montis), first and second floor plans, Sonoma (CA-1440).

General Mariano Vallejo House (Lachryma Montis), elevations, Sonoma (CA-1440).

Cady House, Sonora (CA-116).

Sonora continued

with board-and-batten siding, four-bay front, one story, gable roof extended over front porch. Built 1850s; demolished. 1 ext. photo (1934).

Italia Hotel (Dr. Lewis Gunn Adobe) (CA-1135). Washington St., between Church and June Sts. Adobe and wood frame, nine-bay front, two stories, gable roof extended over two-story veranda, paneled box columns, second-story balcony across three central bays, ground floor has nine doors in trabeated wood frames. Built 1853–54 as an adobe, enlarged later. 1 ext. photo (1934).

Jewish Cemetery (CA-38-7). Yaney Ave. between Lower Sunset Dr. and Seco Sts. Rock walls, brick pillars and wrought-iron gates at entrance leading to lane lined with cypresses. Built 1850s. 4 sheets (1934, including plan, elevations, sections, details; for elevations of gravestone see drawing for Mountain View Cemetery, CA-38-11); 7 photos (1934).

Leonard, Thomas, House (CA-1512). Wood frame with channeled siding, one-and-a-half stories, low-pitched gable roof with cross gable dormer, nine-bay veranda with chamfered columns and fan brackets. Not located. 1 ext. photo (1934).

McCormick House (CA-1111). Wood frame with channeled siding, four-bay front by two bays deep with two rear additions, L-shaped, two stories, gable roof, two-story front porch, railing and chamfered posts with molded caps at second floor, one-story veranda at side. Built 1850s; demolished. 3 ext. photos (1934).

McDonald House. See Sugg House (CA-1137).

Methodist Church (CA-1567). Wood frame with clapboards, one story, gable roof, tower with paired pilasters, steeple, entrance in pedimented enclosed portico. Built 1852. Demolished 1922. 1 photocopy of undated photo.

St. James Episcopal Church (CA-1141). Washington at Snell Sts. Wood frame with board-and-batten siding, one story, high gable roof, front corner tower with two-stage corner buttresses, open belfry with pointed arches and high spire, bracketed hoods over entrance and tower door, tripartite lancet windows with diagonal leading, two-stage buttresses on sides. Built 1859, seventh parish of the California Episcopal Church, oldest Episcopal Church in state; hoods removed, new pointed archway over entrance. 2 ext. photos (1934). SHL

St. Patrick's Church (CA-189). 127 W. Jackson St. Wood frame, one-and-a-half stories, gable roof,

central entrance tower with louvered belfry and spire, round-headed stained glass window over entrance, two round-headed windows flanking tower, fanlight over door; interior has barrel vault, apse, side aisles, rear balcony. 1 ext. photo of general view from across town (1934), 1 int. photo (1934).

Second House (CA-1140). Dodge and Stewart Sts. Wood frame with channeled siding, paneled door in plain surround, transom window, rest of building not ascertainable. 1 photo, detail of door (1934).

Stockton Record Building (CA-1690). Brick, one story, three-bay front, parapeted roof, tin canopy over sidewalk. Built late 19th c. 1 photocopy of 1937 photo.

Store Building (Gem Café) (CA-1688). East side Washington St. Stone masonry, three-bay front, one story, flat roof, local schist laid in large flat slabs, storefront of late 19th-c. design with Eastlake-type ornament. Stone portion built 1856 as Wells Fargo Building by Emanuel Linoberg; facade remodeled. 1 photocopy of undated photo.

Sugg House (Sugg-McDonald House) (CA-1137). 37 Theall St. First level adobe faced with brick, second level wood frame with channeled siding, three-bay front in gable end, two-and-a-half stories, gable roof, two-story front veranda continuous on sides as one-story porch, one-story gabled rear addition. Adobe brick portion built in 1857 by William Sugg. Second floor added in 1880s; served as boarding house prior to 1918. 1 ext. photo (1934).

Town of Sonora (CA-1195). One- and two-story buildings, residential and commercial, with church and school buildings. 2 photocopies of photos (ca. 1860, 1923), 1 photocopy of 1853 lithograph.

Union Democrat Building (CA-1691). Stone or concrete, one story, three-bay front, flat roof with parapet, intricate cast-iron threshold. Demolished 1982. 2 photocopies of 1937 photos.

Sonora vicinity □ Tuolumne County

Lime Kiln (CA-195). Open shed with broadly pitched hip roof open at top in center supported by square wood posts with diagonal braces. Deteriorated by 1934; demolished. 1 ext. photo (1934).

Stone Dam (CA-188). Coursed ashlar and rubble wall of dam with waterfall. Old State Highway 49, 1½ miles N. of Jamestown. 2 photos (1934).

Soquel □ Santa Cruz County

Congregational Church (CA-1192). Wood frame
with beveled siding, one-bay front by three bays
deep, one story, gable roof, projecting central
square tower of two stages with spire, bracketed
roofs, round-arched louvered vent near top of
first stage, windows have architraves with
molded heads and label stops, doors in base of
tower; single nave with recessed sanctuary
framed with molded arch, wooden pews. Built
1868. 2 ext. photos (1936), 1 int. photo (1936).

South Pasadena □ Los Angeles County

Casa de José Pérez (Adobe Flores) (CA-33). 1804
Foothill Blvd. Plastered adobe, stone foundations,
asymmetrical U shape, 81' (five-bay front) ×
67;', east wing wood frame veneered in brick,
patio open at north end, gable roof originally
shingled now tiled, doors and windows not original. West wing built 1839 for Esteban Pérez;
front part of house built 1843 for Manuel Gar-
fías, second owner; east wing later; altered in

1919 by Carleton M. Winslow, Sr. 5 sheets (1936,
including plan, elevations, details); 6 ext. photos
(1936); 1 data page (1937). NR

Miltimore House (CA-1988). 1301 S. Chelton Way.
Stuccoed wood frame, approx. 38' × 44' with
one-story ells, two stories, flat parapeted roof,
wood and glass doors, paired and triple casement
windows with hopper transoms in wood frames,
paved terraces with pergolas supported by Doric
columns extend to south, stark exterior with no
ornament. Built 1911, Irving J. Gill, architect. 6
sheets (1969, including aerial isometric, plans,
elevations); 6 data pages (1969).

Spadra □ Los Angeles County

See entry for Casa Ricardo Vejar under Los Angeles.

Springfield □ Tuolumne County

House (CA-1148). Wood frame with clapboards,

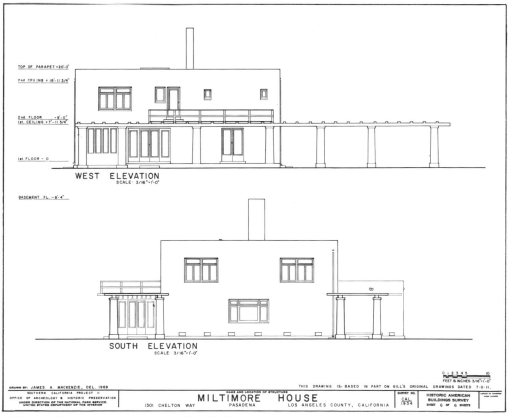

Miltimore House, South Pasadena (CA-1988).

Springfield continued

three-bay front, T-shape, one-and-a-half stories, gable roof, pedimented center pavilion has pilasters at corners, raking cornice and returns, entrance has simplified classical architrave, sidelights and transom window. Built 1850s. 1 ext. photo (1934).

School (Methodist Church (CA-1149). Horseshoe Bend and Springfield Rd. Brick, two bays by three bays, square, high one story, hipped roof, corners reinforced with extra layer of brick, two wooden doors with transom lights on front, wood lean-to. Built 1854; first used as church, then armory and school. 3 ext. photos (n.d., 1934, 1937).

Spring Valley □ San Diego County

Bancroft House (CA-431). 9050 Memory Lane. Museum. Plastered adobe and wood, approx. 32′ × 18′ with 6′ wide porch across front, one story, shingled gable roof extended over porch, recessed wood and glass doors and windows; two rooms entered by doors from the porch, larger room has cobblestone hearth, period furnishings and memorabilia. Built ca. 1856 for A. S. Ensworth, a Justice of the Peace; later owned by Capt. Rufus K. Porter who named Spring Valley and ran a dairy; from 1885–1918 owned by Hubert H. Bancroft, California historian; restored after 1963 by Spring Valley Chamber of Commerce. 2 ext. photos (1964), 2 int. photos (1964); 6 data pages (1965). NHL, SHL

Stent □ Tuolumne County

Town of Stent (also called Poverty Hill) (CA-1577). Mostly one-story, wood-frame buildings, residential and farm buildings. Town has disappeared. 1 photocopy of early 1900s photo.

Stockton □ San Joaquin County

Avon Theatre (CA-1593). NE corner Main and California Sts. Plastered brick, seven bays by nine bays, three stories, flat roof with embellished parapet, alternating triangular and segmental pediments above bracketed cornice, round-arched windows paired except at corners, bays separated by Corinthian pilasters, second-story balcony with iron railing, ground floor storefronts. Built ca. 1860; demolished. 1 photocopy of ext. 1925 photo.

Barnhart House (CA-1621). SW corner Magnolia and Hunter Sts. Wood frame with horizontal wood siding, two-bay front, two stories, hip roof, two-story polygonal bay window on front, polygonal ell at rear, segmental-arched windows and doors, bracketed entablature with frieze panels. Built ca. 1870, typical Italianate residence; brick front porch probably added later. 1 photocopy of 1939 photo.

Budd, Governor James H., Mansion (CA-1627). Wood frame with horizontal siding, three-bay front with polygonal central bay and ell at rear, two stories, flat roof with polygonal, pagoda-like cupola, bracketed cornice, front porch; side hall, irregular plan. Built 1850s; home of James H. Budd, Governor of California from 1895–99; demolished. 1 photocopy of undated lithograph.

Carson House (CA-1612). Wood frame with clapboards and plank siding, three-bay front, one story, gable roof, brick chimney, front porch with split columns on blocks, rear shed additions. Built ca. 1865, good example of a vernacular pioneer cottage; demolished. 1 photocopy of 1933 photo.

Christian Church (CA-1615). Wood frame with clapboard siding, three-bay front, two stories, gable roof with entrance in gable end, gable extended to form second-story porch, central entrance with triangular hood on brackets. Built ca. 1860, simplified Greek Revival style frequently used during the 1860s for meeting halls; first floor filled in under porch; demolished. 1 photocopy of undated photo.

City of Stockton (CA-1601). Most of the HABS collection for San Joaquin County consists of photocopies of historic photographs from the V. Covert Martin Collection. Martin (1885–1962) was a photographer in Stockton who made his own photocopies and borrowed from many sources. His collection of some 2,000 photos is divided between the Pioneer Museum & Haggin Galleries and the Holt-Atherton Center for Western Studies at the University of the Pacific. The documentation filed with HABS No. CA-1601 consists of 17 photocopies of historic photos (1850–1920), showing street scenes in Stockton. Most of the buildings are gone, victims of urban renewal and freeway construction in the old central business district, which was the subject of most of these photos. Photos of individual buildings are filed by building name (see following entries).

Clark, Dr. Asa, House (CA-1581). Oak and Hunter Sts. Plastered brick, one-and-a-half stories with raised basement, gable roof with decorative bargeboards, L-shaped with two-story crenelated square tower in L, front entrance portico with Tudor arches surmounted by a balustrade, pointed-arch windows in gables and tower. Built 1858, provincial Gothic Revival-style residence; demolished 1901–02. 1 photocopy of 1880 photo.

Columbia House ("Green Dragon") (CA-1580). NW corner Channel and San Joaquin Sts. Wood frame with clapboard siding, seven-bay front, two stories, gable roof, two-story porch across front with balustraded railing at second floor. Built ca. 1852, provincial Greek Revival style, typical of commercial buildings of the period; demolished. 1 photocopy of ca. 1870 photo.

Commercial Hotel (CA-1629). 200 block of Main St. Brick, plastered front, twelve-bay front, two stories, flat roof with raised, enriched parapet at front, ornate bracketed cornice with frieze panels and dentil course, round-arched windows with squeezed pediments on consoles, extended wooden awning with railing at second level, ground-floor storefronts. Built 1860s; demolished. 1 photocopy of 1870s photo.

Creanor, Judge, House (CA-1616). Fremont and Commercial Sts. Wood frame with clapboards, three-bay front, two stories with one-story wings, gable roof, entrance in gable end which has cornice returns and lunette, flat-arched windows, entrance door has sidelights and transom window, one-story porch across front has balustrade above; side-hall plan. Built ca. 1860, good example of simplified provincial Greek Revival style house; demolished 1916. 1 photocopy of 1916 photo.

Eureka Firehouse (CA-1638). Plastered brick, two-bay front, two stories, flat roof with raised parapet ornamented with three finials dividing the bays, heavy segmental cornices with modillions, ground floor has large central, round-arched entrance for engines with flanking side doors with hoodmolds and keystones, second floor embellished central section composed as a Palladian window with molded pilasters and paneled sections on either side of central window, "Eureka 2" in large letters in pediment. Built in 1866, this building, like many of its kind, reflected the importance of its company in its imposing design; demolished. 2 photocopies of 1870s photos show building draped and festooned for celebrations.

First Baptist Church (CA-1583). Brick, three-bay front by four bays, one main story with raised

basement and water table, crenelated gable roof, bay division marked with stepped buttresses and crocketed finials, lancet windows with leaded glass in diamond and fan patterns, projecting central two-story tower capped with spire, crenelated parapets, corner crockets with finials, quatrefoil roundels and other Gothic Revival detail, louvered lancet windows in tower. Built 1860, a well proportioned and detailed brick church in the Gothic Revival style; demolished. 1 photocopy of 1880s photo.

'49 Drug Store. See Holden Store (CA-1634).

Globe Iron Works (CA-1605). Brick, four-bay front by eleven bays, two-story front with one-story rear ell, flat roof with parapet, brick cornice and dentil course on main block, metal awning over first floor. Built ca. 1860, utilitarian Classical commercial building; demolished. 1 photocopy of 1925 photo.

"Green Dragon." See Columbia House (CA-1580).

Hart and Thrift Building (CA-1600). Brick, six-bay front by five bays, two stories, flat roof with parapet, molded entablature with dentil course, second floor of facade has round-arched windows with drip molds single and paired in an A, BB, A, A, BB, A rhythm, metal awning with ornamental "fringe" above first floor, surmounted by balustrade. Built ca. 1860 in a modestly embellished Italianate style typical of substantial commercial houses. Demolished. 1 photocopy of ca. 1870 photo.

Hazelton Library. See Frank Stewart Library (CA-1631).

Holden Store ('49 Drug Store) (CA-1634). El Dorado and Main Sts. Stone, two stories, three-bay front, flat roof with parapet, hoodmolds over flat-arched doors and windows, balcony at second level has iron railing. Built 1850, housed Stockton's first pharmacy; by 1886, three-bay front expanded to seven bays, roof raised, cornice elaborated, balcony extended. Demolished. 1 photocopy of 1858 drawing. See historic photo in City of Stockton (CA-1601-10).

I.O.O.F. Building (CA-1625). El Dorado St. between Weber Ave. and Main St. Brick, eight-bay front, two stories, flat roof with parapet and decorative brick frieze, flat-arched second-floor windows divided by pilasters. Built 1853; one half probably added later; ground floor altered; demolished. 1 photocopy of 1925 photo.

Keyes House (CA-1609). SW corner California and Market Sts. Wood frame with clapboards,

Stockton continued

three-bay front, gable shingled roof. Built ca. 1860, vernacular cottage; demolished. 1 photo-copy of undated photo.

Mansion House (CA-1603). Plastered brick, seven bays by fifteen bays with domed polygonal corner bay lavishly embellished at cornice, three stories, flat roof with ornamental balustraded parapet above a Classical entablature, ground floor storefronts, second floor elliptical-arched windows, third floor round-arched windows with more elaborate hoodmolds; flanking buildings in photo are contemporary and well detailed. Built ca. 1875, this is a fine example of the western mercantile palace of the times; demolished. 1 photocopy of 1885 photo. See also historic photo in City of Stockton (CA-1601-15).

Masonic Temple and R. P. Parker Store (CA-1604). Hunter St. between Main and Market Sts. Plastered brick, three-bay front by seven bays, two stories, flat parapeted roof with bracketed cornice, ground-floor storefronts, second-floor bays divided by paneled pilasters, flat-arched windows with hoodmolds, central front window has paired round-arched sash with hoodmold on label stops. Built ca. 1870; demolished. 1 photo-copy of 1876 photo.

McKee Block (Sterling Corner) (CA-1602). Main and Hunter Sts. Plastered brick, eight bays by eight bays with chamfered corner, three stories, bracketed cornice with frieze panels, molded belt courses, ground floor has round-arched windows and corner entrance surmounted by second-floor balcony on consoles with a balustrade, second-floor windows round-arched with paired round-arched window on corner, third floor round-arched windows. Built 1868–69; demolished 1960s. 1 photocopy of ca. 1870 photo. See also historic photo in City of Stockton (CA-1601-14).

Parker, R. P., Store. Included with Masonic Temple (CA-1604).

Philadelphia House (CA-1607). Plastered brick, three-bay front, two-story front section, three-story rear addition, flat parapeted roof, front section has simple facade with flat-arched windows and second-floor balcony, rear section has seg-mental- and round-arched windows with drip molds and a bracketed cornice. Built probably 1850s, rear addition probably 1860s; demolished. 1 photocopy of 1875 photo.

St. Mary's Cathedral Church (CA-1624). Brick, three-bay front, one story, gable roof with bell cote and stone coping, rose window in the gable, two lancet windows with tracery, transept gable end has one large lancet window with tracery, square three-stage tower in angle of ell, first two stages have buttresses, third stage has pointed-arch louvers; latin cross plan. Built 1865; additions in 1880s and 1893; interior remodeled since 1955 but preserves its Gothic Revival character. The exterior is a good example of Gothic Revival style and preserved the earlier side tower. 1 photocopy of 1876 photo.

San Joaquin County Courthouse (CA-1632). Brick, five-bay front in gable end, two stories, gable roof with pedimented end and triangular vent, wooden polygonal cupola in two stages with an open gallery under the second stage with clockfaces, domes roof and flag pole, front entrance porch with Classical details. Built 1854; demolished. 2 photocopies of 1884 photos.

San Joaquin County Courthouse (CA-1639). Main and Hunter Sts. Brick foundations. Built 1890, E. E. Meyers and son, architects; demolished. 1 photocopy of ca. 1890 photo of courthouse under construction, perhaps taken during corner-stone-laying ceremony.

San Joaquin Firehouse (CA-1640). Weber Ave. and California St. Brick, three-bay front, two stories with square crenelated tower with bartizans over central bay, second floor has crenelated parapet with bartizans, ground floor with round-arched central door flanked by side doors, pronounced archivolt trim springing from paneled pilasters, second floor has large central window with paired round-arched windows set under an encompassing round-arched drip mold with label stops, side windows also have drip molds with label stops. Built 1869; demolished. 1 photocopy of 1880 photo. See historic views in City of Stockton, CA-1601-8 and -9.

Simpson, Andrew, House (CA-1626). NW corner Oak and El Dorado Sts. Wood frame with clap-boards, three-bay front, two stories, gable roof with cornice returns, semicircular louver in gable, paneled corner pilasters, wrap-around one-story porch with round-arched bracing between posts, corbeled brick chimney; L-shaped plan. Built ca. 1860, a good example of the vernacular Greek Revival-style house; demolished. 1 photo-copy of 1925 photo.

Smith, Captain, House (CA-1618). Two structure with common wall: one brick, two stories, gable roof with gable wall dormer, windows have relieving arches and archivolt trim; wooden structure has five-bay front, two stories, hip roof, porch across front with wood posts and brackets.

Built 1870; demolished. 1 photocopy of 1937 photo.

Sterling Corner. See McKee Block (CA-1602).

Stewart, Frank, Library (Hazelton Library) (CA-1631). Market and Hunter Sts. Plastered brick, three bays, one story, mansard roof with gable wall dormers with round-arched niches, center pavilion has round-arched opening with a pronounced molded archivolt and keystone between short fluted pilasters, surmounted by a triangular pediment, surmounted by a balustrade, side bays have round-arched windows at ground floor surmounted by round windows with cross mullions, between pilasters with molded caps. Built 1870; modernized 1940s; demolished. 1 photocopy of 1876 photo.

Terry, Judge Daniel S., House (CA-1582). NW corner Fremont and Center Sts. Wood frame with horizontal siding, three-bay front, two stories, low-pitched roof, bracketed cornice, paneled corner pilasters, one-story porch across front with split columns, segmental-arched windows with flat heads; side-hall plan. Built 1850s; demolished 1924. 1 photocopy of 1876 photo.

Tone, Jack, House (CA-1620). Jack Tone Rd., 11 mis. NE of Stockton. Brick, two or three stories, hip roof, segmental-arched windows. Built 1873. 1 photocopy of 1925 photo.

Trahearne, Washington, House (CA-1596). SE corner El Dorado and Park Sts. Wood frame with channeled siding, two stories, hip roof with gable-roofed ells, two-story polygonal bays on the gable ends feature modillioned cornices and segmental-arched windows, one-story porch at corner has segmental-arched braces between chamfered wooden posts, surmounted by a balustrade. Built 1860, typical Italianate suburban house; moved ca. 1925. 1 photocopy of 1870s photo.

Weber, Captain Charles M., House (CA-1641). Wood frame and adobe, three-bay front by eight bays, two stories, double veranda on three sides has columns with molded caps and X-railing, gable roof with square cupola, one-story addition in front has veranda on three sides and a deck on the roof with balustrade. Built 1850, by the founder of Stockton, this imposing Greek Revival plantation house sat on Weber Point and was surrounded by gardens and onion-domed lattice gazebos within a picket fence; flooding caused the family to move in 1893, after which the house deteriorated and finally burned in 1917. 3 photocopies of photos (ca. 1852, ca. 1915) show

house in original setting and in deteriorated condition.

Strawberry Valley □ El Dorado County

Strawberry House (CA-1682). Placerville Rd. Wood frame, three bays, square, massive shingled hipped roof extended over porch. Built 1850s as hostelry on Placerville Rd; demolished. 2 photocopies of undated photos, 1 photocopy of 1861 drawing of valley.

Susanville vicinity □ Lassen County

Fort Defiance (Roop's Fort) (CA-1310). Log with saddle-notching, one story, shingled gable and gable roof, wood plank doors and one window. Built ca. 1855 by Isaac Roop, first settler, elected governor of the unofficial Nevada Territory, 1859–61; cabin was headquarters of resistance to California's claim of jurisdiction, 1863–64; rebuilt. 2 photocopies of 1925, 1939 photos. NR

Sweetland □ Nevada County

Hotel and Store (CA-1400). Wood frame with horizontal siding over vertical board-and-batten siding, four-bay front by two bays, two-and-a-half stories, gable roof with boxed cornice, one-story gable-roofed side wing, round-arched window with Y-transom tracery. Built ca. 1860; town gone. 1 ext. photo (1934).

Timbuctoo □ Yuba County

Main Street (CA-1546). One-story buildings, mostly wood frame, with false fronts and sidewalk canopies. 1 photocopy of ext. photo (1850s), 1 photocopy of photo ca. 1930.

Wells Fargo Building (CA-1295). Rubble stone with brick front, two-bay front, one story with loft, corrugated metal gable roof with board-and-batten siding in gable end, brick parapet in front, metal canopy over sidewalk supported by wood posts, recessed doors with folding metal shutters. Built ca. 1852. 3 ext. photos (ca. 1936, n.d.).

Tracy vicinity □ Alameda County

Mountain House (CA-1199). Intersection of Mountain House and Grant Line Rds., 1.3 mi. N. of Hwy

Tracy vicinity continued

580. Wood frame with board siding, one story, semi-flat roof with high false front, shed roofed porch across front with wood posts, rear gable-roofed wing, wood-framed windows and doors; rectangular plan, interior altered. Built late 1880s; demolished. 1 ext. photo (1925).

Tragedy Springs □ El Dorado County

Carved Tree Marker (CA-1502). 51 mis. NE of Jackson An 1848 carving in a debarked section of a tree commemorating Mormon scouts murdered by Indians; tree can no longer be located. 1 photography of undated photo.

Tulare □ Tulare County

Commercial Buildings (CA-1794). Two- and three-story masonry structures with flat roofs, arcading, canopies over sidewalks. 2 photocopies of ca. 1900 photos.

Tuttletown □ Tuolumne County

Tuttletown Hotel (Swerer's Store) (CA-1272). Wood frame with channeled siding, two stories with one-story wing, gable roof with cornice returns in gable end; stone outbuilding, two-bay front, gable roof with board-and-batten siding in gable. Built ca. 1855 as commercial center of Tuttletown; only foundations remain next to Rte. 49. 4 ext. photos (1930s, 1934).

Tuttletown vicinity □ Tuolumne County

Farm House (CA-1271). Wood frame with channeled siding, two stories with one-story wing, gable roof, full-length two-story veranda across front with shed roof. Built 1860s; demolished. 1 ext. photo (1934).

Union City □ Alameda County

See entries under Alvarado

Vacaville □ Solano County

Peña Adobe (CA-1198). 2 mis. SW of Vacaville on Peña Adobe Rd. Museum. Adobe with frame addi-

tions, one-and-a-half stories, gable roof extended to cover front porch. Built 1843 on site of ten-square-league Rancho Los Putos that Governor Pío Pico granted to Juan Felipe Peña and Manuel Cabeza de Vaca; frame addition ca. 1864; completed plan and roof ca. 1880; restored 1961–65 by City of Vacaville in cooperation with Solano County and California Medical Facility of State Department of Corrections. 5 sheets (1962, including site plan, plans, elevations, details, sections); 4 ext. photos (1962); 1 data page (1981). NR

Ventura □ Ventura County

Mission San Buenaventura (CA-22). E. Main St. at S. Figueroa St. Brick front wall and tower, adobe side and rear walls, stone buttresses, $51' \times 155'$, one story, gable tiled roof, square tower at front corner rises above building in two stages with round-arched openings and domical roof, round-arched entrance framed by pilasters under pediment. Built 1801–09, ninth mission in chain of 21; rebuilt after earthquake 1812; alterations made ca. 1893 removed in 1957 restoration. 10 sheets (1936, including plot plan, plans, elevations, sections, details); 6 ext. photos (1936), 1 int. photo (1936); 2 data pages (1937).

Vista vicinity □ San Diego County

Casa del Rancho Guajome (CA-43). 2.5 mis. NE of Vista, Guajome Regional Park. Adobe, stone foundations, rectangular with two courtyards, $118' \times 185'$, one story, small two-story look-out, tiled gable roof extends to cover arcaded porch across front windows altered for glazed sash, wood shutters. Built 1852–53 for Col. Cave Johnson Couts; look-out added 1883; restored 1973. 11 sheets (1936, including plot plan, plans, elevations, sections, details); 11 ext. photos (1936), 1 photocopy of architect's plans (ca. 1851); 1 data page (1936). NHL, SHL.

□ *Chapel.* Plastered adobe, one story, L-shaped, $20'$ (one-bay front) $\times 32'$, gable roof, exposed rafter ends. Built 1868. 1 sheet (1936, including plan, elevations, section, details); 1 ext. photo (1936).

□ *Water Tank.* Plastered brick, vertical planks in gable, one story, $17' \times 18'$, gable roof with cupola, door is only opening. 1 sheet (1936, including plan, elevation, details); 1 ext. photo (1936).

Volcano   □   Amador County

Adams Express Building (Sing Kee Store) (CA-1518). Main St. and Consolation. Stone, plastered and scored, two-bay front, one story, gable roof, iron doors. Built ca. 1855; incorrectly called Adam's Express; remodeled with new second floor with projecting balcony at gable end, exterior side stairs. 2 photocopies (1925, n.d.).

Cannon "Old Abe" (CA-1507). Cast in Boston, Mass., by Alger Co. in 1837; this and one other cannon at Shiloh may be two oldest 6-pound cannons in the U.S. 1 photocopy of 1925 photo.

Masonic and I.O.O.F. Building and Store (CA-1345). Main St. Stone, plastered and scored, three-bay front, two stories, gable roof, two-story porch across front, simple balustrade on second floor; one-story stone store adjoining. Built 1856, new balustrade and iron staircase on side building added. 1 ext. photo (1934), 2 photocopies of undated photos.

St. George Hotel (Empire and Eureka Hotel) (CA-1285). Main St., S. end of town. Brick, five-bay front, three stories, hipped roof, three-story wrap-around veranda with balustrades at the second and third floors, double glass doors open to balcony at each floor. Built 1864, an outstanding example of a Gold Rush era hotel. 1 ext. photo (1934), 5 photocopies of undated photos.

Stone Buildings—Ruins (CA-1504). Main St. Stone, random ashlar, some with dressed stone fronts; Keller & Symonds general store with three openings for doors in front; Clute-Grillo building with stone facade remaining and four sets of paneled iron doors and gable roof. Built 1856; ruins. 2 photocopies of 1938 photos.

Stone Store (Cigar Emporium) (CA-1505). Main St. Stone, random ashlar on front, rubble on sides, three-bay front, one story, gable roof, one-story veranda across front, elliptically arched doors with iron shutters. Built ca. 1855; restored 1961–63; now Cobblestone Art Gallery. 1 ext. photo (1934), 1 photocopy of 1938 photo.

Town of Volcano (CA-1510). Small gable-roofed buildings, mostly wood frame, mostly one story. Town founded 1849 as The Volcano, renamed 1850. 1 photocopy of early 1850s photo. SHL

Wine Shop (Sibley's Brewery) (CA-1517). Between Main St. and Jerome St. Dressed stone, three-bay front, one story, gable roof, shed-roofed porch across front. Built 1856 as Sibley's Brewery; restored. 1 photocopy of 1925 photo.

St. George Hotel (Empire and Eureka Hotel), Volcano (CA-1285-1).

Warm Springs □ Alameda County

Cohen, A. A., Hotel, Rancho Agua Caliente (CA-1656). Wood frame with shiplap siding, eight bays by three bays, two stories with attic under mansard roof, dormers. Built 1869 to replace earlier resort buildings destroyed by 1868 earthquake, site of ancient Indian watering place, rancho granted to Fulgencia Higuera in 1834; sold by Cohen in 1870 to Leland Stanford, who converted it into a winery; used as a resort into 1960s; demolished. 1 ext. photo (1940).

Higuera, Abelardo, Adobe, Rancho Agua Caliente (CA-1666). 47885 Wabana Common. Wood frame with drop siding and adobe, three-bay front, two stories, hipped roof with square cupola centered in front with segmental arched windows, front porch with balustrade; central-hall plan. Built c. 1850 by Abelardo Higuera, one of second generation of the Higuera clan of Rancho Agua Caliente, granted in 1834 to Don Fulgencio. Adobe ruinous after 1868 earthquake, rebuilt and remodeled with two-story extension, now Hillview Lodge. 3 ext. photos (1940).

Higuera, Fulgencio, Adobe, Rancho Agua Caliente (CA-1665). Adobe buildings destroyed in 1868 earthquake. Photos show walls of 2-story adobe building with roof collapsed; now vanished. 3 ext. photos (1940).

Warner Springs vicinity □ San Diego County

Kimble-Wilson House (CA-426). Adobe, one story, three-bay front, shingled gable roof, shed-roof porches on three sides. Built ca. 1865, used as store 1875–1908. 3 ext. photos (1960), 1 int. photo (1960).

Warner Ranch (CA-424). San Felipe County Rd. Built ca. 1845 for Jonathan Trumbull Warner who changed his name to Don Juan José Warner and became a Mexican citizen in order to acquire title to property, buildings burned in Indian raid in 1851; rebuilt 1858 to serve as way station for Butterfield's Overland Mail Company. 1 photo of general view (1960); 7 data pages (1963). NHL, SHL.

□ *Ranch House (CA-424).* Plastered adobe and board-and-batten siding, stone foundation, approx. 47' (three-bay front) × 42' with 6' wide veranda across one side and frame addition at rear corner, gable roof with lean-tos at both

sides; hall-less plan, peeled-log ceilings with remnants of painted canvas. 4 sheets (1962, including plan, elevations, sections, details); 2 ext. photos (1960); 3 data pages (1963).

□ *Barn—Trading Post (CA-425).* Adobe and frame, mortise-and-tenon construction, hand-hewn timbers, variety of board sidings, remnants of other walls indicating variable construction periods, approx. 45' × 76', one story, gable roof. 3 sheets (1962, including plan, elevations, sections, details); 1 ext. photo (1960), 1 int. photo (1960); 4 data pages (1963).

Wawona □ Mariposa County

Wawona Hotel (CA-1805). Wood frame with clapboards, thirteen-bay front, two stories, gable roof, two brick chimneys, two-story shed-roofed porch across front, Chippendale railings on both levels. Built 1869–75 as a National Park Service hotel in Yosemite National Park. 1 photocopy of 1903 photo. NR

Weaverville □ Trinity County

Blacksmith Shop (CA-1185). Rough hewn logs let into corner posts, two stories, shingled gable roof, stepped board-and-batten false front, shingled shed roof over front work area, timber crane to one side. Built 1860s; demolished. 1 ext. photo (1937).

Chinese Joss House (CA-1452). State Historic Park. Two structures, both wood frame, temple 20' × 48' with horizontal siding, attendants' quarters 14' × 36' with vertical siding, gable roofs, front portions have stepped gable-end pieces with ornate carved sections, front portion of temple has recessed entrance porch with ceremonial gate of wood in three sections painted to simulate brick, entrance doors have wood panels on either side and above with calligraphy; rectangular plan with ornate and ritualistic interior furnishings. Built 1874 to serve the large local Chinese population. 2 ext. photos (1934), 3 int. photos (1934); 19 data pages, including 11 pages of architectural drawing (1972).

Commercial Buildings—Main Street (CA-1446). One- and two-story brick and wood buildings with one- and two-story wood porches over the sidewalk. Built during the mining boom in 1850s, 1860s, and 1870s, Weaverville is one of the most intact of the mining towns with a few

Commercial Buildings, Main Street, Weaverville (CA-1446).

unusual two-story buildings of divided owner-ship with second-floor access by spiral stairs from sidewalk to upper balcony. 3 photos (1934).

I.O.O.F. Lodge No. 55 Hall (John Cole Building) (CA-1448). Brick, two stories, three-bay front, parapeted roof with bracketed cornice, double glazed doors at street level in deep reveals, two-story hip-roofed front porch with spoked railing, I.O.O.F. symbol beneath porch roof, second-floor reached by spiral stair with railing from side-walk. Built 1856 as store with lodge room above. 2 ext. photos, one with spiral stairs of N.S.G.W. Building in foreground (1934).

Jumper House (CA-1451). Court St. Wood frame with clapboards, four-bay front in gable end, one story, gable roof, three French doors on front, front porch with pierced columns on block bases and molded caps. Built 1850s. 2 ext. photos (1934).

Native Sons of the Golden West Building (CA-1668). Brick stuccoed and scored to resemble stone, three-bay front, two stories, gable roof,

two-story front porch extending over sidewalk with projecting pediment lettered N.S.G.W., sec-ond-floor balustrade with X's between verticals, spiral stair with railing from sidewalk to upper level. Built 1850s. 1 photocopy of 1930s photo.

Old Brewery (CA-1449). Main St. Brick and wood, three-bay front on brick portion, three-bay shed-roofed side addition with clapboards, brick structure of two stories with paneled and dentiled parapet, iron-shuttered openings. Built 1855. 1 ext. photo (1934).

Old Fire Engine (CA-1453). Pumper, largely metal, with hose and wagon tongue. 1 ext. photo (1934).

Store (CA-1450). Adobe and wood frame with horizontal siding, two-bay front, one-and-a-half stories, gable roof, iron-shuttered openings, sim-ple wooden canopy on posts over sidewalk. Built 1850s; demolished. 3 ext. photos (1934).

Trinity County Courthouse (CA-1447). Main and Court Sts. Brick, six-bay front, two stories, para-peted roof with molded brick courses and brack-

Weverville continued
ets, glazed double doors with iron shutters throughout, iron second-floor balcony. Built 1856 as a saloon. 1 ext. photo (1934).

Westport   □   Mendocino County

Houses on Residential Street (CA-1464). Wood frame with horizontal siding, one-and-a-half stories, gable roofs, one-story porches across front. 1 ext. photo (1934).

Westport—General (CA-1463). Town on hillside above the ocean with small one-story buildings, one grander house with two stories, two-story bay windows, hipped roof. 1 photo of general view (1934).

Whiskey Slide   □   Calaveras County

First House (John Noce House) (CA-1489). Wood frame with board-and-batten siding, one story, broad gable roof, massive rough-cut stone chimney in front. Built 1850s for John Noce; demolished, town gone. 1 photocopy of 1925 photo.

Whittier   □   Los Angeles County

Casa de Pío Pico (CA-37-24). 6003 Pioneer Blvd. at Whittier Blvd. Museum and park. Plastered adobe, irregular U-shape with two-story section, 98' × 35', one-story wings forming an open patio with a well, gable roof extended over two-story porch on patio side, exterior stair. Built ca. 1850 for Pío Pico, last Mexican governor of California; house originally had thirty-three rooms, floods of 1867 and 1883–84 destroyed the west wings and corredor; alterations chiefly by Charles Lyman Strong who paved the east patio and dug the well; several out-buildings including the mill and chapel were destroyed and the material used for building a bridge across the river in 1907; house repaired and converted to a museum by the Whittier Museum and Historical Society; more recent restoration efforts by the State Department of Parks and Recreation, refurnishing by Docents of the Whittier Historical Society. 6 sheets (1934, including plans, elevations, sections, details); 7 ext. photos (1934); 1 data page (1937). SHL

Willows   □   Glenn County

*Glenn County Courthouse (CA-1804). 526 W. Sy-*camore St. Plastered stone, three-bay front, Greek cross shape, two stories, central domed cupola with lantern and bull's-eye windows and swags, full Classical entablature, low gable roof with raking, dentiled cornice and Classical balustrade with newels and statuary, round-headed windows with triangular pedimented hoods divided by pilasters, central portion of the facade has pedimented portico with paired columns and a projecting balustraded entrance porch. Built 1900; a notable example of a Classical Revival courthouse. 1 photocopy of 1914 photo.

Wilmington □ Los Angeles County

See entry for Drum Barracks under Los Angeles.

Woodbridge □ San Joaquin County

Arizona State Home for Insane (CA-1636). Wood frame with clapboards, three-bay front in gable end, gable roof with cornice returns, fourth windowless bay added to front, not covered by gable roof, front porch with simple wood posts. 2 ext. photos (n.d.) including street scene.

I.O.O.F. Building (CA-1590). Brick, four-bay front in gable end, two stories, gable roof, second floor has floor-length windows with flat heads on consoles, above is I.O.O.F. set in a panel, above the bracketed cornice is the date 1874, ground floor remodeled. Ground floor built 1860s as the Lavinsky store, second story added 1874. Restored 1982, facade collapsed during restoration, presently being rebuilt. 1 photocopy of 1920 photo.

Woodbridge College (CA-1635). Wood frame with horizontal siding, square with projecting square tower, two stories, hipped and gabled roof, bracketed cornice above which the tower steps back in two stages, tall narrow windows with segmental drip molds on ground floor. Probably built 1870s; demolished. 1 photocopy of 1915 photo.

Woods Hotel (CA-1610). Wood frame with clapboards, six-bay front by two bays, two stories, gable roof with cornice returns, one-story porch across front with simple wood posts, two double entrance doors on ground floor. Built mid 19th c.; demolished. 1 photocopy of 1920s photo.

Woods, Jeremiah, Cottage (CA-1611). Wood frame with clapboards, three-bay front, one story, gable roof with wood shingles, central door. Built ca. 1885, home of founder of Woodbridge and Wood's Ferry. 1 ext. photo (n.d.) which also shows some outbuildings.

Woods Crossing □ Tuolumne County

Farm Buildings (CA-1570). Farmhouse apparently wood frame, two stories, gable roof with cornice returns on gable end; outbuildings of various sizes. Built late 19th c. Not located. 1 photocopy of 1925 photo.

Woodside □ San Mateo County

Filoli (Bourn-Roth Estate) (CA-2117). Canada Rd. Brick, U-shaped, thirteen-bay front, two-and-a-half stories, tiled hipped roof, modillioned cornice, small entrance portico with Doric columns topped by balustrade, four massive arched brick chimneys, round-arched French doors at ground level, expansive formal gardens; spacious rooms, ballroom with walk-in fireplace, renowned chandeliers, hand-painted murals of Ireland. Built 1915–17, Willis Polk, architect. Bruce Porter, landscape designer. 15 ext. photos (1974), 6 int. photos (1974); 4 data pages (1974). NR

Green Gables (Fleishhacker House) (CA-2147). 329 Albion Ave. Wood frame with stucco, two-and-a-half stories, L-shape, hip roof with hipped and gabled dormers, roof covered with irregularly formed shakes molded at eaves to simulate thatching; interior features some carved cabinetwork, mostly painted; landscaped grounds with terraces, ponds, pools, Roman walls. Built 1911, Charles Sumner Greene and Henry Mather Greene, architects; 1916 free-form swimming pool added; 1917 second floor added to servants' wing; 1924 garden room enclosed; 1927 water gardens added; all additions by Greenes; impressive mansion with outstanding sensitivity in its landscape features, water gardens. 28 ext. photos (1975), 10 int. photos (1975), 18 photos of grounds and outbuildings (1975).

La Questa Wine Cellar (CA-2145). 240 La Questa Rd. Fieldstone, two stories set in slope of hill, gable roof. Built 1902. Charles Rosa, stonemason, as wine cellar; rebuilt 1906–09, by Charles Rosa; converted to residence, 1949, Verney O. Chase, architect and engineer, by building wood frame structure on interior. 3 ext. photos (1975).

Woodside Store (CA-2146). Kings Mountain Rd., corner Tripp Rd. Museum. Wood frame with board-and-batten siding, three-bay front, two stories, gable roof, porch on two sides, lean-to additions in rear. Built ca. 1854 for Mathias Parkhurst and Robert Tripp as general store, post office, dental office, saloon, and after 1859 a library; store operated by Tripp until his death in 1909 at age 93. 8 ext. photos (1975), 3 int. photos (1975).

Yosemite National Park □ Mariposa County

Cedar Cottage (CA-1645). Wood frame with clapboards, 76' (eleven-bay front) × 43', two stories, gable roof with hand-split shakes pitches out over two-story porches on three sides, access to rooms from porches; major addition was a shed-roofed room built around a large sequoia tree with a massive stone fireplace in one corner. Built before 1859, acquired ca. 1859 by J. M. Hutchings who added Big Tree Room; leased to Coulter and Murphy who built the Sentinel Hotel in 1876; during the State's administration of the park, the buildings were substantially remodeled, particularly in 1897, but how much the actual appearance was changed is not clear; buildings demolished. 5 sheets (1930s, including plans, elevations, section, details).

Sentinel Hotel (CA-1644). Wood frame with clapboards, 124' × 45', two-and-a-half stories, gable roof with cat walk on ridge, two-story hipped roof porch on three sides, X-railing on second level, spindlework frieze on first level. Built 1876 for Coulton and Murphy; demolished 1960s. 7 sheets (1930s, including plans, elevations, section, details); 1 photocopy of 1904 photo.

Yosemite Chapel (CA-1649). Wood frame with board-and-batten siding, about 26' × 50', shingled high-peaked gable roof with two-stage belfry also shingled, pyramidal base, louvered second stage, witch's cap top, gable-roofed vestibule, rear of building extended in ell containing small chapel and offices. Built 1879 for California Sunday School Association. Charles Geddes, architect, originally located 1 mi. away, moved to present site 1901. 5 sheets (1964, including plan, elevations, sections, details). NR

Sentinel Hotel, Yosemite National Park (CA-1644-1).

Bibliography for
HABS Catalogue

Abeloe, William N. (Hoover, Mildred B., Rensch, H. E., & Rensch, E. G.) *Historic Spots in California*. 1966, Stanford University Press, CA.

Baer, Kurt. *Architecture of the California Missions*. 1958, Berkeley.

Baer, Morley, et. al. *Adobes in the Sun*. 1980, San Francisco.

Baird, Joseph A. *Time's Wonderous Changes: San Francisco Architecture, 1776–1915*. 1962, San Francisco.

Bruegmann, Robert. *Benicia: Portrait of an Early California Town*. 1980, San Francisco.

Burnham, Daniel H., & Bennett, Edward H. *Report on a Plan for San Francisco*. (Edited by Edward F. O'Day), 1905, San Francisco.

Butler, Phyllis. *The Valley of Santa Clara: Historic Buildings, 1792–1970*. 1975, Novato, CA.

Cardwell, Kenneth H. *Bernard Maybeck: Artisan, Architect, Artist*. 1977, Salt Lake City.

Caughey, John W. and LaRee. *Los Angeles: Biography of a City*. 1976, Berkeley.

Corbett, Michael R. *Splendid Survivors: San Francisco's Downtown Architectural Heritage*. (Prepared by Charles Hall Page & Associates for the Foundation for San Francisco's Architectural Heritage.) 1979, San Francisco.

Fogelson, Robert M. *The Fragmented Metropolis: Los Angeles, 1850–1930*. 1967, Cambridge, MA

Gebhard, David. "The Monterey Tradition: History Reordered." *New Mexico Studies in Fine Art* 7: 14–19, 1982.

_____. "The Spanish Colonial Revival in Southern California." *Journal of the Society of Architectural Historians* 26 (May): 131–47, 1967.

_____. "Some Additional Observations on California's Monterey Tradition." *Journal of the Society of Architectural Historians* 46 (June): 157–170, 1987.

_____. "The American Colonial Revival in the 1930s." *Winterthur Portfolio* 22 Summer/Autumn, 1987.

_____. *Schindler*. London and New York. Reprint 1980. Salt Lake City.

Gebhard, David, et. al. *Samuel and Joseph Cather Newsom: Victorian Architectural Imagery in California, 1878–1908*. 1979, Santa Barbara.

Gebhard, David, and Harriet Von Breton. *L.A. in the 30s*. 1980, Salt Lake City.

_____. *Lloyd Wright*. 1971, Santa Barbara.

Gill, Irving J. "The Home of the Future: The New Architecture of the West." *The Craftsman* 30 (May): 140–141, 220, 1916.

Gleye, Paul. *The Architecture of Los Angeles*. 1981, San Diego.

Goodhue, Bertram G. and Carleton M. Winslow. *The Architecture and Gardens of the San Diego Exposition*. 1916, San Francisco.

Hancock, Ralph. *Fabulous Boulevard (Wilshire)*. 1949, New York.

Hannaford, Donald R. *Spanish Colonial or Adobe Architecture of California, 1800–1850*. 1931, New York.

Hart, James D. *A Companion to California*. 1978, New York.

Hatheway, Roger. "El Pueblo: Myth and Realities," *Review, Southern California Chapter, Society of Architectural Historians 1,* no. 1 (Fall): 1–5, 1981.

Hines, Thomas S. *Richard Neutra and the Search for Modern Architecture*. 1982, New York.

Jordy, William H. *Progressive and Academic Ideals at the Turn of the Century*. 1972, New York.

Keeler, Charles. *The Simple Home*. 1904, San Francisco.

Kirker, Harold. *California's Architectural Frontier*. 1960, San Marino.

_____. "The Role of Hispanic Kinships in Popularizing the Monterey Style in California, 1836–1846." *Journal of the Society of Architectural Historians* 43 (October): 250–255, 1984.

Longstreth, Richard. *On the Edge of the World.* 1983, New York, Architectural History Foundation, and Cambridge, MIT Press.

Los Angeles Department of Planning. *City Planning in Los Angeles: A History.* 1964, Los Angeles.

Makinson, Randell L. *Greene and Greene: Architecture as a Fine Art.* 1977, Salt Lake City.

McCoy, Esther. *Five California Architects.* 1960, New York.

_____. *Vienna to Los Angeles: Two Journeys.* 1979, Santa Monica.

Muscatine, Doris. *Old San Francisco: From Early Days to the Earthquake.* 1975, New York.

Neuhaus, Eugene. *The Art of the Exposition.* 1915, San Francisco.

Newcomb, Rexford. *The Franciscan Mission Architecture of Alta California.* 1916, New York.

Padilla, Victoria. *Southern California Gardens.* 1961, Berkeley.

Regnery, Dorothy F. *An Enduring Heritage: Historic Buildings of the San Francisco Peninsula.* 1976, Stanford.

Scott, Mel. *The San Francisco Bay Area: A Metropolis in Perspective.* 1959, Berkeley.

Smith, Kathyrn. "Frank Lloyd Wright, Hollyhock House and Olive Hill, 1914–1924." *Journal of the Society of Architectural Historians* 38 (March): 15–33, 1979.

Smith, Susan Bixby. *Adobe Days.* 1974, Fresno, CA.

Starr, Kevin. *Americans and the California Dream.* 1981, Salt Lake City.

Turner, Paul, et al. *The Founders and the Architects: The Design of Stanford University.* 1976, Cambridge, MA.

Winter, Robert W. "The Arroyo Culture." *California Design 1910,* by Timothy J. Anderson, Eudorah M. Moore, and Robert Winter. Pasadena. Reprint 1980, Salt Lake City.

Adler, David, 137, 164
Albright, Harrison, 207
Allen, Glen, 189
Applegarth, George, 229
Austin, John C., 147

Babson, Seth, 46, 191, 197
Bakewell, John, Jr., and Brown, Arthur, Jr., 78, 81, 160, 207, 211
Barber, Peter J., 51, 247
Beckett, Welton (Wurdeman and Becket), 153
Beelman, Claude, 149
Benson, D. P., 205
Black, Milton, 145
Boring, W. A., 153
Boyd, Thomas, 117
Bryant, Leyland A., 157
Brown, A. Page, 75, 213
Brown, Vincent, 123
Burnham, Daniel H. (also Burnham & Co.), 56, 76, 210, 216
Burrell, Charles, 175
Burton, J. Lee, 155
Burkett, H. E., and Osgood, R. E., 201, 206

Clark, Birge, 179, 181
Cleaveland, Henry W., 47, 210
Clements, Stiles O. (see Morgan, Walls and Clements)
Coffey, Alfred I., 189
Cooper, Henry E., 172
Coolidge, Charles Allerton, 56, 181, 182
Comstock and Trosche, 62, 207, 208
Coxhead, Ernest, 144
Craig, James Osborne, 247
Crain, William and England, Thomas, 228
Cummings, Gordon P., 43, 173, 221
Curlett, William (also Curlett, Eisen, and Cuthbertson), 138, 151

Day, Clinton, 181
Derrah, Robert V., 147
Dodge, George A., 189

Dolliver, J. W., 189

Farquaharson, David (Farquaharson & Kenitzer), 210

Geddes, Charles, 269
Gill, Irving, J. (see also Hebbard, W. S.), 83–85, 142, 148, 171, 200, 204, 205, 206, 207, 250, 259
Goodell, Nathaniel, 46, 62, 192, 193, 197
Goodhue, Bertram Grosvenor, 86, 87, 151, 202
Goodrich, Levi I., 203
Greene, Charles Sumner, and Greene, Henry Mather (Greene and Greene), 69, 70, 183, 269

Harvey, Arthur E., 155
Heineman, Arthur, 152
Hebbard, W. S. (Hebbard and Gill), 205, 207
Hobart, Lewis P., 137, 216
Houghton, J. Franklin (see also Rider, S. A.), 113
Howard, George H., 117

Kenitzer, Henry, 210
Kesling, William P., 155
Kubach, C. U., 154
Kysor, Ezra F., 147, 153

Laver, Augustus, 59, 214
Lemos, Pedro de, 180
Leonard, Joseph A., 217

Maginnis and Walsh, 125
Maybeck, Bernard, 68, 74, 79, 80, 225, 239
Martin, Albert C., 151
Mathews, W. J., 147
McKenzie, Charles S., 125
Miller and Pflueger, 96, 176, 218
Miller, J. R. (also Miller and Pflueger), 211
Miller, Warren P., 159
Morgan, Julia, 183, 251
Morgan, Walls and Clements, 96, 150, 151, 154, 155, 156, 157
Mullet, A. B., 231